Engineering Distributed Objects

Engineering Distributed Objects

Wolfgang Emmerich

London University

John Wiley & Sons, Ltd

Chichester • New York • Weinheim • Brisbane • Singapore • Toronto

Copyright © 2000 by John Wiley & Sons, Ltd,
        Baffins Lane, Chichester,
        West Sussex PO19 1UD, England
        National   01243 779777
        International   (+44) 1243 779777
        e-mail (for orders and customer service enquiries):
        cs-book@wiley.co.uk
        Visit our Home Page on http://www.wiley.co.uk
                      or http://www.wiley.com

Cover illustration: Wassily Kandinsky's "Inneres Kochen" 1925 © ADAGP, Paris and DACS, London 1999. Reproduced with permission from The Solomon R. Guggenheim Foundation, New York.

Other Wiley Editorial Offices

John Wiley & Sons, Inc., 605 Third Avenue,
New York, NY 10158-0012, USA

Weinheim • Brisbane • Singapore • Toronto

Library of Congress Cataloging-in-Publication Data
Emmerich, Wolfgang, Dr. Rer. Nat.
    Engineering distributed objects / Wolfgang Emmerich.
       p. cm.
    Includes bibliographical references and index.
     1. Object-oriented programming (Computer science) 2. Electronic data
processing–Distributed processing. I. Title.

QA76.64. E46 2000
005.1'17–dc21   00-021723

British Library Cataloguing in Publication Data

A catalogue record for this book is available from the British Library

ISBN 0-471-98657-7
Designed by Mark and Sally Spedding, O.O.M.B., Salisbury, Wiltshire
Illustrations by Jenny Chapman
Typeset in 9.5/12 Galliard by C.K.M. Typesetting, Salisbury, Wiltshire
Printed and bound in Great Britain by Biddles Ltd, Guildford and King's Lynn
This book is printed on acid-free paper responsibly manufactured from sustainable forestry,
in which at least two trees are planted for each one used for paper production

Contents

Part II Middleware for Distributed Objects   59

3 Principles of Object-Oriented Middleware   61

Preface

Back in 1995, Richard Soley and Roberto Zicari drew my attention to a new paradigm in object-oriented computing: distributed objects. Roberto and I had worked on distributed object databases for the first half of the 1990s. He convinced me that the success of objects in databases would be repeated for distributed system construction and persuaded me to work with him at LogOn Technology Transfer on promoting the OMG/CORBA standard in Central Europe. Roberto was entirely wrong about the success of object databases, but he was perfectly right about distributed objects. There are now very few organizations that do not use distributed objects as the primitives for building distributed systems. All applications that are built with Microsoft's COM can potentially be distributed; Java has a primitive for distributed objects built into the very core of the language; and significant large-scale, heterogeneous distributed system constructions are achieved with OMG/CORBA.

As part of my work for LogOn, I prepared and delivered CORBA training sessions for the European IT industry. At the same time, I took a lectureship at City University in London and my Head of Department asked me to teach a course on Distributed Systems. When I looked around for a suitable textbook that would not only cover distributed system principles, but also teach the object-oriented perspective in which the staff at LogOn believed, I was rather disappointed when I realized that there was no such book. The emerging books about distributed objects failed to distil the principles that are important when teaching students and the existing textbooks on distributed systems did not mention objects at all. The mere lack of a suitable textbook, however, did not put me off teaching a course on 'Engineering Distributed Objects'; it just meant that I had to develop much more elaborate lecture notes. When I took my current position at University College London, I was given the opportunity to extend and develop my teaching material on distributed objects further and the idea arose to turn the lecture notes into a textbook.

Although I made a lot of improvements to those initial lecture notes during the course of writing this book, I am still rather unsatisfied with the result. At the core of that dissatisfaction lies the lack of an established and mature engineering discipline for distributed object systems. Unlike operating systems, compilers and relational databases, which are more or less well understood by now, software engineers have yet to establish a solid theory and proven engineering methods that guide engineering researchers in building distributed object systems. These things are necessary before we can claim a proper engineering approach towards distributed objects systems. Thus this book can only be the first attempt towards such an engineering approach. It is not uncommon in other engineering disciplines that improvements are made in an incremental and continuous fashion, rather than the revolutionary improvements we sometimes witness in science.

In this spirit, the book aims to distil and highlight the common principles of distributed systems that are based on the object-oriented paradigm and to carefully distinguish the

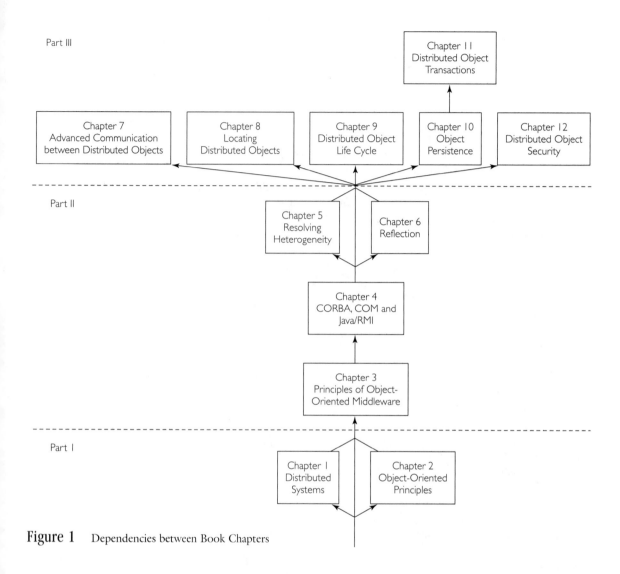

Figure 1   Dependencies between Book Chapters

different perspectives that client programmers, server programmers and systems administrators have on these objects. The book uses the emerging lingua franca, the Unified Modeling Language, to talk about the various aspects of distributed object design and to indicate the support that engineers might expect from object-oriented middleware in the design of their distributed object systems.

How to use this book

There are a lot of books in the market that explain particular distributed object systems to software engineering professionals. This book is written mainly for a student audience. It will be most useful on final year undergraduate programmes or on taught postgraduate courses. Professional software engineers may also find this book useful when they want to understand the common principles that underlie the distributed systems that are constructed following an object-oriented approach.

In order to make the best use of this book, readers will have to be familiar with object-oriented programming in Java or C++. We will occasionally discuss the influence that programming languages have on the design of distributed objects and how systems that utilize multiple programming languages can be built. These discussions will be difficult to follow if readers do not have object-oriented programming skills. We make no assumptions, however, about the knowledge that readers may have about distributed systems. This book will be useful as an introductory text on distributed system construction and we adopt an object-oriented perspective that will enable a smooth transition from first year programming courses, which increasingly choose object-oriented languages.

The book has three parts and each part is broken down into several chapters. When testing the book with a class, we found that about 2–4 hours were required for teaching each chapter. We therefore believe that this book includes sufficient material for 40 hours of lectures on distributed objects.

Figure 1 shows a reading map that presents an overview of the dependencies between the chapters. The first part explains important basic concepts. The Chapter 1 introduces the idea of distributed systems and Chapter 2 explains basic concepts of distributed system construction. Both chapters may be omitted if they have been covered in sufficient depth elsewhere in a curriculum. Chapters 3–6 discuss the principles that are needed for the execution of a distributed object request, that is the invocation of an operation from an object that may reside on another host. Of these, Chapters 3 and 4 are essential to the understanding of Part III of the book. Chapter 5 discusses the different dimensions of heterogeneity and Chapter 6 presents reflection mechanisms that enable object requests to be defined when the client runs. Though we believe these topics are important for understanding the nature of object-oriented middleware, they are not necessary for understanding Chapters 7–12. These chapters discuss solutions to particular problems that are inherent to distributed system construction. They all assume the ability to execute object requests and are largely independent of each other, except Chapters 10 and 11. Chapter 11 discusses transactions and this concept cannot reasonably be discussed without having defined a notion of persistence.

The design of each chapter uses a number of pedagogical features. Each chapter opens with a statement of its learning objectives. During the main body of the chapter, marginal notes are used to highlight definitions and keypoints. At the end of each chapter, a concise summary of the main arguments is given. Self-assessment exercises are provided that are meant to help the reader to validate the understanding of the text; they should be answered with a single sentence. A further reading section relates the material of the chapter to the literature. We have refrained from providing detailed exercises for laboratory or course work as part of the book and refer to the web site that accompanies the book (http://www.distributed-objects.com) for continuously updated material. The web site also contains Powerpoint Slides and hand-outs for each chapter that will help lecturers to prepare a course on distributed objects.

This is the way definitions are highlighted.

Keypoints are typeset like this.

Acknowledgements

The fact that I am the only author of this book is largely misleading; this book is a group effort and it would have not come into being without the help of so many people.

First of all, I would like to thank Roberto Zicari for getting me interested in distributed objects. Without Roberto, this book would not exist. I thank my friend and partner Fabrizio Ferrandina and my colleagues at my current consulting company Zühlke Engineering GmbH for giving me the opportunity to apply so many of the concepts that I write about in this book in industrial practice. Moreover, I would like to thank Stefan Zumbrunn for testing the material of this book in Zühlke's distributed object training courses.

I have to express my gratitude to Steve Wilbur, Head of the Department of Computer Science at University College London, for providing me with the opportunity to develop a course on distributed objects and for enabling me to extend the course material into this book. The department has allowed me to retreat for the extended periods of time that were necessary to complete this book in a timely manner. I want to express my special thanks to Catalin Gruia-Roman of Washington University and to Paolo Ciancarini of University of Bologna for hosting me in those periods. A great thanks also goes to Roberto and Diva for distracting me from writing with cycling and culinary experiences.

I owe great thanks to my former office mate Stephen Morris. His encouragement and continued feedback kept me going whenever I was stuck. The sharp reviews of Gian-Pietro Picco and Thomas Gschwind enabled me to improve the quality of the book considerably. I also thank Neil Roodyn, Ray Welland, Jeff Magee, Mehdi Jazayeri and a number of anonymous reviewers for their feedback. It was fun to work with my colleague, Anthony Finkelstein, on the design of the chapter layout.

I thank the staff at Wiley for their continued support and trust. Simon Plumtree and Gaynor Redvers-Mutton have been extremely helpful in keeping me on track writing this book. Katrina Arens has been of great help in organizing the review process and managing the cover design. Dawn Booth was the most efficient production editor one could possibly have. Shena Deuchars 'debugged' my English and Jenny Chapman turned my initial illustrations into well-designed figures. Mark Spedding turned our amateurish chapter design into the professional layout that the book now has.

Finally, I would also like to thank Lorenzo. When you were two years old, Lorenzo, you made me understand the importance of pictures when you asked me to read your first books to you. I learned as much Italian as you did!

To Cecilia

Part I

Concepts

Part I: *Concepts*

Part I sets the scene for this book and introduces concepts that will be needed in later chapters. Chapter 1 introduces the notion of a distributed system. In order to distil the common characteristics of a distributed system, we study examples of such systems that have been built using the object-oriented paradigm. We discuss the differences between centralized systems and distributed systems and define distributed systems to consist of autonomous components that reside on different machines whose communication is supported by a distribution middleware. Middleware resides between the network operating system and the application and aims to make distribution as transparent as possible to both users and application programmers. Transparency was first defined in the Open Distributed Processing (ODP) standard of the International Organization for Standardization (ISO), which we briefly discuss.

This book assumes that the object-oriented paradigm is used for distributed system construction. Consequently, we focus on middleware that is based on objects. Such systems support an object model and Chapter 2 discusses the basic ingredients of the object model. The construction of distributed objects is often a team effort and engineers have to communicate about objects with their colleagues. We use the Unified Modeling Language (UML) as a notation to describe various aspects of objects and we briefly introduce the UML concepts that we need in Chapter 2. Object-oriented middleware aims to hide the complexities of distribution as much as possible. However, middleware currently does not, and probably never will, achieve complete transparency. We highlight the differences between designing local objects, which communicate locally using method calls, and designing distributed objects in order to avoid some pitfalls that stand in the way of successful distributed object systems.

1

Distributed Systems

Learning Objectives

In this chapter, we will investigate several case studies in order to acquaint ourselves with the principles of distributed systems. We will use these examples to understand the differences between centralized and distributed systems. The decision to opt for a distributed system architecture often arises from particular sets of non-functional requirements. We will investigate these scalability, reliability, performance, heterogeneity and openness requirements in order to comprehend their impact on distributed system architectures. We will recognize the importance of transparency and ascertain the transparency dimensions that are important for the engineering of distributed systems.

Chapter Outline

This book focuses on techniques and principles for constructing distributed systems. Intuitively, a distributed system consists of components that execute on different computers. For the system to appear as a whole, the components need to be able to interact with each other. This is achieved using a computer network. Before we can start investigating how distributed systems can be constructed, we will have to develop an understanding of what characterizes a distributed system. We need to know why we decide to build a system in a distributed way and what principles should be applied during this construction.

The decision to build a distributed rather than a centralized system is often derived from the requirements that the system's stakeholders express. The requirements that drive the decision towards a distributed system architecture are usually of a non-functional and global nature. Scalability, openness, heterogeneity and fault-tolerance are examples of such non-functional requirements. If systems have to be built in such a way that they can scale beyond the load that can be borne by a single computer, then the system has to be decomposed into components that reside on different computers and communicate via a computer network. Sometimes systems are required to be open and able to communicate with other systems, which are probably owned and operated by different organizations. It is not possible to have these components on the same computer in a centralized system, as organizations would not be willing to give up control. Systems also evolve, which means that new components are added over time. Old components, however, may not employ the latest technology, programming languages, operating systems, hardware and network protocols. It is generally impossible to rebuild components over and over again merely to incorporate the latest technology. This leads to heterogeneous systems, where older components remain on the hardware and operating system platforms for which they have been built and form a distributed system with newer components that are written in modern languages and run on newer platforms. Finally, it may be useful to duplicate critical components on different computers so that if one computer fails another one can take over and the overall system availability is not affected.

We study these requirements from different points of view in this chapter. In the first section, we characterize a distributed system by comparing it to a centralized system. We then review examples of distributed systems that have been built in practice. We use these examples to distil the requirements that lead engineers to adopt distributed system architectures and then finally review the facets of transparency that a well-designed distributed system should exhibit.

1.1 What Is a Distributed System?

1.1.1 Ingredients of a Distributed System

Before we can start to discuss how to engineer a distributed system, we have to understand what it is that we aim to construct; we have to give a definition of a distributed system. We have to reason about the differences between distributed systems and centralized systems. We have to find the typical characteristics of a distributed system. Finally, we should understand the motivation for building distributed rather than centralized systems.

Intuitively, a distributed system will have components that are distributed over various computers. A computer that hosts some components of a distributed system is referred to as a *host*. The concept of a host shall then denote all operational components of that computer including hardware and its network operating system software. Figure 1.1 visualizes this idea.

A host is a computer that executes components that form part of a distributed system.

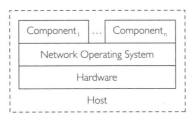

Figure 1.1

Hosts in a Distributed System

A distributed system has more than one component on more than one host. These components need to interact with each other. They need to provide access to each other's services and they need to be able to request services from each other. In theory, the components could do that directly by using the primitives that network operating systems provide. In practice, this would be too complex for many applications. As shown in Figure 1.2, distributed systems usually employ some form of *middleware* that is layered between distributed system components and network operating system components and resolves heterogeneity and distribution.

Middleware is a layer between network operating systems and applications that aims to resolve heterogeneity and distribution.

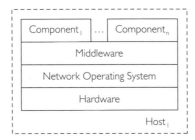

Figure 1.2

Middleware in a Distributed System

Transaction-oriented middleware supports the integration of transactions across distributed databases. Systems in this category include IBM CICS or Tuxedo. Message-oriented middleware systems enable the exchange of reliable message traffic across distributed components. Examples of this class include IBM MQSeries, the DEC MessageQueue or the Java Message Queue. Remote Procedure Calls (RPCs) were standardized by the OSF and supported the invocation of procedures across host boundaries. RPCs were the starting point for the development of object-oriented middleware, which includes the various available OMG/CORBA implementations, Remote Method Invocation (RMI) for Java, and Microsoft's COM. There are also non-mainstream products. These include mobile agent facilities, such as Aglets, implementations of tuple spaces that distributed threads can use to communicate, and so on.

Example 1.1

Middleware Approaches

An excellent understanding of the functionality and behaviour of middleware components is essential for the engineering of distributed systems. Hence, we have dedicated Part II of this book to a detailed discussion and comparison of those middleware systems that support the object-oriented paradigm, that is CORBA, RMI and COM.

A distributed system consists of components on networked hosts that interact via middleware so that they appear as an integrated facility.

For the purpose of this book, we employ a definition that we adapted from [Colouris et al., 1994]. As shown in Figure 1.3, a *distributed system* is a collection of autonomous hosts that that are connected through a computer network. Each host executes components and operates a distribution middleware, which enables the components to coordinate their activities in such a way that users perceive the system as a single, integrated computing facility.

A certain aspect of distribution is transparent if it is not visible to users, application programmers or administrators.

This definition demands a very important property of a distributed system: distribution shall be hidden from users. They shall rather perceive the system as a single computing facility. As we shall see later, it is also desirable to hide the complexity of distribution as much as possible from application programmers. This hiding is referred to as *transparency*. If we achieve this, application programmers can develop applications for distributed systems in very much the same way as they develop applications for centralized systems.

Figure 1.3
A Working Model of a
Distributed System

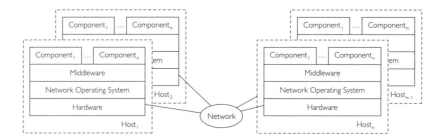

1.1.2 Centralized Versus Distributed Systems

Let us now compare distributed systems with the centralized systems familiar to most readers. The aim of this comparison is to highlight the distinctive characteristics that are often found in distributed systems.

Centralized Systems

Centralized systems have non-autonomous components.

A centralized system may be composed of different parts. However, these parts, such as classes in an object-oriented program, are not *autonomous*; the system possesses full control over its parts at any one time. The parts become operational at the time the system is started and if the system is deactivated or deleted, then all parts of the system will be deactivated or deleted, too.

Centralized systems are often built using homogeneous technology.

Centralized systems are often fairly *homogeneous*. They tend to be constructed using the same technology. Very often the same programming language and the same compiler is used for all parts. The compiler generates the same type of machine code and all parts use the same representation for data. Parts are then either statically or dynamically loaded by the same loader or linker. Communication between parts can be achieved very efficiently using programming language primitives, such as procedure calls or method invocations.

Some centralized systems support multiple users. Database applications are a good example. The database and its forms and reports are a *shared resource*. All users share a centralized system all the time and the system might become overloaded at times.

Multiple users share the resources of a centralized system at all times.

A centralized system can be built to run in a single process. It is even possible to construct it single-threaded and designers can build centralized systems that are not concurrent programs.

There is only a single *point of control* in a centralized system. The state of a centralized system can be characterized by the program counter of the processor, the register variable contents and the state of the virtual memory that is used by the process that runs the system. Centralized systems have a single *point of failure*; either they work or they do not work. Situations where parts of the system are unreachable due to a communication failure generally do not occur.

Centralized systems have a single point of control and of failure.

Distributed Systems

Distributed systems use a more coarse-grained structuring concept; distributed systems have multiple *components* and these may be decomposed further into parts. Components are autonomous; they possess full control over their parts at all times. There is, however, no master component that possesses control over all the components of a distributed system. In order for the distributed system to appear as an integrated computing facility, components need to define interfaces by means of which they communicate with each other.

Distributed systems have autonomous components.

The components of a distributed system need not be homogeneous. In fact, they are often rather heterogeneous. Heterogeneity arises, for example, from a need to integrate components on a legacy hardware platform, such as an IBM mainframe, with components newly-written to operate on a Unix workstation or a Windows NT machine. Components then might be written in different programming languages; mainframe programs are often written in Assembler, RPG or Cobol while new components will be written in Visual Basic, Java or C++. The source of components might be compiled into heterogeneous machine code. The machine code might use different data representation formats. IBM mainframes use a big-endian representation for integers and EBCDIC character codes while most Unix workstations work with a little-endian representation for integers and a 7-bit ASCII or an 8-bit ISO character encoding.

Distributed systems may be built using heterogeneous technology.

In a distributed system there may be components that are used exclusively by a single user (they are known as unshared components). In fact, this is one of the major advantages of distributed systems. If a component becomes overloaded by too many users or too many requests from other components, another component capable of performing the same services can be added to the distributed system and the load can be split among them. Moreover, components can be located so that they are local to the users and other components with which they interact. This locality improves the overall performance of the

Distributed system components may be used exclusively.

distributed system as local communication tends to be more efficient than communication with components that are far away.

Distributed systems are executed in concurrent processes.

As a consequence of component autonomy, **distributed systems execute components concurrently**. Hence, there are generally as many processes involved in the system as there are components. In addition, components are often multi-threaded; they may create a new thread whenever they start to perform a service for a user or another component. In that way the component is not blocked while it is executing a service but is available to respond to further service requests. In addition, the processes of a distributed system are generally not executed on the same processor. Hence, inter-process communication involves communication with other machines through a network. Different levels of abstraction are involved in this communication.

Distributed systems have multiple points of failure.

Unlike centralized systems, distributed systems have **multiple points of failure**. The system may fail because a component of the system has failed. It may also fail if the network has broken down, or if the load on a component is so high that it does not respond within a reasonable time frame. Hence, in a distributed system, situations occur in which parts of the system are fully operational while other parts, which rely on a currently unavailable component, do not function properly.

1.2 Examples of Distributed Systems

In this section, we review case studies of distributed systems. The first three case studies have been developed in industry and are operational. The last example is artificial and will be used to explain concepts throughout the book.

There is an overwhelming body of distributed systems. It is probably fair to say that most of these systems were not developed using the object-oriented techniques that we discuss in this book, for these techniques are still rather new. When we selected the case studies, we deliberately chose case studies that have been built using object-oriented techniques in order to illustrate that it is feasible to deploy object technology for distributed system construction.

1.2.1 Video-on-Demand

A video-on-demand service subscriber can rent videos without having to obtain videotapes. The videos are, rather, transmitted electronically. From a customer's point of view, there are many advantages. The video-on-demand service can be operational 24 hours a day; movies are always available as there is no limitation on physical media; and the time between deciding to watch a movie and the availability of the video is reduced drastically.

Hong Kong Telecom Interactive Multimedia Services have built a video-on-demand service using distributed objects. In this system, the client components that are used to display videos and the server components that load and transmit videos are considered as objects. They are distributed: clients are hosted by set-top boxes in the homes of the customers of the service and several video-on-demand servers were needed in order to make the system scale to its current 90,000 subscribers.

Example 1.2
Hong Kong Telecom Interactive Multimedia Services

The client components in the case study were implemented in Java, which means that they can be downloaded from a web server. Updating the copy on the web server implements migration to new versions of the client. Moreover, Java was chosen in order to ensure that the clients run on a number of different platforms, including web browsers and set-top boxes. The server objects were implemented in C++, mainly because they had to perform efficiently on Unix servers. Hence, the video-on-demand system is a distributed system consisting of heterogeneous components.

Video-on-demand system uses heterogeneous hosts.

The video-on-demand system uses an object-oriented middleware. We will revisit this form of middleware throughout the book. It supports the definition of interfaces of the server objects in a way that is independent of programming language, network and hardware. It manages the communication between client and server objects that is necessary to locate the server that holds a desired video and to select the video to be downloaded.

Video-on-demand system is built using middleware.

The system exhibits all of the characteristics of distributed systems that we discussed in the previous section. The components are autonomous and heterogeneous: client components are written in Java. They operate in web browsers or set-top boxes. The servers operate on Unix hosts. The servers are shared components while each customer has an unshared client object. The system is inherently concurrent, given that there are 90,000 potential users. Although it is unlikely that all subscribers will decide to watch a video at the same time, there are probably several hundred concurrent users at any point in time. Finally, there are also multiple points of failure as each of the set-top boxes/web browsers, the network link or the servers might be overloaded or fail.

Video-on-demand system has all the characteristics of a distributed system.

1.2.2 Aircraft Configuration Management

The scale of aircraft design and manufacturing processes at Boeing demands extensive IT systems. Aircraft return to the manufacturer regularly for maintenance and safety checks. Maintenance engineers therefore require an up-to-date database of the engineering documents for that particular aircraft, covering every part and the models and individual designs in which parts are used. As Boeing constructs approximately 500 new aircraft each year, the database of engineering information has documents about 1.5 billion parts added to it each year. The centralized and mainframe-based system with which the aircraft manufacturer was working was not capable of bearing this increasing load any more and a new system had to be constructed.

Support systems for aircraft configuration management must be scalable.

Example 1.3
Construction of an Aircraft

The above photograph gives an impression of the construction floor where aircraft are built and maintained. A modern aircraft consists of approximately three million individual parts. The process of integrating and maintaining these parts as a cohesive and functional whole is long and complicated for two reasons. First, every aircraft is unique because different airlines have different needs. Operators of scheduled flights, for instance, order aircraft with fewer seats and bigger overhead lockers than charter airlines. Thus, each combination of parts is put together according to specific customer demands. Secondly, in the process of revising a basic design, additional revisions may become necessary in other areas of the design. Substituting one part for another in a specific area may then require the design team to ensure the switch has no detrimental effects in other areas. If changes are required, such further revisions must be looped back through the system until a new stable design is created.

Integration of components from different vendors leads to heterogeneity.

Rather than building components from scratch, Boeing decided to use commercial off-the-shelf components, such as product data management, enterprise resource planning and computer-aided project planning systems. The decision to deploy unmodified third-party software allowed the vendor to use the best available systems. However, in order to build a system that is perceived by its users as a single integrated computing facility, Boeing had to integrate heterogeneous components into a distributed system.

Object-wrapping can be used to integrate off-the-shelf components.

Boeing made a decision early on to integrate its chosen software packages as a whole. They adopted a technique called *object wrapping*. Packages are wrapped with an interface encapsulating large chunks of application functionality, rather than breaking the applications down into smaller business objects and attempting to encapsulate each of these on an individual basis. This approach allowed the project to make rapid initial steps by avoiding extensive application-level revamping and allowed the producer to take full advantage of its decision to buy instead of build. The deployment of a distributed system for the aircraft configuration management system enabled the manufacturer to build a scalable system quickly (because it was composed from existing components). The system will be able to respond to changing needs more easily as new components can be added. Moreover, the system improved the overall performance of aircraft design and maintenance as it is better integrated. Hence, the manufacturer has gained a competitive advantage because it can design, customize and maintain aircraft more swiftly.

The integration was achieved by using an object-oriented middleware to integrate a data centre which will, in the end, have more than 45,000 total users, with as many as 9,000 at any one time. 20 large Sequent database machines run Oracle relational databases to store engineering data. 200 Unix servers host components for the application software and numerous workstations are used to provide construction and maintenance engineers with graphical user interfaces to the system.

Middleware is used to resolve heterogeneity and distribution.

Again, the aircraft configuration management system exhibits all the characteristics of a distributed system. The degree of autonomy in this case study is even higher than in the previous case study as Boeing did not have access to the source code of the components they bought off the shelf. The system is also more heterogeneous with components running on a larger variety of hardware platforms. The system consists of components that operate in concurrent processes. Some of these components are shared (e.g. the components providing the database access) and some components are not shared (the browsers with which aircraft configurations are displayed on a workstation). Again, the system is a concurrent system as the 20 Sequent machines run database servers that are concurrently accessed by the system's users. The system also has multiple points of failure. Any of the databases may be overloaded; the network may fail; or servers operating the aircraft configuration management applications may be unavailable.

Configuration management system has all characteristics of a distributed system.

1.2.3   IT Infrastructure of a Bank

The IT infrastructure in banks are still dominated by mainframe systems. The Swiss bank from which this case study was taken is a very typical example. It needed to integrate application components on these mainframe systems with application components that provide services on more modern platforms.

An example of a service is obtaining the mortgage balance of a customer or executing an equity transaction. Services are provided by reusable components. A component encapsulates a particular application. This application might be a new application or it might be a legacy application that the bank has used for a long time. Components are integrated with other components for the implementation of business processes. The integration of components that reside on heterogeneous platforms, however, means that distributed systems are constructed.

Service architecture consists of heterogeneous new and legacy components.

The bank has used transaction-oriented middleware, which could integrate distributed transactions across multiple hosts. It then decided to migrate towards using an object-oriented middleware in order to implement the service architecture in a systematic way. The components were implemented as distributed and heterogeneous objects. Objects export operations, which are the implementations of services. Objects might request the execution of services from other objects. Objects might combine the results of service

Different types of middleware can be used to resolve distribution and heterogeneity.

Example 1.4
IT Service Architecture of a
Swiss Bank

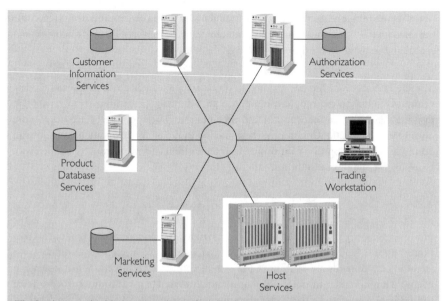

Customer
Information
Services

Authorization
Services

Product
Database
Services

Trading
Workstation

Marketing
Services

Host
Services

The bank runs a highly-integrated set of applications on large Unisys and IBM mainframes. The mainframes process approximately 2 million transactions each day and they host approximately 13,000 different applications. Recently, hardware platforms, such as Unix servers and PCs running various versions of the Windows operating system, were added to the infrastructure. The IT infrastructure used to be product-orientated. Every product that the bank offered was supported by an application. Before a product could enter the market, applications supporting the product had to be written. These applications evolved on different hardware and operating system platforms. Recently the bank has shifted the focus from products to customers. Agents in the bank now want to be able to obtain a customer profile that displays information about all products that the customer has with a bank. This demands integration between the various product-orientated applications. Moreover, agents expect applications to be integrated. By integrating the share trading application with the account management application, the purchase of an equity package can be debited instantaneously to the current account, rather than in an overnight batch. In order to meet these challenges, the bank defined the above service architecture.

requests in order to provide a higher-level service. The object-oriented middleware is used to broker service requests between the heterogeneous objects.

The implementation of this architecture has brought the bank several substantial advantages. It can now integrate applications with each other although they might not operate on one of the mainframes. Hence, the new architecture reduces the time that is needed for the creation of applications supporting new products as now the bank can use modern programming languages and operating systems to write and execute new components. The components that encapsulate applications each have very well-defined interfaces leading to a more maintainable infrastructure. Yet the mainframes and the large body of applications that run on them remain operational and the bank's huge investment in them is preserved.

Again, the bank's IT infrastructure exhibits all the distributed system characteristics that we suggested above. The components are rather autonomous. Some of the legacy components cannot be modified any more. There is a substantial heterogeneity among the components. Hardware platforms range from Unisys mainframes to Unix servers to Windows NT workstations. The bank also used a variety of programming languages including Assembler, Cobol, C, and C++. There are some components that are shared (e.g. the account databases) and others that are not shared (the user interface components to various applications). The system supports some 2,000 users and therefore consists of multiple concurrent processes. The bank is also aware of the possibility of multiple points of failure. To overcome this problem they have made a transaction management system an essential part of the middleware platform upon which they constructed their infrastructure.

The service infrastructure exhibits all characteristics of a distributed system.

1.2.4 Distributed Soccer League Management

While the three previous case studies are real, the distributed soccer league management system that we introduce now is invented. We will use it as a running example throughout this book. Its use is motivated by didactic considerations; we will be able to twist the case study in such a way that we can demonstrate all the concepts relevant to this book. We could not do this with an existing case study.

The purpose of the application is to support a national soccer association in managing soccer leagues. The application has to keep an account of soccer clubs, each of which might have several teams. The soccer clubs maintain the composition of teams. Players need to obtain a license from the soccer association. Teams have to be registered with the soccer association, too. The soccer association also runs national teams that draw their squads by selecting the best players from the teams according to certain selection criteria.

The national soccer league is inherently distributed. The clubs are geographically dispersed. The league management will, therefore, need to provide services for soccer teams to register players and to register teams. The clubs need to provide services to the soccer association so that it can make appointments with players for games of national soccer teams.

The soccer league management application is likely to be rather heterogeneous. This stems from the fact that the different clubs are autonomous. They want to use their existing computing infrastructure to provide the services demanded by the soccer association. Hence, the system will include different flavours of the Windows operating system, some clubs might use Unix machines and the traditional clubs might even have a mainframe. Likewise, different programming languages will be used for the implementation of services demanded by the soccer associations. Some clubs will already have a relational database with all the details that the association wants. They will just use a programming language with embedded SQL. Others will start from scratch; they may buy a package, such as Microsoft Office, off-the-shelf and then use Visual Basic to program an Access database.

The soccer league management system has multiple points of control. Each club manages its teams and players independently from and concurrently with the league management. The component run by the soccer association needs to be multi-threaded; it needs to be able to react to multiple concurrent requests of clubs registering players for a license. Similarly, the components in the clubs need to be able to react to a player appointment request from the component that manages the composition of national soccer teams.

There may be multiple points of failure in our distributed soccer management application. Clubs might not be connected to the soccer association by high-quality network connections, but rather by slow modem or ISDN connections. Computers in particular clubs might be switched off occasionally. This may lead to situations in which the league management system is only partially operational. Thus, a distributed system must be designed in such a way that a failure in one component must not bring down the whole system.

1.3 Distributed System Requirements

In the first section of this chapter, we have briefly compared centralized and distributed systems. The second section has shown common properties of some case studies. In this section we look at distributed systems from yet a different angle. We take an engineering perspective and look at the software engineering process in order to see when the factors that influence the choice of a distributed system architecture need to be identified. We then discuss the requirements that lead to the adoption of a distributed system architecture.

Figure 1.4 shows a system development process that we adopted from [Booch, 1995]. It includes a requirements stage where the system is conceptualized and where the user's requirements are determined. The purpose is to find out what the customer really wants and needs. In the analysis stage, the behaviour of the system functionality is formalized. The results of the conceptualization and analysis stages determine any further stages in the process.

Figure 1.4
Booch's Macro Development Process

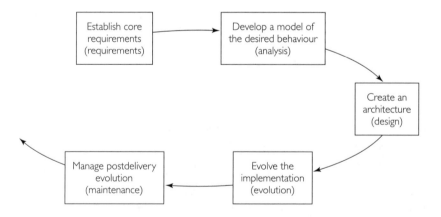

 The need to distribute a system is often derived from non-functional requirements.

The requirements stage involves identifying the functional and non-functional properties that stakeholders demand from a system. Functional requirements are concerned with the functions that the system can perform for its users. Functional requirements can usually be localized in particular components. Following the Boochean approach, functional requirements are then formalized during the object-oriented analysis. Non-functional requirements are concerned with the quality of the system. It tends to be difficult to attribute them to particular parts of the system; they are, rather, global. Non-functional requirements, therefore, have a serious impact on which overall architecture is chosen for the system. This is done during the design stage.

The non-functional requirements that typically lead to the adoption of distributed system architectures are:

1. Scalability
2. Openness
3. Heterogeneity
4. Resource Sharing
5. Fault-Tolerance

It should have become clear by now that the construction of a centralized system is considerably simpler, and therefore cheaper, than building a distributed system. Hence, it is beneficial not to build a distributed system if it can be avoided. However, some non-functional requirements just cannot be achieved by a centralized system. Let us now develop a better understanding of these requirements.

1.3.1 Scalability

When designing a power system, an important factor that engineers have to take into account is the amount of power that the users of the system will draw. This is the same for software architectures. A single generator is inappropriate as the power supply for the National Grid for the same reason that a single PC is inappropriate as a video-on-demand server: neither could bear the load.

The load that a software system has to bear can be determined in many different dimensions. It can be expressed by the maximum number of concurrent users. The Hong Kong video-on-demand service might have to serve up to 90,000 concurrent users when it goes into service. Load can also be defined by the number of transactions that the system needs to execute in a given period. The Swiss bank stated that it would perform up to two million transactions per day. Finally, load can be determined by estimating the data volume that has to be handled by the system. The data volume that Boeing's aircraft configuration management system has to maintain increases by engineering documents for approximately 1.5 billion aircraft parts each year.

For a power system, the meaning of bearing the load is obvious: we expect the system to provide the power when we need it. The same holds for computer systems; in addition to continuing the service, we expect certain qualities of service. *Qualities of service* are concerned with how the function is performed. We expect these qualities even if the system is operating under high load. A clerk in a bank expects the transaction to be completed within a couple of seconds. Likewise, a user of a video-on-demand service expects videos to arrive at a rate of at least 10 frames per second. Otherwise, the service is considered inappropriate.

Scalability denotes the ability to accommodate a growing load in the future.

Software architectures should be designed in such a way that they are stable for the lifetime of the system. The architecture therefore not only has to be able to bear the load when the system goes into production, but a prediction has to be made about how the load will develop during the lifetime of the system. Predictions as to how the load is going to develop are rather difficult. When the Internet was developed, no one estimated the current number of nodes. One of the reasons for the Internet's success is that it can grow to accommodate the increased load; it has a scalable architecture. In general, we refer to system architectures as *scalable* if they can accommodate any growth in future load, be it expected or not.

Distributed system architectures achieve scalability through employing more than one host.

Scalability requirements often lead to the adoption of distributed system architectures. In the Boeing case study, the old mainframe just could not bear the load imposed by an additional 1.5 billion parts each year. It created a bottleneck and had a negative impact on the overall performance of the engineering division. Distributed systems can be scalable because additional computers can be added in order to host additional components. In the Boeing example, 20 Sequent machines share the load of the databases needed to accommodate the overall engineering data. More machines can be added if it turns out to be necessary.

1.3.2   Openness

Open systems can easily be extended and modified.

A non-functional property that is often demanded from a software and system architecture is that it be open. *Openness* means that the system can be easily extended and modified. To facilitate openness, the system components need to have well-defined and well-documented interfaces. The system construction needs to adhere to recognized standards so that system components can be exchanged and the system does not become dependent on a particular vendor. Openness is demanded because the overall architecture needs to be stable even in the presence of changing functional requirements. Institutions that procure a new system want the system to evolve with the institution. They want to preserve their investment rather than throw it away. Hence, it is required that new components can be integrated into the system in order to meet new functional requirements.

The integration of new components means that they have to be able to communicate with some of the components that already exist in the system. In order to be able to integrate components a posteriori, existing components must have well-defined *interfaces*. These interfaces must declare the services that a component offers. A *service* is an operation that a component performs on behalf of a user or another component. Services are often parameterized and the service parameters need to be specified in the interface, too. A *client component* uses such an interface to *request* a service from a *server component*. Note that a component that is a client of some component can itself be a server to other components. Components might be reactive and have to respond to the occurrence of *events* that are detected by other components. A billing component in the video-on-demand server, for instance might have to react to the downloading of a video that is detected by the video database component. In an open system, components need to declare which events they produce so that other components can react to them.

Openness and distribution are related. Components in a distributed system have to declare the services they offer so that other components can use these services. In a centralized system, components may also declare their interfaces so that other systems can use them. The use, however, is often confined to procedure calls. These restrict the requesting component in various ways. A request in a distributed system is more flexible. It can be made from the same or a different machine. It can be executed synchronously or asynchronously. Finally, the requester and the server can be constructed in a heterogeneous way.

Distributed system components achieve openness by communicating using well-defined interfaces.

1.3.3 Heterogeneity

A requirement that occurs frequently for new systems is that they have to integrate heterogeneous components. Heterogeneity arises for a number of reasons. Often components are bought off-the-shelf. Components that are constructed anew might have to interface with legacy components that have been around in an enterprise for a long time. Components might be built by different contractors. In any of these cases, components are likely to be heterogeneous.

Component *heterogeneity* arises from the use of different technology for the implementation of services, for the management of data and for the execution of components on hardware platforms. Heterogeneity can stem from the autonomy of the component builders, from components built at different points of time or from the fact that one technology is better suited for a component than another technology.

Heterogeneity of components can arise in the programming languages, operating systems, hardware platforms and network protocols.

When we revisit the case studies that we have discussed in Section 1.2 we see that most of them involved building distributed systems from heterogeneous components. In the Boeing case, many components were bought off-the-shelf. They were constructed using different programming languages and operated on different hardware platforms. In the bank example, new components had to be integrated with legacy systems for account management that operated on a mainframe. In the video-on-demand system, front-end components were written in Java so as to be portable. Back-end components had to be written in C++ to be high-performant.

The integration of heterogeneous components, however, implies the construction of distributed systems. If the system includes components that need to be executed on their native hardware platforms, the components needs to remain there. To be able to appear as an integrated whole to users, components then have to communicate via the network and heterogeneity has to be resolved during that communication.

Component heterogeneity can be accommodated by distributed systems.

1.3.4 Resource Access and Sharing

Resources denote hardware, software and data. *Resource sharing* is often required in order to render an expensive resource more cost-effective. A Sequent database machine is a highly specialized and, therefore, rather expensive piece of equipment. It becomes cost-effective for Boeing because it is shared by several hundred engineers. Resource sharing also occurs as a consequence of communication and co-operation between users. In the Boeing case study, the construction engineer of the aircraft communicates with the maintenance engineer by means of the database component. It stores the engineering documents that

Often resources, i.e. hardware, software and data, need to be shared by more than one user.

the construction engineer finalized so that they can be retrieved by the maintenance engineer, if necessary.

Security of resource access needs to be considered.

The fact that components are not exclusively used by a single user on a single machine has security implications. It has to be defined who is allowed to access shared data in a distributed system. To be able to do that, a notion of users has to be introduced and systems have to validate that the users actually are who they claim to be. Hence, a secondary requirement is to control access to a resource that needs to be shared. In the Hong Kong Telecom's video-on-demand system, access needs to be controlled so that only authorized users are allowed to download videos; the company wants users to register and pay before they can start to download videos.

The right to access a resource is implemented by resource managers. A *resource manager* is a component that grants access to a shared resource. The video-on-demand server is an example of such a resource manager. It manages the videos owned or licensed by Hong Kong Telecom. It will force users to identify themselves and it will authenticate them against a registered user set. It will only allow authenticated users to download a video.

Distributed objects provide a sophisticated model of resource sharing.

Resource managers and their users can be deployed in different ways in a distributed systems architecture. In a *client-server architecture*, there are servers that manage and provide certain resources and clients that use them. We use a more sophisticated model for resource sharing in this book. It is based on the concept of distributed objects. A distributed object represents and encapsulates a resource that it uses to provide services to other objects. Objects that provide services, in turn, might rely on services provided by other objects. This leads to an architecture that has various layers and is therefore sometimes also referred to as an *n-tier architecture*.

1.3.5   Fault-Tolerance

Hardware, software and networks are not free of failures. They fail because of software errors, failures in the supporting infrastructure (power-supply or air conditioning), abuse by their users, or just because of ageing hardware. The lifetime of a hard disk, for instance, lies between two and five years, much less than the average lifetime of a distributed system.

Operations that continue even in the presence of faults are referred to as fault-tolerant.

An important non-functional requirement that is often demanded from a system is fault-tolerance. *Fault-tolerance* demands that a system continues to operate, even in the presence of faults. Ideally, fault-tolerance should be achieved with limited involvement of users or system administrators. They are an inherent source of failures themselves. Fault-tolerance is a non-functional requirement that often leads to the adoption of a distributed system architecture.

Distributed systems can be more fault-tolerant than centralized systems. Fault-tolerance can be achieved by limiting the effect of failures. If a client in Hong Kong fails to watch a video, it does not necessarily mean that all other users will be affected by this failure. The overall system more or less continues to work. Fault-tolerance of components, such as the video-on-demand server, is achieved by redundant components, a concept referred to as *replication*. If a component fails then a replica of that component can step in and continue to serve.

Given that there are more hosts in a distributed system, each running several processes, it is much more likely that failures occur than in a centralized system. Distributed systems, therefore, have to be built in such a way that they continue to operate, even in the presence of the failure of some components.

Fault-tolerant components are built in such a way that they are able to continue to operate although components that they rely on have failed. They detect these failures and recover from them, e.g. by contacting a replica or an equivalent service.

Distributed systems achieve fault-tolerance by means of replication.

1.4 Transparency in Distributed Systems

The design of a distributed system architecture that meets all or some of the above requirements is rather complicated. Our definition of distributed systems demands that the distributed system appear as a single integrated computing facility to users. In other words, the fact that a system is composed from distributed components should be hidden from users; it has to be transparent.

In addition, it is also highly beneficial to hide the complexity of distributed system construction from the average application engineer as much as possible. They will be able to construct and maintain applications much more efficiently and cost-effectively if they are not slowed down by the complexity introduced through distribution.

There are many dimensions of transparency. These transparency dimensions were first identified in [ANSA, 1989]. Because they were so fundamentally important, they formed an important part of the International Standard on Open Distributed Processing (ODP) [ISO/IEC, 1996]. Figure 1.5 shows an overview. These transparency criteria will be discussed in detail in this section. The figure suggests that there are different levels of transparency. The criteria at lower levels support achieving the transparency criteria at higher levels.

Transparency in distributed systems has several different dimensions.

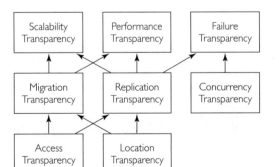

Figure 1.5

Dimensions of Transparency in Distributed Systems

A detailed understanding of the transparency dimensions is useful for several reasons. The dimensions provide a yardstick against which we can measure middleware components. We can use them to review the extent to which middleware systems actually support the application engineer in achieving overall distribution transparency. Moreover, we can use the transparency criteria to review the design of distributed components. They will allow us to distinguish well-designed components from components that cause problems during the operation, administration or maintenance.

1.4.1 Access Transparency

Access transparency means that the interfaces for local and remote communication are the same.

For a distributed system to appear as a single integrated computing facility, the system components have to interact with each other. We assume that a component interacts with another component by requesting execution of a service. *Access transparency* demands that the interface to a service request is the same for communication between components on the same host and components on different hosts. This definition is rather abstract. Let us review some examples of access transparency in Example 1.5.

Example 1.5
Example of Access Transparency

Users of the Unix network file system (NFS) can use the same commands and parameters for file system operations, such as copying or deleting files, regardless of whether the accessed files are on a local or a remote disk. Likewise, application programmers use the same library function calls to manipulate local and remote files on an NFS.

In our soccer management application, a team component offers some services that are implemented by operations. An operation has a name, a parameter list and a return type. The way any of these operations is invoked is independent of the location. Invocation is identical for a club component that resides on the same machine as the team component and for a national component that resides on the host machine of the soccer association.

Access transparency is an important property of a distributed system. A component whose access is not transparent cannot easily be moved from one host to another. All other components that request services would first have to be changed to use a different interface. We will review how access transparency is achieved with middleware in Chapters 3 and 4.

1.4.2 Location Transparency

Location transparency means that service requesters do not need to know physical component locations.

To request a service, components have to be able to address other components. They have to identify the component from which they want to request the service. *Location transparency* demands that components can be identified in service requests without knowing the physical location (that is the host) of the component.

Example 1.6
Examples of Location Transparency

A user of a Unix NFS can access files by addressing them with their full pathname. Users do not have to know the host name or the IP address of the machine that serves the partition of the file system that contains the file. Likewise, application programmers just pass the pathname identifying a file to the Unix library function to open a file and they can then access the file using an internal identifier.

The users of a video-on-demand system do not have to know the name or the IP address from which their client component downloads a video. Similarly, the application programmer who wrote the client component should not have to know the physical location of the video-on-demand server that provides the video.

Location transparency is another primary property that any distributed system should have. If location is not transparent, the administration of the system will become very difficult. In particular, it becomes next to impossible to move components from one server to another. When an NFS administrator decides to move a partition, for instance because a disk is full, application programs accessing files in that partition would have to be changed if file location is not transparent for them. Hence, middleware systems have to support identifying and locating components in such a way that the physical component location remains transparent to the application engineer. We discuss techniques and their implementations for achieving location transparency in Chapter 8.

1.4.3 Migration Transparency

It sometimes becomes necessary to move a component from one host to another. This may be due to an overload of the host or to a replacement of the host hardware. Moving could also be needed due to a change in the access pattern of that component; the component might have to be relocated closer to its users. We refer to this removal of components as *migration*. *Migration transparency* refers to the fact that components can be migrated without users recognising it and without designers of client components or the component to be migrated taking special considerations.

Migration transparency means that a component can be relocated without users or clients noticing it.

In the soccer management application, players tend to move from one team to another. Migration transparency means that components, such as the application managing the national soccer team, do not have to be aware of the fact that the player component has moved to a different team.

Example 1.7
Example of Migration Transparency

Migration transparency depends on both access and location transparency. Migration cannot be transparent if the interface of a service request changes when a local component is moved to a remote host or vice versa. Likewise, migration cannot be transparent if clients need to know the physical location of a component.

Migration transparency depends on access and location transparency.

Migration transparency is a rather important property. It is very difficult to administer a distributed system in which components cannot be freely relocated. Such a distributed system becomes very inflexible as components are tied to particular machines and moving them requires changes in other components. We discuss how migration transparency is achieved in Chapter 9 when we discuss the life cycle of distributed objects.

1.4.4 Replication Transparency

It is sometimes advantageous to keep copies of components on different hosts. These copies, however, need to be tied together. If they maintain an internal state, that state needs to be synchronized in all copies. We refer to copies of components that meet this requirement as *replicas*. The process of creating a replica and keeping the replicas up-to-date with the original is referred to as *replication*. Replication is used to improve the overall

A replica is a component copy that remains synchronized with its original.

performance and to make systems more scalable. Moreover, if one replica fails other replicas can stand in.

Replication transparency means that users and programmers do not know whether a replica or a master provides a service.

Replication should be transparent in a distributed system. *Replication transparency* refers to the fact that users and application programmers are not aware that a service they are using is not provided by an "original" master component, but by a replica. Replication transparency also refers to the fact that application engineers who build a component should not have to take into account that the component might be replicated.

Example 1.8
Example of Replication Transparency

In the video-on-demand service, we could imagine that it would be beneficial to replicate the video database server. In that way, the video-on-demand system scales to accommodate many concurrent users. Replication transparency means that customers who watch a video are not aware that the video is downloaded from a replica server rather than the original server. It also means that the engineers who wrote the client software did not have to design them in such a way that they were capable of contacting a replica rather than the original database. Finally, replication transparency means that the engineer who wrote the database server did not have to build the server in such a way that it could be replicated.

Replication transparency depends on access and location transparency.

Replication transparency depends on access and location transparency in the same way as migration transparency does. Replicas are typically held on different machines from that which hosts the master component in order to distribute the load. To achieve replication transparency, we need the way that services are requested to be the same for the replica and the master and we must avoid clients needing to know the location of either the replica or the master component.

Without replication transparency, the resulting systems will be difficult to use and even more difficult to scale to accommodate a growing load. If replication is not transparent for the construction of components providing a service, it will not be possible to replicate existing components that have not been constructed to be replicated. This complicates administration, as components have to be changed when replication becomes necessary.

1.4.5 Concurrency Transparency

Concurrency transparency means that users and programmers are unaware that components request services concurrently.

When we characterized distributed systems, we pointed out that they are inherently concurrent. Hence, multiple components may exist and operate concurrently. Concurrency of components, however, should be transparent to users and application engineers alike. *Concurrency transparency* means that several components may concurrently request services from a shared component while the shared component's integrity is preserved and neither users nor application engineers have to see how concurrency is controlled. This definition is rather abstract and it needs to be illustrated with a number of examples.

In the bank application (see Figure 1.4), the mainframe will host a component that manages the current accounts of customers. When an equity trader buys equities on behalf of a customer, the costs are debited to the customer's current account. Concurrently, an advisor in the bank might print a statement of the same account. It is transparent for the two users that they are accessing the account at the same time. The application engineers who developed the two components should not have to consider the potential of concurrent accesses to the same account, either. In the soccer league management application, the trainer of a club team might use an application to compose training and playing schedules. That application would request a service to make appointments from individual player components. Concurrently, the trainer of the national soccer team. The users are unaware of each other and the engineers who build the team management applications do not have to take measures to avoid concurrency conflict.

Example 1.9
Examples of Concurrency Transparency

The integrity of resources in the presence of concurrent accesses and updates has to be retained. Potential implications of integrity violations include incorrect financial accounts, money that is lost during financial transactions or soccer players who are unavailable for important games due to a double booking.[1] Hence, concurrency has to be controlled somehow. If concurrency were made visible to users, they would recognize that they are not the sole users of the system. They might even see what other users do. This is only acceptable in exceptional cases (e.g. in computer supported co-operative work systems) but users in general would not be willing to implement concurrency control. If concurrency control were to be implemented by the application engineers, the construction of applications would be much more complicated, time-consuming and error-prone. Fortunately, there are techniques available so that concurrency control can be implemented in a middleware component in such a way that concurrency can be transparent to both users and application engineers. We discuss these techniques and the use of middleware systems that implement them in Chapter 11.

1.4.6 Scalability Transparency

As discussed above, one of the principle objectives to build a distributed rather than a centralized system is to achieve scalability. *Scalability transparency* denotes another high-level transparency criterion and demands that it should be transparent to designers and users how the system scales to accommodate a growing load. Scalability transparency is very similar to performance transparency in that both are concerned with the quality of service that is provided by applications. While performance is viewed from the perspective of a single request, scalability transparency considers how the system behaves if more components and more concurrent requests are introduced.

Scalability transparency means that users and programmers do not know how scalability of a distributed system is achieved.

---

[1] I leave the reader to decide which of these is the worst fault.

Example 1.10
Example of Scalability
Transparency

> The Internet is a good example of a distributed system that scales transparently. The size of the Internet increases daily because new hosts are continuously added. These hosts generate additional network traffic. To improve, or at least retain, the quality of service of the existing sites, the bandwidth of routers and backbone connections is being improved continuously. Through the very careful design of the Internet, however, improving the physical layer does not affect existing nodes or even applications of the Internet. Thus, the Internet scales in a transparent way.

 Scalability transparency depends on replication and migration transparency.

Achieving scalability transparency is supported by replication transparency and migration transparency in the same way as they support performance transparency. If a system supports replication, we can scale it by adding more replicas. Moreover, we can add new hosts and populate them with existing components that we migrate from overloaded hosts.

If scalability is not transparent to users they will be annoyed by degrading performance as the overall system load gradually increases. There might be situations where a system that functions correctly is rendered unusable because it cannot accommodate the load. In banking applications, for example, systems often have to complete batch jobs overnight. If they fail to complete the batch because it is too complex, the bank cannot resume business on the following day. If scalability is not transparent to application developers, a consequence is that the system (often its architecture) has to be changed. These changes tend to be rather expensive.

1.4.7 Performance Transparency

Performance transparency means that users and programmers are unaware how good system performance is maintained.

Another high-level transparency dimension is *performance transparency*. This demands that it is transparent to users and application programmers how the system performance is actually achieved. When considering performance, we are interested in how efficiently the system uses the resources available. These resources can be the time that elapses between two requests or the bandwidth that the system needs. Again, performance transparency is supported by lower-level concepts as it relies on replication transparency and migration transparency.

Example 1.11
Example of Performance
Transparency

> As an example of performance transparency, consider a distributed version of the make utility [Feldman, 1979] that is capable of performing jobs, such as compiling a source module, on several remote machines in parallel. Complex system compilation can be performed much faster using multiple processors. It not only considers the different processors and their capabilities, but also their actual load. If it can choose from a set of processors, it will delegate the compile jobs to the fastest processor that has the lowest load. In this way, the distributed make achieves an even better performance. Programmers using a distributed make, however, do not see or choose which machine performs which job. The way in which the actual performance is achieved is transparent for them.

Replication of components provides the basis for a technique called *load balancing*, which achieves performance transparency. A middleware system that implements load balancing selects the replica with the least load to provide a requested service. The middleware system should perform this balancing decision in a way that is transparent to both users and application programmers. The performance of a system can be improved if components are relocated in such a way that remote accesses are minimized. This usually requires migration of components. Achieving an optimal performance would then demand that access patterns to components are monitored and component migration is triggered when necessary. We achieve performance transparency if the underlying middleware triggers component migration in a way that is transparent to users, application programmers and possibly even administrators.

Performance transparency depends on replication and migration transparency.

Performance transparency is rather difficult to achieve. Only a few middleware systems to date are actually capable of performing load balancing. The reason is that it is genuinely difficult to automatically predict the load that a component is going to cause on a host in the future. Because of that, achieving good performance of a distributed system still requires significant intervention of application designers and administrators.

1.4.8 Failure Transparency

We have identified that failures are more likely to occur in distributed systems. *Failure transparency* denotes the concealment of faults from users, client and server components. Hence, failure transparency means that components can be designed without taking into account that services they rely on might fail. The same consideration also applies to server components. Failure transparency implies that server components can recover from failures without the server designer taking measures for such recovery. As shown in Figure 1.5, failure transparency is a high-level transparency criterion. Its achievement is supported by both concurrency and replication transparency.

Failure transparency means that users and programmers are unaware of how distributed systems conceal failures.

If failures have to be concealed, we have to ensure that the integrity of components is not violated by failures. Such integrity violations are often due to related updates that are only partially completed. We will see that transactions are used to ensure that related changes to different components are done in an atomic way. Transactions, in turn, are implemented based on the mechanisms that achieve concurrency control. We will discuss this in Chapter 11 in more detail. In addition to transactions, replication can be employed to achieve failure transparency. Replicas can step in for a failed component and provide a requested service instead of the original component. When this is done in a way that is transparent to users and client components, failures of components are concealed.

Failure transparency depends on concurrency and replication transparency.

Failure transparency is particularly important for the banking application. Customers will not tolerate it if an automatic teller machine does not deliver the cash they wanted. They also worry whether the teller machine actually debited money from the account without dispensing the cash equivalent. Failures that might occur during a cash withdrawal should be concealed from the customer. The design of the equity trading packages or marketing packages used in the bank should not have to be adjusted to recover from faults. Designers of these applications should be able to assume that components they rely on are or will be made available. Moreover, components that provide services to other components should be re-activated and recover to an earlier consistent state

Example 1.12
Example of Failure Transparency

Failures should be transparent to users; otherwise, they will be unsatisfied with the system. If failures of servers are not transparent to designers of client applications, they have to build measures into their clients to achieve failure transparency for their users. This will complicate the design of clients and make them more expensive and difficult to maintain.

Key Points

▶ Distributed systems consist of a number of networked hosts, each of which executes one or several components. These components use middleware to communicate with each other and the middleware hides distribution and heterogeneity from programmers to some extent.

▶ Developers often do not have the choice to develop a centralized system architecture because non-functional requirements that include scalability, openness, heterogeneity, resource sharing and fault-tolerance force them to adopt a distributed architecture.

▶ We have discussed different dimensions in which distribution can be transparent to users, application designers and administrators. These dimensions are access, location, concurrency, failure, migration, replication, performance and scalability transparency. These provide design guidelines for distributed systems.

▶ The transparency dimensions we identified are not independent of each other. Access, location and concurrency are low-level transparency dimensions. They support higher level dimensions, such as failure, performance and scalability transparency.

Self Assessment

1.1   Name five reasons for building a distributed system.
1.2   What is the difference between a client-server system and a distributed system?
1.3   Is a three-tier architecture a distributed system?
1.4   Why do we not build every system as a distributed system?
1.5   What is the relationship between requirements engineering and distributed systems?
1.6   What are the eight dimensions of transparency in distributed systems?
1.7   What can the transparency dimensions be used for?
1.8   What is the difference between location and access transparency?
1.9   What are the differences between performance and scalability transparency?

Further Reading

Engineering distributed systems follows a development process that is not much different from that for other software systems. Throughout this book, we assume that the reader is familiar with basic software engineering principles and techniques. We recommend [Ghezzi et al., 1991], [Pressman, 1997] or [Jalote, 1991] as a reference. A good introduction to object-oriented software engineering is given in [Jacobson et al., 1992].

The selection of particular distributed system architectures is often driven by non-functional requirements. The requirements engineering process that precedes the design of a distributed system is beyond the scope of this book and we refer to [Sommerville and Sawyer, 1997] as a good reference. Moreover, several software engineering standards, such as those discussed in [Mazza et al., 1994] include practices for good requirements engineering. They define categories of non-functional requirements that influence the architecture of distributed systems.

Other textbooks employ a definition of distributed systems that slightly differs from ours. The reader might deepen the understanding of relevant concepts by comparing our definitions with the ones given in [Sloman and Kramer, 1987], [Colouris et al., 1994] and [Mullender, 1993].

[ANSA, 1989] mentions different dimensions of distributed system transparency for the first time. Transparency dimensions are also discussed in the Open Distributed Processing (ODP) standard of the International Organization for Standardization (ISO) [ISO/IEC, 1996].

2

Designing Distributed Objects

Learning Objectives

In this chapter, we will study the central notion of distributed objects. We will learn about the history of object orientation and how contributions from different disciplines of Computer Science led to distributed objects. We will study the notations defined in the Unified Modeling Language (UML), which we will use to communicate about the design of distributed objects. We will then grasp a meta-model for objects in order to acquaint ourselves with the concepts of distributed objects, such as object types, attributes, operations, inheritance and polymorphism. We will recognize the differences between distributed and local objects in order to understand how the design of objects differs when objects reside on different hosts.

Chapter Outline

2.1 Evolution of Object Technology
2.2 UML Representations for Distributed Object Design
2.3 A Meta-Model for Distributed Objects
2.4 Local versus Distributed Objects

In the last chapter, we introduced the concept of a distributed system. The main constituents of every distributed system are the system components. They offer services to other components, which can request service execution.

In this book, we assume an object-oriented view of distributed systems. Hence, we consider the components of a distributed system to be objects. The object-oriented paradigm is a very appropriate model for a distributed system. Services can be seen as operations that an object exports. How these objects are implemented is of no concern and the type of an object is therefore defined by interfaces. Interfaces may declare the visible state of a component, which can be regarded as a set of object attributes. The concept of references to objects is used for addressing components. Finally, the requesting of a service can be seen as a remote operation invocation.

All aspects of object orientation (concepts, languages, representations and products) have reached a stage of maturity where it is possible to address complex issues of distribution using the object-oriented paradigm. We review the evolution of object-oriented concepts in the next section to indicate exactly where we have now reached. Prior to implementation, all systems necessarily go through preliminary stages of more general analysis and design which, in the case of those that use an object-oriented approach, are now facilitated by the standardized representations offered by the Unified Modeling Language, in particular the diagrams defined in the UML Notation Guide. We discuss those diagrams in the second section. We then discuss a meta-model relevant to distributed objects in order to provide a framework for explaining basic concepts, as now generally understood, and a hierarchy for thinking about how objects are implemented. Once detailed design is underway it is necessary to consider very carefully the differences between centralized and distributed systems and the implications of factors including the life cycle, object references, request latency, security and so on. We discuss what differentiates distributed object design from local object design in the last section.

2.1 Evolution of Object Technology

Figure 2.1 shows an overview of important steps in the development of distributed objects. We can distinguish three strands in object orientation: distributed systems, programming languages and software engineering. Although largely independent, several cross-fertilizations are indicated by the lines that span the boundary of the strands.

Object orientation started in Scandinavia with the development of Simula [Dahl and Nygaard, 1966]. Simula is a programming language that was targeted to the development of simulation programs. Simula includes the concept of a class, which is a type whose instances can react to messages that are defined by operations.

David Parnas presented the idea of a *module* in his seminal paper 'A technique for the software module specification with examples' [Parnas, 1972]. The need for modules is driven by the observation that data structures change more frequently during program maintenance than names, parameters and results of operations. By hiding information about the data structures within a module, other modules cannot become dependent on these modules; they are not affected if data structures have to be changed. These ideas later

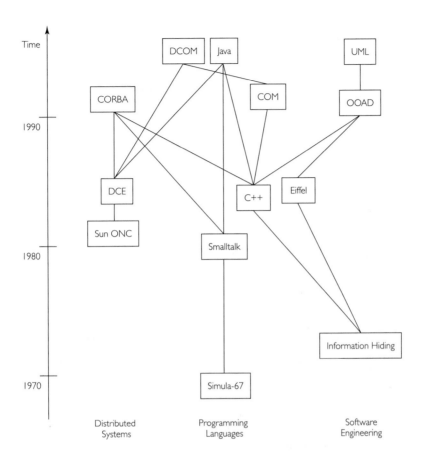

Figure 2.1

The Evolution of Object Technology

influenced programming language designers and led to the inclusion of constructs to restrict the visibility of instance variables and methods in object-oriented programming languages, such as C++, Eiffel and Java.

In the late 1970s, the Xerox Palo Alto Research Center conducted research into novel user interfaces for computers and invented the ideas of desktops, windows and pointing devices, such as mice or trackballs. It became clear that existing imperative programming languages were not well suited for applications that needed to react to events in multiple windows. In response to that problem Smalltalk [Goldberg, 1985] was developed as a new programming language that was centred around the notion of an *object*. Objects were applied to many different problems and Smalltalk implemented the vision that 'everything is an object'. Objects were used to implement the functionality of applications, to store data and to compose the user interface from different components. Objects were even used to manage the evolution of the set of object types that are defined. Smalltalk also included the concepts of inheritance and polymorphism that made it possible to create reusable class libraries, for instance to support user interface management.

Inspired by the success of Smalltalk, several groups introduced object-oriented concepts into procedure programming language, which led to the creation of hybrid object-oriented languages. Bjaerne Stroustrup led a development at AT&T Bell Labs, where his group extended the C programming language with object-oriented concepts into C++ [Stroustrup, 1986]. Although Smalltalk was a conceptually nicer language, C++ was more successful commercially. C++ is a strict superset of C and promised a smoother migration to object-oriented concepts while continuing to use existing C code. C++ is more efficient than Smalltalk. Finally, C++ is a statically typed language, which means that static semantic errors can be detected at compile time, while they are only detected at run-time in Smalltalk.

For several reasons, C++ was, and to a considerable extent still is, rather difficult to use. The language leaves a considerable amount of freedom to programmers. Like Smalltalk, it does not have a rigorous type system, it enables programmers to manipulate object references and it lacks powerful memory management. Eiffel ([Meyer, 1988b]) was defined to overcome these deficiencies. Eiffel supports the notion of 'design by contract'. Contracts are specified in class definitions that are binding for client and server. The contract is enforced by Eiffel's powerful type system. Class definitions not only include static properties of classes but also behavioural definitions, such as invariants and pre- and post-conditions of operations.

The success of object-oriented programming languages motivated the development of notations and a method for applying the object-oriented paradigm in earlier phases of the development. At the end of the 1980s and early 1990s, object-oriented analysis and design (OOAD) methods were defined in order to enable the seamless use of objects from requirements to implementation. About ten methods were defined and the more successful ones included Booch's Object-Oriented Analysis and Design [Booch, 1991], Jacobson's Object-Oriented Software Engineering [Jacobson et al., 1992], Rumbaugh's Object Modeling Technique (OMT) [Rumbaugh et al., 1991] and the Open Method [Henderson-Sellers et al., 1998]. The techniques each used their own notation for objects and they had a different focus on analysis, design or both.

A consortium led by Rational Corporation, which employed Booch, Rumbaugh and Jacobson at the time, defined the Unified Modeling Language (UML) in an attempt to resolve the heterogeneity in object-oriented analysis and design notations. UML includes a meta-model, a semantics definition and a notation guide. UML supports modelling the structure of systems using class diagrams and object diagrams. It also facilitates modelling the behaviour of systems. Interaction diagrams are used for modelling inter-class behaviour. State diagrams are used to model intra-class behaviour. UML was adopted by the Object Management Group (OMG) as an industry standard [OMG, 1997c]. Methods now merely differ in how this standard notation is used during the analysis and design of objects.

Many distribution aspects of objects have their origin in the Remote Procedure Calls (RPCs) that were developed by Sun Microsystems as part of the Open Network Communication (ONC) architecture. In ONC, clients can call procedures that run on remote machines. The interfaces of remote programs are specified in a dedicated interface definition language. Client and server stubs convert complex procedure parameters and results to and from a form that is transmissible via network transport protocols, such as TCP or UDP. Stubs are derived by `rpcgen`, a compiler for the interface definition language.

Other Unix vendors and PC vendors quickly adopted RPCs as a primitive to build distributed systems at a higher level of abstraction than TCP. As part of their effort to standardize Unix, the Open Software Foundation (OSF) also standardized RPCs in the Distributed Computing Environment (DCE). In particular, DCE standardized an external data representation (XDR) for data types that are used in procedure parameters and results. By means of XDR, clients can call remote procedures from servers that have a different data representation. OSF also standardized a number of higher-level services, such as a naming service to locate components and a security service that can be used to authenticate components.

The OMG was created as early as 1989 in order to develop and promote the Common Object Request Broker Architecture (CORBA). CORBA combines the idea of remote invocation with the object-oriented paradigm. An essential part of the CORBA standard is an Object Request Broker (ORB). Objects use ORBs to request execution of operations from other objects. Hence, ORBs provide the basic communication mechanism between distributed objects. These objects may be heterogeneous in various dimensions: the deployment platforms, the operating systems, the networks by which they are connected and the programming languages in which they are written. Hence, ORBs provide the basic communication mechanisms for distributed and heterogeneous objects. The OMG has also standardized interfaces for higher-level services and facilities that utilize the basic communication mechanism to solve standard tasks in distributed systems, many of which support achieving the distribution transparency dimensions identified in the previous chapter.

Microsoft defined its Component Object Model (COM) as an interoperability model for applications that are written in different programming languages. COM objects can be implemented in different programming languages, including Visual Basic, Visual C++ and Visual J++. COM is not fully object-oriented, as it does not include multiple inheritance. COM objects, however, can have multiple different interfaces and this is used as a replacement of inheritance.

The first versions of COM did not support distribution. They served as a basis for integrating heterogeneous objects on the same machine. With the advent of Windows NT4.0, a technology called Distributed Component Object Model was introduced to COM and COM now uses OSF/RPCs to support distributed access to COM objects.

Distribution primitives are tightly integrated with object-oriented programming language features in Java [Winder and Roberts, 1997]. Java includes primitives for Remote Method Invocation (RMI) so that a Java object on one machine can invoke methods from a Java object that resides on a remote machine. RMI also uses stubs and skeletons to perform marshalling, although data representation heterogeneity does not have to be resolved.

We have now very briefly sketched the evolution of object technology. Several of the concepts that we could only touch on here will have to be revisited throughout the rest of the book. We will discuss the principles that underlie Java/RMI, OMG/CORBA and COM in Part II. The use of these middleware systems requires detailed knowledge of the underlying object-oriented concepts as well as object-oriented design notations. We will focus on them in the remainder of this chapter.

2.2 UML Representations for Distributed Object Design

A software engineering method encompasses a notation as well as development heuristics and procedures that suggest how to use the notation. A notation is defined in terms of syntax and semantics. The syntactic part of the notation can be determined in terms of a grammar, be it for a textual or a graphical language. The semantics of a language can be distinguished in static and dynamic respects. The static semantics typically identify scope and typing rules, such as that declarations of identifiers must be unique within a certain scope and that applied occurrences must match particular declarations. The dynamic semantics defines the meaning for different concepts of the notation.

In this section, we discuss the syntax and semantics of the Unified Modeling Language (UML). UML is a notation for object-oriented analysis and design. The Object Management Group standardized UML in 1997. UML consists of a meta-model, the definition of the semantics of concepts identified in the meta-model, and a notation guide that identifies different diagram types that utilize the concepts of the meta-model. The purpose of this section is to introduce a standard notation for communication about objects. We do so by focussing on the diagram types and their use in the process of engineering distributed objects. For a discussion of the UML meta-model and the precise semantics of UML concepts, we refer the reader to the UML literature [Booch et al., 1999, Rumbaugh et al., 1999, Jacobson et al., 1999].

 Different forms of UML diagram are used during the design of distributed objects.

The UML diagram types that we present now are likely to be used during the engineering of distributed objects. For each of them, we discuss its purpose, indicate the main concepts that are available and briefly and informally indicate the semantics of these concepts.

2.2.1 Use Case Diagrams

Use case diagrams capture requirements from a functional perspective.

Use case diagrams are produced during the requirements analysis stage of the system development. A use case diagram (see Example 2.1) has a graphical notation that is used to analyze the system and the different ways in which it is used.

Actors are types of human user or external system.

Analysis begins with the identification of *actors* external to the system. An actor is a generic way of describing the potential users of the system. Actors are represented as stick persons in use case diagrams. In identifying actors, we will need to consider scenarios or situations typical to the system and its use. Note that the users are not necessarily human; they may also be external systems that use an application through its system interfaces. A further important distinction is between actors and users. Actors are types while users denote particular instances of these types.

A use case is a generic description of an entire course of events involving the system and actors external to the system.

A *use case* is depicted as an oval in a use case diagram. The description of the use case is associated with that diagram. Together the use cases in a diagram represent all the defined ways of using the system and the behaviour it exhibits whilst doing so. Again, we separate types and instances for use cases. Each use case is a specific type for how the system is used.

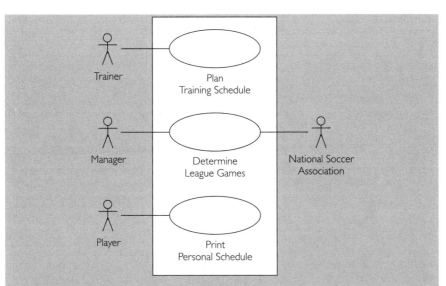

Example 2.1
Use Case Diagram for Soccer
Management

The National Soccer Association is an external system actor. A particular system user, such as the trainer Ottmar, may take on the roles of different actors at different times, for instance Player or Trainer.

A *scenario* denotes an instance of a use case. When a user (an actor instance) inputs a stimulus, the scenario executes and starts a function belonging to the use case.

Actors interact with certain use cases. These *interactions* are recorded in the use case diagram in order to show which users of which types interact with a particular use case. Interactions also identify which types of user have a stake in the functionality that is embedded in a use case. Interactions are depicted as lines.

The identification of interaction between actors and use cases is an important step for the engineering of a distributed system. Actors will need an interface to the system. If actors represent humans they will need a user interface. If they represent external systems, they will need a system interface. In both cases, the interface may need distributed access to a use case. The user interface might be deployed on the web, for instance, and then the user should be able to interact with the system from a browser running on a remote machine. Likewise, the external system might be running on a remote host and should be able to access the use case remotely.

2.2.2 Sequence Diagrams

Use cases are rather abstract and difficult to use for eliciting detailed requirements. A scenario can be seen as particular example of a use case and as such it is more concrete. *Sequence diagrams* are a graphical notation that can be used for modelling scenarios. Example 2.2 shows a sequence diagram that refines a scenario for the Plan Training Schedule use case of Example 2.1. A sequence diagram depicts objects that participate in the scenario and the sequence of messages by means of which the objects communicate.

Sequence diagrams model interaction scenarios between objects in a sequential fashion.

Example 2.2
Sequence Diagram for a Plan
Training Schedule Scenario

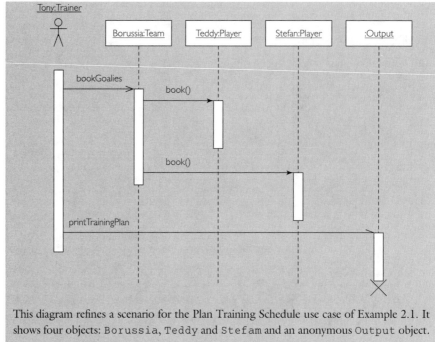

This diagram refines a scenario for the Plan Training Schedule use case of Example 2.1. It shows four objects: `Borussia`, `Teddy` and `Stefam` and an anonymous `Output` object.

Objects in a sequence diagram are displayed as rectangles. The annotation in that rectangle consists of an optional object name and a type identifier, separated by a colon. The annotation of objects is underlined in order to indicate the difference from classes, which are also represented as rectangles. Objects have lifelines that indicate their lifetime. The lifeline is a vertical dashed line that starts at the rectangle. The cross at the bottom of the `Output` object lifeline indicates that the object ceases to exist at that point in time.

 Messages are sent from a client object to a server object to request operation executions.

Messages that are sent from one object to another are shown as horizontal arrows. They are given names that usually correspond to operations of the target object. An arrow with a complete arrowhead shows a synchronous message. In the example, `bookGoalies` is a synchronous message that the trainer of the goalkeepers would send to the team object. `printTrainingPlan` is an asynchronous message because the trainer wants to continue working while the output is processed on a printer. Filled arrowheads indicate local messages that are implemented as procedure calls. The `book` messages that the team object sends to the two players who are goalkeepers are examples of those. Messages are ordered in time. Earlier messages are shown above later messages. A rectangular stripe along a lifeline represents the activation of the object. Activation corresponds to a period when the object performs an action, either directly or by sending a message to another object. The top of the stripe indicates the beginning of activation and the bottom shows when the object is deactivated.

Sequence diagrams can be used during analysis and design.

The use of sequence diagrams is not confined to requirements analysis. Sequence diagrams are also extremely useful to show design scenarios. During analysis, sequence diagrams show what happens in a scenario. In design, sequence diagrams show how a scenario is implemented using objects that can be directly mapped to the target programming language and distribution middleware. These implementation scenarios are used to validate the design and to see whether use cases can actually be implemented with the functionality defined in the design class diagram.

2.2.3 Class Diagrams

Class diagrams are probably the most important form of UML diagram. Class diagrams define object types in terms of attributes, operations and the associations between objects. Hence, class diagrams provide a type-level perspective, while sequence diagrams present examples at an instance-level of abstraction. Class diagrams model attributes, operations and relationships in a static way. The concerns addressed by class diagrams include the visibility of attributes and operations, the type of attributes and the signatures of operations, the cardinality of associations and the like. Class diagrams are a static modelling tool and do not determine dynamic aspects of classes, such as the algorithms of operations. A class diagram is shown in Example 2.3.

Class diagrams define the type of objects in terms of attributes, operations and associations.

The main building blocks of a class diagram are *classes*. A class represents an object type. Classes are shown as rectangles. These rectangles may be divided into three compartments. The top compartment shows the name of the class, the middle compartment identifies the attributes supported by the class and the bottom compartment declares the operations of the class. The attribute and operation compartments may be omitted for reasons of simplicity.

UML class diagrams support the information hiding principle. In accordance with C++ and Java, UML supports different degrees of visibility for attributes and operations. *Public* attributes and operations are displayed with a +. *Public* declarations are freely accessible from outside the class. *Private* attributes and operations are shown using a −. Private declarations cannot be accessed from outside the class scope.

The visibility of attributes can be public or private.

Type and subtype relationships between classes are modelled in UML class diagrams using *generalizations*. They are represented as an arrow with a white arrowhead. The class to which the arrowhead points generalizes the class at the other end of the arrow. The existence of generalizations motivates a third category of visibility. *Protected* operations and attributes are only accessible from within the class and any specialized class. Protected declarations are preceded by a #. In the example, this means that operations inside the scope of class Club can access the inherited name attribute, as its visibility is declared protected in class Organization.

A type may generalize another type.

Associations are shown using lines and they may be given a name. Associations model the fact that one class is related to another class. Most associations are *binary*, which means that they connect two classes. Associations are the most general form of relationship. An *aggregation* is an association that indicates that objects are aggregates of other objects. Aggregation relationships have a diamond at the object that forms the complex object from its aggregates. *Composition* associations are stronger form of aggregations and they determine that the component fully belongs to the composite. This means that there can be only one composite for every component. A filled diamond indicates such a composition.

Associations connect objects and they may have aggregation or composition semantics.

Example 2.3

Class Diagram with Object
Types for Soccer Team
Management

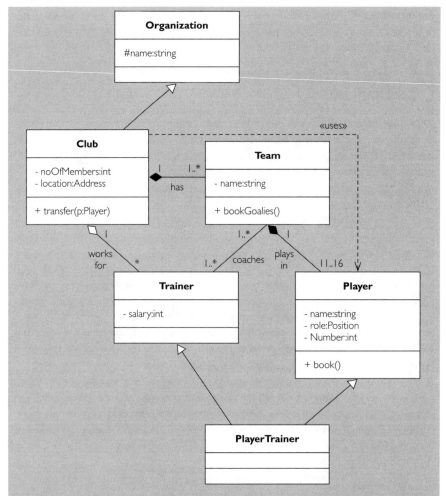

Class `Organization` generalizes class `Club`. The class diagram shows several associations, for instance to indicate that a `Player` plays in a `Team` and that a `Club` has several `Teams`. Association `works for` is an aggregation, `has` is a composition modelling that a `Team` is entirely controlled by a `Club`. A soccer team needs at least 11 and up to 16 players. This is modelled using the cardinality `11..16` at the `Player` end of association `plays in`. The cardinality of `1` at the `Team` end of `plays in` means that players play in exactly one `Team`. An example of a dependency is that `Club` depends on `Player` because `Player` is used as a parameter type in operation `transfer`.

Dependencies indicate
that one object type
depends on another
type.

Dependencies are another form of association. A dependency indicates that a class depends on another class. This dependency is often created by the use of object types in attributes, operation results or parameters. Dependency associations are represented as dashed arrows. They start at the dependent class.

Associations may designate different *cardinalities*. The cardinality determines in how many instances of a particular association an object can participate. If upper bounds are not known, a * is used. A cardinality of zero means that participation in the association is optional.

Associations may have different cardinalities.

We note that class diagrams are used in several circumstances during the engineering of distributed objects. Class diagrams are used during the analysis stage when they determine the relevant properties of objects. In these class diagrams, the object types are modelled from the perspective of what the supported system should do. Class diagrams are also used during the design stage to define the interfaces of distributed objects. As distributed objects are often composed of many local objects, class diagrams may also be used for the design of server object implementations.

Class diagrams are used to capture type-level abstractions in both the analysis and design of distributed objects.

In practice, a class design of a distributed system may have to define several hundred object types. In order to manage the resulting complexity, some structuring mechanism is needed for class diagrams. *Packages* provide such a structuring mechanism. Packages can be used to organize class diagrams in a hierarchical way (see Example 2.4). A package is represented in a class diagram as a folder. Each package is represented by a class diagram at the level below.

Packages are used to structure analysis and design information in a hierarchical manner.

2.2.4 Object Diagrams

Object diagrams are used to show examples of instances of classes that were shown in class diagrams and how they are interconnected. They express the static part of an interaction diagram and we will occasionally use them for this purpose in this book. An object diagram shows objects, which are instances of classes. Objects are represented as rectangles. In order to highlight that these rectangles represent objects, rather than classes, we underline the content of the first compartment, which shows the name and the type of an object. These two are separated by a colon, but if it is not important, the name can be omitted.

Object diagrams show examples of instances of classes.

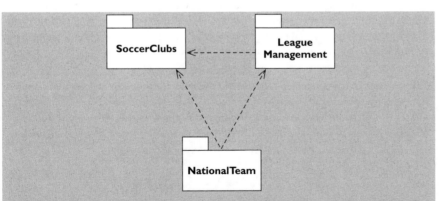

Example 2.4
Use of Packages

Package `SoccerClubs` might be refined by the class diagram shown in Example 2.3. The packages have dependency associations between them. These dependency associations mean that a class in a dependent package uses one or more classes from the package on which it is dependent.

Example 2.5
Object Diagram

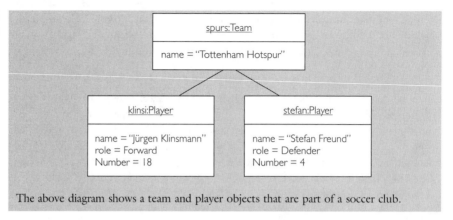

The above diagram shows a team and player objects that are part of a soccer club.

The second compartment in an object representation shows the attributes. Unlike in a class diagram, where the name, type and initialization are shown, the attribute representation in an object diagram only shows the name and the current value of the attributes. Because it is not necessary to specify the operations of objects (they are all specified in the classes of the object), the rectangles in object diagrams generally only have two compartments. Finally, object diagrams may show links that interconnect objects. A link is an instance of an association. As such, it needs to meet the constraints of the association, such as the cardinality.

2.2.5 State Diagrams

State diagrams model the dynamic behaviour of objects from a type level of abstraction.

Class diagrams model objects statically. UML *state diagrams* model the dynamic behaviour of objects. State diagrams provide support for describing the temporal evolutions of objects in response to interactions with other objects. This is achieved by modelling the various states of an object and identifying possible transitions between these states. State diagrams in UML are essentially equal in power to statecharts, which were first introduced by [Harel, 1987]. Harel extended the notion of finite state machines by composite and concurrent states. These extensions avoid the explosion in the number of states and transitions that are known from finite state machines.

The representation of statecharts in state diagrams takes the form of a collection of rounded rectangles (the states) and directed edges (the transitions). Each state diagram is associated with one class. It models the states that instances of the respective object type can be in. Note that not all classes need a state diagram. They are only required if classes model objects that maintain a state in such a way that the order in which operations may be executed depends on those states.

The transitions between states may be annotated. By convention, these annotations have two optional parts that are separated by a slash. The first part is a condition, which is given in square brackets. If present, the condition must hold for the transition to be enabled. The second part of a transition annotation denotes the operation that is executed during that transition.

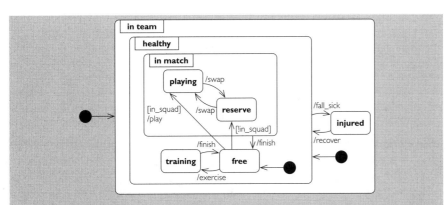

Example 2.6
State Diagram with Composite States

The transition between `free` and `playing` is annotated. The condition `[in_squad]` is true if the trainer has designated the player to play when the game kicks off. State `in team` is a composite state. Transition `fall_sick` is allowed from every substate of `healthy`: a player can acquire an injury when he is playing in a game, during a training session or during spare time. He may even acquire a cold when sitting on the reserve bench. After having recovered from an injury, a player's state is the default `free`.

A *composite state* is represented as a rounded rectangle with embedded states. State diagrams do not impose any restrictions on the number of nested component states. Transitions leading from one component state to another mean that that transition is allowed from every substate of the composite state.

States may be composed of other states.

Default states determine the initial states of a composite state. Default states are designated by the unlabelled transition that originates at a filled circle.

State diagrams can be composed by nesting a state within another state. This essentially reduces the number of transitions as a transition leading from a state subsumes transitions from all substates that it entails. State diagrams also support *parallel states*. Parallel states are

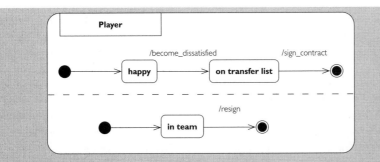

Example 2.7
State Diagram with Parallel States

Two threads of computation proceed independently within a `Player` object. Initially, a player is happily playing in a team. The player may then at some time in point become dissatisfied and be put on the transfer list, while still playing in the team. When the player finds a new team, the player will sign a contract with the new team and resign from the current contract. Again, there is not necessarily any particular order in which these two actions have to be carried out.

used whenever two concurrent threads proceed independently. Without parallel composition the independent states would have to be combined and this generally leads to an explosion in the number of states. Hence the aim of parallel composition is to reduce the number of states. A parallel composition is shown in Example 2.7.

2.3 A Meta-Model for Distributed Objects

In this section, we discuss the concepts that are needed for defining distributed objects. In order to avoid confusing the different levels of abstraction that are involved, we show the reference model of the OMG Meta-Object Facility [OMG, 1997a] in Figure 2.2. At the lowest level (Level 0), there are individual distributed objects. These are capable of performing services upon requests from other objects. They are instances of object types defined at Level 1. Object types specify the common properties of these similar objects.

Figure 2.2
Objects, Types, Meta-Object Models and Meta-Object Facilities

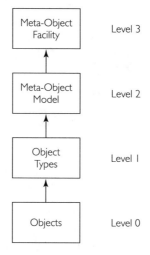

Object types are instances of a meta-object model (Level 2). This is the level where most of the concepts we define in this section are situated. We note that there are many meta-object models. Examples include the meta-model of the Unified Modeling Language or the object models that are used in object-oriented programming languages. They all differ slightly in the way they treat inheritance, polymorphism, static or dynamic typing and failure handling. Thus a need arises to be able to formalize meta-object models and a meta-object facility (Level 3) is used for that purpose. The reader should be aware of the existence of meta-object facilities, but we are not going to use such a formal meta-object facility because it does not aid in comprehending the concepts. In this section, we use UML to show how these concepts are applied. Thus we use concepts of Levels 0 and 1 to exemplify the meta-model concepts that we introduce in this section.

2.3.1 Objects

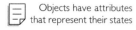 Objects have attributes that represent their states

An *object* has a set of attributes that together represent the *state* of the object. Attributes need not be accessible from other objects; they are then private or hidden. Hiding attributes is encouraged because it achieves data abstraction as demanded by Parnas. Data stored in hidden attributes can only be accessed and modified by operations; other objects cannot become dependent on the internal data structures of an object and they can be changed without affecting other objects. This is particularly important if objects are designed and maintained in a distributed setting, possibly by different organizations. Objects may export a set of operations that reveal the state of attributes or modify their values. Other objects may request execution of an exported operation.

and operations that may modify the states.

An attribute may be seen as a pair of operations. The first operation is used to store data in the attribute and the second operation returns data from the attribute. Each attribute has a *name*. Names should be chosen to reveal the semantics of the data stored in the attribute. A name is used to identify an attribute within the context of an object. To be useful for this purpose, attribute names should be unique within an object. Attributes also have a type. The type determines the domain of the attribute. Attributes can only store and return values that are from the domain induced by the attribute's type.

An attribute is a mapping between an object and a value; it is characterized by a name and a type.

Object-oriented meta-models often provide concepts that support the hiding of attributes. A *public attribute* is visible outside the object and may be accessed and modified by other objects. This defeats data abstraction and public attributes should be used very carefully. A *private attribute* is not visible outside the object and can only be accessed in operations of the object. Some object-oriented meta-models also support *read-only attributes* whose visibility lies between public and private attributes; the value can be accessed from outside the object but only be modified by operations of the object. Attributes may also be *constant*. This means the value is determined during creation of the object and it is never changed.

klinsi:Player

name = "Jürgen Klinsmann"
role = Forward
Number = 18

A soccer player object may have certain attributes, such as a name, a role and a number worn on the back of a shirt. Some of these attributes may not be visible to the outside.

Example 2.8
Soccer Player Object

Some object-oriented programming languages support the concept of class variables, which are sometimes referred to as static member variables. These variables retain state information that is common to all instances of a type. We note that this concept is not appropriate for distributed objects, which are generally distributed across different hosts; class variables or static member variables would lead to the need to distribute updates of this state to all those hosts where instances reside.

Distributed objects do not have class or static variables.

Objects have a unique *object identifier* that is assigned to the object when it is created. Objects generally retain their identity throughout their lifetime. An *object reference* is a handle that a client has on an object. Clients use object references to reference the object, for instance when they want to request an operation. An object has just one identity but there may be many references to the object.

Objects have one unique identifier but may have multiple references.

Object-oriented meta-models distinguish between object identity and object equality. Two objects are *equal* if they comply to some equivalence rule. This can be as simple as 'store the same data' or more complicated and application-dependent, such as 'equality of complex numbers expressed in cartesian and polar coordinates'. They may still have a different identity. Objects addressed by two different object references are *identical* if they have the same object identity. Two identical objects are also equal but the reverse may not hold.

There are usually many different perspectives on the same object. Stakeholders consider different properties of an object as important. A player is interested in his or her schedule, while the soccer association is more interested in the player's license number. During object-oriented analysis, analysts try to define the overall functionality of an object; they are concerned with *what* an object can do. During object-oriented design, it is determined *how* an object works. Designers incorporate decisions about the environment in which the object resides. Yet, designers are not interested in how operations are implemented. They are merely interested in the interface the object has with other objects. Programmers implementing an object in an object-oriented programming language, in turn, focus on the way operations are implemented. Most of the object-oriented concepts that we discuss now apply to objects in all the different perspectives. This conceptual continuity is, in fact, one of the strongest advantages of the object-oriented approach to engineering distributed systems.

2.3.2 Types

Object Types

Object types specify the common characteristics of similar objects.

It would be inappropriate to declare operations and attributes individually for each object. Many objects are similar in structure and behaviour. They have the same attributes and operations. There may be many soccer player objects, for example, and all of them have the same attributes and operations; only their object identity and the values of their attributes differ. *Object types* specify those characteristics that are shared by similar objects.

Object types define a contract that binds the interaction between client and server objects.

[Meyer, 1988b] considers object types as *contracts* between clients and servers. This notion is particularly useful in distributed systems where client and server objects are often developed autonomously. The object type of a server object declares the attributes and operations that it offers. Automatic validation can determine whether or not client and server implementations obey the contract that is embedded in the type definition. The concept of object types therefore contributes greatly to reducing the development times of distributed objects.

Objects are instances of object types.

Objects are *instances* of types. By means of the instance relationship, we can always get information about the attributes and operations that an object supports. Object-oriented meta-models differ in whether each object has one or several types. They may also differ in whether the instance relationship can change during the lifetime of an object.

Object types are specified through interfaces that determine the operations that clients can request.

The type of a distributed object is specified through an *interface*. The interface defines all aspects of an object type that are visible to client objects. These include the operations that the object supports and the attributes of the object. The interface of an object type defines a set of *operations* by means of which the data stored in attributes of the object are modified.

Operations do not have to modify an object's state; they may just compute a function. The execution of an operation may rely on operations provided by other objects.

Example 2.9
An Object Type Specification
Through an Interface

«Interface» **Player**
- readonly name:string - readonly role:Position - readonly Number:int
+ void book(in d:Date) raises AlreadyBooked

The above UML diagram shows the interface of `Player` objects. The diagram uses the stereotype `<<Interface>>` to indicate that the definition is an interface rather than a class. It defines the attributes and operations that are important for soccer players.

An operation has a *signature*, which determines the operation's name, the list of formal parameters and the result that the operation returns. Typed object-oriented meta-models will assign formal types to parameters and results. These formal types are used to check that the parameters that are passed to an operation during invocation actually correspond to the parameters that the operation expects. The same ideas apply to the return value of an operation. It may be typed in order to restrict the domain from which operations can return values.

The signature specifies the name, parameters, return types and exceptions of operations.

Operations also have a visibility. *Public operations* are visible to other objects; they may request their execution. *Private operations* are hidden from client objects. Execution of a private operation may only be requested by other operations of the same object.

Not all operations supported by an object type need to be included in an interface.

Non-Object Types

The management of distributed objects imposes a significant overhead. Unlike programming languages, which can treat object references as memory addresses for objects, object references in distributed systems also have to include location information, security information and the like. It would, therefore, be largely inappropriate to treat simple data, such as boolean values, characters and numbers as distributed objects. Likewise, it is advantageous if complex data types can be constructed from simpler data types without incurring the overhead imposed by objects. Yet, the idea of having a contract, which defines how these data can be used, applies as well. These considerations underlie the concept of *non-object types*, which can be atomic types or constructed types. Instances of these non-object types are *values* rather than objects. Values do not have an identity and cannot have references.

Meta-models for distributed objects also include types that are not objects.

Object-oriented meta-models will include a small number of *atomic types*. Although different types are supported by different meta-models, most will include types such as `boolean`, `char`, `int`, `float` and `string`. Atomic types determine a set of operations that can be applied to atomic values. Examples of these are the boolean operators AND, OR and NOT.

Constructed types are built from atomic types or object types by applying a *type constructor.*[1] The type constructors provided by object-oriented meta-models will again vary. They are likely to include records, arrays and sequences of simpler types. Again, a fixed set of operations may be applied to constructed types. Records may have a selection operation so that an individual element of the record can be selected. Likewise, sequences may have an iteration operation that visits each element of the sequence.

2.3.3 Requests

An object request is made by a client object in order to request execution of an operation from a server object.

Conceptually, an *object request* is a triple consisting of an object reference, the name of an operation and a list of actual parameters. An object request is similar to a method invocation in an object-oriented programming language. Both eventually execute an operation and pass actual parameters to the formal parameters of the operation. Requests, however, involve a more significant overhead: they have to resolve data heterogeneity; they need to synchronize client and server; they may cause network communication; and a server object may not be active and may have to be started before it can execute the request. As all this takes considerably longer, we want to distinguish between method invocations and object requests.

Like method invocations, requests may be parameterized. The request passes actual parameters from the client object to the server object. If client and server object reside on different hosts, parameters have to be transmitted via the network. If client and server are hosted by different hardware platforms, the data representation of request parameters may have to be translated. Request parameters might also be used to pass the results of the operation execution from the server to the client. Again, network communication and data representation translation might be required.

The number of parameters a client has to pass and their types are determined by the signature of the requested operation. For each formal parameter that is declared in the operation signature, the request has to include a compatible actual parameter. The engineering of distributed systems is considerably simplified if the compiler used for developing clients validates that the types of actual request parameters match the formal parameters declared in the signature of the requested operation declaration.

Example 2.10
Object Request

Let us reconsider the trainer who wants to book a training appointment with a soccer player. To make such a request, the trainer object has to have an object reference to the soccer player object. The trainer will then request a booking by providing the name of operation `book` as well as a value of type `Date` as an actual parameter. If the player and trainer objects are located on different machines, the request is transferred to the server host and the actual parameters are transmitted via the network to the server object. The server object, in turn executes the operation and transmits the result (whether the booking operation was successful) back to the client object.

---

[1] Type constructors should not be confused with constructors that create objects.

2.3.4 Exceptions

Requests may not always be executed successfully. Requests may fail for reasons that we discussed in the previous chapter. When we discussed failure transparency in that chapter, we demanded that failures should be concealed from application programmers and users alike. While it is highly desirable to hide failures from application programmers, it might not always be possible. Failures, however, must be hidden from users. Client programmers, therefore, have to react to those failures that the middleware cannot handle itself. Thus, the meta-model should include a mechanism for notifying clients about the details of a fault. *Exceptions* are such a mechanism.

Exceptions notify clients about failures that occur during the execution of an object request.

Exceptions are data structures for details about failures. An exception is *raised* by a server object or by the distribution middleware. Exceptions are transferred via the network from the server or middleware to the client. When a client checks for the occurrence of an exception we say that the client *catches* the exception. When an exception occurs, the client can use the exception's data structures in order to find out what went wrong.

We can distinguish *system* from *type-specific* exceptions. System exceptions are raised by the middleware. They inform about system failures, such as an unreachable server object. A server object may raise type-specific exceptions when the execution of a request would violate the object's integrity. The server object would then not complete the operation execution and inform the client about this failure by means of an exception. In theory, these situations could be avoided if the client always enquired whether the server would complete an operation. In practice, this is too slow because two requests are needed, one for the enquiry and another one for the request itself. Remember that requests involve a significant overhead and the number of requests has to be minimized. Hence, clients request an operation and are prepared for the failure of the operation.

Let us reconsider the operation to book a soccer player. That operation might raise an exception `AlreadyBooked` if the player has already been booked at the requested date and time. The data structures associated with `AlreadyBooked` might include vacant time slots that are adjacent to the ones requested. By using exceptions rather than an explicit enquiry about free time slots and a successive booking, the trainer object uses one rather than two requests.

Example 2.11
Exception Definition

The designer of a server object should be able to signal to designers of client objects that they should catch certain exceptions. Hence, meta-models often extend signatures for operations with an exception clause. That clause enumerates all the exceptions that the operation is allowed to raise.

In fact, exceptions are part of the contract between server and client object. By using an operation whose signature includes exceptions, the client object is obliged to catch the declared exceptions. Unless it catches them, the client does not know if the operation has been executed successfully. As exceptions highlight these obligations, designers of server objects should use exceptions to indicate failures. Explicit error parameters or operation results do not convey this obligation to check and therefore the use of exceptions is preferred.

Exceptions are part of the contract between client and server objects.

2.3.5 Subtypes and Multiple Inheritance

A subtype inherits all attributes, operations and exception definitions from its supertype.

Exceptions, attributes and operations are defined for object types. Object types may have exceptions, attributes and operations in common with other types. A subtype has all the attributes, exceptions and operations declared for its supertype; the subtype *inherits* these attributes from the supertype. The subtype may add attributes, exceptions and operations and become a specialization of its supertype.

A subtype can inherit from more than one supertype.

An object type may inherit from more than one supertype. This concept is referred to as *multiple inheritance*. If the component model supports multiple inheritance, the inheritance relationship between object types is a graph, rather than a tree. As an example, consider a soccer player who is also a trainer (as occurs in many amateur teams). A type `PlayerTrainer` would, therefore, be a subtype of both `Player` and `Trainer`.

Although very elegant at first glance, multiple inheritance can cause problems (see Example 2.12). Multiple inheritance can lead to name clashes if a subtype inherits two properties from two different supertypes or if an operation inherited from a common supertype is re-defined on one branch and not re-defined on another branch.

Example 2.12
Name Clash with Multiple Inheritance

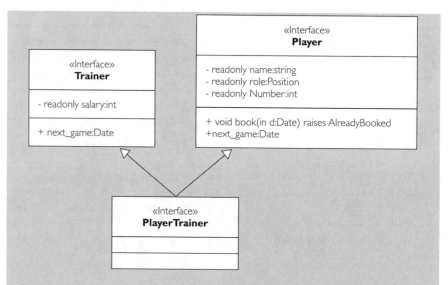

Both types `Player` and `Trainer` define an operation `next_game` that returns details about the next game in which the player or the trainer have to engage. This leads to a name clash in type `PlayerTrainer`. If a client of a `PlayerTrainer` object requests execution of `next_game` it is unclear whether the operation should be taken from `Player` or from `Trainer`.

The concept of subtypes is one of the strongest advantages of object-oriented meta-models, for several reasons. First, the design and successive implementation of object types can be reused in different settings where types can be extended in new subtypes. This increases development productivity considerably. Secondly, changes to common attributes, exceptions and operations are easier to manage, because they only affect one object type. Thirdly, subtyping supports different levels of abstractions in a design of distributed objects and they become easier to understand. Finally, whenever an instance of a particular type is expected, for example as a parameter or in an attribute, instances of all subtypes can be used. Hence, subtyping enables polymorphism.

2.3.6 Polymorphism

Object types restrict the domain of attributes and parameters. Object models that support *polymorphism* not only allow instances of the attribute or parameter type to be assigned to attributes and parameters, but also instances of all the type's subtypes.

Polymorphism means that an attribute or parameter can refer to instances of different types.

Example 2.13
Polymorphism

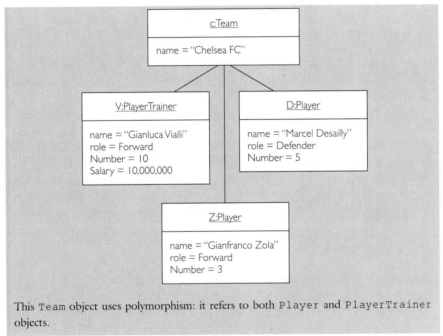

This Team object uses polymorphism: it refers to both Player and PlayerTrainer objects.

Subtypes may adjust inherited operations to fit the subtype's needs. This is achieved by redefining operations. *Redefinition* is achieved by declaring the operation with the same name and the same signature in the subtype and implementing it in the subtype. The correct operation is chosen by means of late binding.

Late binding means that it is decided at run-time, rather than at compile-time, which operation executes in response to a request. The decision is based on the dynamic type of an object. The search for an operation to implement a request starts at the type from which the object was instantiated. If that type does not implement the operation, the next supertype is searched until a supertype is found that does implement the operation.

Late binding means that it is decided at run-time which operation executes a request.

Late binding is often used together with polymorphism. Clients use operations that are defined for the static type of an attribute or parameter. At run-time, instances of subtypes may be assigned to the attribute or parameter. If the attribute or parameter is used in a request, late binding is used to determine which operation actually performs the request.

2.4 Local versus Distributed Objects

The design of local objects that reside in centralized applications is reasonably well understood. The software industry has agreed on UML as a notation that is highly suitable for such designs. CASE tools are available that support editing the different UML diagram types and provide code generation facilities that map to C++, Java or Smalltalk. In this section, we explain the differences between designing local and distributed objects to avoid pitfalls.

Example 2.14
Differences between Local and Distributed Objects

Some time ago, we were called in to advise on some problems with a distributed design for an engineering data warehouse. The purpose of the warehouse was to manage engineering diagrams for drilling-rigs, pipelines and pumping-stations for a new oil-field exploration in the North Sea. Circles represented reactors and polylines represented pipes that connected reactors. A typical diagram included some 50,000 such objects.

The designers had used a CASE tool to model all the objects that occurred in these applications. The CASE tool even supported the generation of interface definitions for distributed objects.

The team happily used that functionality and implemented types that enabled each of these objects to be requested remotely. We were called in when the team detected performance problems and were surprised that loading a diagram took several minutes. The reason for these problems was that points of polylines in the engineering diagrams were enabled as server objects. This was an unnecessary overhead as the points were never remotely accessed. They were not aware of the request latency that is inherent to distributed objects.

2.4.1 Life Cycle

 Creation, migration and deletion of distributed objects is different from local objects.

If an object in a non-distributed application wants to create another object, it applies an object creation operator to a class or an object type. The operator invokes a constructor, which then creates the object. The new object will reside on the same host and in the same process space as the object that requested its creation. The object also will not leave that virtual machine until a point in time when it is deleted. Therefore, object creation is considered an implementation problem.

Now consider a client object in a distributed application that wishes to create objects on some other host. Object creation operators and constructors are not capable of achieving this. We need to use them as primitives for designing object types that are capable of creating objects elsewhere. Hence, distributed object creation is a design problem.

The principle of location transparency in this context also means that where to create objects should be determined in such a way that neither client nor server objects have to be changed when a different host is designated to serve new objects.

If a host becomes overloaded or needs to be taken out of service, objects hosted by that machine need to be moved to a new host. This is referred to as *migration*. Migration is a problem that does not exist with local objects. Migration has to address machine heterogeneity in hardware, operating systems and programming languages.

Objects in a non-distributed application may be deleted implicitly by garbage collection techniques, which are available in Java, Eiffel or Smalltalk. As we will see in Chapter 9, distribution complicates the application of garbage collection techniques, since it would require that objects know how many other distributed objects have references to them. It is rather expensive to achieve referential integrity in a distributed setting and therefore most distributed object systems do not fully guarantee referential integrity. This has implications on the design of client objects, as they have to be able to cope with the situation that their server objects are not available any more.

In summary, the distributed object life cycle has to consider object creation, migration and deletion. We will discuss techniques, interfaces and protocols for the distributed object life cycle in Chapter 9.

2.4.2 Object References

In object-oriented programming, references are handles to objects that are implemented through memory addresses. The fact that pointers are memory addresses may be visible (as in C++) or hidden (as in Smalltalk, Eiffel or Java). In any case, pointers are rather lightweight structures and there is usually no big penalty for having many pointers to objects.

Object references are larger for distributed objects than for local objects.

References to distributed objects are more substantial data structures. They need to encode location information, security information and data about the type of objects. Orbix, a rather lightweight implementation of CORBA, uses 40 bytes for an object reference. Hence, Orbix demands ten times the memory for an object reference than is needed for a pointer in a 32-bit architecture. The difference may increase to a factor of 100 for middleware that supports security and needs to pass authentication information with each object reference.

These considerations have a number of implications for the design of distributed object-based applications. First, applications cannot maintain large numbers of object references since they would demand too much virtual memory on the client side. Secondly, the distribution middleware has to know all object references and must map them to the respective server objects. Given the size requirements of object references it seems unfeasible to have a large number of server objects and a large number of references to them. When designing distributed object-based applications we have to bear this in mind and minimize the number of objects. We should choose the granularity of objects such that both clients and middleware can cope with the space implications of object references.

2.4.3 Request Latency

An object request in an object-oriented programming language is implemented through a member function call. Performing a local method call on a modern workstation requires less than 250 nanoseconds. In addition, programming language compilers are built in such a way as to optimize method invocations by including the code in the calling code (inlining) when appropriate, thus eliminating the need for a call. Hence, the overhead of calling a method is negligible for the design of an application.

A distributed object request is orders of magnitude slower than a local method invocation.

Example 2.15
Interfaces for Local and Remote
Iterations

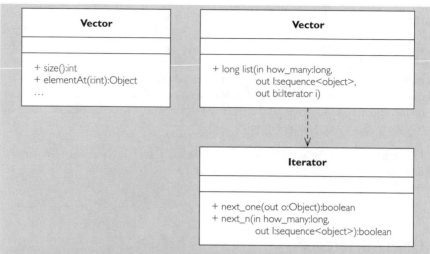

The diagram on the left depicts an excerpt of class `Vector` of the Java `util` package. `Vector` exports an operation `elementAt` that returns the object at a particular position in the vector. Operation `size` returns the number of elements in the vector. An iteration that visits all elements in the vector can then be implemented in a loop ranging from 0 to `size()-1`. Assuming just-in-time compilation of the Java byte code for this loop, the overhead of invoking `elementAt` for a vector with 1,000 elements will be roughly 250 microseconds, which is negligible. On the other hand, if the request for `elementAt` comes a thousand times from a `Vector` object on a remote host, the overhead would be roughly half a second and this is no longer negligible.

The diagram on the right shows a better design. Operation `list` returns a sequence of object references that contains at most the number of elements specified by the parameter `how_many`. If the vector has further elements, `list` also returns a reference to a `BindingIterator`. The iterator can be used to obtain further sequences of elements. This design solves the performance problem because a sequence containing many object references can be transferred at once. Local operations provided for that sequence would then be used to visit the elements of that sequence. If we were to obtain the 1,000 elements in batches of 100 each, the overhead would be 10 remote invocations plus 1,000 local calls to obtain the elements from the sequence. We can assume that the size of an object reference is somewhere below 500 bytes so that the overall size of the returned list will be less than 64KB. Transmitting this amount of data does not considerably increase the overall time of the request. Thus the performance of this approach requires $10 \times 500 + 1000 \times 0.25 = 5250$ microseconds. Hence, the performance of this design will be 100 times better than the naive solution we discussed above.

This is considerably different when requesting an operation from an object that resides on a different host. The overhead of such a request is between 0.1 and 10 milliseconds, depending on the technology that is being used. We have measured an object request brokered by Orbix between two SPARC Ultra servers connected with a 100 Mbit network. Approximately 500 microseconds were needed for that request. Hence, object requests take about 2,000 times as long as local method calls and this overhead is not negligible during the design of distributed objects. Example 2.15 presents the impact on the design.

In order to optimize poor performance, designers need to have quite deep knowledge about the particular approach that is used to solve distribution, as well as about the problem domain. In the above example, we had to make assumptions about the overall cost of a simple object request, the size of the representation of an object reference and the increase of latency depending on the size of the transmitted information. Without this basic knowledge and understanding of how distributed object requests are implemented, designers cannot reasonably build efficient systems. We discuss this in the chapters of Part II

Request latency has to be taken into account when designing distributed objects.

2.4.4 Object Activation

Objects created with an object-oriented programming language reside in virtual memory between the time when they are created and when they are deleted. This is inappropriate for distributed objects for the following reasons:

Distributed objects may not always be available to serve an object request at any point in time.

1. Hosts sometimes have to be shut down and then objects hosted on these machines have to be stopped and re-started when the host resumes operation;
2. The resources required by all the server objects on a host may be greater than the resources the host can provide; and
3. Depending on the nature of the client application, objects may be idle for a long time and it would be a waste of resources if they were kept in virtual memory all the time.

For these reasons, we consider two operations in addition to the principal life cycle operations we discussed above. These are activation and deactivation. *Activation* launches a previously inactive object, brings its implementation into virtual memory and thus enables it to serve object requests. *Deactivation* is the reverse operation: it terminates execution of the object and frees the resources that the object currently occupies.

Activation brings previously inactive objects into main memory so that they can serve an object request.

We note that activation may increase the latency of requests further. If an object has to be activated prior to being able to serve a request, the time needed for that activation increases the request latency. This time depends on the operating system of the server host. Very often this is the time needed to start an operating system process, which is quite significant. It is, therefore, important to devise and implement policies that minimize the need for activation and deactivation.

The overhead of activation adds considerably to the latency of object requests.

Activation and deactivation of distributed objects should be transparent to users and programmers of client objects. Activation and deactivation may also be transparent to administrators if they are fully implemented by a distribution middleware. This requires, however, that administrators provide sufficient installation and policy information to enable the middleware to implement activation and deactivation. That installation and policy information includes a repository for object implementations as well as activation and deactivation strategies.

Activation and deactivation should be transparent.

Activation and deactivation is, however, often not transparent to designers of server objects. Some server objects expose a state at their interface. Even objects that do not export any attributes might have an internal state. Upon deactivation, that state must be stored on

Stateful objects have to be persistent.

persistent storage so that it can be retrieved upon activation. Hence, designers of such server objects must make provisions for the state to become persistent upon deactivation and to be retrieved upon activation. Persistence of distributed objects can be achieved in the same way as with local objects. Techniques include serialisation and storage in a file system, mapping to relational databases or mapping to object databases. We discuss such techniques in Chapter 10. Persistence of distributed objects, however, has to be integrated with the implementation of activation and deactivation.

2.4.5 Parallelism

Objects that are written in an object-oriented programming language are usually executed sequentially in a process on a host. Some object-oriented programming languages and many operating systems support concurrent programming by offering threads that can be used to execute objects concurrently. Threads implement an interleaved model of concurrency that enables multiple threads to share the same processor. Figure 2.3 shows an example of three processes A, B and C that are executed in an interleaved way on one processor. Only one process is active at a time and a scheduler switches between these processes. Hence, it is not possible to accelerate a job by distributing it across multiple threads. The threads will all be executed on the same processor and that processor restricts the performance of the job.

Figure 2.3
Interleaved Model of
Concurrency

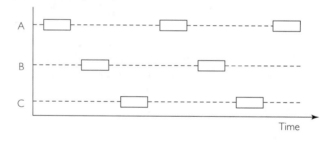

Distributed objects often
execute in parallel.

If a host has more than one processor, threads may actually physically execute in parallel. The client object that requests a service always executes in parallel with the server object. If it requests services in parallel from several server objects that are on different machines, these requests can all be executed in parallel. Hence, distribution has the potential to decrease considerably the elapsed real time needed for a job. This can be achieved if the tasks performed by operations are rather coarse-grained so that the overhead for request latency is small compared to the time needed to perform an operation.

Concurrency may have
to be controlled.

Interleaved concurrent execution of two operations may lead to integrity violations, such as inconsistent analysis or lost updates. Given that distributed objects are executed concurrently all the time we may have to control concurrency if the integrity of objects is at risk. Unlike objects stored in databases there is no central control in a distributed system that implements concurrency control. It is therefore necessary for designers of distributed objects to be aware of and implement concurrency control within the server objects they build. We discuss techniques and protocols for concurrency control in Chapter 11.

2.4.6 Communication

In object-oriented programming, requests are implemented as methods call. Such calls block the calling object until a point in time when the result becomes available. Distributed object communication aims at mimicking method calls as closely as possible. Hence, the default form for object requests is synchronous communication and the client is blocked until the server object returns the result.

There are different communication primitives available for distributed object requests.

Due to the request latency inherent to communication between distributed objects it might be inappropriate to force a client to await completion of a request; additional forms of synchronization are needed. They might optimize synchronization for those operations whose signatures indicate that no results have to be transmitted to the client. When designing interfaces it might therefore be advantageous to take such optimizations into account.

Communications between objects in a centralized application occur between two peers. For a method call there is just one caller and one called operation. Again, this is the default for communication between distributed objects and it is referred to as peer-to-peer communication.

Peer-to-peer communication might not always be appropriate for distributed objects, where often multiple distributed objects need to communicate with each other. Hence, distributed object communication primitives need to be designed that facilitate communication between groups of objects. Moreover, it might be advantageous if multiple requests to one or several objects can be processed at once. We focus on advanced communication, that is non-synchronous communication, communication between groups of objects, and request multiplicity in Chapter 7.

2.4.7 Failures

In the previous chapter, we argued that distributed systems fail more often than centralized systems. This has a number of implications on the design of distributed objects. Unlike objects in centralized applications, distributed objects have to be designed in such a way that they cope with failures. One could take the point of view that the underlying middleware should aim at minimizing failures and implement requests with exactly-once semantics. With exactly-once semantics the middleware would guarantee that every request is executed once and only once.

Distributed object requests are more likely to fail than local method invocations.

While it is generally possible for a system to implement exactly-once semantics, there is a clear trade-off. An implementation of exactly-once would generally need to rely on persistent storage of requests and thus it would add considerably to the complexity of request implementation. As a result, request latency would be increased further. This might not be appropriate for applications that need a low request latency but can tolerate lost requests. The approach taken by most middleware systems is therefore that they implement at-most-once semantics as a default. This means that they execute every request at most once but they tell clients when a request has failed. Additionally, they provide further mechanisms that designers can use to ensure higher or lower level request reliability. We will revisit request reliability in Chapter 7.

Different reliabilities are available for distributed objects.

Clients need to check
whether servers have
executed a request

The fact that requests may fail, of course, implies some obligations for the design of a client. Unlike method calls, clients cannot assume that requests have been executed properly when the request returns control to the client. They have to check for exceptions that occurred while the request was executed. Clients sometimes also have a sequence of requests that should be done either together and completely or not at all. As an example, consider a funds transfer from one account to another account. It is usually composed of a debit and a credit operation. If after the debit operation is completed successfully the credit operation fails then the effect of the debit operation should also be undone in order to avoid an erroneous balance on the accounts. To make sure that such a sequence of requests is performed completely or not at all is supported by the concept of transactions. Clients have the obligation to declare the beginning and the end of a transaction.

Designers of server objects have to build server objects in such a way that they can participate in transactions. They must make provisions to undo the effect of changes. All the server objects that participate in a transaction must have successfully completed their operations before the effect of a transaction can be made permanent. In Chapter 11, we discuss protocols and interfaces that are used for the implementation of distributed transactions.

2.4.8 Security

 Distribution of objects
makes them vulnerable
to security attacks.

Centralized applications that are written using object-oriented programming languages often deal with security at a session level. They request users to identify themselves during an authentication procedure at session start and then they trust that the user will not make the session available to unauthorized users.

Distributed objects may communicate over insecure networks, where attackers can openly access network traffic. In this setting it is far more important than in centralized systems that both client and server objects can be certain that they are actually interacting with the object with which they think they are interacting. In addition, different users might make requests of a distributed object in parallel. These requests will then be performed in an interleaved way. Hence, it is not sufficient to authenticate at a session level but individual requests might have to be authenticated. Moreover, server objects have to be able to decide whether a user or client that has requested execution of an operation is authorized to execute that request. Hence, they have to control access to their operations. Finally, they might have to generate irrefutable evidence that they have delivered a request to a client in order to be able sustain claims for payment for the service provided during that request.

 Security has to be
considered during the
design of distributed
objects.

All these problems affect the design of both the client and the server object. As security impacts the design of both server and client objects, we will discuss encryption techniques as basic primitives for implementing security. We will discuss in Chapter 12 the techniques and interfaces that support authentication, auditing, access control and non-repudiation services that can be used in the design of distributed objects.

Key Points

▶ A component model defines how services are defined, how the externally visible state of a component is determined, how components are identified and how services are requested. In this book we take an object-oriented perspective on distributed systems. Hence components are considered as objects. Objects communicate using object requests. A client object may request the execution of an operation or access to an attribute from a server object.

▶ We have very briefly introduced the Unified Modeling Language. It includes a set of graphical notations that are useful for expressing object models from different perspectives. We have discussed use case diagrams, which can be used to identify the need for system interfaces. Sequence diagrams are used to model scenarios of object interactions. Class diagrams can be used to model the static properties of classes, in particular the attributes and operations of a class and the association the class has with other classes. State diagrams express the internal state of distributed objects as well as transitions between these states. These diagrams support the design of, and the communication about, distributed objects.

▶ We have discussed the ingredients of a meta-object model for distributed objects. This included operations, attributes, exceptions, subtyping, multiple inheritance and polymorphism. Instances of the meta-object model are object types that designers of distributed systems have to determine. These types define properties that their instances have in common.

▶ We have discussed the differences between designing centralized objects that are implemented with an object-oriented programming language and distributed objects. These differences were many-fold. The life cycle of distributed objects is more complicated as location information has to be considered. References to distributed objects are more complex as they have to be able to locate objects and because security and type information may have to be added. The latency of requests from distributed objects is about 2,000 times greater than the overhead of calling a method locally. Objects might have to be activated prior to serving a request and they might have to be deactivated if they are no longer used and this adds further to the request latency. Distributed objects have a potential for performing tasks faster than centralized objects due to real parallelism. To cope with request latency, there will have to be additional forms of communication between synchronous and peer-to-peer requests. Distributed objects may fail and therefore both client and server objects have to be built in such a way that they can tolerate failures. Finally, distributed objects communicate via possibly insecure networks and therefore they have to be designed in such a way that security and privacy is not affected.

Self Assessment

2.1 What is an object?

2.2 What is an object type?

2.3 What is an object request?

2.4   What is the difference between an object and an object type?

2.5   How are services modelled in an object-oriented meta-model?

2.6   Why does a meta-object model for distributed objects also include non-object types?

2.7   Give examples when you would use polymorphism in the design of distributed objects.

2.8   In which stage of the software process would you utilize UML use case diagrams?

2.9   What are UML sequence diagrams used for?

2.10   What is the difference between private, protected and public declarations in UML class diagrams?

2.11   What consistency relationships have to hold between sequence diagrams and class diagrams?

2.12   Explain reasons why distribution has to be considered during the design of distributed objects.

Further Reading

The OMG object model is described in the Object Management Architecture Guide [Soley, 1992]. It also includes an exhaustive and comprehensive glossary of object-oriented terminology. A detailed description of the object model of Microsoft's COM is provided by [Box, 1998] and Chapter 5 of [Grimes, 1997] explains the extensions that enable distributed access to COM objects.

The Unified Modeling Language was adopted as an OMG Standard in November 1997. The OMG maintains an extensive web site with about ten documents on UML. The most important of those are the UML Semantics Guide [OMG, 1997a] and the UML Notation Guide [OMG, 1997c]. While these are the definite references about UML, they are not the most readable introductions. [Booch et al., 1999] define a user guide to the UML. [Rumbaugh *et al.*, 1999] provide a reference manual to the UML and [Jacobson *et al.*, 1999] discuss a software development process model that uses the UML. A thorough introduction to UML is also provided by [Muller, 1997] and a very concise overview is given by [Fowler and Scott, 1997]. [Quatrani, 1998] discusses how to use a CASE tool in order to develop UML models.

It is important that readers are aware that distributed systems are always parallel systems. A lot of work has been done on building concurrent systems and there is no need for us to elaborate on that. The theoretical foundations for building parallel and concurrent systems have been laid by the work of [Hoare, 1978] on CSP and [Milner, 1989] on CCS. A very practical approach to concurrency using design patterns and Java's thread model is discussed in [Lea, 1997]. [Magee and Kramer, 1999] pursue an engineering approach to the design and implementation of concurrent object-oriented programs that is very similar to the techniques we present for distributed objects in this book. Magee and Kramer introduce FSP, a process algebra for finite state processes, and describe systematic transformations of FSP specifications into concurrent Java implementations.

Part II

Middleware for Distributed Objects

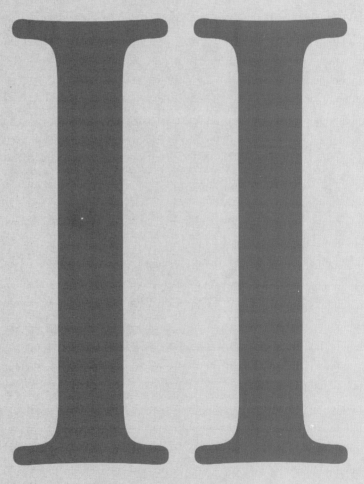

Part II: *Middleware for Distributed Objects*

The second part of the book is centred around a single question: How does object-oriented middleware enable an object that resides on one host to request an operation execution from an object that resides on a different host? The chapters in this part study different aspects of this question.

Chapter 3 introduces the principles of object-oriented middleware. We review the principal tasks that object-oriented middleware must perform by using the ISO/OSI reference model. We discuss the support that network operating systems provide for the construction of object-oriented middleware and we see that middleware implements the session and presentation layers of the reference model.

Chapter 4 presents three examples of object-oriented middleware and discusses their similarities and differences. We use the framework that was established in the previous chapter to compare systems that implement the Common Object Request Broker Architecture (CORBA) of the Object Management Group, Microsoft's COM and Java's Remote Method Invocation (RMI). We present and compare their object models and show the different architectural components that they provide to enable synchronous object requests to be made between distributed objects.

Objects that reside on different machines may be heterogeneous. Their hosts may use different processor architectures and different operating systems. The objects may be written using different programming languages and they may not even be connected to the same middleware. These different forms of heterogeneity should be transparent to the application programmer. In Chapter 5, we discuss the different forms of heterogeneity and show the principles that middleware uses to resolve them.

Object requests may be defined at different stages. Very often, they are defined statically at the time when a client program is compiled. Such static definition is achieved using a local method call to an operation from a 'stub' that was generated by the object-oriented middleware. There are, however, situations when it becomes necessary to defer the definition of object requests until run-time. Chapter 6 presents the principles of dynamic object requests, namely dynamic invocation and reflection mechanisms, that middleware provides for request definition at run-time.

3

Principles of Object-Oriented Middleware

Learning Objectives

The communication between objects that are distributed across a network is enabled by middleware. In this chapter we will grasp the basic principles of such middleware. We will learn that middleware is a layer between the network operating system and distributed applications. We will understand how middleware relates to the ISO/OSI reference model. We will comprehend why middleware is built upon the transport layer and how it implements the session and presentation layer. We will acquaint ourselves with different forms of middleware and understand the origins of object-oriented middleware. We will finally investigate the process of developing distributed objects using object-oriented middleware.

Chapter Outline

In the previous chapter, we discussed the design of objects. We argued that object-orientation provides a suitable component model for distributed systems. We have identified object requests as the most important concept; it enables a client object to request execution of an operation from a server object. In distributed systems, client and server objects generally reside on different hosts. Hence, object requests may have to be communicated via a network that connects the hosts.

Computer networks facilitate the physical interchange of electrical or optical signals as packets of information. They detect and may even correct transmission errors. A network implements the routing of packets between different hosts and takes care of the composition of such packets into byte streams or fixed-length messages. Network support is built into most modern operating systems. We, therefore, refer to them also as *network operating systems*.

Application engineers could use network operating systems to exchange information based on sending fixed-length messages or writing into a byte stream. Many distributed systems are actually built this way and for systems that need non-standard features or that are performance-critical this is appropriate. It is, however, often not advisable to do so; there is a substantial conceptual gap between the capabilities of network operating systems – reading and writing from and to byte streams – and what designers are interested in – requesting operations from remote objects. If network operating systems are used directly the application engineer will have to bridge this conceptual gap. This is time-consuming, error-prone and distracts the designer's attention from the real problems.

Middleware is layered between network operating systems and distributed applications in order to bridge this gap. Middleware provides the application designer with a higher-level of abstraction. Middleware implements this higher level of abstraction based on primitives that are provided by network operating systems. While doing so it hides the complexity of using a network operating system from application designers. The idea of middleware is not new. Many different types of middleware have been suggested and built and are being used in industrial practice. In this book we are mainly concerned with object-oriented middleware. Object-oriented middleware facilitates object requests between distributed objects. It implements requests by using primitives provided by network operating systems.

This chapter explains the principles of middleware and then takes an object-oriented perspective. We first look at networks, the base upon which middleware is built. We investigate the different forms of middleware that exist: transaction monitors, message-oriented middleware and remote procedure calls. We then take an object-oriented perspective on middleware and finally discuss the development support that object-oriented middleware systems provide.

3.1 Computer Networks

3.1.1 ISO/OSI Reference Model

The Open Systems Interconnection (OSI) reference model was defined in 1977 by the International Organization for Standardization (ISO). It identifies the need for standardiza-

Application
Presentation
Session
Transport
Network
Data link
Physical

Figure 3.1
The ISO/OSI Reference Model

tion of the communication between hosts built by different manufacturers. We do not want to discuss the ISO/OSI reference model in full detail but rather recall the basic principles that we will refer to later. The ISO/OSI reference model is a layered architecture in which each layer builds on abstractions provided by the layer below. Figure 3.1 shows a graphical overview of the model.

The *physical layer* specifies the mechanical, electrical and optical behaviour of the plugs and sockets of a physical interface to the network. Implementations of the physical layer perform functions in order to signal, modulate and synchronize the transmission of bits over the physical network. In addition, it may perform error detection by monitoring the quality of the electrical or optical signals received.

The physical layer is concerned with the transmission of bits over a physical circuit.

Conceptually, a network is a graph of interconnected nodes. The *data link layer* implements edges in these graphs. These nodes may be routers, switches or computers. It maps the physical connection provided by the physical layer into a layer that can transmit packets from one node to another in a relatively error-free manner. The data link layer provides error correction based on physical error-detection primitives provided by the physical layer.

The data link layer implements a single connection between two computers.

While the data link layer is concerned with node-to-node connections, the *network layer* implements the connection of multiple nodes into a network. As such, it is concerned with routing messages along multiple edges in the graph of nodes. Thus, the network layer isolates the higher layers from data link considerations and implements connections between arbitrary nodes of the network.

The network layer implements the interconnection of multiple nodes in a network.

The *transport layer* adds the capability of mapping longer messages or even continuous sequences of data onto these package-routing capabilities. If the network layer does not provide reliable package routing then transport layer implementations add such reliability. Transport layer implementations also map transport layer identifiers onto network addresses.

The transport layer adds the ability to route longer messages between two hosts.

Some transport layer implementations are connection-less. For these transport layers, the *session layer* provides facilities to establish and maintain connections between two or more distributed components. If the transport layer implementation is connection-oriented, the session layer merely uses the connection mechanisms of the transport layer.

The session layer establishes and maintains connections between distributed system components.

The presentation layer resolves differences in data representation and provides the ability to transport complex data.

Being able to transmit streams of bytes between two or more distributed system components might not be sufficient for the communication between two or more components. Very often these components want to communicate high-level data structures, such as records, arrays and sequences. These higher-level data structures need to be converted into a form that can be transmitted via a connection that can transmit streams of bytes. Moreover, components might be implemented on heterogeneous hosts. Heterogeneous hosts may use considerably differing representations for atomic data structures. Mainframes, for example, use big-endian representations for integers while Unix workstations tend to use little-endian representations. *Presentation layer* implementations resolve such differences in the representation of information between distributed components.

The application layer provides application functionality.

The *application layer* is concerned with distributed components and their interaction. In the setting of this book, the application layer will be implemented using distributed objects. The object types are defined according to the meta-model of the respective object-oriented middleware. The middleware provides an interface definition language that can express all the concepts of the meta-model. Distributed objects request operation execution from each other and the presentation layer implementation is used to resolve heterogeneity and to map complex request parameters onto a form that can be transmitted via the transport layer.

We are going to review the transport layer of the model in more detail now. Transport layer implementations provide a sufficiently powerful basis for implementing distribution middleware. Middleware systems are therefore typically layered above the transport layer and they implement the presentation and session layers.

3.1.2 Transport Layer

Network operating systems may provide different implementations of the transport layer. This is motivated by the differing characteristics of network layer implementations upon which transport layers are implemented. Moreover, different kinds of application may have different and sometimes conflicting requirements for the transport layer.

We generally distinguish *connection-oriented transport layer* implementations from *connection-less transport layer* implementations. Connection-oriented transports maintain a connection between two distributed components on behalf of upper layers. They provide operations to open and close a connection, to write data into such a connection and to read data from such a connection. Connection-oriented transports, therefore, provide upper layers with a mechanism to exchange data through streams of bytes. Connection-less transports provide upper layers with the capability of sending fixed-length messages between distributed hosts. These messages are referred to as *datagrams*. If a connection-less transport protocol is used, implementations of the session layer are needed to associate sent and received messages with certain applications.

Different implementations of the physical, data link and network layers may provide differing degrees of reliability. An optical wire, for example, that is used with an Asynchronous Transfer Mode (ATM) network implementation would typically provide a higher degree of reliability than an analogue and noisy telephone line that is used with a Serial Line Internet Protocol (SLIP). As upper layers need to be provided with a considerable degree of reliability, the transport layer needs to implement reliable transport even if the underlying network is unreliable. If a reliable network were used, on the other hand, implementing reliability also in the transport layer would reduce the performance of distributed applications unnecessarily. If a reliable physical or data link layer is being used, it is not necessary to implement error correction in the transport layer. However, most operating systems can interact with different data link layers and they use the same transport layer for all of them.

Unix operating system implementations generally provide two different implementations for the transport layer. These are the Transmission Control Protocol (TCP) and the User Datagram Protocol (UDP). TCP is connection-oriented and provides a reliable form of transport. It is now also available for Microsoft's operating systems. UDP is connection-less and it provides unreliable transport of data. Whether TCP or UDP is best used depends on whether or not an application needs to retain the connection for longer periods of time. Applications, such as `rwho`, which checks for logins on all hosts of a local area network, use UDP in order to avoid having open connections to large numbers of computers. Applications, such as `ftp`, that need a reliable connection for prolonged periods of time establish TCP connections.

TCP is a connection-oriented transport protocol; UDP is a connection-less transport protocol.

Transmission Control Protocol

TCP provides upper layers on one host with the ability to write unstructured data into a stream of bytes so that upper layers of a component on another host can read data from that stream. At the same time, the second component can write unstructured data to be returned into the stream so that upper layers of the first component can read the result.

TCP provides bi-directional streams that distributed systems can write to and read from to exchange data across hosts.

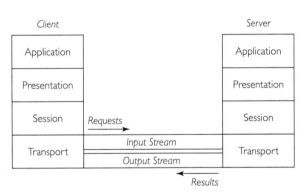

Figure 3.2
Usage of TCP for Distributed System Interactions

Figure 3.2 sketches the use of bi-directional TCP byte streams for distributed requests between a client and a server components. After having opened a bi-directional channel, the presentation layer of the client maps service parameters into a form that can be transmitted via a stream of bytes. It then writes the parameters into the input stream. The presentation layer implementation in the server component reads from the input stream and reconstructs the request parameters. Upon completion of the request, the presentation layer implementation of the server component transforms the request results into a stream of bytes and writes those into the output stream. The presentation layer implementation of the client component then reads from the output byte stream and re-constructs the results. The client then closes the TCP connection.

The implementation of TCP has to map the higher-level of bi-directional byte streams onto capabilities that the network layer implementation provides. TCP is often layered on top of the Internet Protocol (IP). IP supports the routing of packets between hosts. Network layer implementations may not retain the sequence of packets as they may be sent along different routes. Two IP packets, for example, might arrive in the reverse order to that in which they were sent. Hence, the implementation of TCP for IP will have to buffer packets on the receiving host and sort them on the basis of sequence numbers, so that the overall order of bytes is retained.

 TCP adds reliability to unreliable network protocols but is less efficient than UDP.

TCP is often used with unreliable network protocols. To provide a higher degree of reliability to upper layers, it implements several reliability mechanisms. In order to detect transmission errors, TCP applies checksums to all transmitted data. It uses these checksums and sequence numbers to detect missing, defect and duplicated packets. TCP employs a re-transmission strategy so that it can usually recover from errors of the underlying network protocol implementation in a way that is transparent to the programmer implementing an upper layer.

Transport layer implementations are available to the middleware programmer in the form of *sockets*. Sockets are available on all Unix workstations and servers as well as the various Microsoft operating systems. On Unix and Windows, there are two different types of socket, SOCK_STREAM and SOCK_DGRAM. Sockets of type SOCK_STREAM provide the programming interface to TCP. A combination of an Internet domain name and a port number identifies a socket. The socket interface includes operations to create sockets and to bind port numbers and domain names to a socket.

User Datagram Protocol

UDP provides the ability to send fixed-length messages between distributed system hosts.

UDP is a relatively simple transport layer implementation. It provides the capability to send messages containing blocks of bytes with a fixed length to other distributed components. UDP provides a slightly lower level of abstraction than TCP. While TCP is connection-oriented, UDP is connection-less. Moreover, UDP only provides a uni-directional flow of messages.

Figure 3.3 sketches how a middleware implementation uses UDP for the implementation of interactions between distributed system components. The middleware does not have to open a connection between client and server components. It rather decomposes the request data into a (usually) small number of request datagrams. The middleware then uses UDP to transport these request datagrams to the host of the server object, where the request information is decoded and processed. The result of the operation is then treated in the same way and sent as a UDP message back to the requester.

Depending on the message size of the UDP implementation (usually 9 KB) and the package size used in the underlying network (for example the IP maximum transfer unit is 1500 bytes for ethernet-based adapters), UDP implementations have to fragment messages into one or more network packets. UDP does not guarantee that the messages arrive in the order they were sent. UDP buffers messages for the receiver in the order of their arrival. Senders of messages must, therefore, encode a sequence into the message contents to enable upper layers on the receiving host to re-establish the original sequence.

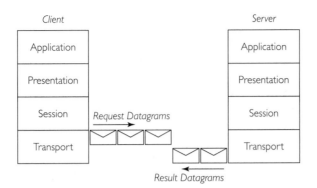

Figure 3.3
Usage of UDP for Distributed
System Interactions

UDP provides a checksum field so that receivers know that the packets that they receive contain the correct data. Unlike TCP, however, UDP adds no further delivery guarantee to the network layer implementation. It is therefore, often used in local area networks in which the physical, data link and network layer implementations provide sufficient degrees of reliability already. As a direct result, UDP is an efficient protocol, as it does not spend any resources on error-detection and correction. Moreover, there is no overhead for connecting and listening to connections. As object requests can often be represented in byte packets of 9 or 18 KB, one or two UDP packets are sufficient for sending an object request. This makes UDP a particularly attractive protocol for the implementation of object requests for middleware that is used over high-quality networks, such as many local area networks.

UDP does not add reliability, but is more efficient than TCP.

In order to implement object requests with UDP, middleware vendors use sockets. The programming interface to UDP on Unix systems is provided by sockets of type SOCK_DGRAM. With a socket of that type, middleware implementations can use sendto in order to send a datagram of a given length to a receiving socket on another host. A middleware implementation on that host might call recvfrom in order to read the datagram from the socket.

3.2   Types of Middleware

We have now developed an understanding of the transport layer. If application engineers had to rely directly on transport layer implementations, such as TCP or UDP, they would have to implement the communication between distributed system components based on writing to and reading from byte streams or fixed-length messages. We regard this as inappropriate for the following reasons:

Distributed system construction directly on top of a transport layer is rather difficult.

1. The communication will often need to send complex parameters, such as records, character strings or arrays. Application engineers would have to map those to sequences of bytes.
2. Different encodings of data types in memory might be used if clients and server objects are not deployed on the same hardware platform and if they are not written in the same programming language. Application engineers would have to map those onto each other.

3. Parameters and return values might refer to other distributed system components. Application engineers would have to implement object references in terms of Internet domain names, port numbers and additional addressing information.

4. Application developers and administrators would have to implement component activation, that is the ability of a server component to respond to a client request even when it is not currently running in an operating system process.

5. Given this referencing and encoding, type safety is an important concern. *Type safety* denotes the guarantee that an operation requested by a client is actually implemented by a server component and that the actual parameters supplied by the client must match the service definition. Achieving type safety manually is quite tedious and error prone, particularly if client and server objects are developed by different engineers.

6. After sending the request, the client object needs to wait for the result to come back, either from the output stream in TCP or by a reply message in UDP. Again, implementing this synchronization manually is rather tedious and error prone.

7. Sometimes there are qualities of service required that cannot be guaranteed by the network level. It may, for example, become necessary for different service requests to be implemented in an atomic fashion, that is either completely or not at all.

Middleware simplifies distributed system construction by implementing the presentation and session layers.

Fortunately, application engineers do not have to engage in these activities but can rely on distribution middleware. Middleware maps complex parameters passed to service requests into a transmittable form; resolves heterogeneity; resolves logical component addresses to Internet domain names and port addresses; and synchronizes client and server objects. While doing so, middleware implements the session and presentation layers of the ISO/OSI reference model.

The requirement to build applications in a heterogeneous and distributed setting is not new. Solutions for resolving heterogeneity and distribution in the form of middleware have been available for some time, too. The available middleware can be classified into three major categories: transaction-oriented, message-oriented and object-oriented middleware. Their differences can be explained by their initial goals.

3.2.1 Transaction-Oriented Middleware

Transaction-oriented middleware is often used with distributed database applications.

Transaction-oriented middleware supports transactions across different distributed database systems. Hence, this type of middleware is often used in architectures where components are database applications. Transaction-oriented middleware uses the two-phase commit protocol [Bernstein et al., 1987] to implement distributed transactions. The products in this category include IBM's CICS, BEA's Tuxedo and Transarc's Encina. These products assume that participating database management systems implement the two-phase commit protocol.

The Open Group have adopted a standard for Open Distributed Transaction Processing (DTP). DTP is widely supported by relational and object-oriented database management systems and transaction-oriented middleware. [X/Open Group, 1994] defines the XA-Protocol for two-phase commit.

Being able to integrate updates in distributed databases also provides the foundation for fault-tolerance and load-balancing [Birman, 1997]. Many transaction-oriented middleware systems use distributed transactions to maintain replicated databases on different servers. Updates to these databases are synchronized using distributed transactions. Load-balancing is used to direct queries to the least-loaded replica.

In Chapter 11, we will discuss transactions between distributed objects. These distributed object transactions build on the XA-Protocol of the DTP standard and are now widely available in distributed object middleware, too.

Object-oriented middleware has transaction-oriented middleware capabilities.

3.2.2 Message-Oriented Middleware

Message-oriented middleware supports the communication between distributed system components by facilitating message exchange. Products in this category include IBM's MQSeries, Sun's ToolTalk and NCR's TopEnd. Client components use these systems to send a message in order to request execution of a service to a server component. The content of such a message includes the service parameters. Another message is sent to the client from the server to transmit the result of the service.

A strength of message-oriented middleware is that this paradigm supports asynchronous message delivery very naturally. The client continues processing as soon as the middleware has taken the message. Eventually the server will send a message including the result and the client can collect that message at an appropriate time. This achieves de-coupling of client and server and leads to more scalable systems.

Message-oriented middleware is used when reliable, asynchronous communication is the dominant form of distributed system interaction.

A further strength of message-oriented middleware is that it supports multi-casting; it can distribute the same message to multiple receivers in a way that is transparent to clients. This is a useful primitive for implementing event notification and publish/subscribe-based architectures.

Message-oriented middleware systems achieve fault-tolerance by implementing message queues that store messages temporarily on persistent storage. The sender writes the message into the message queue and if the receiver is unavailable due to a failure, the message queue retains the message until the receiver is available again.

Object-oriented middleware initially did not achieve this degree of fault-tolerance, but only supported synchronous communication with at-most-once semantics. We will discuss in Chapter 7 the integration of message-oriented middleware and object-oriented middleware, which achieves reliable and asynchronous object requests.

Object-oriented middleware is starting to be integrated with message-oriented middleware.

3.2.3 Remote Procedure Calls

Remote Procedure Calls (RPCs) were invented in the early 1980s by Sun Microsystems as part of their Open Network Computing (ONC) platform. RPCs are operations that can be invoked remotely across different hardware and operating system platforms. Sun provided remote procedure calls as part of their Sun OS, an early Unix implementation. Sun sub-

An RPC is a procedure call across host boundaries.

mitted RPCs as a standard to the X/Open consortium and it was adopted as part of the Distributed Computing Environment (DCE).

 The origin of object-oriented middleware is RPC.

Remote procedure call systems are the origin of object-oriented middleware. In some systems, RPCs are even used to implement distributed object requests. We now study how remote procedure calls implement the presentation and session layers so that we can, in the next section, discuss how object-oriented middleware extends remote procedure call systems.

Interface Definition Language

RPCs are clustered in RPC programs.

The server components that execute RPCs are called *RPC programs*. The RPC program has an interface definition that defines procedures that can be called remotely. Interface definitions also define data types of arguments that can be passed to remote procedures. The DCE standard includes an interface definition language that is used to define these exports in a way that is independent of programming languages. Example 3.1 shows an interface definition in Sun's RPC interface definition language.

Example 3.1
RPC Program that Handles Soccer Player Data

```
const NL=64;
struct Player {
  struct DoB {int day; int month; int year;}
  string name<NL>;
};
program PLAYERPROG {
 version PLAYERVERSION {
  void PRINT(Player)=0;
  int STORE(Player)=1;
  Player LOAD(int)=2;
 } = 0;
} = 105040;
```

The above interface definition defines a struct type for soccer Player data, which may then be passed as a complex procedure parameter to an RPC program.

Presentation Layer

 RPC presentation layer integration maps application data structures onto a homogeneous and transmissible form.

The presentation layer implementation of RPCs maps application data structures, such as the Player data structure, into a form that can be transmitted via the transport layer. This involves two principal tasks: resolution of data heterogeneity and mapping of complex data structures into blocks or streams of bytes. An overview of the tasks for the presentation layer implementation of middleware is given in Figure 3.4.

As we have seen in Chapter 1, distributed systems are often deployed across different hardware platforms. Some of these platforms use different representations for representing data. One of the principal responsibilities of the presentation layer is to resolve this data heterogeneity between client and server objects. We will study the techniques for data heterogeneity resolution that are used in object-oriented middleware in Chapter 5.

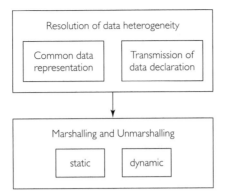

Figure 3.4
Tasks Achieved by the
Presentation Layer
Implementation

After having resolved heterogeneity, the presentation layer transforms the high-level data structures that are passed as request parameters into a form that can be transmitted by the transport layer implementation. The required transformation process is commonly referred to as *marshalling*. The presentation layer also implements the reverse mapping, that is the reconstruction of complex data structures from a sequence or block of bytes. This mapping is referred to as *unmarshalling*. Example 3.2 shows an example of marshalling and unmarshalling operations written in C++. In practice, this code is generated by the interface definition language compiler rather than hand-written, but we believe it is important that the reader understands what the generator needs to achieve. We have, therefore, deliberately not used the C++ iostream functionality in order to demonstrate more clearly what needs to be done.

The mappings between application and transport data representations are called marshalling and unmarshalling.

```
char * marshal() {
  char * msg;
  msg=new char[4*(sizeof(int)+1) + strlen(name)+1];
  sprintf(msg,"%d %d %d %s",dob.day,dob.month,dob.year,
                           strlen(name),name);
  return(msg);
};
void unmarshal(char * msg) {
  int name_len;
  sscanf(msg,"%d %d %d %d ", &dob.day,&dob.month,&dob.year,
                           &name_len);
  name = new char[name_len+1];
  sscanf(msg,"%d %d %d %d %s",&dob.day,&dob.month,&dob.year,
&name_len,name);
};
```

Example 3.2
Marshalling and Unmarshalling of
Complex Data Structures

The operation `marshal` transforms player data into a sequence of bytes and the operation `unmarshal` performs the reverse operation. Similar operations are performed by every client and server stub.

Marshalling can be implemented statically or dynamically.

The parameters that have to be marshalled obviously depend on the operation signatures of the server objects. Hence, marshalling is specific to the particular remote procedures. The way data heterogeneity is resolved is operation-specific for the same reason. A choice arises as to when marshalling and resolution of data heterogeneity is implemented. It may be implemented statically at compile time (that is, operations for marshalling and resolving data heterogeneity may be compiled and linked into client and server objects) or determined dynamically at run-time (that is, the particular signature of an operation exported by a server object may be interpreted).

Client and server stubs are static implementations of marshalling and unmarshalling.

Stubs are generated by remote procedure call systems in order to implement type-specific concerns, such as marshalling and operation dispatch. The input to that generation process is an interface definition that defines the formal parameters of the procedures exported by an RPC program. In that way, stub generation solves the problem that presentation layer implementations are needed for each object type. RPC systems on Unix provide an interface definition language compiler, called `rpcgen`, that generates pairs of stubs, a *client stub* and a *server stub*. The client stub resolves heterogeneity of the actual procedure parameters and marshals them. Moreover, it unmarshals the result and reproduces the native data representation for the client. Likewise, the server stub unmarshals the actual procedure parameters and maps them to the native data representation of the host where the RPC program is executed. When the procedure result becomes available it is returned to the server stub, which resolves heterogeneity and marshals it into a transmittable form.

Session Layer

The session layer implementation needs to enable clients to locate an RPC server. This can be done statically or dynamically. The binding in Example 3.3 is static because the hostname is determined at compile time. Static binding is fairly simple, but is not location transparent and thus it limits migration and replication transparency. With dynamic binding, the selection of the server is performed at run-time. This can be done in such a way that migration and replication transparency are retained. Each host of a Unix network that supports RPCs runs a particular daemon called `portmap`. Any RPC server registers its programs with the `portmap` daemon that runs on the host. Clients can contact a single

Example 3.3
Client Program using RPC to Invoke an Operation

```
print_person(char * host, Player * pers) {
  CLIENT *clnt;

  clnt = clnt_create(host, 105040, 0, "udp");
  if (clnt == (CLIENT *) NULL) exit(1);
  if (print_0(pers, clnt)==NULL)
  clnt_perror(clnt, "call failed");
  clnt_destroy(clnt);
}
```

The above C code creates a client stub for the RPC program in Example 3.1 that uses a UDP connection to connect to `host`. If the creation succeeds, it calls the stub with `print_0`.

portmap daemon, to check whether the server supports a particular program or to get a list of all programs that reside on the server. Clients can also broadcast a search for a program to all portmap daemons of a network and the portmap daemons with which the program is registered will respond. In that way the client can locate the server program without knowing the topology of the network. Programs can then easily be migrated from one server to another and be replicated over multiple hosts with full transparency for clients.

Another design choice is related to *activation*. The activation policy defines whether a remote procedure program is always available or has to be started on demand. For startup on demand, the RPC server is started by the inetd daemon as soon as a request arrives. The inetd requires an additional configuration table that provides for a mapping between remote procedure program names and the location of programs in the file system. If an RPC program is always available, requests will be handled more efficiently because startup overheads do not arise. On the other hand, it uses resources continuously.

Activation policies determine how servers are enabled to perform requests.

3.3 Object-Oriented Middleware

Object-oriented middleware evolved more or less directly from the idea of remote procedure calls. The first of these systems was the OMG's Common Object Request Broker Architecture (CORBA), and then Microsoft added distribution capabilities to its Component Object Model (COM) and Sun provided a mechanism for Remote Method Invocation (RMI) in Java. The development of object-oriented middleware mirrored similar evolutions in programming languages where object-oriented programming languages, such as C++ evolved from procedural programming languages such as C. The idea here is to make object-oriented principles, such as object identification through references and inheritance, available for the development of distributed systems.

Interface Definition Language

Every object-oriented middleware has an object model, which has more or less the features that we discussed in Chapter 2. It has an interface definition language (IDL) that has language constructs for all concepts of the respective object model. While the details of the object models and interface definition languages differ slightly, they have several concerns in common. We discuss the differences when we consider interface definition languages and object models in detail in Chapter 4 but now discuss the commonalities.

Every object-oriented middleware has an interface definition language.

A disadvantage of remote procedure calls is that they are not reflexive. This means that procedures exported by one RPC program cannot return another RPC program. Object-oriented middleware provides interface definition languages, where interfaces define object types and instances of these types are objects in their own right. This means that a server object that implements an object type can return other server objects, as shown in Example 3.4.

IDLs support the concepts of object types as parameters; failure handling; and inheritance.

Object-oriented middleware further extends remote procedure call programs in the way they handle failures. Sun's RPCs return null pointers when the remote procedure call fails. This does not allow the middleware or the server object to inform the client why a failure

Example 3.4
Object-Oriented Interface to
Handle Player Data

```
interface Player : Object {
  typedef struct Date {
    short day; short month; short year;
  };
  attribute string name;
  readonly attribute Date DoB;
};
interface PlayerStore : Object {
  exception IDNotFound{};
  short save (in Player p);
  Player load(in short id) raises (IDNotFound);
  void print(in Player p);
};
```

Objects of type `PlayerStore` return a reference to another server object in operation `load`. It raises an exception if a player with the given identifier cannot be found. Both `Player` and `PlayerStore` inherit from `Object`.

occurred. Object-oriented middleware has more sophisticated failure-handling mechanisms. It uses exceptions to inform clients about the details of a failure that occurs while an object request is executed. The object models and interface definition languages of object-oriented middleware all support inheritance. This means that common operations and exceptions can be defined in one interface and other interfaces can inherit these operations and exceptions. In particular, all object-oriented middleware has root types from which every interface inherits a set of common operations.

Presentation Layer Implementation

The presentation layer implementation of object-oriented middleware is very similar to that of RPCs. Object-oriented middleware also supports client and server stubs, which perform marshalling and resolve heterogeneity of data representation.

 Object-oriented middleware presentation layers need to map object references to the transport format.

The only serious difference between the presentation layer implementation of object-oriented middleware and RPCs concerns the handling of object references. The transport layer protocol of an object-oriented middleware needs to define representations of object references. They need to be marshalled and unmarshalled in a similar way to application-level data structures.

Session Layer Implementation

The session layer implementation of object-oriented middleware is slightly more complex than that of remote procedure calls. The implementation provides the connection between multiple objects over one or several connections established by the transport layer. In more concrete terms, the tasks performed by the session layer implementation are the mapping of object references to hosts, an implementation of primitives for activation and deactivation of objects, the invocation of the requested operation and the synchronization of client and server.

Transport layer implementations, such as TCP and UDP, use addressing schemes based on host names and port numbers. Remote procedure call systems use the `portmap` daemon in order to map between service names and host names. To achieve this mapping, service names defined by system administrators have to be unique. Object-oriented middleware extends the basic idea of portmaps in several respects. First, addressing of server objects is based on object references. Secondly, these object references are generated by the middleware rather than an administrator. Finally, the session layer implementation of object-oriented middleware maps object references to hosts in a fully transparent way.

Session layer needs to map object references to hosts.

Client objects always identify the object from which they request the service by an object reference. That object reference is an essential part of the request and is always transmitted with an identification of the requested operation and the request parameters. The client side of the middleware implementation uses the object reference to locate the host where the server object resides. The session layer then connects to the server side implementation of the middleware that resides on that host. The server side implementation of the object request broker contains a component that we refer to as an *object adapter*. There is usually at least one object adapter on each host. Among other tasks, object adapters implement object activation and deactivation. (Please review the concepts of activation and deactivation introduced on Page 53.)

Session layer implements object activation policies in the object adapter.

The object adapter implements the mapping of object references to active object implementations (that is, implementations that are executing). This mapping is achieved as follows. Upon arrival of a request for an object in its realm, the object adapter checks whether the object is active (that is, whether the object implementation is being executed by an operating system process). If it is not, the object adapter looks up how to start the implementation of the object in an *implementation repository* or *registry*. The actual startup may be achieved in many different ways. The adapter might launch a separate operating system process for the object, spawn a new thread of an existing process or dynamically link a library to itself. Once the adapter has started or otherwise identified the operating system process executing the object implementation, it forwards the request to that object.

Object adapters need to be able to start up servers, which register in an implementation repository or registry.

The object needs to invoke the requested operation. This is referred to as *operation dispatch*. To dispatch the operation, the object implementation will need to partially decode the request information that has been transmitted via the network and passed on by the object adapter. That request information will include an identifier of the requested operation and so the object knows which operation to call in the implementation of the server object.

Session layer needs to implement operation dispatch.

The session layer implementation on both sides also needs to achieve the synchronization between client and server objects. Object requests are, by default, synchronous forms of communication. This means that the middleware has to force the client object to wait until the server object has completed executing the request and has produced a result or notifies with an exception that it is unable to satisfy the request. We note that there are also non-synchronous forms of communication and we have deferred their discussion to Chapter 7. The implementation of synchronization in a middleware system is conceptually part of the session layer, both at the client and the server. The client side needs to wait for requests to be

Session layer needs to implement synchronization.

completed before it gives control back to the client; the server side needs to signal completion of the request to the client side.

We note that some of the above concerns that need to be addressed by the session layer implementation are specific to object types, while others are not. Objects of different types have different operations and each of these operations is likely to have different parameter lists and return types. Hence, the implementation of calling the requested operation on the server side has to be implemented in a different way for each different object type. The mapping of object references to hosts, the activation and deactivation and the synchronization between client and server object can therefore be provided completely by the middleware.

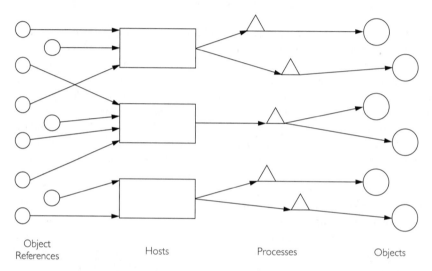

Figure 3.5

Mappings Implemented by the Session Layer

Object References   Hosts   Processes   Objects

These considerations are summarized in Figure 3.5. The session layer implementation of an object request broker first finds the host on which to execute the request. This decision is generally based on object references which identify a host, either directly or indirectly. It then contacts the object adapter on that host which locates or activates the process in which the object resides. The server process then identifies the object and finally the session layer implementation of the object implementation ensures that the requested operation is executed. This is the point when the session layer passes control to the presentation layer, which handles complex data structures of operation parameters and the results the operation wishes to pass back to the client.

3.4 Developing with Object-Oriented Middleware

In this section, we discuss how object-oriented middleware facilitates the development of distributed objects. The organization of this section is driven by a development process for

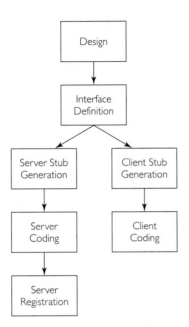

Figure 3.6
Design and Implementation
Process for Distributed Objects

distributed objects, which is sketched in Figure 3.6. The rectangles represent different process activities and the arrows represent precedence relationships between activities.

The process starts by designing the server objects based on requirements that existing and future client objects may have. The design could be done using a Computer Aided Software Engineering (CASE) tool that supports an object-oriented design notation, such as the Unified Modeling Language. Hence, class diagrams are designed that show the relationship between server objects and client objects and that indicate the static structure of object types in terms of operations and attributes. Sequence diagrams might be used to model scenarios of how client objects interact with server objects. State diagrams might indicate constraints on the order in which server object operations can be requested.

The next step of the process transforms the information acquired in class diagrams into interface definitions. An interface definition governs the structure and behaviour of server objects. The way interfaces are defined depends on the particular object-oriented middleware system that is being used. The transition from class diagrams into interface definitions may be partially automated if the CASE tool supports code generation of interface definitions. The generated interfaces then need to be refined by the server object designer. We discuss the definition of interfaces in detail in Section 3.4.1.

Client and server object programmers then use the interface definitions designed in the previous step in order to generate stubs. For a client object, a client stub serves as a local proxy for a server object. This means that the client object can call the client stub with local method or procedure calls. For a server object, a server stub serves as a local proxy for client objects. The stubs implement the presentation and session layers that we have discussed in the previous section. We review the generation of stubs in Section 3.4.2.

The classes from which client objects are instantiated use client stubs in their implementation. They make object requests by calling a client stub. The client class therefore has to import the client stub. Depending on the programming language chosen for the client, this may be done using a C++ include directive or a Java import statement.

The server object programmer uses the stub in order to implement the object. Depending on the programming language chosen for the server implementation, the classes that implement the server object type might inherit from an abstract class defined in the server stub or it might implement a server stub interface.

In centralized applications, the operating system loader achieves that object implementations are available when they are needed. With distributed objects, an object adapter is responsible for that and it relies on an implementation repository. Server object implementations have to be registered with an implementation repository. Then the distribution middleware knows where to locate the objects and how to activate them.

3.4.1 Interface Definition

In Chapter 2 we argued that the object-oriented paradigm provides a suitable component model for building distributed systems. We have outlined typical constituents of a meta-model for distributed objects. A meta-model defines concepts that determine properties of object types. In fact, each object-oriented middleware defines its own meta-model. Examples include the OMG object model defined for CORBA, Microsoft's Component Object Model (COM) and the object model for Java Remote Method Invocations (RMI).

IDLs provide language constructs for all concepts of their underlying object model.

Object-oriented middleware systems need to provide facilities for designers to instantiate their meta-models. The instantiations are type definitions for distributed objects. Middleware may use a programming language for this purpose or it may provide an explicit interface definition language (IDL). IDLs are typically not computationally complete. They do not provide language constructs that are needed to implement objects.

Interface definitions add considerable detail to class diagrams.

We note that the interface definition adds considerable detail and thus refines the class diagram, such as that shown in Example 2.3. In particular, the interface definitions include exceptions, definitions of constructed types, such as Address, refined parameters of operations and implementations for the various associations.

Interfaces can be seen as contracts that govern the interaction between client and server objects.

Interface definitions play an extremely important role in the engineering of distributed objects. [Meyer, 1988b] considers type definitions as contracts between the clients that wish to use a service and the objects that provide the service. The object implementations in fact are under an obligation to implement the interfaces, provide the declared operations, respect their formal parameter lists and raise only those exceptions that are declared in the interface. Clients are under an obligation to call only those operations that have been declared in an interface, pass actual parameters that match the formal parameters declared in the interface, and to catch all the exceptions that are declared.

Interfaces are also the basis for distributing type information.

The declarations provided as part of an interface definition are also used by the middleware itself. In particular, for dynamic invocations when requests are only defined at run-time, middleware systems need to safe-guard that both clients and server actually obey the contract. Moreover, there are situations where the middleware needs to translate requests between formats used by different middleware systems and it usually needs to have type information to do that. We will see in Chapter 6 that middleware systems store interface definitions for that purpose and provide a programming interface so that interface definitions can be accessed.

While all object-oriented programming languages have types or interfaces, interface definitions have a more specific role for distributed objects; they are the principle source from which middleware systems generate client and server stubs and thus they provide the basis for the automatic implementation of those presentation and session layer tasks that are type-specific.

Client and server stubs are automatically derived from interfaces.

3.4.2 Stub Generation

We have already discussed the role of stubs in the presentation and session layer implementations of remote procedure calls. Also object-oriented middleware use client and server stubs for the implementation of presentation and session layers. From a development point of view, we can consider them from a different perspective. For a client developer, a stub represents the server object. From a server object, the server stub represents the client object. Stubs are, in fact, incarnations of the proxy design pattern that was identified in [Gamma et al., 1995]. A proxy is placeholder that hides a certain degree of complication. Client and server stubs hide the fact that an operation execution is being requested in a distributed fashion. The client stub resides on the same host as the client object and the server stub resides on the same host as the server object. The implementor of the client object may, therefore, call the client stub using a local method call. Likewise, the server stub calls the server object using a local method call and the server and client stub implementations implement the distributed communication transparently for client and server object developers.

Client and server stubs are proxies for servers and clients.

Figure 3.7 shows the differences between a local method call and an object request that is implemented using client and server stubs. With a local method call, parameters are passed from the caller to the called operation via mechanisms, such as the hardware stack. The call is executed using some jump operation that is supported by the processor. Object requests, which are executed remotely, utilize stubs to perform the marshalling and unmarshalling, the resolution of heterogeneity and the synchronization of client and server objects.

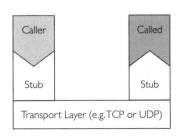

Figure 3.7
Method Calls versus Object Requests

Stubs are generated
by the IDL compiler
that is provided by
the middleware.

Stubs are always generated by a compiler that the middleware provides for its respective interface definition language. Part of every compliant CORBA implementation is a CORBA/ IDL compiler that generates stubs. Note that server stubs in CORBA are referred to as server skeletons. Every COM implementation comes with a Microsoft IDL compiler that generates the COM client and server stubs. The approach taken in Java/RMI is slightly different in that it provides a compiler that generates stubs from the Java class definition, without the involvement of an intermediate interface definition.

Example 3.5
Stub Generation Process

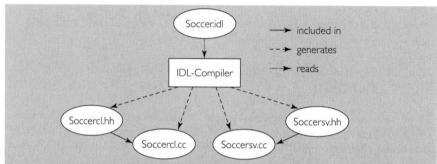

The CORBA interface definition contained in file `Soccer.idl` is translated into stubs and skeletons that can be used for client and server object development in C++. The IDL compiler generates four files: two for the client stubs and two for the server stubs. With the CORBA/C++ language binding, each stub is itself a class; the first file of each pair includes the class definition and the second one the class implementation.

3.4.3 Implementation of Client Objects

A static object
request is made by a
client calling a local
method of a client
stub.

Client objects make an object request by invoking a client stub. Hence they use a local method call for defining that request. This implies that the request is fully defined at the time the source code of the client is compiled. We therefore refer to this kind of request definition as *static request definition*.

The invocation of a stub implies a dependency of the client code from the stub. Hence, the stub has to be generated before the client code can be compiled. Moreover, the client code needs to be recompiled whenever the stub has been changed, for example due to a change in the interface definition of the server object.

Stubs are typed and
thus compilers can
check type safety.

We demand object requests to be *type safe*. Type safety means that at run-time the server object will be able to meet those requests that have been accepted at compile time. Without type safety we could experience run-time errors due to requests of unavailable operations or wrong actual parameters. When compiling a client object source in a type-safe setting, we expect the compiler to detect requests that are not supported by the server object and wrong actual parameter lists. This is generally achieved by using statically-typed languages, such as Ada, C++ or Java. Using these languages, we will import or include the stub class declaration and the compiler will check any static request definition against the class declaration. Because the client stub class declaration directly evolved from the interface definition, programmers can be certain that they only make requests that are actually supported by the interface of the server object.

Because client stubs are invoked by the client, the client has to be bound with the object code for the client stub. Because the client stub generally relies on the object-oriented middleware to resolve the generic part of the presentation and session layer implementations, some middleware libraries also have to be bound with the client.

For any operation included in the interface, the operation in the client stub generally has the same signature as the operation in the server object. This supports linking the server object directly with the client when it is known at linking time that remote access will not be needed. Hence, the identity of operation signatures means that static object requests achieves access transparency. From an engineering point of view, it is a good idea to define interfaces between subsystems using an interface definition language, even though the interfaces might not be used in a distributed setting. The availability of interfaces, however, simplifies distribution of these components considerably.

 Stubs can achieve access transparency.

The identity of the signatures of client stubs and server objects also enables the middleware to make optimizations based on the location of objects. If client and server objects reside on the same host, there is no need to use client and server stubs and the network for the communication of object requests. Indeed, that would be far too inefficient. Sophisticated object-oriented middleware implementations therefore shortcut the network and invoke the server object directly if it is located on the same host. Again, this is considerably simplified by access transparency.

 Middleware may shortcut a stub if server and client reside on the same host.

3.4.4 Implementation of Server Objects

The implementation of interfaces has to solve the problem that a generated server stub needs to call the object implementation in a type-safe way. We would like the compiler that we use for translating the server object to detect typing problems, such as missing parameters or parameters of the wrong type for the invocation of server objects in the same way as for the invocation of client stubs.

 The generated server stub has to call the server implementation that an application builder designed.

There are two approaches to the implementation of server objects in a type-safe way: interfaces and inheritance. Both approaches achieve that the server stub calls the server object.

Interfaces and inheritance make server object implementations type-safe.

Not all object-oriented programming languages support the concept of interfaces and inheritance may be used with these languages. For implementation by inheritance, the middleware generates an abstract class as part of the server stub. This abstract class has abstract operations that declare the operation signature but are not implemented by the class. Pure virtual member functions may be used in C++ and deferred operations may be used in Eiffel. The class implementing the server object is then defined as a subtype of this abstract class. The server stub will have a reference that is statically of the abstract class but refers dynamically to an instance of the server object.

The programming language compiler used for the server implementation will check that the redefinition of abstract operation meets the declarations of the respective operations in the

Example 3.6
Type-Safe Implementation of
Server Objects

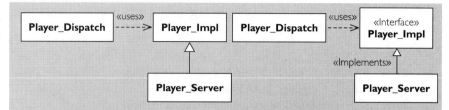

The diagram on the left shows how inheritance is used in classes `Player_Dispatch` and `Player_Impl`, which are contained in the server stub for object type `Player`. Class `Player_Server`, which implements the IDL type `Player`, implements all deferred operations defined in `Player_Impl`.

The diagram on the right shows an interface-based implementation with the relationships of interfaces and classes involved on the server side. For an IDL interface `Player`, an IDL compiler might produce a server stub class `Player_Dispatch`, whose purpose is to unmarshal parameters. `Player_Dispatch` then calls the requested method from the server object. The static type of the object reference used in that call would be of type `Player_Impl`, which is an interface implemented in class `Player_Server`.

abstract superclass. The implementation of `Player_Dispatch`, for example, would have a reference of static type `Player_Impl`, which at run-time refers to an object of type `Player_Server`. Hence, this inheritance approach is another way to achieve type-safe implementations of server objects.

Several modern programming languages, such as Java, provide a mechanism for interfaces and a particular implementation relationship between interfaces and classes. These programming language interfaces should not be confused with the interfaces for distributed objects that are written using an IDL in a way that is independent of programming languages. Programming language interfaces are a particularly useful vehicle for the type-safe implementation of server objects. Following this approach, the IDL compiler generates a programming language interface that includes all operations exported by the IDL interface. The server object implementation then declares that it implements the programming language interface.

This approach achieves the required type safety, because the compiler used for translating the implementation of the server object checks that it correctly implements the interface that was derived by the IDL compiler. In Example 3.6, a Java compiler used for compiling `Player_Server` validates that the interface `Player_Impl` is implemented correctly. As `Player_Dispatch` uses `Player_Impl`, we have achieved that the generated class can safely call the hand-coded class.

3.4.5 Server Registration

 Server objects must be registered in the registry or implementation repository of the middleware.

Object activation as discussed above might necessitate the object adapter to start a server object implementation. Once the server objects have been compiled, they need to be registered with the object-oriented middleware. The purpose of this registration is to tell the object adapter where to find the executable code for the object and how to start it.

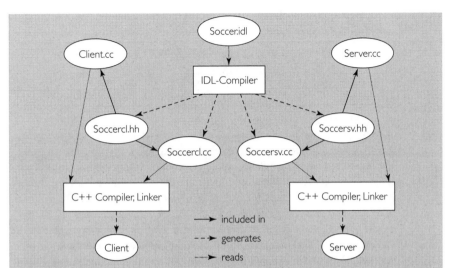

Example 3.7
Use of Stubs for Client and
Server Object Development

The client implementation in file Client.cc includes Soccercl.hh so as to enable the compiler to check consistency between the declaration and use of client stub implementations. When translated into an executable, Client.cc is linked with the object code of the client stub that is generated from file Soccercl.cc. Likewise, the implementation of the server object includes the class definition of the server stubs that are stored in file Soccersv.hh and the object code of the server stub is linked with the object code of the server object.

How server implementations are registered largely depends on the particular middleware and on the operating system on which it runs. The details are not important for this textbook and we focus on the principles only.

The registration is generally done by a system administrator, who maintains an *implementation repository*. The implementation repository is somewhat similar to the inetd daemon of remote procedure calls. It associates objects, which are usually identified by an object reference, with some instructions on how to start up the *servant* in which the server object executes. There is an implementation repository on each host. The middleware provides administration tools to maintain the implementation repository. These tools enable administrators to browse through the list of servants that are registered on a particular host. Moreover, they allow administrators to register new server objects and to delete existing server objects.

There are several examples of these implementation repositories. Microsoft's COM relies on the registry that is part of the Windows operating system. Likewise, Java provides activation interfaces that are used with RMI. They are implemented in the Java RMI daemon, which plays the same role as the object adapter in CORBA. Although the CORBA specifications do not explicitly prescribe it, many CORBA implementations do include an implementation repository with respective administration tools.

Key Points

▶ We used the ISO/OSI reference model to explain where conceptually object-oriented middleware is situated and we identified that the middleware is built on top of the transport layer.

▶ We discussed non-object-oriented forms of middleware. These include transactional and message-oriented middleware as well as remote procedure calls.

▶ Object-oriented middleware implements the session and presentation layers of the ISO/OSI reference model.

▶ The session layer implementation uses connections between two hosts to establish a connection between two objects residing on that host. In order to achieve that, it implements an object adapter which knows about all active server objects on a particular host and is capable of activating and deactivating objects. Finally the session layer implements the synchronization of requests between two objects.

▶ The presentation layer implementation of an object-oriented middleware implements the transport of complex request parameters and results and the resolution of heterogeneous data representation.

▶ We discussed the main activities of the development process for distributed objects. These include the interface definition, the generation of client and server stubs, the coding of client and server objects and the registration of the server object.

▶ The interface is defined using an interface definition language that is an essential part of most object-oriented middleware. The middleware provides a compiler that checks interfaces on syntactic and static semantic consistency and produces client and server stubs.

▶ Client and server stubs contribute to achieving type safety of request. On the client side, this is concerned with ensuring that the client only requests operations that are declared in the interface and that the client passes correct actual parameters. On the server side, type safety is concerned with ensuring that the server object implements the interface definition correctly.

▶ We identified the need for an implementation repository that stores the information on how an object adapter can activate server objects prior to these server objects serving requests.

Self Assessment

3.1 Name the seven layers of the ISO/OSI reference model.

3.2 On which layer does object-oriented middleware build?

3.3 Which layers does the middleware implement?

3.4 Give reasons why it is not a good idea to use the transport layer directly.

3.5 What concerns does the session layer implementation of object-oriented middleware address?

3.6 What are the two principal tasks that the presentation layer implements?

3.7 What concerns are specified in the interface definition that are typically not determined in an object-oriented design using UML?

3.8   What are the principal products that an interface definition language compiler produces?

3.9   What is type safety?

3.10 How do client and server stubs contribute to achieving type safety?

3.11 Name three non-object-oriented classes of middleware.

3.12 When would you use which class of middleware?

Further Reading

There are many books about networks and it is impossible to list them all here. [Tanenbaum, 1989] provides an excellent introduction to the ISO/OSI reference model and we highly recommend it. Though we suggested in this chapter that it is not a good idea for an application programmer to use network programming capabilities directly, it may be worth considering [Stevens, 1990] for a detailed description of TCP, UDP and the socket programming interface. The reader may then be able to fully appreciate how much easier the development of distributed systems becomes through the use of object-oriented middleware.

We have only been able to give a very brief overview of other classes of middleware and refer the reader to the extensive literature. One of the earliest transaction monitors was IBM/CICS and we refer to [Summerville, 1987] for a discussion of its use. [Hall, 1996] provides a good introduction to the use of Tuxedo, one of the market leading transaction server products, for the construction of client–server architectures. Recently, Microsoft launched a transaction monitor product and a discussion of its application is provided by [Hillier, 1998].

There is a large body of literature about remote procedure calls. A good introduction is included in [Colouris et al., 1994]. Remote procedure calls were standardized by the Open Group as part of the Distributed Communication Environment (DCE). A good introduction to DCE is provided by [Schill, 1993].

4

CORBA, COM and Java/RMI

Learning Objectives

We will now familiarize ourselves with the three most prominent examples of object-oriented middleware; the Common Object Request Broker Architecture (CORBA) of the Object Management Group (OMG), Microsoft's Common Object Model (COM) and Sun Remote Method Invocation (RMI). We will study these systems in order to understand how the principles that we learned in the previous chapter are applied in practice. We will focus particularly on how they implement an object request between a client and a server object and highlight how the middleware systems achieve transparency of requests. While doing so, we will grasp the differences and similarities between the object models and architectures that these middleware systems use.

Chapter Outline

In the previous chapter, we explained the principles of object-oriented middleware. We outlined the relationship of middleware to the ISO/OSI reference model and we saw that the presentation and session layers are implemented by middleware. We discussed the concept of marshalling and unmarshalling. We saw how stubs implement marshalling and unmarshalling in the middleware implementation of the presentation layer. We studied different forms of middleware and how they have led to the development of object-oriented middleware. We also discussed how object identification is implemented in middleware as part of the session layer implementation. We saw how developers use middleware to generate stubs from interface definitions and how they build these stubs into executable distributed objects.

In this chapter we take a closer look at three particular examples of object-oriented middleware. We investigate CORBA, COM and Java/RMI and show how the principles discussed in the previous chapter are used and applied in practice. CORBA is a specification standard for middleware that is implemented in about a dozen products. COM is Microsoft's component object model and provides support for invoking operations from remote objects. Java/RMI is the mechanism for remote method invocation that has become available in version 1.1 of the language specification.

We follow a common structure for the discussion of each of these middleware systems. We begin by presenting the meta-object model that the system supports. While the systems all support the concepts of object types and instances thereof, they differ in their approach to inheritance and the handling of failures. The meta-object models provide the semantic foundations for the interface definition languages, which are used to define object types. We then discuss the architecture of the middleware and we review in particular how a request is executed at run-time.

The separate treatment of these three object-oriented middleware approaches in this chapter may suggest that they are competing against each other and that one will eventually 'win' and replace the other two. We rather believe that there is room for all three to co-exist and that the choice of a middleware for a particular platform will be quite a simple one. The object-oriented middleware of choice for mainframes and Unix platforms that are often chosen for mission-critical and high-availability applications is CORBA. Internet and e-commerce applications that need to be portable across a large number of platforms will most likely choose some form of Java platform and COM is the middleware of choice for distributed systems that are developed for Windows operating systems.

In Chapter 5, we will discuss how middleware systems resolve heterogeneity, which may arise in data representation and programming languages. In that chapter, we will pay particular attention to the interoperability and interworking specifications that enable the co-existence that we mentioned above. In this chapter, we discuss static approaches to object requests and in Chapter 6 we will present how object requests are determined at run-time. All chapters in Part III then discuss how these middleware systems help in solving particular design problems.

4.1 CORBA

The CORBA specifications are defined by the Object Management Group, a non-profit organization that has more than 800 members at the time of writing this book. The first specification adopted by the OMG was the Object Management Architecture (OMA) [Soley, 1992]. The OMA, shown in Figure 4.1, defines a reference model for distributed objects and classifies objects into different categories. CORBA supports heterogeneous and distributed objects. Communication between objects is achieved through an object request broker, which aims to hide heterogeneity and distribution as far as possible.

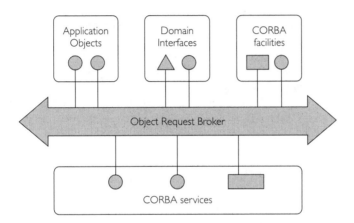

Figure 4.1
The OMG Object Management Architecture [Soley, 1992]

The second substantial specification that the OMG produced is the *Common Object Request Broker Architecture* (CORBA) [Object Management Group, 1995]. This specification defines the interface definition language for CORBA and identifies a number of programming language bindings. These bindings determine how client and server objects can be implemented in different programming languages and we will discuss them in detail in Chapter 5. The CORBA specification also defines object adapters that govern object activation, deactivation and the generation of object references.

An important design goal of CORBA is to overcome heterogeneity.

After the initial version of the CORBA specification had been adopted, the OMG started working on the *CORBAservices* specification [Object Management Group, 1996]. A service, in OMG terminology, is a basic mechanism that enables the construction of distributed systems. The OMG has adopted more than a dozen CORBAservices so far. These support locating objects, creating and moving objects, push-type communication between objects, managing relationships between objects, controlling concurrent access to objects, managing distributed transactions between objects and securing access to objects. We will discuss the incorporation of these services into architectures for distributed objects in Part III of this book.

More recently, the OMG has adopted interface specifications that are useful but, unlike the CORBAservices, not mandatory for the construction of a distributed system. The OMG refers to these interfaces as CORBAfacilities. They include interfaces for a distributed help system, for a facility to input Asian character sets, and a facility for establishing operating system independent printing and spooling.

At the time of writing this book, the OMG has started focussing on specific interfaces for vertical market domains (*Domain Interfaces*). The OMG has set up task forces for market domains, such as electronic commerce, finance, telecommunication, transport and health care. Some of these specifications have been adopted already. Examples include the Currency interface prepared by the Finance Domain Task Force and the Air Traffic Control Display Manager defined by the Transport Domain Task Force.

4.1.1   Meta-Object Model and Interface Definition

The CORBA object model is defined in the Object Management Architecture Guide. We explain it by highlighting the differences and additions of the CORBA Object Model to the more general meta-object model for distributed objects that we used in Chapter 2. We will strive to explain the particular design choices that the OMG made together with their rationale. We encourage readers to review the concepts that were introduced in Chapter 2.

Alongside the discussion of the meta-object model, we will introduce CORBA IDL, an interface definition language with constructs for all concepts of the CORBA object model that is independent of all programming languages. Application builders use IDL to define export interfaces of objects and to group these interfaces into more coarse-grained modules. The OMG has standardized language bindings between IDL and C, C++, Smalltalk, Ada-95, Java and OO-Cobol. The programming language bindings are used both for implementing server objects and for accessing server objects from clients and we will discuss them in Chapter 5 when we discuss how programming language heterogeneity is resolved.

Objects

 CORBA objects have a unique identifier, but multiple object references.

Each CORBA object has a unique object identifier. There may be many object references to a CORBA object. CORBA object references are opaque to clients, that is client objects do not know the content of object references. In order to make an object request, i.e. request the execution of an operation from a server object, a client has to have a reference to the server object. Object references support location transparency as clients can request operations from referenced objects without having to know where the object is physically located. The physical hostname is embedded in the reference in order to enable CORBA implementations to locate the server object, but this information is hidden from the client.

 CORBA object references are persistent.

CORBA object references are generated and then managed by CORBA object request brokers. In particular, the broker stores object references persistently. This means that the object reference remains valid, even though the server object might currently be deactivated. When the reference is used for a request, the broker will use the object reference to locate the server object and re-activate it if necessary.

Types

The CORBA object model is statically typed. This means that all attributes, parameters and operation return values have a static type, defined using CORBA IDL. The rationale for this static typing is that it enables type safety to be checked in those situations when strongly typed programming languages are used for client and server object implementations: The types identified in the interfaces are then mapped to static types in the programming language representations of client and server objects. In the case of Java, Ada-95, C++ and C, the programming language compilers actually validate that the interfaces have been respected by client and server objects.

CORBA's object model is statically typed.

Object types in the CORBA object model have a unique name. The name is introduced in IDL using the keyword `interface`. The interface then contains operation, attribute, type and exception definitions that belong to the object type. In addition to object types, the CORBA object model defines a number of atomic types. These are represented in IDL as `boolean`, `char`, `short`, `long`, `float`, `string`.

More complex types can be constructed from object and atomic types using type construction mechanisms. These constructed types can be given new names using the `typedef` construct. The type constructors are declared in IDL using the keywords `sequence`, `struct`, `array` and `union`. Instances of these complex types are complex values that do not have their own identity and cannot have references. The rationale of this decision is that the object model should support designers in passing complex values from a client to a server object or vice versa. If sequences and arrays were treated as objects, they would be passed by reference and the values would need to be transferred with additional object requests.

CORBA supports complex types whose instances are values that are not remotely accessible.

```
typedef struct _Address {
  string street;
  string postcode;
  string city;
} Address;
typedef sequence<Address> AddressList;
interface Team { ... };
```

`Address` is a structure that consists of three string fields: `street`, `postcode` and `city`. `AddressList` is a type for a sequence of address values. The interface `Team` defines an object type.

Example 4.2
Type Declarations in CORBA

The name of an interface has to be unique throughout the distributed system. When interfaces are developed in a distributed and autonomous fashion, it could easily happen that two interfaces have the same name. The CORBA object model supports the concept of *modules* that restrict the scope in which declarations are valid. Modules are declared in IDL using the keyword `module` and they may contain interface definitions, type definitions, constant definitions and exception definitions. Hence, distributed development teams would typically agree a set of module names and could then freely choose the names of identifiers within the scope of their modules.

Modules are used to restrict the scope of identifiers.

The CORBA object model allows for *nested modules*. These are modules that are contained in other modules. Nested modules provide a mechanism for breaking down the complex modules that could occur in sizeable development projects into manageable units.

As it may be necessary to access declarations, such as types, from within the scope of other modules, the CORBA object model includes the concept of scoped identifiers. A scoped identifier is a sequence of module names followed by a regular identifier. Scoped identifiers are declared in CORBA IDL by delimiting identifiers that occur in these sequences by "::".

Example 4.2

Use of Modules to Avoid Name Clashes

```
module Soccer {
  typedef struct _Address {
    string street;
    string postcode;
    string city;
  } Address;
};
module People {
  typedef struct _Address {
    string flat_number;
    string street;
    string postcode;
    string city;
    string country;
  } Address;
};
```

Address is defined twice. Ambiguity is avoided by declaring the address type in the scope of different modules. Other IDL code may refer to addresses for soccer applications by Soccer::Address and to addresses of people by People::Address

Attributes

Attributes make state information of server objects accessible to client objects.

The CORBA object model includes the concept of attributes. They are used to make the state of server objects accessible to clients. Conceptually, the CORBA object model regards each attribute as a pair of operations. Client objects use one operation to read the state of the attribute while the other operation enables a client to modify the attribute.

Attributes are defined in CORBA IDL using the keyword `attribute` followed by the static type of the attribute and the name. Scoping in IDL is rather strict and identifiers have to be declared before they can be used. The type of the attribute has to be known before the attribute can be used. Forward declarations may be used to declare that certain types exist so that they can be used before they are fully defined.

The CORBA object model is a model for interface definitions. As such it does not need to support private or protected attributes. All attributes that are declared in the interface are accessible to clients. Hidden attributes of a server object are not included in the interface definition; they are only declared in the object type's implementation using a particular programming language.

CORBA supports the concept of read-only attributes. The value of a read-only attribute can be read, but it cannot be modified. Read-only attributes, therefore, correspond to only one operation, which supports returning the attribute value. In CORBA IDL, read-only attributes are declared by preceding the attribute declaration with the keyword `readonly`. In the example, `noOfMembers` is readonly while attribute `Teams` can be modified.

Readonly attributes cannot be modified by client objects.

The CORBA object model also supports the concept of constants. These are read-only attributes, whose value is not even changed by the server object implementation. Accessing a constant on the client side, therefore would not necessarily require an object request to be executed. The declaration of constants in IDL is very similar to C and C++; constants are introduced by the keyword `const` followed by the constant name and the literal determining the constant value.

```
interface Player;
typedef sequence<Player> PlayerList;
interface Trainer;
typedef sequence<Trainer> TrainerList;
interface Team {
   readonly attribute string name;
   attribute TrainerList coached_by;
   attribute Club belongs_to;
   attribute PlayerList players;
   ...
};
```

The forward declarations of interfaces `Player` and `Trainer` enable us to define `PlayerList` and `TrainerList`, two types for sequences of object references. Attributes are defined within the scope of an object type. Attribute `name` cannot be modified by clients of `Team` while attributes `coached_by`, `belongs_to` and `players` can be modified.

Example 4.3
Attribute Denition in Interface Types

Operations

The CORBA object model supports operations. They are defined for object types. An operation has a return type, an operation name, a list of parameters and a list of exceptions that the operation may raise. The CORBA object model does not support private or protected operations for the same reason that it does not support private or protected attributes. Operations of a server object that should not be made available to clients are just not declared in the interface of the object type.

CORBA operations specify the services that clients can request from server objects.

Operations can have three different *kinds* of parameters. An `in` parameter specifies that the client submits an actual value that is not modified by the server. An `out` parameter indicates that the server object produces a parameter value during the object request. An `inout` parameter allows the client to pass an actual parameter value that is modified by the server

CORBA operations may have in, out, or inout parameters.

during the request execution. This explicit indication of the request parameters is used for various purposes. It is more expressive than the pointers or reference declarations of C++. Explicit parameter kinds are also used to signal memory allocation and de-allocation obligations to the client or server programmer.

 CORBA does not support overloading to avoid complicating the programming language bindings.

The CORBA object model does not support the concept of overloading that is known from other object models, such as C++ or Java. Overloading means that different operations may have the same name as long as the parameter lists are different. Overloading is not supported because it does not add much to the expressive power of the interface definition language and complicates the binding to programming languages, such as C or Cobol, that do not support overloading.

Example 4.4
CORBA operation definitions

```
interface Team {
   ...
   void bookGoalies(in Date d) ... ;
   string print();
};
```

Team defines operations bookGoalies and print that can be requested from client objects.

Requests

 CORBA object requests are used to invoke a particular operation by a server object.

A request in the CORBA object model identifies the server object by an object reference to that object. It also determines the name and the actual parameters of the requested operation.

CORBA requests might also pass information about the environment in which they are executed. For example, a request may pass the identification of the transaction context in which the request executes or the security profile of the principal making a request from the client to the server object.

Static CORBA object requests are defined when the client is compiled; dynamic object requests are defined when the client is run.

CORBA supports the definition of requests at both compile-time and run-time of the client. The former are referred to as static requests and the latter are called dynamic requests. Static CORBA requests are determined by invoking a client stub. Dynamic requests are defined by setting the request parameters using a standardized dynamic invocation library. We will discuss dynamic definition of CORBA requests in more detail in Chapter 6.

 Execution semantics of CORBA object requests is at-most-once.

Object requests in CORBA have at-most-once semantics. This means that if an error is indicated to the client, the server object may not have executed the requested operation. If no error is indicated, the client can assume that the operation has been successfully executed by the remote object.

Failure Handling

CORBA raises an exception if a failure occurs.

The CORBA object model supports exceptions in order to inform clients about faults that occur during a request. The CORBA standard defines approximately 25 system exceptions. These are raised by the object request broker run-time environment when it detects failures, such as disconnected network connections, server objects that cannot be started due to a lack of memory and the like.

Type-specific exceptions inform client objects about an object request that has been aborted when it would otherwise lead to an integrity violation.

```
exception PlayerBooked{};
interface Team {
  ...
  void bookGoalies(in Date d) raises (PlayerBooked);
  ...
};
```

Example 4.5
Exceptions in CORBA

The type-specific exception `PlayerBooked` in class `Team` will be raised by operation `bookGoalies` in order to prevent an integrity violation of booking the goalkeepers at a date when they are not free.

Subtypes and Multiple Inheritance

The CORBA object model supports multiple inheritance of object types. Inheritance in IDL is declared for an object type by enumerating the names of direct supertypes after the types interface name. Following the C++ terminology, inheritance in CORBA is public, which means that all attributes and operations of all supertypes are also exported by its subtypes. In addition, inheritance is virtual. This means that operations are bound dynamically and what is used to implement an operation is only decided at run-time.

CORBA supports multiple inheritance.

As we have seen in Chapter 2, the support of multiple inheritance might lead to conflicts, such as name clashes and incorrect repeated inheritance. The OMG object model excludes these situations and obliges the designer of an interface to resolve them. IDL compiler implementations detect these situations and issue static semantic errors.

The inheritance hierarchy in the CORBA object model has a single root. This root is the interface `Object`, which is pre-defined by the CORBA specification. The rationale for this is that type `Object` provides a mechanism to specify attributes and operations that every CORBA server object should have. These include the ability to duplicate object references to the object and to provide mechanisms for genericity that we will discuss in Chapter 6. If the definition of a supertype is omitted for an IDL interface it is assumed implicitly that it inherits from `Object`.

Every CORBA object inherits from `Object`.

Polymorphism

Every CORBA attribute or variable has a *static type*, which is the type defined for the attribute or parameter when its interface definition is compiled. Every CORBA object has a *dynamic type*, which is the object type from which the object was instantiated. The CORBA object model supports a restricted form of polymorphism, which in effect

The CORBA object model is statically typed.

Example 4.6

Inheritance in CORBA

```
interface Organization {
  readonly attribute string name;
};
interface Club : Organization {
  exception NotInClub{};
  readonly attribute short noOfMembers;
  readonly attribute Address location;
  attribute TeamList teams;
  attribute TrainerList trainers;
  void transfer(in Player p) raises (NotInClub);
};
```

Club is declared as a subtype of Organization and inherits the name attribute. It then adds attributes and operations that are specific to Club. Organization implicitly inherits from Object.

means that attributes and parameters whose static type is an object type may refer at run-time to objects which are of different types. Unlike Smalltalk, the CORBA object model restricts polymorphism in such a way that the dynamic types have to be subtypes of the static types of variables. Given the inheritance hierarchy shown in Example 2.3 on Page 38, it is possible to assign an object that is an instance of Club to an attribute that has the static type Organization.

Polymorphism is often used together with redefined types. Redefinition in CORBA is restricted to operations. It is not possible to redefine the static type of an attribute. Moreover, the signature of an operation cannot be changed, for example by specializing the type of a parameter. This strict redefinition rule ensures that polymorphism in CORBA is type-safe; it cannot lead to an assignment of an object that is a supertype of the static type of the attribute or parameter that it is assigned to.

4.1.2 Architecture

This section focuses on the architectural components of an object request that are involved in executing a request at run-time.

Figure 4.2 shows the components of a CORBA-based application that are involved in requests at run-time. The central component of the CORBA architecture is an *object request broker* (ORB). An ORB receives a request to invoke an operation from a client object and forwards that request transparently to the server object. In particular, the ORB locates the server object based on the object reference provided by the client, transmits the request parameters to the server and returns the request results to the client object.

Marshalling and unmarshalling is performed by client stubs and implementation skeletons.

Marshalling and unmarshalling of request parameters is performed by the *dynamic invocation interface, client stubs* and *implementation skeletons*, which are CORBA's server stubs. Client stubs and server skeletons are generated by an IDL compiler, which is an integral component of every CORBA product. The dynamic invocation interface supports the

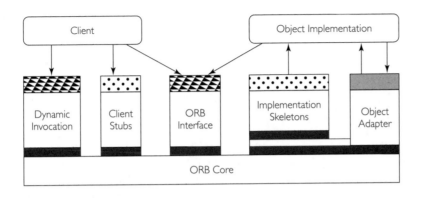

Figure 4.2
CORBA Architecture [Object Management Group, 1995]

definition of requests at run-time, which we will discuss in detail in Chapter 6. While doing so, the dynamic invocation interface interprets run-time type information in order to determine the marshalling algorithms.

The CORBA specification supports several object adapters. The *Basic Object Adapter* (BOA) was adopted as part of the first version of the CORBA specification in 1992. The BOA defines how server objects register with an ORB, how the ORB generates references for a server object and how server objects are activated and deactivated. The BOA, however, was under-specified in the first CORBA specifications which lead to incompatible BOA implementations in the first CORBA products. The OMG has rectified this problem with the adoption of the *Portable Object Adapter* (POA) as part of the CORBA 2.2 specification. The POA defines registration, activation and deactivation more precisely and also supports persistent objects.

 Object adapters support object activation and deactivation.

The *ORB Interface* includes a set of types that both client and server objects use for initialization purposes. Clients can, for example, use the ORB Interface to obtain a set of initial object references; servers use the interface to select an object adapter. The ORB Interface also specifies the common root type `Object` whose operations and attributes every CORBA object inherits. Moreover, the ORB Interface specifies the operation of the Interface Repository, which we are going to discuss in detail in Chapter 6.

ORB Interface includes the Interface Repository and is used for initializing clients and servers.

Any CORBA-compliant object broker directly achieves access and location transparency. Access transparency is achieved because the client stubs have exactly the same interface as the server objects. Hence client programs do not have to be changed when they switch from invoking a client stub to invoking the server object directly. A big advantage of CORBA is that it achieves location transparency. It is achieved because all the client needs to make an object request is a reference of the server object. Clients do not have to have any knowledge

CORBA achieves access and location transparency.

about the host on which the server object resides. In Chapter 8, we will discuss how clients obtain these object references in a location-transparent way. CORBA also supports other forms of transparency when it is used together with the CORBAservices. We will discuss this in Part III, when we discuss how to use the CORBAservices to solve various design problems.

4.2 COM

Microsoft presented the first version of COM during the OLE Professional Developer's Conference in 1993. With Windows NT4.0, Microsoft introduced distribution capabilities into COM. These mechanisms were initially referred to as Network-OLE, DCOM and Active/X in the (marketing) literature, but they are now commonly subsumed under the term COM. They will be referred to as COM+ in future versions of the Windows operating system. As we will see later in this section, Microsoft did not invent the distribution mechanism from scratch but rather relied on, and extended, OSF/DCE's remote procedure calls.

In order to be able to appreciate the design decisions for COM, it is important to understand the overall goals that Microsoft wanted to achieve when they set out to develop a component object model. The main goal derives from the observation that the object models of current object-oriented programming languages are too weak to support reuse of changing components. In particular, the models do not support binary encapsulation and binary compatibility.

COM supports binary encapsulation.

Binary encapsulation means that the machine code representation of server objects can evolve independently from its clients. Object-oriented programming languages, such as C++ and Java, support syntactic encapsulation at the source code level. A programmer of a server object can declare instance variables to be private and then client objects cannot access these instance variables. If a server programmer adds a private instance variable to an object, however, the code of all clients needs to be re-compiled because the memory needs for instances of the server object have changed. This is highly inappropriate for a company such as Microsoft. Microsoft wants to be able to evolve objects that are part of its operating systems and applications and ship them in new releases, service packs and patches to its customers. These new versions are installed on millions of hosts on customer sites. Additional software that third parties might have provided should continue to work without re-compilation, even if Microsoft modifies the binary representation of objects. Hence, binary encapsulation is one of the key requirements that drove the development of COM.

COM defines memory layout of objects to force different compilers to produce interoperable binary code.

Binary compatibility means the ability to use the machine code of an object that was created using one program development environment when developing client code in a different environment. While this could also be achieved by standardizing the machine code representation for a particular programming language, different mechanisms are needed for binary compatibility between different programming languages, such as C++ and Visual Basic.

The principal mechanism of COM for achieving both binary encapsulation and binary compatibility is the separation of interfaces from implementations. Clients see objects only through interfaces which do not compromise any implementation details. Interfaces are defined using MIDL, Microsoft's interface definition language, which evolved from RPC/IDL.[1] Implementations of objects may be written in any programming language with a language binding to MIDL. These are currently Visual C++, Visual Basic and Visual J++.

4.2.1 Meta-Object Model and Interface Definition

We will introduce and discuss the concepts of COM and the constructs of MIDL using a running example. To facilitate comparison between COM and CORBA, we use the same example that we used for the introduction of OMG/IDL.

Objects

COM defines the concepts of interfaces, implementations and classes. These three concepts that should be carefully distinguished.

A *COM interface* defines a protocol through which client objects can communicate with a server object. These interface definitions are at a type-level of abstraction. By convention, interface names always start with an I. COM interfaces have 128-bit physical names that are referred to as UUIDs, These UUIDs are unique in both time and space and are generated by a COM utility. The generation algorithm achieves uniqueness by incorporating ethernet adapter Ids, the time of generation and some random numbers.

 COM interfaces have a unique physical identifier (UUID).

```
[ object, uuid(1CF2B120-547D-101B-8E65-08002B2BD115)]
interface ITeam : IUnknown {

  . . .

};
```

Example 4.7
Interfaces in Microsoft COM

A *COM implementation* is a class of a programming language that implements an interface. COM defines programming language bindings to C++, Visual Basic and Microsoft's variant of Java. These bindings govern how these languages are used to implement MIDL interfaces. Instances of a COM implementation are referred to as *COM objects* and they are instances of classes in the respective programming languages. In our example, a C++ class Player implementing interface IPlayer is a COM implementation.

Note that, unlike CORBA, COM does not support the concept of object references. COM objects are identified by pointers to main memory locations. These pointers are called *interface pointers*. At that location there would be either the server object, if clients and servers reside in the same address space, or a proxy. Proxies are COM's equivalent to CORBA client stubs.

 COM objects are identified by pointers to main memory locations where either the object or a proxy is located.

---

[1] We use the acronym MIDL throughout this book to refer to Microsoft's interface definition language to avoid confusion with the OMG/IDL, which is considerably different. We note, however, that the COM and CORBA literature refer to MIDL and OMG/IDL simply as IDL.

COM implementations
may implement several
interfaces.

An implementation may implement several interfaces. In our soccer management application, for example, we might have a class `PlayerTrainer` that implements both the `IPlayer` and `ITrainer` interfaces and that would be used for those trainers that are still active players.

COM classes manage
the life cycle and are
able to locate objects.

COM classes are named implementations that represent instantiable types. COM classes should not be confused with implementations, which are classes of a programming language that are used to implement interfaces. COM classes expose one or several interfaces and often provide the principal mechanism to create or locate COM objects. In our example, there would be COM classes for trainer, club, team and player objects. By means of these classes, new club, team, trainer and player objects could be created and interface pointers to these objects could be obtained.

COM classes are instantiated in *class objects*. Each COM class needs to have at least one class object. These objects are singleton objects, which means that there is generally only one instance of the COM class available in a particular domain.

A COM class has a physical name, which is used by a client to obtain COM objects. These names are referred to as CLSIDs. Like UUIDs, they are unique in both space and time and they are generated by COM using the same algorithm that is used for UUIDs.

Figure 4.3 uses the Unified Modeling Language to summarize the relationships between the concepts that we have just introduced. An implementation implements one or several interfaces. Interfaces are identified by a UUID. An implementation can be instantiated by several COM objects, which are referenced by their location in main memory. Class objects are instances of COM classes and they are used to create and locate COM objects.

Figure 4.3
Relationships between
Interfaces, Implementations and
Classes

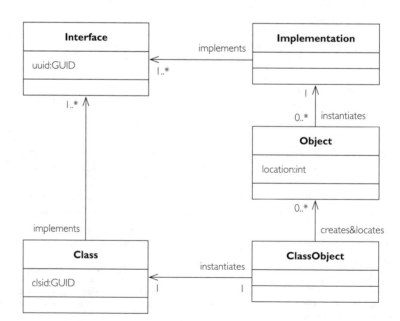

The COM object model and MIDL do not have equivalents to CORBA's modules. Recall that the purpose of CORBA's modules was to limit the scope of the visibility of identifiers in order to avoid name clashes between interfaces. The COM object model distinguishes logical and physical identifiers. Logical identifiers may clash with each other as the internal identification is purely achieved using physical identifiers, such as UUIDs and CSLIDs which are uniquely generated by COM. Hence the mechanism to limit the scope of identifiers that was needed for CORBA is unnecessary in COM. The price to pay for this, however, is the exposure of cumbersome 128-bit integers in any interface and object implementation.

COM does not need a module mechanism.

```
typedef struct tagAddress {
  BSTR street;
  BSTR postcode;
  BSTR city;
} ADDRESS;

interface ITeam : IUnknown {
  ...
  [propget] HRESULT CoachedBy([out] ITrainer *val[3]);
  [propput] HRESULT CoachedBy([in] ITrainer *val[3]);
  [propget] HRESULT Players([in] long cMax, [out] long *pcAct,
    [out,size_is(cMax),length_is(*pcAct)] IPlayer *val);
  [propput] HRESULT Players([in] long cElems,
                            [in,size_is(cElems)] IPlayer *val);
  ...
};
```

Example 4.8
Type Construction in COM

The parameter of operation `CoachedBy` is a fixed length array. It is appropriate to use a fixed length array as soccer teams generally have up to three coaches.

The output parameter of the second `Players` operation is a conformant array. We use a conformant array here because the operation needs to compute the output parameter and we do not know how many players the team has.

The parameter to the first `Players` operation is an open array.

Types

COM's object model is statically typed and the MIDL compiler checks for static semantic errors. Interface pointers have a dynamic type and they can only be used to request operations that are exported by that specific type. This is checked statically by the compilers used to build clients. COM supports base types and a limited number of type constructors. *COM base types* are atomic types. They are defined in a platform-neutral manner and include `boolean`, `byte`, `small`, `short`, `long`, `float`, `double`, `char` and `enum`.

There are fewer type construction primitives available in COM than there are in CORBA. COM supports records and arrays. Records are defined in MIDL using the `struct` construct. COM supports three different forms of arrays, depending on whether they will

COM has fewer type constructors than CORBA.

be used as input or output parameters. *Fixed length* arrays specify the dimension of the array at the time the interface is compiled.

Conformant arrays allow their dimension to be specified at run-time. The caller sets the array and passes the number of elements of the array as the first parameter. The attribute of the second parameter `size_is` then specifies that array `val` has as many elements as were passed as the first parameter. *Open* arrays provide a way to specify both the capacity of an array and the actual size of the array via additional parameters. This supports passing arrays of varying size as input and output parameters of an operation. A client requesting an operation would tell the COM object in the first parameter the dimension of the array that is available and in the second parameter would specify how many elements are contained in the array passed as the third parameter.

Attributes

 COM treats attributes as operations.

Unlike CORBA, COM does not support the specification of attributes for interfaces. Exposing instance variables at the interface would break the binary encapsulation that is valued so highly in COM. Instead, COM supports the use of property operations. By using the `[propget]` and `[propput]` keywords in front of an operation, the interface designer specifies that the only purpose of this operation is to obtain or modify, respectively, an attribute. Some programming language bindings then map these operations to instance variable access and modifications.

Example 4.9
Attribute in a COM Interface

```
interface ITeam : IUnknown {
   [propget] HRESULT Name([out] BSTR val);
   ...
};
```

Operations

 Operations that are declared in an interface are visible to all clients.

Like CORBA, COM does not have any primitives to define the visibility of operations. All operations that are declared in a COM interface are available to clients. There is, however, a way to hide operations of a COM object from clients. This is simply not to expose them in any interface that the COM object implements. COM's flexible interface mechanism can also be exploited to provide client-specific views on COM objects. To do this with CORBA, implementations would use multiple inheritance to inherit from the implementation skeletons of more than one interface. Thus, multiple interfaces in COM provide similar expressiveness as multiple inheritance in CORBA.

 COM operations have in, out and inout parameters.

Operations can have parameters. In MIDL, the parameterization is annotated by attributes given in square brackets. `[in]` parameters are supplied by clients, `[out]` parameters are returned by the COM object to a client and `[in,out]` parameters are supplied parameters that are modified by the COM object. In this respect, the COM and CORBA object models are very similar.

```
interface ITeam : IUnknown {
  ...
  HRESULT BookGoalies([in] DATE *d);
  HRESULT Print();
};
```

Example 4.10
Operations in COM

Requests

By convention, COM operations return a 32-bit integer that encodes whether or not operations have been successfully executed. Hence, unlike CORBA operations, they do not have a return type that can be used to encode application semantics and out parameters have to be used instead.

HRESULT indicates request success or failure.

An object request in COM is essentially an operation invocation. If the COM object from which operation execution is requested resides on the same host and is dynamically linked to the client object process then the request will actually be a local method call. If client and server object do not execute in the same process or reside on different hosts, the request is executed using Microsoft's version of a remote procedure call. This means that the request is executed by marshalling the request parameter at the client side, then, if necessary, activating the server object, potentially on a different host and then unmarshalling the request parameters on that host. The server then performs the operation, the server stub marshals any parameters with an [out] attribute and returns them via inter-process or network-communication primitives to the client stub. The client stub then unmarshals the results and returns them to the client.

Like CORBA, COM supports the static definition of requests when the client is compiled. This is inappropriate for environments that need to interpret requests at run-time, such as VisualBasic Script or JavaScript. COM therefore also supports the definition of dynamic requests at run-time by means of its pre-defined IDispatch interface. We will discuss this in Chapter 6 in full detail.

COM supports both static and dynamic operation invocations.

Like CORBA object requests, COM operation invocations have at-most-once semantics. This means that if an error is indicated to the client, the operation might not have been executed. If no error is indicated, clients can assume that the operation has been successfully executed by the COM server object.

COM operation invocations have at-most-once semantics.

Failure Handling

The COM object model supports dealing with failures by means of results of COM operations. COM includes a pre-defined type HRESULT to indicate successful or erroneous execution of an operation. HRESULTs are essentially 32-bit integer values that are returned from server objects to clients. The bits of these HRESULTs are partitioned into four fields as indicated in Figure 4.4.

Severity Code	Reserved	Facility Code	Information Code
31	30-29	28-16	15-0

Figure 4.4
Sections of Information in HRESULT

The highest-level bit indicates success or failure. A zero in this bit indicates that the operation succeeded, otherwise it failed. If the HRESULT is interpreted as a signed long, values greater than or equal to zero indicate success and values smaller than zero indicate failure. The second partition is used internally by COM and is not available to client or server programmers. The facility field indicates, in Microsoft's terminology, the particular 'technology' that the success or failure indication relates to. Examples of these technologies include structured storage or persistence. The least significant two bytes in the information code partition are used to pass the error information itself.

A number of HRESULTs are pre-defined in the COM library as constants of long numbers. These include S_OK, S_FALSE, S_FAIL, S_NOTIMPL and S_UNEXPECTED. In order to encode these results, COM uses the least significant 9 bits of the information code partition. In addition, server programmers may define their own HRESULT using the macro MAKE_HRESULT provided by the COM library.

Example 4.11
Using HRESULT

```
const HRESULT CALC_E_PLYBKED=
    MAKE_HRESULT(SEVERITY_ERROR,FACILITY_ITF,0x200+1);
```

The constant CALC_E_PLYBKED is defined as an error for a facility interface and has value 0x201. The interface facility denotes an error code that is unique within the context of an interface. The addition of 0x200 to an error code is necessary in order to avoid clashes with the COM reserved error codes.

 COM HRESULTs are less expressive than exceptions to explain reasons for failure.

COM's handling of failures is considerably less powerful than the approach using exceptions that was chosen for CORBA for several reasons. First, CORBA interfaces declare the application-specific error conditions that may occur in the raises clause for each operation. Client programmers that use COM cannot tell that they have to check for certain error conditions as there is no association between HRESULT values and particular operations. Secondly, in the CORBA object model, data structures may be passed from the server to the client in order to give detailed information about an error. In COM this is essentially confined to a binary flag indicating that an error has occurred. Finally, the treatment of error-codes as fields of bits, some of which are reserved while others are not, might be efficient but is not exactly the correct level of abstraction for the design of distributed objects.

Inheritance

 COM supports single interface inheritance.

COM supports interface inheritance. For example, IClub inherits from IOrganization. Every COM interface, in fact, has to inherit from another interface and the interface inheritance hierarchy forms a tree with one root.

Every COM interface inherits from IUnknown.

The root interface is IUnknown, shown in Figure 4.5. IUnknown has three operations that every COM object needs to implement. QueryInterface checks whether an object reference supports a particular interface. AddRef and Release increase and decrease the number of references that there are to an object. Every COM object, therefore has to count how often it is referenced so that objects without a reference are deactivated.

```
// unknwn.idl - system IDL file
[local, object, uuid(00000000-0000-0000-C000-000000000046]
interface IUnknown {
  HRESULT QueryInterface[in] REFIID riid,
                        [out] void **ppv);
  ULONG AddRef(void);
  ULONG Release(void);
}
```

Figure 4.5
COM Root Interface
IUnknown.

Microsoft has chosen not to support multiple inheritance for interfaces. Hence, every interface except for IUnknown inherits from one and only one other interface. There are several reasons for that. First, the mapping between COM and RPCs for remote communication would be much more complicated if COM supported multiple inheritance. Secondly, the object code produced by different compilers for the implementation of multiple inheritance is considerably different and that would conflict with one of the major design goals of COM: binary compatibility. Finally, COM's multiple interfaces can be used to implement multiple inheritance.

COM, however, makes extensive use of multiple inheritance for implementations in C++. The MIDL compiler generates a C++ class for each interface. This class is pure virtual, which prevents clients from instantiating it. Any object that implements this interface has to inherit from this class and implement the pure virtual member functions that correspond to the COM operations. As objects may implement multiple interfaces, the object implementation has to inherit from all pure virtual classes that were derived from the interfaces (as in Example 4.13).

Polymorphism

COM supports polymorphism in the same way as many other object models, such as Java. In the soccer application, all the operations that are available for organizations are also available for clubs. Clients wishing to request operations using the IOrganization interface may, in fact, request the operations from an object implementing IClub.

The distinction of interfaces and implementation in COM enables a further form of polymorphism, because COM interfaces can have multiple implementations. For example, we

```
[object, uuid(1CF2B120-547D-101B-8E65-08002B2BD118)]
interface IOrganization : IUnknown {
  [propget] HRESULT Name([out] BSTR val);
};
[object, uuid(1CF2B120-547D-101B-8E65-08002B2BD116)]
interface IClub : IOrganization {
  ...
};
```

Interface IClub inherits the attribute access operation Name from interface IOrganization.

Example 4.12
Inheritance Relationships
between COM Interfaces

Example 4.13

Implementation of Two Interfaces

```
#include "Soccer.h"
class TrainerPlayer : public ITrainer, public IPlayer {
private:
    char* name; // name is the same in ITrainer & IPlayer
    short Number; //for IPlayer
protected:
    virtual ~TrainerPlayer(void);
public:
    TrainerPlayer(void);
    IMPLEMENT_UNKNOWN(TrainerPlayer)
    BEGIN_INTERFACE_TABLE(TrainerPlayer)
        IMPLEMENTS_INTERFACE(ITrainer)
        IMPLEMENTS_INTERFACE(IPlayer)
    END_INTERFACE_TABLE(TrainerPlayer)
    void train(); // ITrainer method
    void book(); // IPlayer methods
};
```

Class `TrainerPlayer` implements both interfaces `ITrainer` and `IPlayer` as they were defined in Example 2.3. Assuming that the COM interface definitions are stored in a file `Soccer.idl`, the MIDL compiler would have generated a file `Soccer.h`. This file would include the pure virtual class definitions for `ITrainer` and `IPlayer`. Class `ITrainer` would demand implementation of method `train` and class `IPlayer` would demand implementation of method `book`. This implementation is achieved in class `TrainerPlayer` because it is a subclass of both `ITrainer` and `Player` and implements the two respective methods. The uppercase identifiers `IMPLEMENT` are preprocessor macros that declare which interfaces `TrainerPlayer` implements.

could use different C++ classes to implement the `IPlayer` interface in order to implement the differences between goalkeepers, strikers and sweepers.

Type coercion means dynamic type casts that are supported by the `QueryInterface` operation.

When using polymorphism, it sometimes becomes necessary to use the same object through a different interface. This is supported by COM's *type coercion*, which is a form of dynamic type cast. Type coercion denotes the ability to dynamically modify the type of an object reference. Type coercion is supported by the `QueryInterface` operation of `IUnknown`, shown in Example 4.5. The first parameter denotes the UUID of an interface. When `QueryInterface` is requested, the object checks whether it implements that interface and if so returns a reference to an interface pointer, whose dynamic type is the requested interface. Using `QueryInterface`, clients can safely cast between the different interfaces that an object implementation supports.

4.2.2 Architecture

As shown in Figure 4.6, there are three principal ways that COM implements operation execution requests. COM chooses these transparently for the client programmer depending on the location of the server object. If the server object is available in a dynamic link library

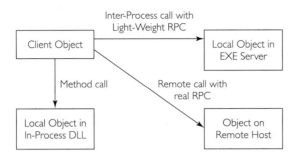

Figure 4.6
COM Implementations for Object Requests

(DLL) on the same host, the DLL is loaded if necessary and the object request is implemented as a local method call. If the server object is located on the same host, but executes in a different process (EXE Server), COM uses a light-weight remote procedure call mechanism, which performs marshalling and unmarshalling but does not use the network as a transport. Finally, if the server object is not available locally, COM implements the object request using full-blown remote procedure calls. This is the most complicated case and deserves further discussion.

Figure 4.7 shows the architecture of the distributed COM that is used to implement object requests from remote hosts. The architecture is layered and the figure associates the components with layers of the ISO/OSI reference model.

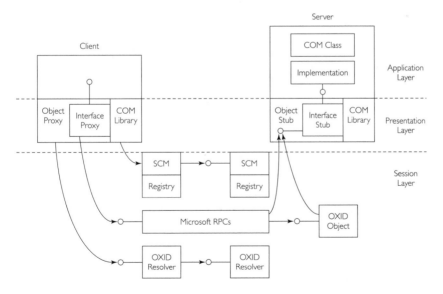

Figure 4.7
Architecture of Distributed COM

At the application layer, a client object possesses a pointer to an interface proxy. This is shown by the little circle that is connected to the interface proxy. The server includes an implementation of the interface and a COM class, which is capable of creating new instances of the implementation and which can locate these instances.

At the presentation layer, the architecture shows an object proxy, an interface proxy and the COM library on the client host and an object stub, an interface stub and the COM library on the server host. The *object proxy* is capable of marshalling and unmarshalling pointers and creates an interface proxy for the particular interface through which the request is sent. The *interface proxy* is capable of marshalling and unmarshalling the parameters of all operations contained in the interface with which it is associated. Hence, object proxies and interface proxies together perform the task that is performed in CORBA using the client stub. COM needs these two different concepts due to its ability to have different interfaces for the same object. The presentation-layer on the server-side mirrors the client-side. The *object stub* is capable of marshalling object references and of creating interface stubs. *Interface stubs* unmarshal and marshal operation parameters for the interfaces they are associated with and call the requested operation. Hence, object stubs and interface stubs perform similar tasks as the implementation skeleton in CORBA. Finally, the *COM library* provides the primitives to create or locate an interface pointer to clients. Object proxies, interface proxies, object stubs and interface stubs are generated by the MIDL compiler in the same way as CORBA client stubs and implementation skeletons are generated by an OMG/IDL compiler.

The session layer implementation of COM is concerned with object activation and the mapping of interface pointers to RPC bindings and references of server objects for remote method invocation purposes. The COM library includes the function `CoGetClassObject`, which is the client interface for activation. It takes a CSLID and a UUID as input parameters and returns an interface pointer to an activated class object that implements the identified interface. Activation of remote objects is achieved by the *Service Control Manager* (SCM), an instance of which executes on each host of COM server objects. To implement a call to `CoGetClassObject` the COM library contacts the local SCM which consults the local registry about a server path name and contacts the SCM on that server, which starts the object.

For the implementation of the various mappings, the server-side SCM associates objects with an *object exporter identifier* (OXID). That identifier is used by the *OXID resolver* on the server host to associate an object with a particular RPC binding. Then an object reference is created that uniquely represents the interface pointer on the server host. The SCM on the server side then marshals the interface pointer and returns it to the client-side which unmarshals it and updates the information in the object proxy. The client-proxy calls the OXID resolver on the client-side in order to obtain a cached mapping of the OXID and the RPC binding. The RPC binding is then returned to the object proxy so that future object requests can be performed without the involvement of SCM, registry and OXID resolvers.

We note that this architecture achieves both access and location transparency. Access transparency is achieved because the implementation of every COM interface operation in an interface proxy has exactly the same signature as the implementation itself. This is, in fact one of the pre-conditions for COM being able to transparently use in-process servers, EXE-servers and remote objects. Location transparency is achieved, because all a client needs to have in order to request an operation is an interface pointer. The object proxy and the interface proxy on the client-side encapsulate the location information that was provided during activation.

4.3 Java/RMI

Java is an object-oriented programming language developed by Sun Microsystems. Java is a hybrid language in that it is both compiled and interpreted. A Java compiler creates byte-code, which is then interpreted by a virtual machine (VM). Java was designed to be highly portable. This portability is achieved by provision of different VMs that interpret the byte code on different hardware and operating system platforms. The first releases of Java confined communication between objects to within one VM. With the arrival of version 1.1 of the Java Development Kit, this shortcoming was removed.

That version of Java includes an Application Programming Interface (API) known as *remote method invocation* (RMI). RMI enables a client object that resides in one Java VM to invoke a method from a remote server object that resides in a different Java VM. As these VMs may actually execute on different hosts, Java/RMI must be regarded as an object-oriented middleware and we can consider remote method invocations in Java to be object requests between Java objects that are distributed across different Java VMs.

RMI enables Java objects to invoke methods across different JVMs.

Again, we want to understand the rationale that drove the design and implementation of Java/RMI. These include a high-level primitive for object communication, a smooth integration with the Java object model and the reliance on Java VMs for the resolution of heterogeneity.

The original language specification only included network communication primitives at the level of abstraction of UDP datagrams and TCP streams. While the flexibility these primitives provide for distributed object communication are necessary in a few application areas, the language designers wanted to provide a higher-level communication primitive that supports distributed object communication at the level of abstraction of remote method invocations.

Remote method invocation is defined in such a way that it can be tightly integrated with the rest of the Java language specification, development environment and the Java VM. This implies that only minor changes and extensions could be made to the Java object model.

In particular, the language designers did not want to give up the assumptions that the same byte code is executable by different Java VMs and that heterogeneity is resolved entirely by these VMs. Hence, remote method invocations can assume a homogeneous representation of data across all hardware and operating system platforms. Java/RMI was also not designed to support remote method invocation between Java objects and objects written in any other object-oriented programming language. Java/RMI assumes that both client and server object are written in Java and execute in a Java VM.

Java/RMI is meant to be a rather lean provision of distribution capabilities on top of the Java VM. Sun are providing higher-level services on top of RMI. One such set of services is Jini [Arnold et al., 1999], which supports application construction for portable hosts with, for example, transactions and event notification services. Another example are the Enterprise Javabeans [Monson-Haefel, 1999], which aim to provide component-based development support for server components by combining Javabeans with RMI and adding higher-level services, such as transactions, persistence and security.

4.3.1   Meta-Object Model and Interface Definition

Java/RMI does not have a dedicated IDL.

Given the homogeneity requirements discussed above, there is no need for an interface definition language. Even prior to the definition of RMI, Java already included a distinction between interfaces and classes. Hence, unlike CORBA and COM, Java/RMI does not have an interface definition language but rather uses the Java language itself.

Packages in Java restrict the scope of declarations.

Java provides a mechanism that is similar to CORBA modules for restricting the visibility of declarations. This scoping mechanism is referred to as *packages*. There are two perspectives on packages in Java. First, the package to which the declarations contained in a file contribute must be identified. Declarations contained in other packages then need to be scoped with the package name. If we want, for example, to declare a remote interface, we declare it as an extension of `java.rmi.Remote`. Having to specify the fully scoped name all the time can be avoided using an `import` statement, that is usually included at the beginning of a Java source. These import statements may include wildcards in order to make all declarations included in a package visible.

Objects

Java/RMI enables a client object to invoke methods from a remote server object. Both client and server objects are written in Java. However, unlike local method calls, which may be governed by a class definition, the contract for a remote method invocation is always determined by an interface.

In order to make a remote method invocation, client objects have to possess a reference to a remote object. While references to non-remote objects are merely addresses, references to remote objects include further information, such as the location of the host on which the server object resides. The differences between local and remote object references, however are transparent to programmers of client objects.

Client objects obtain references for remote server objects using the Java/RMI registry. The *registry* is a naming service. Server objects can bind their object reference to a name. Client objects use the registry to resolve a name binding and obtain the reference. We will discuss the principles of naming in Java further, in Chapter 8.

Types

Java is a strongly-typed language and has a static type system. Java supports *atomic types*, such as `int`, `float`, `double` and `char`. Java object types include both classes and interfaces.

Java interfaces that extend Remote declare methods that can be invoked remotely.

An *interface* is an object type that is implemented by one or several other classes. Interfaces are used extensively for remote method invocations. A server object that wishes to be accessible remotely has to implement at least one Java interface, which directly or indirectly extends the pre-defined interface `java.rmi.Remote`. `Remote` does not declare any operation but defines the abstraction of being remotely accessible. Interfaces that extend `Remote` are generally referred to as *remote interfaces*. The RMI specification refers to instances of classes that implement a remote interface as *remote objects*.

```
package soccer;
import java.rmi.*;
interface Team extends Remote {
  ...
}
```

Example 4.14
Interfaces in Java

In the new package `soccer`, the import statement makes all declaration of package `java.rmi` visible to remote interface `Team`. Classes that implement `Team` are remote classes and instances of these classes are remote objects.

Although Java/RMI treats remote objects in the same way as other objects in many respects, it makes some important differences. For parameter-passing purposes, Java/RMI handles remote object types in a different way from non-remote object types. A *remote object type* is a class that implements a remote interface. A *non-remote object type* is class that does not implement a remote interface.

Attributes

Java interfaces cannot define attributes. This is appropriate for interfaces of remote objects in general because attributes need to be transformed and marshalled and attribute accesses can fail. COM interfaces cannot have attributes for the same reason and the CORBA object model considers attributes in terms of their accessor operations. In order to provide access to instance variables of server objects, therefore, designers of remote objects have to write access operations (see Example 4.15).

RMI does not have any
mechanisms for
attributes.

```
import java.rmi*;
interface Team extends Remote {
   String name() ... ;
   ...
}
```

Example 4.15
Attribute Access Operations in
Java Remote Interfaces

The operation `name` returns the attribute value of a remote object of type `Team` as a string.

Operations

Operations in Java are referred to as *methods*. A client object can request execution of all those methods that are declared in all remote interfaces of the class of the server object. Note that that class may have additional public operations, which can be invoked locally but which are not available to clients that reside in other VMs.

Operations that should be remotely accessible must not include any parameter types of classes that implement remote interfaces. The operations should therefore only have atomic, non-remote object types and remote interfaces. The semantics of a remote method

Parameters of remote
methods must not include
types of remote classes.

invocation is very close to a local method invocation, with one important exception: the mechanism for passing objects to a remote object is different from that of a local method call.

 Java uses different parameter-passing mechanisms for remote and local method invocation.

Parameter-passing of atomic types has a call by value (CBV) semantics for both local and remote methods. This means that the called method works with a copy of the value. Objects are passed using call by reference (CBR) to local method calls, which means that rather than passing the object to the invoked method, only the object reference is passed. Hence, both the invoking and the invoked method work with the same object. This is different for some remote method invocations. Passing a non-remote object to a remote method will copy the passed object. As a consequence non-remote object parameters always have to be serializable; their classes have to implement the `java.io.Serializable` interface.

Example 4.16
Operations in Java Remote Interfaces

```
import java.rmi.*;
import java.io.*;
class Date implements Serializable {...}
interface Team extends Remote {
    void bookGoalies (Date d) ...;
    void print () ...;
}
```

Operation `bookGoalies()` of interface `Team` has a parameter of type `Date`, which is a non-remote object type. When the date is passed to `bookGoalies()` it is passed by value and any interactions of method `bookGoalies` with the date are performed locally using the copy of the date. To be able to pass the date by value, the run-time environment has to serialize the date, which is why `Date` implements `java.io.Serializable`.

Passing a remote object to a remote method has call by reference semantics again. Hence, objects that implement the `Remote` interface are not copied but remain on the same host. The following table summarizes this discussion.

Figure 4.8
Parameter-Passing in Java Local and Remote Method Invocations

Parameter	Atomic type	Non-remote object type	Remote object type
Local Call	CBV	CBR	CBR
Remote Call	CBV	CBV	CBR

At first glance, it seems strange to use a different semantics for passing remote and non-remote objects. There are, however, good reasons, why the designers of Java/RMI made this choice. First, a remote object that is passed to a method on some other machine has the capability of being accessed remotely and therefore it can be passed by reference; the semantics of parameter-passing can be the same as in the case of a local method invocation. Secondly, non-remote objects are, by definition, not accessible from remote objects.

Hence, it would not be possible to pass non-remote objects by reference to a method that might be executed on a different machine; that method could never invoke any operations from the object passed. One option would have been not to support passing non-remote objects at all. But this deprives application builders of a useful capability. The ability to pass an object by value is useful because it can reduce future network traffic as the server can invoke operations from that object locally. This improves efficiency and reduces the network load.

Although the inventors of Java/RMI had good reasons to define this semantics, there are various things of which application designers need to be aware:

1. Any non-remote object that is to be passed to a remote object must implement the Serializable interface. This has to be defined at the time the non-remote object is implemented. In particular, engineers have to foresee whether the object will potentially have to be passed to remote objects that are built in the future.
2. When passing non-remote objects to a remote method, programmers have to be aware that any changes the remote method makes to the object will not be reflected on local copies of the object.
3. When passing remote objects to a remote method, programmers have to be aware that clients see any changes the remote method makes to the object.

Requests

Object requests in Java are remote method invocations. Like CORBA object requests and COM operation invocations, Java requests have at-most-once semantics. This means that if an error is indicated to the client, the remote method might not have been executed. If no error is indicated, clients can assume that the method has been successfully executed by the remote object.

Java remote methods are executed with at-most-once semantics.

Unlike COM and CORBA, however, Java only supports static remote method invocations, which means that a Java remote method invocation can only be defined at the time the client object is compiled. Java does have a reflection API which can be used to make dynamic local method invocations. However, the reflection API (at least in version 1.2 of the Java language specification) is not integrated with Java/RMI; it is not possible to pass the meta-data that is needed for a dynamic request across to a remote object, as it does not implement Serializable. We expect, however, that this deficiency will be removed in future versions of Java/RMI.

Unlike CORBA and COM, Java does not support definition of remote method invocations at run-time.

Failure Handling

Failures that occur during Java remote method invocations are communicated to the client using exceptions. Exceptions are not specific to Java/RMI but are a general-purpose mechanism that Java provides for notifying failures to callers. Any operation included in an interface that extends Remote has to declare that it may throw a RemoteException. Instances of this exception class can be used by clients to obtain a detailed error message, as well as any nested exceptions, such as network or I/O exceptions that caused the remote method invocation to fail.

Remote methods must declare that they may throw RemoteException.

Example 4.17

Exception Declaration in a
Remote Interface

```
import java.rmi.*;
class PlayerBooked extends Exception {};
interface Team extends Remote {
  String name() throws RemoteException;
  Trainer[] coachedBy() throws RemoteException;
  Club belongsTo() throws RemoteException;
  Player[] players() throws RemoteException;
  void bookGoalies(Date d) throws PlayerBooked,
                                  RemoteException;
  void print() throws RemoteException;
}
```

All operations in `Team` raise `RemoteException`. In addition, `bookGoalies` raises `PlayerBooked`, a type-specific exception that extends `Exception`.

Remote methods
throw additional
exceptions.

Remotely-accessible methods may declare that they raise type-specific exceptions as part of the interface definition. Type-specific exceptions are generally used to notify abortions of operation executions that would otherwise lead to integrity violations. These type-specific exceptions have to extend `Exception`.

Subtypes and Multiple Inheritance

Java supports inheritance in that a class may *extend* another class. Java does not support multiple inheritance for classes, but allows multiple inheritance for interfaces. This means that an interface may extend several interfaces.

Remote interfaces can
inherit from remote
and non-remote
interfaces at the same
time.

The ability to extend more than one interface makes it possible to have an interface that extends a remote interface and also a non-remote interface. This is allowed as long as all inherited operations declare that they may throw `RemoteException` and that they meet the requirement of not using remote classes as parameters or result types. The semantics of this interface inheritance is then that those operations that are inherited from non-remote interfaces are also available remotely.

Polymorphism

Java supports polymorphism that is statically-restricted by inheritance. Any variable, parameter or result type has a static type. Assignments to these are possible if the static type is a supertype of the static type of the object that is being assigned. This constraint ensures type safety.

With multiple interface inheritance, it becomes possible to have polymorphism between remote and non-remote objects. For example, we could declare an array of `Organization` that contains references to `Club` objects and non-remote objects whose classes only implement `Organization`.

```
import java.rmi.*;
import java.io.*;
interface Organization {
  public String name() throws RemoteException;
}
class Address implements Serializable{
  public String street;
  public String postcode;
  public String city;
} ...
class NotInClub extends Exception{}
interface Club extends Organization, Remote {
  int noOfMembers() throws RemoteException;
  Address location() throws RemoteException;
  Team[] teams() throws RemoteException;
  Trainer[] trainers() throws RemoteException;
  void transfer(Player p) throws RemoteException,NotInClub;
}
```

Example 4.18
Inheritance between Java
Remote Interfaces

Interface Club is an example of multiple interface inheritance. It extends both the non-remote interface Organization and the remote interface Remote. It is, therefore, possible to obtain the name of a club remotely through method name that is inherited from Organization.

4.3.2 Architecture

Figure 4.9 shows an overview of the architecture of Java/RMI. Clients start remote method invocations through a local method call to a stub. Like client stubs in CORBA and interface proxies in COM, stubs are type-specific and include all the remote methods that are available from the remote object on the server side. Clients obtain references of remote objects by means of naming, which is implemented in the registry. Server objects register their object references with the registry so that clients can locate them. Server objects may be activated explicitly by some administrator or implicitly when a remote method invocation is made for that object. In the latter case, the object has to be able to be activated and use activation interfaces to register itself. During activation, the activation interfaces call the object's

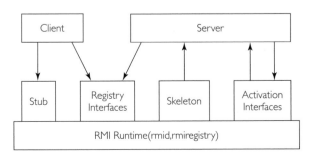

Figure 4.9
Architecture of Remote Method
Invocations

constructor and enable the object to restore its state. Once an object is activated, control is passed to the skeleton which invokes the desired remote method.

Stubs and skeletons perform marshalling and unmarshalling of parameters.

The Java/RMI architecture has many similarities with the CORBA architecture, in the initial definition of which Sun participated. Stubs and skeletons are specific to the type of a remote server object that implements a remote method invocation. Stubs and skeletons have to perform the marshalling and unmarshalling of invocation parameters and hence implement the presentation layer. Like CORBA and COM, Java/RMI provides a mechanism to generate stubs and skeletons from the interface definition in a fully automatic way. The Java/RMI specification demands the availability of `rmic`, a compiler that produces stubs and skeletons. Unlike CORBA's IDL compiler and the MIDL compiler that is part of COM, `rmic` does not work on interface definitions but generates the stubs and skeletons from the class that implements an interface. Hence, the byte code of stubs has to be shipped to client developers, rather than the interface definitions that are distributed to developers of CORBA and COM clients. This is appropriate as Java/RMI can assume that stubs are always called by other Java objects, while CORBA client stubs and COM proxies have to be generated for the programming languages in which a client object is written.

The `Registry` interfaces provide the functionality that server objects use to register their object reference. Client objects can then use the registry to obtain object references of server objects in a location-transparent way. We will revisit the registry interfaces when we discuss location services in Chapter 8.

Activation interfaces support on-demand activation and deactivation of object references.

The session layer implementation of Java/RMI supports object activation on demand through the activation interfaces. They avoid the need for Java/RMI server objects to be in memory all the time and enable them to be activated on demand. These interfaces are only included from Java/RMI version 1.2. Activation can be achieved fully transparently as shown in Figure 4.10.

An important concept for object activation is the *faulting reference*. It is an intelligent reference to a remote object that resides within a stub. A faulting reference contains an *activation identifier*, which provides sufficient information to activate the object. It also contains a *live reference* to the remote object, which is possibly void. If the faulting reference is used in a remote method invocation it checks whether the live reference actually refers to an activated object. If that is the case, the life reference is used to forward the method invocation to the remote object. If the life reference is invalid, the activation identifier is used to find the remote host on which the object is to be activated. Each host has an *activator* to which the activation identifier is passed. Activators in Java/RMI are thus similar to CORBA object adapters and SCMs in COM. The activator uses the identifier to look up an *activation descriptor*. It determines in which Java VM the object is to be activated, the class name of the object, a URL for the byte-code of the class and some initialization data for the object. If the desired VM is not running, the activator starts it. It then passes the activation descriptor to an *activation group* that exists in each Java VM. The activation group then loads the byte code from the URL, constructs the object and initializes it with the data provided. It returns the remote reference to the activator, which notes that the object is now running. The activator, in turn, returns the object reference to the faulting reference in the client's stub, which updates its life reference.

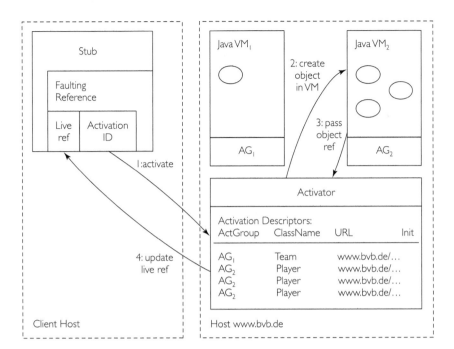

Figure 4.10
Activation of Remote Objects in Java/RMI

Location transparency is achieved in Java/RMI through remote object references. Clients do not have to have any knowledge about the location of server objects. They only need to obtain an remote object reference from the registry and use it to invoke remote methods. We will discuss in Chapter 8 how Java object references can be obtained and we will see that the default provision that is available in Java does not support location transparency. The fact that there are different call semantics for non-remote object types means that access transparency is also not fully achieved because clients have to be aware of the fact that they are calling a remote or a local method. Thus Java/RMI is inferior in this respect compared to COM and CORBA.

Java remote method invocations are not fully location and access transparent.

Key Points

▶   CORBA, COM and Java/RMI enable client objects to request operation executions from distributed server objects. These operations are parameterized and detailed parameter-passing mechanisms are specified.

▶   Java/RMI is different from CORBA and COM in that it integrates non-remote objects into the object model. This is achieved by modifying the standard Java parameter-passing mechanism into the model and by passing non-remote objects by value.

▶   CORBA, COM and Java/RMI all use a form of reference to identify server objects in a location-transparent way. CORBA objects are identified by object references, COM objects are identified by interface pointers and Java/RMI objects are identified by faulting references.

▶ The object models of CORBA, COM and Java/RMI all separate the notion of interfaces and implementations. The separations are rather more strict in CORBA and COM, where there are separate languages to define interfaces and where implementations can be written in different programming languages.

▶ The object models of all three object-oriented middleware systems support inheritance. They all specify a common root that they use to give common properties to any object references. This root is `Object` for CORBA, `IUnknown` in COM and `Remote` in Java/RMI.

▶ In all three approaches, attributes are treated as operations. This may be implicit, as in CORBA, or explicitly incorporated by the designer using COM and Java/RMI.

▶ All object models have support for dealing with failures during object requests. CORBA and Java/RMI define standard exceptions and support the definition of type-specific exceptions as part of the interface definition. COM defines HRESULTs, which are 32-bit integers, and gives designers designated areas in these integers to use for type-specific exceptions.

▶ All object models are statically typed and support a restricted form of polymorphism. In all models it is possible to assign an object to a variable of a different type as long as the variable's static type is a supertype of the dynamic object type.

▶ All three middleware systems provide generators for client and server stubs to implement the presentation layer. CORBA uses client stubs and implementation skeletons. COM uses interface proxies and interface stubs. In Java/RMI they are referred to as stubs and skeletons.

▶ CORBA, COM and Java/RMI all support the on-demand activation of server objects. CORBA achieves this through the object adapters; in COM it is implemented by the Service Control Manager; and in Java/RMI the activator implements activation.

Self Assessment

4.1   What are the similarities between the object models of CORBA, COM and Java/RMI?

4.2   What are the differences?

4.3   Why do COM and Java/RMI not have attributes in their interface definition languages?

4.4   How does CORBA get around this problem?

4.5   Why do all middleware systems support detection and handling of failures?

4.6   How does object activation work in CORBA, COM and Java/RMI?

4.7   Explain the reasons why CORBA, COM and Java/RMI distinguish interfaces from implementations.

4.8   Explain why the form of restricted polymorphism that is available in CORBA, COM and Java/RMI is type-safe.

Further Reading

There are numerous books on CORBA. They are mostly aimed at the professional market and they provide in-depth explanations of how CORBA works. [Mowbray and Zahavi, 1995] explains lessons learned from using CORBA in the DISCUSS project at MITRE. [Orfali et al., 1996] and [Orfali et al., 1997] are more readable versions of the CORBA specifications. [Vogel and Duiddy, 1997] focus on the use of CORBA with Java as a client and server programming language. [Siegel, 1996] provides a number of case studies that use CORBA for building distributed systems.

There are numerous books about COM that are also targeted at the professional market. A very carefully written introduction is provided by [Box, 1998]. [Grimes, 1997] presents a very technical view of the distribution capabilities of COM and guides the reader into developing distributed COM components. [Roodyn and Emmerich, 1999] report on the successful application of COM for systems that integrate real-time data feeds in financial information systems.

RMI extends the Java language. For programmers familiar with C and C++, [Flanagan, 1997] provides a quick reference to Java. A thorough introduction to Java for beginners is given by [Winder and Roberts, 1997]. The Java/RMI specification is available from [RMI, 1998]. An introduction to the first version of the Java/RMI specification can be found in [Hughes et al., 1997]. [Jackson and McClellan, 1999] show a number of examples that utilize Version 1.2 of the Java/RMI specification. A good introduction to the activation interfaces of Java/RMI is provided by [Couch, 1999].

Lewandowski discusses frameworks for component-based client–server computing in [Lewandowski, 1998]. While CORBA, DCOM and Java/RMI are covered and described in considerable detail, the article does not discuss requirements for middleware systems and also does not attempt a comparison between CORBA, DCOM and Java/RMI.

There are further comparisons of middleware available in literature, but to the best of our knowledge, they only cover CORBA and DCOM and focus only on a certain aspect rather than trying to give a comprehensive comparison. [Watterson, 1998] gives a very high-level overview of DCOM and JavaBeans. [Chung et al., 1998] compares in great detail the architecture of CORBA and DCOM and how they process object requests.

5

Resolving Heterogeneity

Learning Objectives

We will recognize the different reasons why heterogeneity may arise. It may result from using different programming languages to implement objects, from using different middleware systems for distributed object communication, or from using different hardware platforms to host objects. We will grasp the principles and techniques for resolving such heterogeneity. We will comprehend the degree of transparency that object-oriented middleware achieves in resolving heterogeneity. We will understand how programming language bindings to a common interface definition language resolve differences in programming languages between client and server objects. We will learn about interoperability and interworking protocols that facilitate the integration of different types of object-oriented middleware. Finally, we will study standard data representations, application-level transport protocols and virtual machines in order to know how they resolve heterogeneous data representations. We will realize that the resolution of these different dimensions of heterogeneity can be achieved by the middleware in a way that is transparent to the application programmer.

Chapter Outline

5.1 Heterogeneous Programming Languages
5.2 Heterogeneous Middleware
5.3 Heterogeneous Data Representation

The case studies we discussed in Chapter 1 have revealed that a distributed system may consist of rather heterogeneous objects. The bank system case study deployed objects on hardware platforms ranging from PCs to mainframes. Moreover, the distributed objects in that case study were implemented in programming languages as diverse as Cobol, C and Visual C++. The bank system was, in fact, not built using just one object-oriented middleware; it utilizes heterogeneous middleware implementations at the same time. These observations suggest that there are several possible forms of heterogeneity of distributed objects.

Heterogeneity may arise from the use of different programming languages. Programming languages have differing underlying object models, some support multiple inheritance and others do not. Programming languages vary in the way they pass parameters and some support both static and dynamic binding while others bind entirely dynamically. When distributed systems are built using different programming languages, the object models need to be unified.

Heterogeneity may arise due to the use of different middleware systems. It may be necessary, for reasons of availability on particular platforms or due to performance consid- erations to utilize more than one middleware in the same distributed system. Middleware may differ, for example, in the way it implements object references or object adapters. In Chapter 4, we have also seen that the different middleware systems support different object models.

Heterogeneity may arise in the different formats that are used for storing attributes, para- meters and result types of requests. The data format is often dependent on the host of the server object and on the programming language that is used to write the object.

It is the middleware that should resolve the above dimensions in which heterogeneity can occur. The resolution should be transparent to the application developer. This means that the application developer will be able to focus on the semantics of distributed objects and that the middleware will do the legwork of mapping different character sets onto each other, swapping the order of bytes if necessary and mapping different object models onto each other. Thus this chapter addresses issues that are important for appreciating how the middleware achieves resolution of heterogeneity. It can be ignored if application programmers are fortunate enough to be able to develop distributed object systems in a completely homogeneous setting.

We now look at issues of heterogeneity in more detail with a view to outlining basic techniques for their solution. We present the idea of different programming language bindings to a common object model as a mechanism to resolve programming language heterogeneity. We discuss the concepts of interoperability and interworking that resolve the heterogeneity between the different object-oriented middleware systems that we presented in Chapter 4. We introduce the concept of a standard data representation that is used for data exchange between different hardware platforms; we present a notation by means of which data representations can be specified and we discuss the idea of a virtual machine that resolves operating system and data representation heterogeneity.

5.1 Heterogeneous Programming Languages

When integrating legacy components with newly-built components, it often occurs that different programming languages need to be used. Legacy components are often encapsulated in so called *object wrappers*, which implement a mapping between an object-oriented interface definition and whatever integration mechanisms the legacy component offers. These object wrappers then have to be written in the programming language of the legacy component. Consider as an example, the bank system case study. Account management applications were written in Cobol to execute on the Unisys host. Interfaces were defined to these applications using CORBA/IDL. These interfaces then had to be implemented in wrappers. The wrapper implementation therefore had to be in Cobol as well. Clients for these account management applications, however, were the trading system written in Visual C++ and the various relational database applications, which were written in C and embedded SQL. Legacy integration is not the only reasons why language heterogeneity occurs. Programming interfaces to components that are bought off-the-shelf may only exist in certain programming languages. Another reason may be that the programming language that is best suited to one component is unsuitable for the other, as was the case in the Hong Kong video-on-demand system. Therefore, the need to integrate components written in heterogeneous programming languages arises in many projects.

COM and CORBA use different programming language bindings to their respective interface definition languages. This is a static approach and requires re-generation of stubs for each different programming environment that clients may use. Java does not have this heterogeneity problem. With Java/RMI alone, it is not possible to have clients or server objects of a remote method invocation that are not implemented in Java. Before we study these approaches in more detail we will now look at the dimensions in which heterogeneity can occur among different programming languages.

Different programming languages may have to be used to build a distributed object system.

5.1.1 Examples of Heterogeneity

Object Model Differences

The programming languages that are used today have largely different approaches to typing. Smalltalk, for example, does not have a static type system; objects only have a type at run-time. Smalltalk therefore does not (and cannot) attempt detection of type safety at compile time and it is possible to pass an object as an actual parameter to a method that the method does not expect. Hence, explicit type checks are needed when objects are used in Smalltalk expressions. Such checks are not necessary in statically-typed languages such as C++, Ada-95 and Java. Programmers using these languages declare types of variables and parameters, which enables the compiler to compute a type for any expression. Unless this type is explicitly manipulated, for example by a type cast, compilers can raise typing errors for source code that assigns an expression to a variable or parameter of incompatible types. If a client of a statically-typed server is written using a dynamically-typed language, requests will not necessarily be type-safe. This is aggravated by the fact that the programmers of server

The type systems of programming languages are different.

objects who are using a statically-typed language often rely on the fact that the compiler has performed type checks on the parameters that are being passed.

Different programming languages have different type construction capabilities. C++ supports templates and Eiffel supports genericity. C and Modula-2 have a fair number of type constructors to express records, arrays and unions. Java only supports arrays and Smalltalk does not have any type constructors. If programmers of server objects offer operations that have complex types, programmers of client objects that are using a language with less expressive type construction capabilities will find it difficult to pass appropriately-constructed parameters.

Modula-2, Ada-95 and Java distinguish between interfaces and implementations. Eiffel has abstract classes and C++ has pure virtual classes, both of which can be considered as interfaces, too. Smalltalk, C and Pascal do not have such a distinction. The lack of interfaces in these latter languages complicates the integration with the former class of languages.

Procedural programming languages, such as Pascal, C and Modula-2 do not support inheritance. All object-oriented languages support some form of inheritance. The way inheritance is supported, however, differs between these languages. Eiffel supports multiple inheritance. Both Eiffel and Java enable operations to be redefined by specializing parameter types and redefined operations are still bound dynamically. C++ supports multiple inheritance and operation redefinition without any restrictions on the parameter types. The result, however, is that those operations can only be bound statically. Java supports single inheritance among classes but multiple inheritance of interfaces. Smalltalk only supports single inheritance. The different forms of inheritance and its absence in procedural languages make it difficult to decide which operations are available from a server object in a setting where different programming languages are used for the implementation of objects.

Imperative languages do not support dynamic binding, but some of them, for example C, support type casts by means of which polymorphism can be implemented. Object-oriented languages all support polymorphism and dynamic binding, though the details differ. In C++ the programmer can decide whether operations should be bound statically or dynamically. In Eiffel and Smalltalk the programmer does not have this choice. The existence of different late-binding strategies in different programming languages again makes it difficult to tell which operation is going to be executed in a heterogeneous setting. The different late-binding strategies often also lead to machine code representations of objects.

Machine Code Representations

In addition to the above differences between object models, there may even be differences in the implementation of the same programming language that lead to problems. These are generally caused by different development environments and compilers that generate machine code in an incompatible way. We now review some examples of those.

At run-time, the code of the operations that server objects can perform is represented in the machine code representation for the processor of the host on which the object resides. As we have seen there may be different types of hosts in distributed systems and these often have different processor architectures as well. In the bank system example, the machine code

Margin notes:

Different programming languages have different type construction capabilities.

Some programming languages distinguish between interfaces and implementations.

Programming languages treat inheritance in different ways.

Programming languages differ in when operation calls are bound to operations.

Binary representation generated by compilers of the same language may differ.

Machine code representation may be hardware platform dependent.

representation for a Unisys processor cannot execute on an MVS machine, the code for a Sun SPARC processor cannot execute on a PC, and so on. Hence, when moving an object from one machine to another machine, the machine code representation of the object needs to change so that its operations can be executed on the new processor.

One of the most serious problems that occurs with different development environments are varying implementations of late binding. Late binding is often implemented using virtual function tables. Even for the same programming language, the layout and use of these virtual function tables differs greatly between development environments. If client and server objects use different table layouts the dynamic binding mechanisms are incompatible and late binding does not work.

Late binding may be implemented in different ways.

The order in which attributes are defined in the object source code is generally not relevant for the semantics of the object. At run-time, however, the order in which attribute values are located in the object's memory is indeed relevant because attribute access and manipulation operations generally need to know the offset from the base address of the object in order to fetch or put a value. The order in which attributes are arranged, however, is not standardized for most object-oriented languages and may differ between different development environments. This leads to different offsets for objects that are generated by different environments and generally inhibits attribute access and modifications of a server object to be carried out by client objects that were compiled with different environments.

The memory layout of objects and the position of attributes may differ.

5.1.2 Programming Language Bindings

We have already seen that object-oriented middleware supports a common object model and that it has a language to express interfaces of server objects in a way that is binding for clients and servers. This is a first and important step towards resolving the heterogeneity of programming languages.

A programming language binding determines how IDL constructs can be used in a client or server object implementation.

A common interface definition language reduces the complexity of integrating n different programming languages from $(n \times (n-1))/2$ bindings between different programming languages to n bindings between a programming language and the interface definition language. Figure 5.1 shows this difference for six programming languages. Integration is further simplified by the way that the interface definition languages are carefully chosen to be mapped relatively easily to a variety of programming languages.

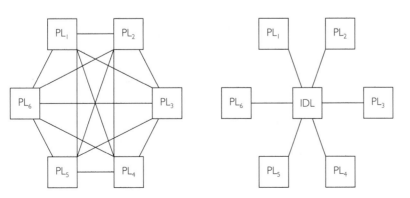

Figure 5.1
Reduction of Complexity of Heterogeneity Resolution by IDL

Figure 5.2

Programming Language Bindings
to CORBA/IDL

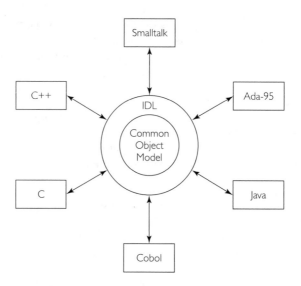

The CORBA specification includes six programming language bindings. CORBA implementations, though, only have to implement one of these bindings to comply with the
specification. This resolves programming language heterogeneity because it allows the client
and the server objects that are involved in an object request to be written in different
programming languages. Rather than discussing each of the language bindings in Figure
5.2 in detail, we focus on the underlying principles of the approach. In order to illustrate
the discussion, we use our soccer management example and show how CORBA's C++
language binding is used to implement both client and server objects.

We approach programming language bindings from different perspectives. From a
language-design point of view we discuss how they map between the programming language
object model and the middleware object model. At an implementation level this mapping
manifests itself in mapping particular constructs of the programming language to IDL
constructs and the other way around. From an architectural point of view we discuss
where programming language bindings are implemented and how these implementations
are used at the different interfaces between middleware and client or server objects.

Mapping Object Models

Bindings of
programming
languages to an IDL
need to be bi-
directional.

As suggested by the double arrows in Figure 5.2, bindings need to be *bi-directional*. This is
because programming language representations of a request on the client-side need to be
mapped to IDL in order to govern the request. Likewise, the IDL constructs that are used
during a request need to be mapped to the programming language constructs used by the
server object to implement the request.

Distributed object
models are statically
typed.

The object models of all middleware that we discussed in Chapter 4 are statically typed.
The object types are defined as interfaces. The programming language bindings map
middleware object types to the types of client and server stubs. These stubs are generally
treated as classes in object-oriented programming languages and they have a well-defined
interface that is used by client and server implementations.

We have seen that object references are essential for making object requests. Hence, bindings need to determine how object references are represented in a particular programming language. In most programming language bindings, the object references representation of the server object is encapsulated in client stubs. These stubs are objects themselves and pointers to these objects can be used to make requests.

Bindings define how object references are implemented.

```
#include "soccer.hh"
int main(int argc, char* argv[]) {
  Team * t;
  Player *goalkeeper, *centreforward,
  char * output; ...
}
```

Example 5.1
Client Stubs in the C++ Language Binding to CORBA/IDL

The above code uses the C++ programming language binding to CORBA/IDL. The client stub types `Player` and `Team` have directly evolved from the IDL types. The client includes the C++ header file `"soccer.hh"`, which defines the stub classes. The variable declarations in the main program of the example of the client declare pointer variables to client stubs of types `Team` and `Player`. Our example assumes that `Team` and `Player` client stubs have been initialized, either by creating new objects or by locating these objects.

Unlike CORBA, COM does not support attributes. Attributes that exist in the CORBA object model are mapped to operations, rather than instance variables, in all programming language bindings. This is for several reasons. First, attributes may have a structured type and they would then have to be marshalled and unmarshalled in the same way as operation parameters or results. Secondly, attribute accesses or updates could fail for the same reasons as operation calls and these failures should be treated in the same way. Thirdly, treating them as operations gives flexibility to the server object designer as to how the attribute should be implemented. It could be implemented within the server object as an instance variable, but could also be mapped to a value stored in a database. Finally, CORBA attributes may be declared as `readonly` and if they were not encapsulated this semantics could not be enforced in most programming languages.

Attributes are always represented as operations.

```
try {
  output=goalkeeper->name();
  cout<<"Obtained reference to player "<<output<< end;
  delete output;
} catch(const Exception &e) {
  cerr << "could not obtain player names" << endl;
  cerr << "Unexpected exception " << e << endl;
}
```

Example 5.2
Attribute Access of C++ Language Binding to CORBA/IDL

An example of an attribute access operation is `goalkeeper->name()`, which retrieves the value of the name attribute of an object of type `Player`.

IDL operations are commonly mapped to operations in the programming language. These operations are available from the client and server stubs. The parameters of these operations and their results are mapped accordingly. In this respect, programming language bindings

Operations are represented as procedures or methods.

determine the mapping of atomic types and structured types. Static object requests are then implemented by locally invoking the methods that are available from the client stub.

Exceptions are represented as exceptions or as explicit output parameters that have to be evaluated.

The mapping of exceptions in CORBA/IDL is rather complicated. This is due to the fact that not all programming languages support exceptions. Even the earlier versions of the C++ language definitions did not include exceptions. Hence, programming language bindings generally determine two strategies for mapping exceptions. The first, and most obvious one, is to use programming language exceptions where they are available. Then all system exceptions are treated as exception classes and further exception classes are generated for the type-specific exceptions. The exception classes are arranged in a type hierarchy with one particular root. This root is `Exception` in case of the CORBA C++ binding. The second strategy is to use an additional output parameter by means of which server objects can communicate failures to the client. The C++ programming language binding for CORBA allows both strategies and we have used the first one in Example 5.3. Therefore object requests are encapsulated in C++ `try/catch` clauses.

Example 5.3
Object Request with C++ Language Binding to CORBA/IDL

```
try {
    t->add(goalkeeper,1);
    t->add(centreforward,10);
} catch(const Exception &e) {
    cerr << "could not add players to team" << endl;
    cerr << "Unexpected exception " << e << endl;
}
```

In our C++ client, the IDL operation `add()` that is available for team objects is statically requested by invoking `add` from the client stub of type `Team`. If an error occurs, the catch clause will be executed and `e` refers to the exception object.

Resolution of multiple inheritance depends on the inheritance model of the programming language.

COM, CORBA and Java/RMI all support inheritance. The CORBA object model even supports multiple inheritance. A programming language binding therefore also has to define how inheritance of the middleware is represented to the client object and how it is implemented by server objects. This is straightforward if both the middleware and the programming language support single inheritance. But there may be also be situations where the programming language does not support inheritance. CORBA, for example has a programming language binding to C and it needs to define how inheritance is reflected in C. The principle that is used most commonly is the static resolution of inheritance during IDL generation. During this resolution process, the IDL compiler generates operations not only for the object type, but also for all the supertypes. This technique can also be applied if multiple inheritance of the middleware object model has to be reduced to single inheritance in the programming language. Then operations inherited via a second or third supertype are statically included in the interface. Example 5.4 shows how multiple inheritance can be resolved statically into single inheritance.

All programming language bindings assume the existence of a common root object.

We have also seen that in all middleware object models there were a few operations that all objects have in common. All CORBA object types inherit from `Object`, all COM interface types inherit from `IUnknown` and all Java/RMI remote interface types inherit from `Remote`. These operations are implemented in common supertypes for client and server

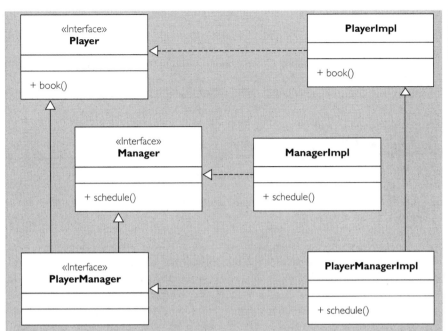

Example 5.4
Resolution of Multiple
Inheritance in Programming
Binding

The diagram above shows an interface `PlayerManager` that inherits from both `Manager` and `Player`. The implementation of these interfaces in a programming language that only supports single inheritance is shown on the right-hand side. The programming language binding defines `PlayerManagerImpl` to inherit from `PlayerImpl` and statically copies the operation `schedule` that `Manager` defines into the class `PlayerManagerImpl`.

stubs. In our example, the client stub types `Player` and `Team` actually inherit from type `Object`.

Implementation of Language Bindings

Now that we have discussed how programming language bindings are defined we can focus on how and where they are actually implemented in the middleware. Bindings are implemented in two different ways that are complementary to each other; they are implemented in application programming interfaces with corresponding libraries and in IDL compilers that generate client and server stubs.

We have seen that all middleware has a finite number of interfaces that client and server objects use to communicate with the middleware. Examples of those are the ORB Interface, the Dynamic Invocation Interface and the Object Adapters in CORBA or the Service Control Module in COM. These middleware interfaces are expressed in the interface definition language of the middleware's IDL and need to be used from different programming languages, too. As they are not dependent on the types of client or server objects, it is sufficient that vendors who implement the middleware deliver an implementation for each middleware interface and each programming language binding. This implementation usually

Middleware offers
application
programming interfaces
to both client and server
objects.

comprises an interface definition in a particular programming language and a library that is linked with the client and server code.

Middleware also includes
compilers that generate
programming language
definitions for stubs and
skeletons from the IDL.

The above approach does not work for those interfaces between middleware and client or server objects that are type specific. These are the client and server stubs, which are generated by the IDL compilers. As the IDL compilers are part of the middleware, an obvious approach is, therefore, to implement the programming language binding in these compilers. Middleware vendors may choose to provide a different compiler for every programming language binding or they may offer a command-line parameter that can be used to command which binding is to be chosen. In this way it can be achieved that stubs have an interface in the programming language in which client and server objects are written.

Access Transparency

Programming language heterogeneity is resolved through multiple programming language bindings. The bindings implement the mapping of the programming language's object model to the middleware's object model. For a summary, let us revisit Figure 4.2 on Page 97 to illustrate this. The programming language bindings are relevant at every interface between the middleware and client or server objects. For CORBA, programming language bindings define how the dynamic invocation interface, the ORB interface and object adapters are implemented in interfaces in a programming language. The CORBA programming language bindings also define how client stubs and server skeletons are generated for one particular programming language.

Resolution of language
heterogeneity is
transparent for
programmers involved.

The resolution of programming language heterogeneity is transparent for the client and the server programmers. It is transparent to a client programmer that the server object may be written in a different programming language. Likewise it is transparent to a server object programmer that requests to perform an object's operation may come from clients written in different programming languages. This transparency is achieved by the fact that both client and server programmers only need to use one programming language binding.

5.2 Heterogeneous Middleware

In Chapter 4, we saw three different examples of object-oriented middleware and it is likely that new object-oriented middleware will be developed in the medium to long term. The availability of different object-oriented middleware may present a selection problem, but sometimes there is no optimal single middleware, and multiple middleware systems have to be combined. This may be for a variety of reasons.

Different middleware
may be required due to
available programming
language bindings.

The integration problem that is to be solved by object-oriented middleware may be such that different programming languages have to be utilized. Not all middleware, however, can be used with every programming language. There are, for example, several CORBA implementations that can only be used with Java as a programming language and others can only be used with C++. COM is only available for C++, Visual Basic and Microsoft's dialect of Java. RMI cannot be used with any other programming language than Java. The mix of programming languages may be such that there is not a single middleware that supports them all and that more than one middleware has to be used.

The ease with which legacy or off-the-shelf components can be interfaced with middleware may vary. PC components, for example, may have an OLE or COM interface that makes COM the middleware of choice. Other components may already have a published CORBA interface, which makes it desirable to use CORBA with these components. If existing COM and CORBA components have to be integrated with each other, it would be desirable to use both COM and CORBA and let COM and CORBA sort out the details of the integration.

Different middleware may be required due to integration with existing systems.

A further factor that can necessitate several middleware systems might be the availability for particular hardware platforms. COM is available for Windows and a few UNIX implementations. There are CORBA implementations for almost all hardware and operating systems, though the availability of a particular CORBA implementation is usually more restricted.

Different middleware may be required due to availability on hardware platforms.

Implementations of the different middleware approaches have greatly varying performance characteristics. Java/RMI has been built for deployment on fast local area networks, because it is rather expensive due to the interpretation of byte code, distributed garbage collection and its call by value semantics for non remote parameters. COM is extremely fast with in-process and non-remote deployments. There are some CORBA implementations that leave a very small footprint in memory and perform extremely efficiently on local area networks. Other CORBA implementations implement the CORBA security specification, use reliable transport protocols and have been targeted to wide area deployment. When building large-scale distributed systems, it may be desirable to use different middleware systems for communication in the local area network and for wide area communication. Hence, the need arises to utilize more than one middleware product. When using more than one middleware, however, access transparency should be maintained. It should, for example be transparent to a programmer writing a COM client object that the server is implemented using a CORBA product.

Different middleware may be required due to different performance profiles.

5.2.1 Examples of Heterogeneity

Although it is desirable, the technologies that we have discussed do not support objects that are distributed across more than one middleware. Figure 5.3 emphasizes this limitation as the objects connected to one middleware are isolated and unable to communicate with objects that are connected to another middleware. We now investigate the problems.

As we have seen in the previous chapter, the details of the object models that are supported by COM, CORBA and Java/RMI differ to a considerable extent. As a consequence, the interface definition languages that are used with these middleware systems also differ. We have seen that Java/RMI does not have a dedicated interface definition language and CORBA/IDL is considerably different from, and more expressive than, Microsoft IDL.

Object models and IDLs differ.

The three approaches also vary in the way they implement object references. The implementation of object references is not specified in the CORBA standard and vendors are free to choose an appropriate representation. Also the Java/RMI object references are incompatible with COM object references. Using the technology we have discussed so far, it is

Object references are represented differently.

Figure 5.3
Limitations Imposed by
Heterogeneous Middleware

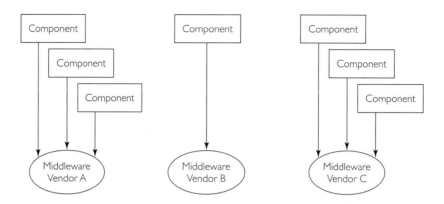

Figure 5.3
Limitations Imposed by
Heterogeneous Middleware

therefore not possible to use the reference to a CORBA server object from a COM client or to have a Java object that uses Java/RMI to invoke an operation from COM server.

 Data heterogeneity is
resolved in different
ways.

In further sections of this chapter, we will see that the different middleware systems also use different approaches to resolve data heterogeneity which occurs as a consequence of different hardware and operating system platforms. These are incompatible with each other, too.

 Different underlying
transport protocols are
used.

Moreover, the transport protocols that are being used by the different middleware approaches may vary. Java/RMI uses byte streams that are supported by the networking packages of Java. CORBA vendors have complete freedom to choose a transport layer implementation to build upon. Indeed, there are CORBA implementations that use a large variety of different transport protocols. COM uses Remote Procedure Calls (RPCs) to achieve marshalling, unmarshalling and synchronization.

5.2.2 Interoperability

 Interoperability
denotes the ability of
different
implementations of
middleware to work
together.

Middleware specifications, such as OMG/CORBA, leave ample room for varying implementations. This is important from a commercial point of view, as vendors can use this freedom to build products that are better in certain respects than other implementations of the specification. Yet, for the reasons outlined above, different implementations of, for example CORBA, should be homogeneous enough to be integrated. *Interoperability specifications* define the protocols that middleware vendors have to implement so that different middleware can participate in the same object request.

Being able to assume that the different middleware systems that may participate in the same object request are different implementations of the same specification helps in facilitating this integration. In particular, we can assume that they have the same object model and that they treat failures in the same way. They may be different, however, in the way they implement object references and in the transport protocol upon which they are built. Hence interoperability specifications have to address these concerns.

Figure 5.4 shows how the limitations discussed above are overcome. Different middleware systems participate in object requests, which are represented as dashed arrows in the figure. These requests are implemented by the middleware systems talking to each other via inter-

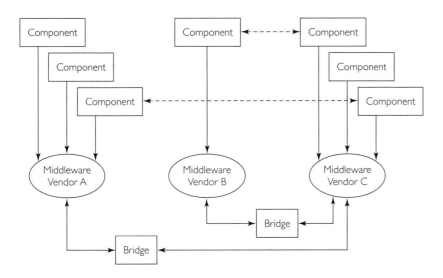

Figure 5.4
Interoperability between Middleware Systems

operability bridges. The fact that the server object is connected to a middleware from a different vendor, however, is transparent for client programmers. Client and server objects communicate only with their middleware as they did before and bridges between different middleware are used to resolve the remaining heterogeneity.

Bridging

The purpose of a *bridge* is to translate a request from the domain of one middleware implementation to another implementation. While doing so, bridges generally map the representation of object references that are valid in the domain of one implementation to references to the same object in the representation of another middleware implementation. Often different implementations are used in different security domains. When bridges interconnect them they enable objects in one security domain to access objects that are contained in another security domain. Thus bridging different middleware implementations also raises security issues, which we discuss in detail in Chapter 12.

Bridges translate a request from one middleware to another.

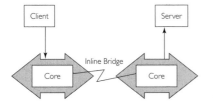 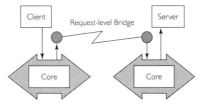

Figure 5.5
Request and Inline Bridging for Interoperability Purposes

There are different forms that bridges can take. Figure 5.5 shows an inline bridge and a request-level bridge. *Inline bridges* are built into the core of the middleware and implement standardized interoperability protocols. They use the internal application programming interfaces of the middleware and therefore they cannot be built by application programmers but rather have to be provided by middleware vendors.

Bridges that are built into the middleware are called inline bridges.

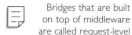

Bridges that are built
on top of middleware
are called request-level
bridges.

Request-level bridges, on the other hand, are built on top of a middleware implementation and they use the published specification of the middleware. Request-level bridges can be added by application programmers in order to implement interoperability for a middleware that does not itself implement a standardized interoperability protocol.

Request-level bridges usually consist of two half-bridges, which are shown in Figure 5.5 as grey circles. Each of these half-bridges contains a proxy, that is a surrogate object. The surrogate on the left is a surrogate for the server that is invoked by the client using the client's middleware. The other surrogate is the client's representation in the server's middleware. Both client and server surrogates use standard mechanisms to communicate with the middleware. These can be either static or dynamic requests. Static requests are type-specific. Such bridges are also known as *type-specific bridges*. Dynamic requests can be formulated in a type-independent way and such bridges are also known as *generic bridges*. Each of these half-bridges uses a mechanism outside the middleware to communicate with its respective other half. A simple implementation would be to link the server skeleton from one middleware to the client stub from the other middleware. However, this approach is not very efficient as marshalling and unmarshalling is performed more often than necessary. An efficient implementation of request-level bridges is quite involved, because all the problems that are otherwise resolved by the middleware and that we have discussed in Chapter 3 have now to be addressed by the bridge designer. Request-level bridges are therefore only used as a last resort in the case that the middleware does not implement an interoperability protocol.

CORBA Interoperability Protocols

The specification of interoperability is important for the CORBA standard. Unlike COM, which Microsoft tightly controls, the CORBA standard is freely available and is implemented by many different vendors. Similarly, Java/RMI is a specification that is implemented by different vendors. It is planned that Java/RMI will rely on the CORBA interoperability protocol family to achieve interoperability between different RMI implementations but also between Java/RMI and CORBA. We therefore discuss the CORBA interoperability protocol family now.

Figure 5.6
Interoperability Protocol Family
of CORBA

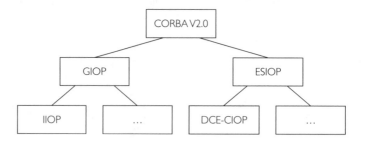

Figure 5.6 shows an overview of the CORBA interoperability protocols. There are two categories of protocols: Environment-Specific Inter-ORB Protocols (ESIOPs) and General Inter-ORB Protocols (GIOPs). ESIOPs support the exploitation of implementation-specific assumptions. The DCE-CIOP, for example assumes that OSF/DCE remote procedure calls are used as an underlying transport. GIOPs are applicable for the integration of any CORBA

products and define CORBA interoperability based on the formats of messages that are transmitted using particular transport layers. All GIOP protocols standardize the formatting of messages that are used to implement object requests, replies and control messages and their representation using particular families of transport protocols. The Internet Inter-ORB Protocol (IIOP) is the most important instantiation of GIOP that assumes use of TCP as a transport protocol. Support of IIOP is mandatory for any CORBA product and is therefore widely available. Also the specification of interoperability between Java/RMI and CORBA is based on the IIOP protocol. This is why we now focus on the discussion of the GIOP and IIOP protocols.

The GIOP defines the contents and structure of a number of message types for ORB interoperability. GIOP assumes the availability of a connection-oriented transport protocol. The different instantiations of GIOP adapt these to particular connection-oriented transport protocols. Transport protocols that are used with GIOP need to meet the following criteria:

1. The transport should be connection-oriented and connect the ORB on the client side with the ORB on the server side. Connection is always initiated on the client side, prior to the client ORB sending the message with the request data through the connection. The ORB on the server side receives this request message, activates the server object, invokes the requested operation and then sends a reply message that includes the operation result or any exception details;
2. If necessary the two ORBs may share the same connection across multiple requests. This is possible because each request message uniquely identifies the requested server object;
3. Request and reply messages do not have to be totally ordered. GIOP supports message-overlapping and uses unique request identifiers to map request and reply messages onto each other; and
4. Connection resources may be re-used by ORBs after they have notified each other about request cancellations and connection shutdown, for which GIOP defines the necessary message types.

GIOP Message Types

The GIOP defines eight message types. These are used for transmitting request data (`Request`), data containing the result of the request (`Reply`), for transmitting request or reply parameters that were too long to fit into one message (`Fragment`), for finding out where request and reply messages are (`LocateRequest` and `LocateReply`), for cancelling a request (`CancelRequest`), for closing the transport connection (`CloseConnection`) and for transmitting details about failures and exceptions (`MessageError`). Of these eight message types, we only consider the request and reply messages in order to show how interoperability messages are defined.

For interoperability to work, the format of these messages, down to the last bit, has to be agreed between the different CORBA vendors. The OMG uses its own technology for this purpose. The messages are defined as CORBA/IDL structures. The Common Data Representation (CDR) defines how IDL types are represented in a byte stream and achieves an unambiguous definition of the IDL message across different hardware platforms that may

Interoperability defines the format of messages that are exchanged between different middleware implementations.

use different number representations or character encodings. We discuss the CDR in
Section 5.3.2.

```
module GIOP {
  struct Version {
    octet major; octet minor;
  };
  enum MsgType_1_1 {
    Request, Reply, CancelRequest, LocateRequest, LocateReply,
    CloseConnection, MessageError, Fragment
  };
  struct MessageHeader_1_1 {
    char magic [4];
    Version GIOP_version;
    octet flags; // GIOP 1.1 change
    octet message_type;
    unsigned long message_size;
  };

  struct RequestHeader_1_1 {
    IOP::ServiceContextList service_context;
    unsigned long request_id;
    boolean response_expected;
    octet reserved[3];
    sequence <octet> object_key;
    string operation;
    Principal requesting_principal;
  };
  enum ReplyStatusType {
    NO_EXCEPTION,USER_EXCEPTION,SYSTEM_EXCEPTION,LOCATION_FORWARD
  };
  struct ReplyHeader {
    IOP::ServiceContextList service_context;
    unsigned long request_id;
    ReplyStatusType reply_status;
  };
};
```

The eight message types each have a *GIOP message header*, shown in Figure 5.7. The
purpose of the header is to declare that this message is a GIOP message in field magic
and to identify which version of the GIOP protocol it uses. It declares the type of which it is
an instance in field message_type. Moreover it indicates how long the message is. The
header also declares whether little or big endian representations are used to encode numbers.

A *GIOP request message* adds a request header and a request body to the GIOP message
header. The purpose of the request message is to transmit all information that is needed by
the receiving ORB to identify the server object and request the execution of the desired
operation from the server object. The request header includes a request identifier that is used

to match request and reply messages. It declares an interoperable object reference that the server can use to identify the object and whether a response is expected. The request header also encodes the name of the operation or attribute and information about the principal, who is requesting the execution. This is needed for security purposes and will be discussed further in Chapter 12. The request body includes a structure encoding all in and inout parameters in the order in which they were specified in the IDL declaration. In the request message it is not necessary to pass values for out parameters. These are included in reply messages.

A *GIOP reply message* adds a reply header and a reply body to the GIOP message header. The header specifies the identifier of the request message in order to enable the ORB on the client side to match the request to a reply message that it sent out earlier. Moreover, it includes an indication whether the operation was executed successful, whether a system or user exception was raised or whether the request was forwarded to yet another ORB. The reply header also includes a service context that is used to pass information that is specific to CORBAservices, such as transaction contexts and security contexts. The reply body includes the result or exception data that needs to be passed to the client. If the reply status indicated no exception, the reply body includes the return value of the operation followed by any out and inout parameters in the order in which they were included in the IDL declaration of the replying operation. If the reply status indicates a user or system exception, the body contains the exception data structures.

IIOP

Using the messages of the GIOP, an ORB on the client side can forward a request to an ORB on the server side and receive the reply. The declaration of the messages in IDL and the mapping to CDR precisely define the byte stream that is to be exchanged between the client- and server-side ORBs. Different vendors have to stick to these specifications in order to get a CORBA-compliance certificate. What remains to be done is to define how these messages are transmitted using particular transport protocols. The Internet Inter-ORB Protocol (IIOP) defines this adoption for the Transmission Control Protocol (TCP), a protocol commonly used across the Internet.

 IIOP is the implementation of GIOP for transport with TCP.

The main purpose of the IIOP protocol is to define TCP-based connection management. In order to send, for example a GIOP request message from a client-side ORB to a server-side ORB, the client has to initiate a TCP connection to a server-side ORB. In order to do that, the client-side ORB has to know the host name of the server-side ORB and a TCP port number on which the server-side ORB is listening for connection requests. Client-side ORBs would need to use different host names and port numbers for different server objects. Hence, they are encoded together with the object-reference. The IIOP specification defines profiles for Interoperable Object References (IORs), which include the TCP address information that another ORB needs to initiate a connection, in addition to the reference data. The IDL declaration for IOR profiles is shown in Figure 5.8.

 IIOP standardizes how TCP connections are established.

Whenever an object reference passes an inline IIOP bridge, the bridge adds the TCP information to the object reference and encapsulates that information in an IOR profile. The host is the Internet Domain Name of the host; for example, the host on which this

Figure 5.8

Interoperable Object Reference
Profiles

```
module IIOP {
  struct Version {
    octet major;
    octet minor;
  };
  struct ProfileBody_1_1 {
    Version iiop_version;
    string host;
    unsigned short port;
    sequence <octet> object_key;
    sequence <IOP::TaggedComponent> components;
  };
};
```

book is written is `amon.cs.ucl.ac.uk`. The `port` number is an unused port number that is determined by the system administrator of the server-side ORB at installation time. The object reference information is stored in the `object_key`. The client-side ORB then uses this profile as the object reference of the server object and does not interpret the object key any further.

Transparency of CORBA Interoperability

CORBA
interoperability is
transparent to client
and server
programmers.

We note that CORBA interoperability through IIOP is transparent to the designer of client objects and the designer of server objects alike. This is because CORBA interoperability is resolved entirely at the intersection between the presentation and the transport layers. It is resolved by standardizing the way that requests are marshalled and unmarshalled onto messages that are sent through TCP. This is two layers below what client and server object designers see.

5.2.3 Interworking

Interworking defines
how different
middleware standards
are integrated.

Interoperability specifications determine how different implementations of the same middleware specification work together. It is, however, also desirable to support the integration of middleware systems that implement different specifications. It may, for example, be necessary to have some COM components on a Windows NT desktop application request operations from CORBA server objects. *Interworking* specifications integrate middleware systems that implement different specifications. The main goal of interworking is to enable a client object in the realm of one middleware to access the services provided by a server object in a different middleware. The designer of the client object should not be aware that the server object resides in a different class of middleware.

Figure 5.9 shows the principle of interworking. The aim is to provide clients that use the object-oriented middleware A with a native object reference in A to a server object that resides in the middleware B. The mapping is achieved by giving clients a reference to a view object whose implementation contains a bridge that uses an object reference in B. The aim of interworking products is to generate these view objects from the interface written in the interface definition language for middleware B.

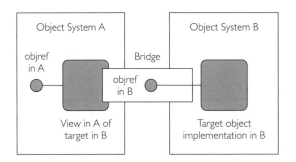

Figure 5.9
Interworking Architecture

The main task that an interworking specification has to achieve is the mapping of the different object models. The view object that the client accesses is an object of one object model and the server object is an object of a different object model. We have seen in Chapter 4 that there are many similarities between the COM and CORBA object models. Both are based on objects and both support the specification of parameterized operations whose execution can be requested by remote client objects. There are, however, also considerable differences between the object models that complicate the interworking specification between COM and CORBA. The CORBA 2.2 specification defines interworking between CORBA and Microsoft's middleware. It not only defines interoperability with COM but also with its predecessor, OLE Automation. The specification contains the necessary details to enable COM and OLE objects to be clients of CORBA server objects and vice versa. While doing so, the specification instantiates the abstract interworking architecture in four ways (see Figure 5.10). The differences between the OLE Automation and CORBA object models are even more pronounced. Interworking specifications are in general more complicated than interoperability specifications because they have to define how the different middleware object models map onto each other. This involves mapping the following items:

Interworking is more difficult to achieve than interoperability.

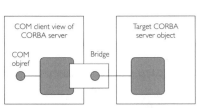

a) COM client object of CORBA server object

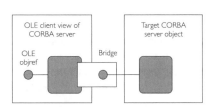

b) OLE client object of CORBA server object

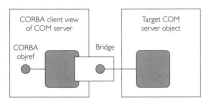

c) CORBA client object of COM server object

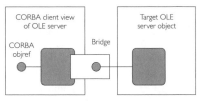

d) CORBA client object of OLE server object

Figure 5.10
Interworking between COM, OLE Automation and CORBA

Atomic Types. Both COM and CORBA support a limited set of atomic types. The mapping between these is very straightforward; most atomic types even have the same name in CORBA/IDL and MIDL, except for `octet` in CORBA/IDL, which is called `byte` in MIDL. The mapping of enumeration, strings, arrays, structs and unions is again very straightforward because these type constructors exist in both object models. CORBA `sequence` types may be unbounded and there is direct support for unbounded sequences in COM. Hence sequences are mapped to a structure with length, size and a pointer to a conformant array (refer to Page 110) containing elements that resulted from the mapping of the sequence's base type.

Exceptions. We have already identified that one of the major differences between the COM and the CORBA object models is their approach to handling failures. COM supports 32-bit values of type `HRESULT` to indicate success or the occurrence of a particular failure. CORBA uses exceptions for this purpose. The ability to return exception data structures from CORBA cannot be reflected as a 32-bit HRESULT. Hence, the CORBA→COM mapping treats exceptions as structures that are added as the last parameter to operations that may raise a type-specific exception. For system exceptions, particular `HRESULT` values are identified.

Interface Definitions. CORBA object types are mapped to COM interfaces. Operations and attributes that may exist in a CORBA object type are mapped to operations in COM. The parameters of CORBA operations are mapped to parameters of the COM operation in a straightforward manner. Given that return types of COM operations are reserved to pass HRESULTs, the return type of a CORBA operation is reflected as an additional out parameter in the operation's COM equivalent.

Inheritance. Single inheritance between two CORBA interfaces is mapped onto interface inheritance in COM. This is simplified by the fact that both object models assume the existence of a common root. CORBA's `Object` maps to COM's `IUnknown` interface. CORBA, however, also supports multiple inheritance, which does not exist in COM. Instead, an implementation of a COM object would implement multiple interfaces that are not related at the object level. The interworking specification, therefore, defines that CORBA interfaces that inherit from multiple other interfaces are mapped to COM interfaces that inherit from `IUnknown` and the operations that would have been inherited are simply duplicated in the implementations.

Interworking specifications are implemented by compilers that translate from one IDL into another. The mapping between object models that is part of an interworking specification is implemented in a compiler. The designer of the COM component would use this compiler to obtain the interfaces from a COM point of view. Likewise, the CORBA designer would use the compiler to translate MIDL into CORBA/IDL. From then on the designer would be unaware that the objects are implemented in a different middleware.

Transparency of Interworking

Interworking can be achieved in a way that is transparent to client and server programmers. Our definition of interworking demanded that it is transparent to clients that they request operation executions from a server connected to a different middleware. Likewise, it has to be transparent to server programmers that their objects provide services to client objects that reside in a different middleware.

The various instantiations of the COM/CORBA interworking architecture do meet this requirement. Implementations of this interworking specification provide compilers that implement the mapping of the different object models that we sketched above. For example, a COM client programmer can be given an MIDL interface definition that is automatically derived from a CORBA/IDL interface definition and vice versa.

5.3 Heterogeneous Data Representation

Before we start explaining techniques that may be used for resolving data heterogeneity, we show some examples of data heterogeneity. These include different data representation formats due to different hardware or differing representations of complex data structures in run-time environments of different programming languages.

5.3.1 Examples of Heterogeneity

A long integer (32 bits) on the Unisys mainframe of the bank system would be represented in a 'big-endian' representation. This means that the highest significant byte is at the end of a four-byte sequence. The RISC processors that are built into modern Unix servers also use a big-endian representation. The same integer has a 'little-endian' representation with the lowest-significant byte at the end of the sequence on an Intel-based Unix or Windows NT machine.

Different hardware platforms have different representations for integers.

Example 5.5
Little- and Big-Endian Representations of Long Integers

The co-existence of little- and big-endian data representations in a distributed system has strong implications for the way data is exchanged between objects residing on heterogeneous hosts. If a long integer is to be passed as an object request parameter from an object on a Unisys mainframe to an object on a Windows NT PC, a data conversion has to be made in order to switch the order of bytes.

Over time, many different encoding schemes for character sets have evolved. Some mainframes still use the 8-bit Extended Binary Coded Decimal Interchange Code (EBCDIC). Unix systems may use the 7-bit American Standard Code for Information Interchange (ASCII) or the extended 8-bit ISO-8859-1 Latin-1 character set. Windows NT uses the 16-bit Universal Character Set (UCS), more recently introduced as part of the ISO-10646 standard. Apart from western character sets, UCS can also accommodate characters from Greek, Cyrillic, Hebrew and most Asian languages.

There are different encoding schemes for character sets.

The differing ways in which long integers are represented in the bank and soccer systems.

Little Endian memory — n+3 n+2 n+1 n — sign

Big Endian memory — n n+1 n+2 n+3 — sign

Example 5.6

EBCDIC, ASCII, ISO-8859-1 and UCS Character Encodings

	P	r	e	u	ß	e	n		M	ü	n	s	t	e	r
EBCDIC	D7	99	85	A4	A2 A2	85	95	40	D4	A4 85	95	A2	A3	85	99
ASCII	50	72	65	75	73 73	65	6E	20	4D	75 65	6E	73	74	65	72
ISO-8859-1	50	72	65	75	DF	65	6E	20	4D	FC	6E	73	74	65	72
UCS	0050	0072	0065	0075	00DF	0065	006E	0020	004D	00FC	006E	0073	0074	0065	0072

The name of a German soccer team encoded in 8-bit EBCDIC, 7-bit ASCII, 8-bit ISO-8859-1 and 16-bit UCS (shown in hexadecimal numbers).

This heterogeneity in character sets causes problems when characters or character strings have to be transferred between hosts. EBCDIC and ASCII are incompatible and have to be mapped onto each other. A strong inclusive relationship exists between characters supported by ASCII, Latin-1 and UCS. This means that every ASCII character is also a Latin-1 character and every Latin-1 character is also a UCS character. Hence, characters do not have to be transformed from ASCII into Latin-1 and from Latin-1 into UCS. However, the reverse does not hold and UCS characters need to be encoded if they are to be transformed into Latin-1 and Latin-1 characters need to be encoded if they are to be transferred into an ASCII representation.

Complex types are encoded differently in different programming languages.

A third form of data heterogeneity may arise due to the way complex data types are implemented by the run-time environment of programming languages.

Example 5.7

Pascal and C Representations of a Character String

Pascal memory		3	a	b	c	

C++ memory		a	b	c	\0

The above figure shows the representation of the same character string in Pascal and C. The Pascal representation begins with the number of characters included in the string, while the C representation starts with the first character and terminates with a byte that is zero.

Even if the way complex types are implemented is the same, the resulting representation may still be different due to heterogeneity of the object types.

Middleware should convert data in a transparent way.

As a result, data may have to be converted when middleware transfers object request parameters and results from one host to another. This transformation requires type information and it therefore has to be done before request parameters are marshalled. Hence, conceptually this transformation is performed by the presentation layer implementation.

There are three principle ways that this conversion can be done. It can be performed implicitly by middleware that utilizes a standard data representation. It can be resolved explicitly at the application level by declaring the type of data in a different way and it can be resolved by the platform on which the middleware executes, for example through abstract virtual machines. We now examine each of those.

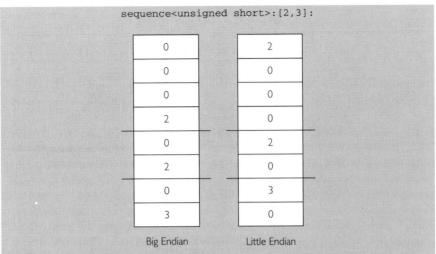

sequence<unsigned short>:[2,3]:

Big Endian   Little Endian

Example 5.8
Little- and Big-Endian
Representations of a Sequence

The above figure shows an example where a sequence of C unsigned short numbers is represented in the same way, but on machines with little-endian and big-endian representations.

5.3.2 Resolution in the Presentation Layer

Standard data representations are used to map between data representations that are specific to the host or programming language. As shown in Figure 5.11, the middleware performs two mappings; the native representation of one host or programming language of the client maps onto the standard data representation and the standard data representation maps onto that of the host or programming language of the server object. Note that these mappings may be necessary even if the client and the server reside on the same host, if they are written in different programming languages.

A standard data representation is an agreed intermediate format.

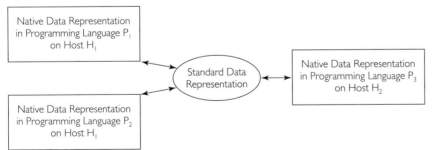

Figure 5.11
Mappings between Native and Standard Data Representations

The overhead of these two mappings may be unnecessary if object requests are implemented by different middleware from the same vendor. Then the vendor could take advantage of implementation knowledge for a more efficient mapping between the native representations. A standard data representation is, therefore, generally only necessary to achieve integration between middleware products of different vendors and is often determined as part of a middleware interoperability standard.

Several different forms of standard data representations have been proposed and are being used with different object-oriented middleware. Sun Microsystems defined the external data representation (XDR) as part of its Open Network Computing environment. XDR was extended by X/Open during the adoption of the Distributed Computing Environment into the network data representation (NDR). DCOM uses NDR as its standard data representation for exchange between heterogeneous DCOM implementations. The General Inter-ORB Protocol of the CORBA standard defines a Common Data Representation (CDR) that is used for those object requests that cross the boundary object request broker between two. This means that CDR is involved if a client object requests an operation execution from a server object that is connected to a different object request broker.

Mapping to and from a common data representation is done in the presentation layer.

The mappings between native and standard data representations are part of the presentation layer implementation of an object-oriented middleware. More precisely, the mappings determine how native data representation formats are mapped into a standardized format when they are marshalled into a byte stream and how these byte streams containing data in a standard representation are unmarshalled into native data representation formats.

Figure 5.12
Alignment of OMG/IDL Atomic Data Types

Type	Alignment	Type	Alignment	Type	Alignment
char	1	long	4	double	8
octet	1	long long	8	boolean	1
short	2	float	4	enum	4

Standard data representations need to define a format for all data that is transmitted during an object request from a client to a server or vice versa. This can be data of all types that can be expressed using the object model of the respective middleware. The definition of standard data representation formats is, therefore, driven by the capabilities for type definitions determined in the object model of the middleware. As we have seen in Chapter 4, these object models all include a set of atomic types and have a way to denote object references. And object references and atomic types can be combined in type constructors.

The approach taken by these standard representations is to define how values of each atomic type are represented in a byte stream, how object references are represented in a byte stream and how these representations are concatenated for each of the type constructors supported by the object model. The approaches taken by the different standardized data representations are all very similar and we can examine one archetypal example to understand the principles. We choose CORBA's CDR for that purpose.

CORBA's atomic data types are encoded in multiples of 8-bit values. As shown in Figure 5.12, CDR defines an *alignment* for each atomic data type that determines how many bytes on a marshalled byte stream are occupied by values of these types. That alignment also determines the index of the byte stream where data of atomic types may start. This may lead to gaps in the byte stream that carries undefined data but it can be used to accelerate the implementation of specific instruction to move atomic data into and out of these byte streams.

The mapping of characters is complicated by the number of different character encodings that are used in practice. The approach taken in CORBA is therefore to first let the two ORBs agree on a common transfer scheme (CTS) that will then be used for character encodings. Characters are transformed into the CTS on the client-side and they are transformed from the CTS on the server side.

The CORBA CDR, in fact, defines two mappings for atomic types that represent numbers. The first one is for big-endian representations and the second one is for little-endian representations. CORBA implementations declare during request marshalling whether they use little- or big-endian representation. This has the advantage that the computationally-intensive reversing of byte orders is not necessary when request data is sent between two little-endian or two big-endian hosts.

Unnecessary reversal of endian types can be avoided if two mappings are defined.

The mapping of complex types that can be constructed using CORBA's type constructors determine the order in which component data are copied into and out of the byte stream. For example, CDR defines that a record (`struct`) is encoded by copying its elements in the order in which they are declared. As another example, CDR defines that sequences are preceded by an unsigned long that indicates the number of elements of the sequence and then the elements are encoded in the order they occur in the sequence.

	Big Endian	Little Endian	Byte
12345 (short)	0x30 0x39	0x39 0x30	0 1
123456789 (long)	0x07 0x5B 0xCD 0x15	0x15 0xCD 0x5B 0x07	0 1 2 3
1234567890123 (long long)	0x00 0x00 0x01 0x1F 0x71 0xFB 0x04 0xCB	0xCB 0x04 0xFB 0x71 0x1F 0x01 0x00 0x00	0 1 2 3 4 5 6 7

Example 5.9
Encodings of Data Types in CORBA's CDR

The above figure shows examples of different length integers that are supported by CORBA and how they are encoded in little and big-endian representation. Floating-point numbers are represented in the IEEE standard format and again there are little- and big-endian representations. Octets are bytes, which are uninterpreted and transferred into the byte stream without any conversion. Boolean values occupy one byte; TRUE is represented as 1 while FALSE is represented as 0. Enumeration types are mapped to longs and represented as such.

CORBA object references are opaque data structures; CORBA vendors do not have to disclose how they implement object references to application programmers or to other vendors. Hence, a reference to an object that is valid within an ORB of one vendor is meaningless within an ORB of a different vendor. The CDR therefore introduces the concept of interoperable object references (IORs). An *interoperable object reference* includes a set of *profiles* that allow references to be annotated with the ORB in which they are valid. Figure 5.13 shows the type definition of interoperable object references in CORBA/IDL.

Figure 5.13
CORBA/IDL Definition of
Interoperable Object
References

```
module IOP {
  typedef unsigned long ProfileId;
  const ProfileId TAG_INTERNET_IOP = 0;
  const ProfileId TAG_MULTIPLE_COMPONENTS = 1;
  struct TaggedProfile {
    ProfileId tag; sequence <octet> profile_data;
  };
  struct IOR {
    string type_id;
    sequence <TaggedProfile> profiles;
  };
```

An IOR includes the type name of the object as a string and a sequence of profiles. Each profile has a `ProfileID` that is given by the OMG to ORB vendors. It contains a sequence of bytes that defines the object reference in the format supported by the ORB of that vendor. Whenever an interoperability bridge needs to pass an object reference from a client ORB to a server ORB it creates a 'proxy' reference containing the IOR. If that proxy reference is passed to another ORB, the proxy reference and the server ORB `ProfileID` are added as another profile to the IOR. In this way, it becomes possible to trace the original object. As the IOR and profiles are standard CORBA records they can be encoded in CDR using the mechanisms that we discussed.

5.3.3 Resolution in the Application Layer

 Middleware can only resolve heterogeneity if it knows how data are structured.

If heterogeneity is resolved by middleware, the middleware must understand the construction of the complex data structures that are transmitted during requests. The complex data structures must, therefore, be exposed to the middleware in the form of type definitions in the interface definition language. Then the middleware can perform transformations to a standardized data representation format transparently for the application developer.

There may be good reasons why application developers choose not to disclose the structure of the application data to the middleware. In the example of the Boeing aircraft configuration management system, bulk engineering data has to be transmitted between database servers and the engineering workstations. The application developers have chosen not to expose the structure of the data for the following reasons:

1. CORBA does not have to perform any computation with the engineering data that it transfers.

2. The interface definition between the server database and the engineering workstation, which had to be defined in CORBA/IDL, would have been unnecessarily complicated. They would have slowed down the compilation time for the interface definition and increased the number of client and server stubs that would have had to be generated;

3. Transforming the data from its native representation into the types defined in IDL would have imposed an unnecessary overhead; and

4. Transmission of the complex data structures would have required complicated marshalling and unmarshalling and, therefore, would have been much slower than just transmitting a byte stream.

If the middleware is unaware of the internal structure of the data that it transfers, we call this *uninterpreted data*. The problem of resolving data heterogeneity, however, also exists for uninterpreted data. In the Boeing example, data representations on the engineering workstations are likely to be different from the representations that prevail on Sequent database machines. In this subsection, we therefore study principles for resolving data heterogeneity at the application level.

The techniques and languages that have been developed for resolution of heterogeneity at the application level are often domain-specific. In this way they can provide support for data manipulation and heterogeneity resolution that is geared towards the application area and the particular type of complex data that are handled and need to be transmitted in that application domain.

Domain-specific languages may be used to structure complex application data.

There are several examples of such domain-specific approaches. STEP [ISO 10303-1, 1994] is defined as a standard mechanism for the exchange of engineering data and was, in fact, used in the Boeing configuration database. ASN.1 [ISO 8824-1, 1998] is used to define messages that are exchanged in communication protocols and is extensively used in telecommunication. SGML [ISO 8879, 1986] and XML [Bray et al., 1998] allow the definition of markup languages that can be used to define structured documents. XML is a simplified version of SGML and will be used widely for exchange of structured information over the Internet. We now take a closer look at XML and we will then generalize the principles and see how they apply in the other approaches.

XML facilitates the resolution of data heterogeneity. By definition, any XML document is a stream consisting only of ISO 10646 characters. This definition facilitates exchange of data in a heterogeneous setting. In order to facilitate the exchange of other atomic data types, such as integers and floating-point numbers, distributed components transform them to and from a UCS representation.

XML supports the definition of a set of markup tags relating to the content of documents, thus delivering both extensibility and potential for validation. Markup tags can be defined for different type constructors so that complex data structures can be built. Thus XML provides a data standard that can encode the content, semantics and schemata for a wide variety of cases – whether as a wire format for sending data between client and server, a transfer format for sharing data between applications, or a persistent storage format on disk.

XML provides a set of element types, which serve to define types of documents and are referred to as Document Type Definitions (DTDs). A DTD contains a set of rules to control how documents and tags are structured, which elements are presented and the structural relationship between the elements for documents of a particular type. A DTD contains the definition of the syntax of an XML document, that is DTDs are schemas for documents.

XML provides a general method for describing data. It allows identification, exchange and processing of distributed data in a manner that is mutually understood. Programmers can build simple parsers to read XML data, making it a good format for interchanging data. It is designed to be used straightforwardly over the Internet and to support a wide variety of applications. XML maintains the separation of presentation details from structured data and, therefore, it allows the integration of data from diverse sources. XML seeks to achieve a compromise between flexibility, simplicity, and readability by both humans and machines.

The XML specification refers to two components: the XML processor and the XML application. The XML processor is the parser that loads the XML document and any related files, checks to make sure that the document follows all the necessary rules (set forth in its DTD), and builds a document tree structure that can be passed on to the application. The XML application acts upon the tree structure and processes the data it contains. XML parsers are available as off-the-shelf components. Applications can then navigate the parse tree of the structured document using an application programming interface that is known as the *document object model* (DOM).

DOM [Apparao et al., 1998] defines the logical structure of a document and how to access and manipulate it. DOM allows programmers to build documents, navigate their structures, and add, modify, or delete elements and content. In DOM, the documents have a logical structure that is similar to a tree. However, DOM is a logical model that may be implemented in any convenient manner, not necessarily as a tree. The name *Document Object Model* reflects the modelling of documents using objects and the model encompasses the structure of a document and its behaviour. DOM identifies the interfaces and objects used to represent and manipulate a document, the semantics of these interfaces and objects, and the relationships and collaborations among these interfaces and objects. DOM consists of two parts: DOM Core and DOM HTML. The DOM Core contains interfaces for accessing and manipulating XML documents and serves as the basis for DOM HTML. The DOM HTML contains interfaces for accessing and manipulating HTML contents.

XML has been used to define numerous domain-specific document types, which are referred to as *instances*. Figure 5.14 shows how some examples relate to HTML, XML and SGML. The *Chemical Markup Language* (CML) [OMF, 1998] has been defined to express the composition of molecules in XML. The *Bioinformatic Sequence Markup Language* (BSML) [Spitzner, 1998] is an XML DTD that is used for the storage and exchange of graphical genomic data. The *Open Financial Exchange* (OFE) markup language is defined for the exchange of structured financial data. The *Mathematical Markup Language* (MML) [Ion and Miner, 1998] is defined for exchanging mathematical formulae in a structured way. The *Stream-based Model Interchange Format* determines a standard structure for the exchange of UML models and was adopted by the OMG as the *eXchange of Model Information* (XMI) specification [Object Management Group, 1998d].

The DTD in Figure 5.15 defines that a `Package` may either be empty or consist of a name, a visibility and, among other components, a sequence of `ownedElements`.

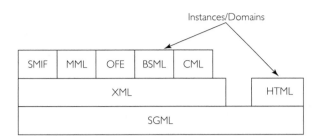

Figure 5.14
Domain-Specific XML Instances

```
<!ELEMENT Model_Management.Package (
        Foundation.Core.ModelElement.name,
        Foundation.Core.ModelElement.visibility,
        ...
        Foundation.Core.Namespace.ownedElement*)?>
<!ELEMENT Foundation.Core.Namespace.ownedElement (
        Foundation.Core.Class |
        Foundation.Core.Interface |
        Foundation.Core.Attribute |
        Foundation.Core.BehavioralFeature |
        Foundation.Core.Operation
        ...)>
<!ELEMENT Foundation.Core.Class (
        Foundation.Core.ModelElement.name,
        Foundation.Core.ModelElement.visibility,
        Foundation.Core.Namespace.ownedElement*,
        ...)>
<!ELEMENT Foundation.Core.ModelElement.name
        (#PCDATA | XMI.reference)* >
<!ELEMENT Foundation.Core.ModelElement.visibility EMPTY >
<!ATTLIST Foundation.Core.ModelElement.visibility
        xmi.value (public | protected | private) #REQUIRED>
```

Figure 5.15
Excerpt of XMI Specification for
Exchange of UML Models

An `ownedElement` can be a `Class`, an `Interface`, an `Attribute`, a `BehaviouralFeature`, an `Operation` and further components. A `Class` has a name, a visibility and again a sequence of `ownedElements`. A name is either a character sequence or a reference to an XML element. The visibility is defined as an empty element that has an attribute whose values can be either `public`, `protected` or `private`.

XMI and the other XML instances have in common that they support the definition of application-specific structured text that can be parsed by an XML parser and can then be traversed by application components using DOM. This can be exploited for the encoding of complex data structures that are then transmitted using object-oriented middleware. In the example of the UML models, we could envisage two UML CASE tools that are distributed across two heterogeneous platforms. If one tool has to transmit model information to the other, it would encode the UML model using the XMI DTD and then pass it in an object request using a byte stream parameter. Heterogeneity is resolved by the fact that both tools use an agreed format — a sequence of UCS characters — to and from which locally-used character sets and numbers are transformed. The use of a byte stream as a request parameter minimizes the performance overhead on the part of the middleware.

Application-level resolution is appropriate if complex data structures would create too big a marshalling overhead.

Example 5.10
XML Document Excerpt that is
an Instance of XMI DTD

```
<Model_Management.Package>
  <Foundation.Core.ModelElement.name>
   Soccer
  </Foundation.Core.ModelElement.name>
  <Foundation.Core.ModelElement.visibility xmi.value="public">
  </Foundation.Core.ModelElement.visibility>
  <Foundation.Core.Class>
   <Foundation.Core.ModelElement.name>
    Team
   </Foundation.Core.ModelElement.name>
   <Foundation.Core.ModelElement.visibility xmi.value="public">
   </Foundation.Core.ModelElement.visibility>
   <Foundation.Core.Attribute>
    ...
   </Foundation.Core.Attribute>
   <Foundation.Core.Operation>
    ...
   </Foundation.Core.Operation>
   ...
  </Foundation.Core.Class>
</Model_Management.Package>
```

This is an instance of the XMI document type definition in Figure 5.15. It represents an excerpt of the UML class diagram that was shown in Example 2.3 on Page 38. Using XMI, we have represented a UML model, a very complex data structure, in a standardized way with a byte stream of UCS characters.

The XML approach to application-level transport protocols is, in fact, very similar to the other approaches. XML, SGML, ASN.1 and STEP all support the definition of a domain-specific syntax that can be used for the exchange of structured information. Like UCS in XML, they all specify standard representations for a set of limited atomic data types. There are also domain-specific instances available. STEP defines *Application Protocols* for several engineering domains, such as the spatial configuration of process plants. ASN.1 defines instances for different forms of encoding rules. ASN.1 type definitions are often transmitted together with ASN.1 instances of these types. Which of these application level transport protocols is chosen depends on the application domain and the availability of domain-specific type definitions. The principles for using them with object-oriented middleware are the same; the middleware does not interpret the structured information that it transfers and merely treats them as, possibly long, sequences of bytes.

5.3.4 Resolution by Platform

Homogeneity of objects
can be achieved by
virtual machines.

We have discussed two approaches where data heterogeneity was resolved in the presentation and application layers. The third way to resolve data heterogeneity among different hardware platforms and operating systems is to introduce a platform above the operating system that is not concerned with distributed communication but solely with interpretation of code and data in a standardized form. Such a platform is often referred to as a *virtual machine.*

The concept of virtual machines is not new. IBM's mainframe operating system, CMS, included the concept of a virtual machine whose purpose was to give each user that shared the mainframe a virtual computer. UCSD Pascal [Overgaard and Strinfellow, 1985], an early Pascal compiler, produced P-code that was then interpreted on different hardware by a virtual machine called the P-System. Virtual machines had a renaissance with Java's success. The JVM primarily achieves portability of Java byte code across many different hardware platforms. The required standardization to achieve this portability, however, also resolves data heterogeneity problems. Let us therefore focus on those parts of the JVM specification [Lindholm and Yellin, 1998] that contribute to this resolution.

The JVM specification resolves data heterogeneity by precisely standardizing the representation of Java's atomic data types, type construction primitives and object references. This precise specification does not leave any room for interpretation by different implementors of Java virtual machines. Hence all data that are passed as parameters to Java remote method invocations have the same representation, by specification, even if they are executed within two separate virtual machines.

The Java virtual machine achieves homogeneity of distributed objects.

The JVM specification defines the representations for Java's atomic types as follows:

1. `boolean` is represented as an `int`;
2. `byte` values are 8-bit signed two-complement integers;
3. `short` values are 16-bit signed two-complement integers;
4. `int` values are 32-bit signed two-complement integers;
5. `long` values are 64-bit signed two-complement integers;
6. `char` values are 16-bit UCS characters;
7. `float` values are 32-bit IEEE 754 floating-point numbers; and
8. `double` values are 64-bit IEEE 754 floating-point numbers.

The reader will recall that object references that can be transmitted as parameters of remote method invocations have to refer to remote objects. Object references to non-remote object references cannot be used as parameters as these objects are copied by value. The implementations of remote references that are generated by `rmic` implement `RemoteRef`, a subtype of interface `Serializable`. Hence, the serialization protocol defines the representation of remote references.

Java only has one type constructor, which allows construction of arrays of varying length. The JVM specification does not demand how arrays are to be represented in memory. It rather specifies the behaviour of a set of array manipulation instructions. These include creation of new arrays, access to elements of arrays, storage in array elements and access to the length of an array.

Unlike COM and CORBA, Java/RMI can pass objects by value to remote method invocations. These objects may have instance and class variables that can contain atomic values, references to other serializable objects or arrays of atomic values and references. For any of those, the data representation is standardized as stated above. The order in which these are arranged in the transmitted byte stream is defined by the classes itself in the implementation of `readObject` and `writeObject`, which are demanded by `Java.io.Serializable`.

We have now seen that any data that can be passed as a parameter to a remote method invocation either already is or can be constructed from a standardized data representation. Hence Java/RMI does not have to take any explicit measures to resolve heterogeneity. This is entirely resolved by the execution platform, the JVM.

Key Points

▶ We have identified three dimensions in which heterogeneity can occur. These are different programming languages, different middleware and different data representation schemes.

▶ CORBA and COM resolve programming language heterogeneity by defining a common object model and providing an interface definition language. Bindings then define a bidirectional mapping between the middleware object model and the programming language object model.

▶ The implementation of programming language bindings is achieved in application programming interfaces and interface definition language compilers.

▶ Middleware heterogeneity is resolved by interoperability and interworking specifications. Both enable middleware that is provided by different vendors to implement jointly a single object request.

▶ Interoperability specifications define protocols that govern how different implementations of the same middleware jointly implement object requests. Interoperability specifications can be defined at different degrees of detail. The CORBA interoperability specification defines a family of protocols.

▶ The GIOP protocol defines the detailed layout for types of message that are exchanged across a connection-oriented transport.

▶ The IIOP protocol instantiates GIOP for TCP/IP-based connections and defines how an object request broker at a client can establish a connection with a server-side ORB using TCP/IP. The IIOP protocol is also used to implement interworking between Java/RMI and CORBA.

▶ Interworking specifications govern how different middleware systems participate in one object request. An interworking specification has to define how the object models of the participating middleware map onto each other. The COM/CORBA interworking specification does that for COM and CORBA.

▶ Data heterogeneity that may be induced due to different processor architecture or as a result of using different programming languages can be resolved in three ways: at the presentation layer, at the application layer and by the platform.

▶ A resolution at the presentation layer maps heterogeneous data representations into a standardized form, such as XDR, CDR or NDR. This approach is used between different implementations of COM and different implementations of CORBA.

▶ Data heterogeneity resolution can be achieved at the application layer if explicit representations of the data types are sent together with object requests.

Mechanisms that allow types to be expressed above the presentation layer, such as XML, SGML, STEP and ASN.1, can be used for that purpose.

▶ Data heterogeneity may also be resolved by the platform. Java/RMI is an example where this approach is used. The Java Virtual Machine specification defines precisely how data is to be represented. Hence, implementations of the JVM for different operating systems resolve data heterogeneity and RMI does not have to take data heterogeneity into account.

Self Assessment

5.1   We have argued that the approach of using language bindings to a common IDL reduces the number of language mappings. When is this not the case?

5.2   What is the position with respect to transparency if there is no common interface definition language?

5.3   How is multiple inheritance in CORBA/IDL treated in the Ada programming language binding?

5.4   What is the difference between interworking and interoperability?

5.5   Explain situations in which you would wish to use more than one middleware.

5.6   How does the designer of a client object use IIOP?

5.7   What is a bridge?

5.8   What are the differences between inline and request-level bridging?

5.9   What type of bridging is prescribed by the COM/CORBA Interworking specification?

5.10   Identify the three ways to resolve data heterogeneity.

5.11   Explain the difference between little-endian and big-endian data representations.

5.12   CORBA does not convert little- into big-endian representations when sending a message. Where is the conversion done? What is the advantage of this approach?

5.13   COM and CORBA resolve data heterogeneity using a standardized data representation. Under which circumstances would you choose to resolve data heterogeneity yourself at the application layer?

5.14   Is it possible to resolve data heterogeneity, middleware heterogeneity and programming language heterogeneity in a way that is completely transparent to client and server object programmers?

Further Reading

The six programming language bindings of CORBA/IDL to C, C++, Smalltalk, Ada, Cobol and Java are specified in detail in Chapters 19–24 of [Object Management Group, 1998c]. The bindings are defined for both client and server object implementation.

[Barret et al., 1996] suggest a different approach to resolving language heterogeneity. They argue that there are rarely more than three programming languages involved in a distributed system and that it is then cheaper to define peer-to-peer interoperability links between the languages. A similar problem to that of language heterogeneity for distributed objects also exists for object persistence. Object database systems provide the database technology that is necessary to store objects persistently. The ODMG-93 specification [Cattell, 1993] standardizes such databases. Object databases can be accessed, queried and modified from programs that are written in different programming languages. The approach that the ODMG-93 standard uses for object databases to resolve this programming language heterogeneity is very similar to the ideas presented here. They define an Object Definition Language (ODL) by means of which the schema of an object database can be specified and the standard then determines three bindings of programming languages to ODL. The interoperability between different CORBA implementations is specified in Chapters 10–14 of [Object Management Group, 1998c]. The interworking specification between CORBA and COM is provided in Chapters 15–17 of the same specification. A more easily readable introduction to COM/CORBA interworking is provided by [Rosen et al., 1998].

There is a substantial amount of literature available on standardized data representations. The Common Data Representation of CORBA is defined in Chapter 13 of [Object Management Group, 1998c] as part of the General Inter-ORB Protocol definition. The transformation of character sets is defined in the general introduction to interoperability in Chapter 11 of that specification.

The Network Data Representation (NDR) is an extension of XDR and was adopted as part of the Remote Procedure Call Standard that is contained in the Distributed Computing Environment (DCE). NDR is specified in Chapter 14 of [Open Group, 1997].

The use of a markup language for client–server applications is discussed in [Chang and Harkey, 1998]. A good introduction to XML is provided by [Bradley, 1998].

6

Dynamic Object Requests

Learning Objectives

In this chapter, we will understand the differences between static requests, which are defined when clients are compiled, and dynamic requests, which are determined when a client is executed. We will become acquainted with dynamic invocation interfaces and the reflection primitives that are needed for dynamic requests. We will see how dynamic invocation interfaces are used and we will recognize the importance of providing type information at run-time for the type safety of dynamic object requests. We will comprehend how dynamic requests can be used for the definition of generic clients that can interact with any type of server object. We will acquaint ourselves with the reflection primitives that are available in current object-oriented middleware and understand their similarities and differences.

Chapter Outline

6.1 **Motivating Examples**
6.2 **Dynamic Invocation**
6.3 **Reflection**
6.4 **Designing Generic Applications**

An object request that
is defined when the
client is compiled is a
static request.

In Chapter 3, we introduced the concept of a client stub that can be invoked using a local method call in order to make a request. This local method invocation defines the request at the time when the client is compiled. The object-oriented middleware systems that we discussed in Chapter 4 use such client stubs. All these middleware systems provide compilers that generate client stubs from an interface definition of the server object and in that way make sure that actual parameters passed to the client stub match the formal server object parameters. The generation of client stubs from interface definition induces a dependency. It means that client objects cannot be built before the server object is defined. It also means that client objects might have to be re-compiled when the server interface changes.

There may be a variety of reasons why it is undesirable to have this dependency. It may be necessary to define a client object that can request operations from any type of server object. Such clients are often defined before the interfaces of their server objects are known. It may also be undesirable to couple client objects tightly with the interfaces of server objects. Particularly in applications that have to execute non-stop it is not possible to shut down a client object just because the signature of its server object has changed, recompile it and then restart it.

An object request that
is defined when the
client executes is a
dynamic request.

In this chapter, we will study another type of primitive, dynamic object requests. Dynamic object requests do not assume the existence of a client stub. They explicitly treat requests as objects and use dynamic invocation interfaces provided by middleware to define object requests 'on-the-fly', that is while the client object executes. Thus dynamic invocation interfaces provide designers with the ability to defer the definition of an object request from compile-time to run-time of the client object.

One of the benefits of the static invocation with client stubs is that the compiler with which the client is compiled can establish type safety; it can check whether the requested operation is actually exported by the server object and whether the actual parameters passed match the formal parameters that the server expects. When requests are defined at run-time, the client compiler cannot perform such checks. In order to make type-safe dynamic invocations, client programmers have to formulate run-time enquiries using a reflection interface that makes the type definitions of the server object available at run-time.

We start with examples that demonstrate the need for genericity. We then outline the principles of dynamic invocation and review how it is achieved in CORBA and COM. We then present principles for handling reflection and again review how this information is made available in current middleware. We finally discuss how these two primitives are exploited for the construction of generic applications.

6.1 Motivating Examples

6.1.1 Object Browser

Assume that you are in the position of a vendor of an object-oriented middleware. You want to deliver the middleware and a development environment. Among other tools, this environment should include an object browser so that developers can inspect the state of the

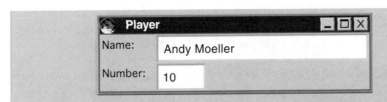

The object browser used for the development of our soccer management application shows the state of an object of type `Player` by showing the values of the player's `Name` and `Number` attributes.

server objects that they construct. Example 6.1 shows the user interface of such an object browser.

This browser will be constructed by the vendor of the middleware. The types of objects to be shown in the browser will be defined by users of the middleware after the middleware has been installed. Hence, the interfaces are defined a considerable amount of time after the browser has been compiled. This means that the browser cannot make any assumptions about the types of object that it is going to display. In particular, it does not have an interface definition of the types from which a client stub could be derived. This browser is an example of a generic object. It needs to defer the definition of requests that obtain attribute values to the time when it is executed. The browser will also need to enquire about type information at run-time so that it knows about the type of the object and can find out which attributes the object has.

6.1.2 Generic Request-Level Bridges

In the previous chapter, we introduced the concept of bridges that are used to mediate between middleware of different vendors. We saw that inline bridges are built into the object-oriented middleware in order to implement an interoperability or interworking specification. We also discussed request-level bridges, which can be built by application developers.

Let us assume that we want to write user interfaces to our soccer management application in Java and that some of the soccer management servers are written in COM. Assuming we do not want to use Microsoft's variant of Java so that we remain compatible with standard Java, we would have to interface our Java user interface components with the COM server objects. We could do that by building request-level bridges.

Request-level bridges can either be built in a type-specific or a generic way. Type-specific bridges are server objects that call a client stub that was produced using the server's middleware. In our example, a type-specific bridge is a Java object that invokes server operations using COM interface proxies. It is appropriate to build type-specific bridges if only a few object types should be made available in the realm of another middleware. If, however, all soccer management server objects should be made available in Java, as in our example,

Example 6.1
Object Brower

Example 6.2
Generic Request-level Bridge

type-specific bridges are inappropriate. This is because new bridges have to be added whenever a new type of soccer management server object becomes available. Moreover, bridges would have to be modified whenever the interface of a server object changes.

Generic bridges overcome this problem. They do not rely on the invocation of client stubs or interface proxies to forward requests. Generic bridges use primitives available from the middleware to create requests during run-time. In our example, a generic bridge would request operation invocation from the soccer management server components using COM's dynamic invocation interface.

6.2 Dynamic Invocation

6.2.1 Principles

Any object request, whether it is static or dynamic, has to define the following items:

Dynamic object requests have to define the same concerns as static requests.

1. The server object from which operation execution is requested;
2. The name of the operation whose execution is requested
3. The actual parameters of the request execution; and
4. A data structure that is made available for the operation results.

Static requests define these by invoking a client stub. Dynamic invocation interfaces do not assume the availability of client stubs in order to determine the operation whose execution is requested from a server object. Instead, they invoke the dynamic invocation interface that is exported by the object-oriented middleware. Dynamic invocation interfaces have to find a different representation for the above items.

The server object can be identified as an object reference. The operation can be identified using its IDL name or as an internal representation that is derived from that name. Actual parameter lists can be provided as sequences of name–value pairs and the operation result can be deposited at some address that is provided by the client. The dynamic invocation interfaces then invoke the identified operation from the identified server object and pass the parameter list as part of the request. Upon return, the parameter list includes the output parameters and the operation result is made available to the client.

Dynamic object requests are prone to violating type safety.

There is, however, a problem with the type safety of this approach. In the example of the object browser, the attribute value retrieval operations whose names are passed as arguments to the dynamic invocation interface must actually be exported by the object to be browsed. The type of the object, therefore, must actually export the operation that is requested and the numbers and types of the actual parameters must match the formal parameter list of the exported operation. For static requests, the interface and programming language compilers ensure type safety, if the programming languages are statically typed. In order to ensure type safety for dynamic requests, access to type information is needed at run-time.

For this reason, an interface for dynamic requests in a middleware is always accompanied by a repository or registry that manages object type definitions. That repository is able to respond to enquiries of clients about the type of server objects. The object browser, for instance, first consults the repository and enquires about the attribute value retrieval operations that are exported by the type of the object to be displayed. That information can then be used to make type-safe dynamic requests.

 Clients need reflection interfaces to enquire about type information at run-time.

In the next two sections, we review how these principles are applied in CORBA and COM. We will introduce CORBA's Dynamic Invocation Interface (DII) and COM's `IDispatch` interface. Both of these interfaces support the definition of object requests at run-time. Although Java supports a Reflection API that would in principle be capable of handling dynamic requests, this API is not yet integrated with RMI.

6.2.2 Dynamic Invocation in CORBA

Let us revisit Figure 4.2 on Page 97 for an overview of the components of CORBA that are involved in object requests. On the client side, these are client stubs, the dynamic invocation interface (DII) and the ORB interface. We discussed the use of client stubs for static requests in Chapter 4. The DII and the ORB Interface enable clients to make dynamic requests.

Unlike the client stubs that implement static requests, dynamic requests in the CORBA DII are themselves objects. Figure 6.1 shows an overview of the interactions between client, request and server objects. A client object creates a `Request` object in order to request the execution of an operation dynamically. The creation of the request object is supported by any CORBA object. The `Request` object supports defining the actual parameters for the requested operation. `Request` objects export operations that enable the client object to issue the request. The operation result can also be determined from the request object.

Dynamic CORBA object requests are themselves objects.

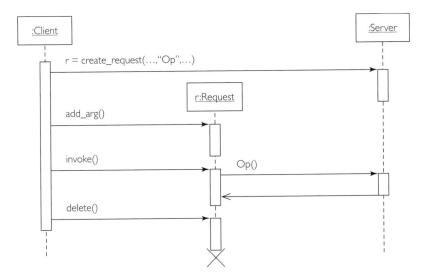

Figure 6.1

Client and Server Interactions for Dynamic Invocations in CORBA

Figure 6.2
Interface of CORBA Root Object Type

```
interface Object {
    Status create_request (
        in Context ctx, // context object for operation
        in Identifier operation, // intended operation
        in NVList arg_list, // args to operation
        inout NamedValue result, // operation result
        out Request request, // newly created request
        in Flags req_flags // request flags
    );
    InterfaceDef get_interface ();
    ...
};
```

⊙━ Every CORBA object can create request objects.

Figure 6.2 shows the interface that is needed for the creation of Request objects. This is the CORBA type Object, which is defined as part of the ORB interface. It includes an operation that creates a Request object. Every CORBA object inherits this operation. Therefore, any CORBA object can create a Request object. The operation to create requests has parameters to determine the operation identifier and a list of name value pairs (NVList) that are used as actual parameters. It produces as an output parameter the desired request object.

Figure 6.3
Interface of CORBA Request Objects

```
interface Request {
    Status add_arg (in Identifier name, // argument name
                    in TypeCode arg_type, // argument data type
                    in void * value, // argument value to be added
                    in long len, // length/count of argument value
                    in Flags arg_flags // argument flags
                );
    Status invoke (in Flags invoke_flags); // invocation flags
    Status delete ();
    Status send (in Flags invoke_flags);// invocation flags
    Status get_response (in Flags response_flags // response flags
                        ) raises (WrongTransaction);
};
```

⊙━ Dynamic invocation interface supports making a request and obtaining a result.

Figure 6.3 shows the interface for object type Request. The interface provides an operation add_arg to add further arguments, so that further request parameters can be added. The interface also exports operations invoke and send, which are used to issue the dynamically-defined request. These two operations differ in their synchronization and we will discuss this difference in detail in Chapter 7. The client can use the result, once the request is completed, and the request object can be disposed of.

⊙━ The client designer decides whether the object request is static or dynamic.

Whether a request is static or dynamic is entirely decided by the designer of the client. Designers of CORBA server objects do not have to take any measures in order to support dynamic requests. In fact, from a server object's point of view, the distinction between dynamic and static requests does not exist and server objects cannot distinguish whether a request was made through a client stub or a request object.

6.2.3 The COM IDispatch Interface

COM also supports the dynamic definition of requests. The motivation for COM is partly architectural. Microsoft wanted to make COM components available for use from languages such as JavaScript or Visual Basic Script. These scripting languages are used extensively to customize applications that are built around Microsoft's Office Applications. JavaScript and Visual Basic Script are not compiled but interpreted. This means in particular, that there is no executable machine code for client objects, which are written in these scripting languages. Hence, there is no executable code to which the server's interface proxies could be linked. This demanded a mechanism that supports the invocation of COM methods without the need for interface proxies.

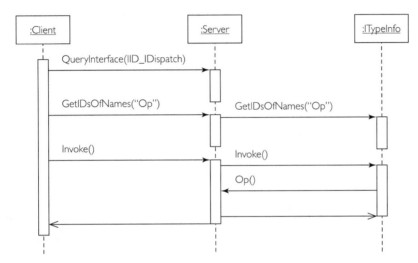

Figure 6.4
Client and Server Interactions for Dynamic Invocations in COM

Figure 6.4 is a sequence diagram that presents an overview of how dynamic object requests are achieved in COM. It shows all main invocations that are needed for a COM client object to invoke an operation from a COM server object dynamically. The client first checks whether the server supports dynamic invocation by querying interface IDispatch. The client then obtains an identifier for the operation that it wants to invoke and passes that identifier to the Invoke operation that performs the dynamic object request.

This dynamic invocation mechanism is encapsulated in an interface that is called IDispatch, shown in Figure 6.5. Operations of those COM objects that implement IDispatch can be invoked dynamically. Interfaces that inherit from IDispatch are referred to as *dual interfaces* because they can be accessed both dynamically and statically. The two IDispatch operations that are needed for dynamic invocation are GetIDsOfNames and Invoke. Example 6.3 shows such a dual interface for soccer player objects.

Dynamic invocation in COM is based on tokens that identify operation and parameter names. Such a token is referred to as a DISPID in COM. Operation GetIDsOfNames implements a mapping between character strings and DISPIDs. A client wishing to make a dynamic invocation uses this operation to obtain the tokens that correspond to the opera-

COM clients pass DISPID tokens to identify the operation that needs to be called.

Figure 6.5

COM IDispatch Interface

```
typedef struct tagDISPPARAMS {
  [size_is(cArgs)] VARIANTARG *rgvarg; //Array of arguments
  [size_is(cNamedArgs)] DISPID *rgdispidNamedArgs; //arg dispIDs
  unsigned int cArgs; //Number of total arguments
  unsigned int cNamedArgs; //Number of named arguments
} DISPPARAMS;

interface IDispatch : IUnknown {
  ...
  HRESULT GetIDsOfNames([in] REFIID riid,              //reserved
          [in,size_is(cNames)] LPOLESTR *rgszNames,//method+pars
          [in] UINT cNames,                            //No of Names
          [in] LCID lcid,                              //locale ID
          [out,size_is(cNames)] DISPID *rgdispid); //name tokens
  HRESULT Invoke([in] DISPID dispID,          //token of op
          [in] REFIID riid,                   //reserved
          [in] LCID lcid,                     //locale ID
          [in] unsigned short wFlags,         //method, put or get
          [in,out] DISPPARAMS *pDispParams,   //logical pars
          [out] VARIANT *pVarResult,          //logical result
          [out] EXCEPINFO *pExcepInfo,        //IErrorInfo pars
          [out] UINT *puArgErr);              //type errors
};
```

Example 6.3

Dual COM Soccer Player
Interface

```
[object, dual, uuid(75DA6450-DD0E-00d1-8B59-0089C73915CB]
interface DIPlayer: IDispatch {
  [id(1),propget] HRESULT Name([out] BSTR val);
  [id(2),propget] HRESULT Number([out] short val);
  [id(3)] HRESULT book([in] Date val)
};
```

tion name and to all parameter names. The parameter name tokens are then used to create a DISPPARAMS structure, which contains two lists, one with the actual arguments and the other with the tokens of the parameter names.

DISPIDs render
dynamic object
requests more type-
safe and efficient.

The use of these tokens has two main advantages over CORBA's approach of just character strings: it contributes to type safety and is more efficient. Clients will get to know before making the dynamic invocation whether or not the server object actually supports the operation whose execution the client requests. The tokens are implemented as integers which means that the dynamic invocation can be implemented more efficiently as integers are easier to compare than character strings. The price for this, however, is the additional invocation to get the token information.

The dynamic operation invocation is performed by calling Invoke. The client identifies the operation that is to be called using the operation name's DISPID and passes the data structure of type DISPPARAMS in order to provide the actual parameters. A C++ implementation of the IDispatch operations is shown in Example 6.4.

```
class Player : IPlayer {
  LONG m_cRef; // COM reference count
  ITypeInfo *m_pTypeInfo; //pointer to type description
  //IUnknown, IDispatch & DIPlayer Methods omitted for brevity

  Player(void) : m_cRef(0) {
    HRESULT hr; ITypeLib *ptl=0;
    hr=LoadRegTypeLib(LIBID_SoccerLib,1,0,0,&ptl);
    hr=ptl->GetTypeInfoOfGuid(IID_DIPlayer,&m_pTypeInfo);
    ptl->Release();
  }
}

STDMETHODIMP Player::GetIDsOfNames(REFIID riid, OLECHAR
                                   **pNames,
                                   UINT cNames, LCID lcid,
                                   DISPID *pdispids) {
  return(m_pTypeInfo->GetIDsOfNames(pNames,cNames,pdispids);
}

STDMETHODIMP Player::Invoke(DISPID id, REFIID riid,
                            LCID lcid, WORD wFlags,
                            DISPPARAMS *pd, VARIANT *pVarResult,
                            EXCEPINFO *pe, UINT *pu) {
  void *pvThis = static_cast<IPlayer*>(this);
  return m_pTypeInfo->Invoke(pvThis,id,wFlags,pd,
                             pVarResult,pe,pu);
}
```

Example 6.4
Implementation of `IDispatch` operations in C++

The constructor of class `Player` initializes the reference to the type library that is stored in `m_pTypeInfo`. The reference is then used to delegate calls to `GetIDsOfNames` and `Invoke` to the type library.

We note that dynamic invocation is not transparent to COM server object designers. Unlike CORBA designers, they have to take explicit measures to make their server objects available for dynamic invocation; they have to implement the `IDispatch` interface. This implementation is, however, straightforward because the designers can rely on a powerful COM component, the type library.

Dynamic object requests are not transparent to COM server programmers.

6.3 Reflection

The dynamic invocation interfaces that we have just discussed facilitate dynamic requests. Clients can request the execution of operations, if they only know the name of the operation. This leads to a new problem: how do clients discover the operations that an object supports? Speaking in terms of our object browser example, how can the browser find out which

Clients need to enquire whether the servers support the operations that they want to request dynamically.

attributes the object has. This information is a necessary pre-requisite to be able to obtain the attribute values using the dynamic object requests.

In this section, we discuss the provision of type information in CORBA and COM through reflection interfaces. We reveal the principles of reflection and we discuss how they are applied in CORBA's Interface Repository and COM's `ITypeInfo` interface.

6.3.1 Principles

The interface definition language compilers of object-oriented middleware collect type information at the time when server interface definitions are compiled. They use that type information for consistency checks between the interfaces, for example to check whether the supertype identified in an interface does exist. That type information is also extremely useful during compilation of client and server object implementations. It can be used to ensure that the operations that a client object requests are provided by the server object and that the operations that a server object implements are indeed the ones that are declared in the interface. Hence, the type information has to be stored between compilation of the interface and compilation of the client or server object implementation. This storage is achieved by associating types with classes and non-object types that are included in the client and server stubs that the IDL compiler produces. It is then captured again by the compilers that are used to compile client and server object implementations.

We have seen in the previous section, that it is not sufficient to retain type information only until the client is compiled. The information may also be needed at the time when the client is executed.

Reflection interfaces provide details about the type of the server object at execution time. Reflection information is provided by some programming languages. In Smalltalk, everything is an object. This means in particular that the classes that define structure and behaviour of objects are objects themselves and that at run-time the classes can be traversed to discover the features of an object. Java has a Reflection API that can be used, for example, to enquire about the operations that an object supports. Also the latest language definition of C++ includes limited reflection capabilities that are referred to as *run-time type information*; it enables the type of an object to be identified during execution time.

Reflection interfaces of programming languages cannot be used. The particular type information that has to be provided at run-time depends on the object model of the programming language, or in our case of the object-oriented middleware. The details of the type information provided for CORBA has to be different from the one for COM, which is again different from the one that should be available for Java/RMI. For this reason, we cannot rely on the reflection capabilities that are provided by a programming language. It would be provided based on the object model of that programming language rather than the object model of the middleware that we use. Moreover, we may wish to write clients using compilers that do not support the latest C++ language definition or using languages, such as Visual Basic, C or Cobol, that do not provide reflection information at all. Hence, we will have to demand that the object-oriented middleware that we use provides all the type information that was available at the time the interface definition was compiled also at the time when the client executes.

A question that arises is how are we going to organize the storage and the access to reflection information? The type information to be provided is that expressed in the interface definition. A natural choice is then to orient the structure of the reflection information along the structure of interface definitions. The nesting of declarations in interface definitions induces some hierarchy that we can exploit to organize the reflection information. In that way, we achieve a strong correspondence between the structure of the static interface definition and the dynamic provision of type information.

Reflection interfaces structure type information according to interface definition languages.

It is during compilation of interface definitions that all necessary reflection information is available. Middleware vendors have to implement the reflection information provision partly in the interface definition language compilers. The compilers gather the type information during static analysis of the interface definition and then have to store the type information in such a way that it can later be retrieved by the middleware when reflection interfaces are used to query a server object's type at client execution time.

DL compiler gathers reflection information and stores it persistently.

The particular query operations that have to be provided depend again on the object model of the middleware. In general, the reflection information has to be able to identify the type of an object. It should then be able to inform clients about the attributes that the object has and which operations the object can execute. For each operation, the details about the parameter list, result types and exceptions that it may raise should be accessible.

6.3.2 The CORBA Interface Repository

CORBA provides reflection through its *Interface Repository* (IR). The Interface Repository is an integral part of the CORBA standard and it has to be implemented by any CORBA-compliant product. The Interface Repository is filled by the CORBA/IDL compiler with type information. The detailed format that is used to store that type information is not specified by the standard, though it is assumed that it is some representation of the interfaces' Abstract Syntax Trees (AST).

Reflection is supported in CORBA's Interface Repository.

Abstract Syntax Trees

Abstract syntax trees (ASTs) are the principal data structures of any compiler. An AST is an abstract representation of the parse tree that is created by a compiler during syntax analysis (see Example 6.5). ASTs omit irrelevant information about concrete syntax and focus on the relevant contents of the compiler input. Nodes in ASTs of the CORBA Interface Repository represent declarations of the compiled interface definition. Nodes in the Interface Repository have a type that reflects the type of the declaration. Edges leading from one node to another indicate the nesting relationship between IDL declarations. Nodes have attributes that are used for storing declaration identifiers.

Interface repository operations mirror IDL abstract syntax tree.

In order to enable client programmers to access the Interface Repository, AST node types are specified in IDL itself. The standard IDL programming language bindings can be used to access the Interface Repository from within the programming language in which the client is written. The UML class diagram in Figure 6.6 shows an overview of the types defined for the Interface Repository. Type `IRObject` encapsulates the common properties of all IR node types. The node type `Container` represents common properties of those

Interface Repository types are defined in CORBA/IDL.

Example 6.5

Interface Definition as an
Abstract Syntax Tree

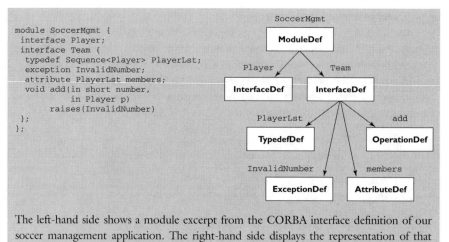

```
module SoccerMgmt {
  interface Player;
  interface Team {
    typedef Sequence<Player> PlayerLst;
    exception InvalidNumber;
    attribute PlayerLst members;
    void add(in short number,
             in Player p)
         raises(InvalidNumber)
  };
};
```

The left-hand side shows a module excerpt from the CORBA interface definition of our soccer management application. The right-hand side displays the representation of that excerpt as an abstract syntax tree.

nodes that reflect declarations that may contain nested declarations. Examples of those are modules, which may contain other modules or interface definitions. `Repository` is the type for root nodes of each Interface Repository. Node type `Contained` implements the common properties of those nodes that represent declarations that are contained within other declarations, such as operation declarations or type declarations.

Figure 6.7 shows the interface for type `InterfaceDef`. InterfaceDef is probably the most important type of the CORBA Interface Repository, as it provides the information about object types. It can be used to obtain references to interface definitions of all supertypes of the interface and it can provide a description of the interface. This `FullInterfaceDescription` contains a list of all attributes and all operations that are contained in the interface.

Figure 6.6

Types of Abstract Syntax Tree
Nodes

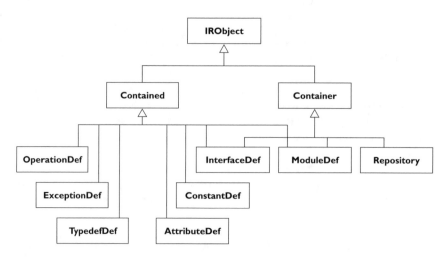

```
interface InterfaceDef : Container, Contained, IDLType {
    attribute InterfaceDefSeq base_interfaces;
    boolean is_a (in RepositoryId interface_id);
    struct FullInterfaceDescription {
        Identifier name;
        RepositoryId id;
        RepositoryId defined_in;
        VersionSpec version;
        OpDescriptionSeq operations;
        AttrDescriptionSeq attributes;
        RepositoryIdSeq base_interfaces;
        TypeCode type;
    };
    FullInterfaceDescription describe_interface();
    ...
};
```

Figure 6.7

Interface Definition of CORBA `InterfaceDef`

Locating Type Information

The most important type of information included in the Interface Repository concerns the type of objects. Clients frequently wish to enquire about an object type and therefore they need to locate an interface definition. There are three ways that the Interface Repository supports this. Client objects that have an object reference can directly obtain a reference to the type of the object. Client objects can perform queries to locate type information that they know by name. Client objects can also navigate the Interface Repository and discover all the type information that is registered.

To obtain the type of an object, clients use the operation `get_interface`, which each object inherits from `Object` as shown in Figure 6.2 on Page 151. `Get_interface` returns a reference to an `InterfaceDef` object. This reference refers to the node in the Interface Repository that contains the type of the object. In our soccer management example, if we had a reference to an object of type `Player`, we could obtain the reference to the interface definition for this type by requesting execution of `get_interface` from this object.

The `Container` object type of the Interface Repository includes two query functions: `lookup` and `lookup_name`, shown in Figure 6.8. Clients use these functions to perform associative searches for type declarations. Operation `lookup` takes as a parameter a scoped name. Clients use this operation if they know the name of the interface they are looking for and if they know in which modules the interface is contained. To locate the interface definition of `Player` in our example, a client would use the scoped name `SoccerMgmt::Player`. Operation `lookup_name` searches for identifiers that are declared somewhere in the Interface Repository. Clients can restrict the depth of the search and also limit the search results to declarations of a particular kind. To find the `Player` interface definition object using `lookup_name`, we would pass `Player` as the search name, limit the definitions we are interested in to `InterfaceDef` and restrict the search to

```
module CORBA {
    typedef sequence <Contained> ContainedSeq;
    interface Container : IRObject {
     // read interface
     Contained lookup (in ScopedName search_name);
     ContainedSeq contents (
                    in DefinitionKind limit_type,
                    in boolean exclude_inherited);
     ContainedSeq lookup_name (
                    in Identifier search_name,
                    in long levels_to_search,
                    in DefinitionKind limit_type,
                    in boolean exclude_inherited);
     ...
    };
    ...
};
```

two levels. The contained sequence that is returned would then include a reference to the interface definition of `Player`.

Finally, if we do not have an object reference whose type we want to explore and if we do not know the name of the type that we are looking for, we can explore the Interface Repository in a navigating way. Every inner node in the Interface Repository is of type `Container`, or a subtype thereof. As such it exports the operation `contents`, which we can use to enumerate the declarations that are known at the node. If we applied `contents` to the module definition node, we could obtain the two interface definitions for types `Player` and `Team`. We could then apply `contents` to the `Player` interface definition and we obtain the four children `PlayerLst`, `InvalidNumber`, `members` and `add`.

Once a client object has found the appropriate interface definition, it can use operations provided by `InterfaceDef` to enquire about details of the object type. `InterfaceDef` exports an operation `describe_interface` that returns a list of attribute descriptions and a list of operation descriptions. The attribute descriptions include for each attribute its name and type. An operation description includes the operation name, a description of the parameter list, the return type and the list of exceptions that the operation may raise.

6.3.3 The COM Type Library

 The COM reflection interface relies on type library files that the MIDL compiler produces.

Similarly to the CORBA/IDL compiler, the MIDL compiler can also be instructed to generate information that is then provided through reflection interfaces. The compiler generates tokenized type information in a type library file (ending in `.TLB`). These type library files are then read by the COM run-time environment and the information contained therein is made available to clients during execution time. Then clients can discover the unknown type of a server object. We now discuss the interface that COM provides to this type library. An overview of the interfaces that are part of the type library is shown in Figure 6.9.

Figure 6.9
Classes involved in the COM
Type Library

The entry point for access to the COM reflection interface is the type library. Its interface is `ITypeLib`. It includes operation `GetTypeInfoOfGuid`, which can be used to obtain a reference to an object implementing `ITypeInfo` for a type identified by its GUID. We have used this operation in the constructor of `Player` that we showed in Example 6.4.

The `ITypeInfo` Interface

`ITypeInfo` is the main interface to the COM type library. In fact, we have come across `ITypeInfo` already when we discussed dynamic invocation in COM and we have seen how to use `invoke` from `ITypeInfo` in order to make a dynamic request. In addition to enabling dynamic invocation, `ITypeInfo` provides the mechanisms to discover the type of server objects. The operations that are relevant for that purpose are included in the excerpt of `ITypeInfo` shown in Figure 6.10. Objects that implement `ITypeInfo` provide the type information for a particular COM object.

As we have seen in the previous section, the COM reflection interface is based on tokens, called `DISPID`s. The interface provides for mappings between these tokens and standard identifiers. `GetIDsOfNames` provides a mapping between identifiers and tokens and `GetNames` implements the reverse mapping. Using `GetTypeAttr`, a client can obtain a descriptor of type `TYPEATTR`, an excerpt of which is shown at the top of Figure 6.10. That descriptor provides information about the number of operations (`cFuncs`) that the type exports and the number of attributes (`cVars`) that the instances of the type have. `GetFuncDesc` and `GetVarDesc` return the descriptors describing operations and attributes.

The COM Type Library maps DISPIDs to operation and parameter names.

Locating Type Information

The COM Type library provides two ways to make reflection enquiries: direct access to an object's type and primitives for iteration through all definitions that are included in the type library. In order to directly access the `ITypeInfo` object that encapsulates the type information for an object, clients use the `GetTypeInfoFromGuid` of the `ITypeLib` interface. Because a reference to the type information object is used quite heavily for objects that implement dual interfaces, the reference is often kept in an instance variable of these objects, as we have done in the `Player` object shown in Figure 6.4.

An iteration over all type information objects included in a type library is supported by the `ITypeInfo` interface. Its `GetTypeInfoCount` operation returns the number of declarations included in the library and operation `GetTypeInfo` can be used to obtain the reference to the type information objects at a particular index in the library.

Figure 6.10

COM ITypeInfo interface

```
typedef struct FARSTRUCT tagTYPEATTR {
    ULONG cbSizeInstance; // The size of an instance of this type.
    USHORT cFuncs;         // Number of functions.
    USHORT cVars;          // Number of variables or data members.
    USHORT wMajorVerNum;   // Major version number.
    USHORT wMinorVerNum;   // Minor version number.
    ...
} TYPEATTR;

typedef struct tagFUNCDESC {
    DISPID memid;          // member
    [size_is(cScodes)] SCODE *lprgscode; // output parameter
    [size_is(cParams)] ELEMDESC *lprgelemdescParam;
    FUNCKIND funckind;    // specifies virtual, static or dispatch
    INVOKEKIND invkind;   // indicates if this is a property function
    short cParams;         // total number of parameters
    short cParamsOpt;      // total number of optional parameters
    short cScodes;         // number of permitted return values
    ELEMDESC elemdescFunc; // return type of function
    ...
} FUNCDESC;

interface ITypeInfo : IUnknown {
  HRESULT GetFuncDesc( UINT index, FUNCDESC **ppFuncDesc);
  HRESULT GetIDsOfNames( OLECHAR **rgszNames,
                          UINT cNames, DISPID *pMemId);
  HRESULT GetNames(DISPID memid, BSTR *rgBstrNames,
                   UINT cMaxNames, UINT *pcNames);
  HRESULT GetTypeAttr(TYPEATTR **ppTypeAttr);
  HRESULT GetVarDesc(UINT index, VARDESC **ppVarDesc);
  HRESULT Invoke(VOID *pvInstance, DISPID memid, USHORT wFlags,
                 DISPPARAMS *pDispParams, VARIANT *pVarResult,
                 EXCEPINFO *pExcepInfo, UINT *puArgErr);
  ...
};
```

6.3.4 Summary

The COM type library and the CORBA Interface Repository are very similar.

The COM type library and the CORBA Interface Repository apply the same principles. They both treat type information in a reflective way; they provide them as objects in order to make them accessible to client programs. They both create a hierarchical structure of these type objects and provide operations to traverse this hierarchy.

The CORBA Interface Repository is

The COM type library provides a lower level of abstraction than the CORBA Interface Repository. The COM type library is a restricted three-level hierarchy consisting of libraries, interfaces and interface components. The CORBA Interface Repository has arbitrary levels of nesting, as modules may be included in other modules. Moreover, the COM type library does not have query operations in support of associative lookup of identifiers. For COM, these query operations have to be implemented on top of the iteration primitives that are provided.

slightly more powerful than the COM type library.

6.4 Designing Generic Applications

The construction of generic applications demands that clients do not have any static knowledge about the server objects from which they request operations. Clients rather need to discover this knowledge through reflection interfaces. *Generic distributed applications* use the primitives that provide run-time type information for that purpose. They then exploit that knowledge and create object requests dynamically.

In this section, we summarize the discussion of this chapter by means of an example. We show how the object browser that we introduced at the beginning can be implemented in both CORBA and COM.

Using CORBA

An object browser that is constructed with CORBA should be capable of displaying any CORBA server object and should show the server's attributes and their values. The only assumption that the designer of the browser can make is that the server object is of type `Object`. Example 6.6 shows how CORBA's dynamic invocation interface and the Interface Repository are used together to construct the object browser. Note that the client object does not use any specific operations of the server object.

Using COM

Example 6.7 shows the UML sequence diagram with the interactions that are necessary to construct the browser with COM. The basic assumption that we need to make is that all the interfaces are dual and that all objects implement `IDispatch`. If we can make this assumption, we can obtain the attribute names and values for the server object without having to know its type.

Summary

The object browser example shows how to build generic applications. We have seen how to discover type information through reflection interfaces. We have then used that type information to make correct object requests dynamically. From an architectural point of view this allows us to build components that do not need client stubs. This form of genericity is supported by both CORBA and COM.

In general, this approach now offers a second choice to designers of distributed objects. They can either use static invocation using stubs or they can use dynamic invocation. In

Example 6.6
Object Browser with CORBA
DII and IR

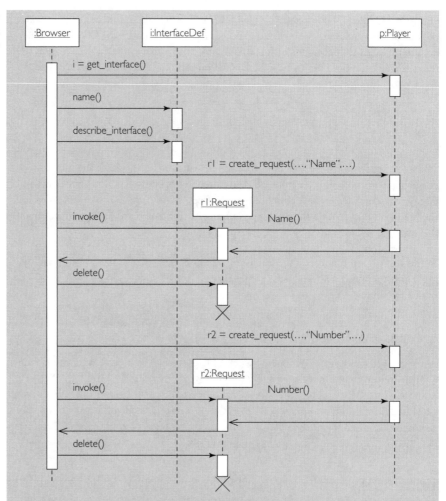

The browser uses the Interface Repository to enquire the type of the server object. The browser obtains a reference to the interface definition of the object by using the `get_interface` operation, which every CORBA object inherits from `Object`. From the interface definition, it obtains the name of the type which is displayed in the title bar of the browser window. It then gets a `FullInterfaceDescription` of the interface and uses the list of attribute descriptions. It then creates a `Request` object for each attribute name using the DII. The `Request` object executes the attribute access operation when the `invoke` operation is called. For the `Player` object, two request objects are created: one requests the name of the player and the other obtains the player's number. After completion of the object request, both `Request` objects are deleted.

deciding which approach to use, designers will have to consider the trade-offs between the two approaches. There is a trade-off between time efficiency and development costs on the one hand and space efficiency and genericity on the other. Because of the complicated usage and the less efficient performance of dynamic object requests, designers decide in the majority of cases in favour of static requests.

The dynamic invocation interfaces of COM and CORBA consume both more development and more execution time than the static invocation interfaces. This is due to the explicit creation and deletion of request objects and the interpretation of marshalling. If we consider the sequence diagrams in Examples 6.6 and 6.7, we will see that there are about ten invocations necessary to make two requests. This compares to two static invocations of a client stub. Hence, we can assume that the development of clients that use the DII is much more expensive. It is also more expensive for another reason. With static invocation, the compiler that is used to compile the client checks for type safety of the approach. The

Dynamic object requests are more expensive to develop and execute more slowly.

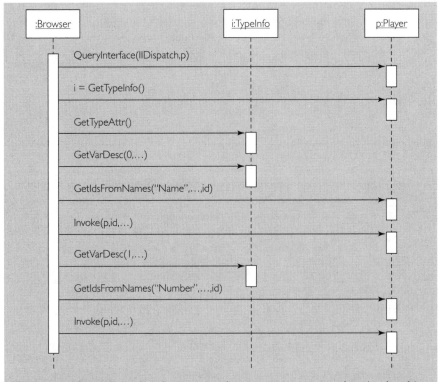

Example 6.7
Browser with COM Type Library and IDispatch

The browser first ensures that the server implements IDispatch, otherwise the object cannot be dynamically invoked and we cannot display its attribute values. It then obtains the type information for the object by invoking the GetTypeInfo operation. It returns an interface pointer to the ITypeInfo implementation that governs the type of the player object. The browser then obtains the type attribute for that player object. This descriptor says how many attributes the object has and that we need tokens 0 and 1 to access the attributes. We obtain the name of these attributes using the GetVarDesc operation from the ITypeInfo implementation. To obtain the attribute values, we use COM's dynamic invocation. We then need to obtain the DISPIDs of the attribute access operations. We do so by passing the attribute names to the GetIDsfromName operation, invoked through the IDispatch interface. The browser then invokes the Invoke operation from the player object and passes the DISPIDs of the attribute accessor operations. The Invoke operation produces an output parameter that contains the desired attribute values.

compiler used to compile dynamic invocations cannot perform such checks as operation names are passed as strings. Hence errors that might have been found at compile-time with static invocation are only detected as run-time exceptions with the dynamic invocation interface.

Dynamic object requests can be used when the client object is defined before the server object.

On the other hand, the applications that can be built using dynamic invocation interfaces and reflection interfaces can be made more robust against changes. We will not have to modify the object browser if, for example, we add an attribute to player objects. We do not even have to stop the browser to accommodate this change. With static invocations, we would have to generate a new client stub and modify the browser by invoking the access operation for the new attribute. If there are many different object types to be viewed, the browser does not have to use all client stubs for these object types and in that way the object code of the browser will be smaller and use less resources.

Key Points

▶ There are situations where clients objects cannot afford to use client stubs to make an object request. Generic clients may have to be capable of handling any type of object; clients may have to be built before the interface definitions of their server objects are available; clients may have to be particularly robust against changes of server objects; or clients may be written in interpreted languages that cannot be linked to a client stub.

▶ Dynamic invocation offers an interesting alternative to the static invocation that is made when invoking a client stub.

▶ Dynamic invocation is well supported by COM and CORBA. Dynamic invocation is transparent for CORBA server programmers, while COM server developers have to define the interface as dual and implement the IDispatch operations. The current version of Java/RMI does not support dynamic invocation, as the Java Reflection API is not yet integrated with RMI.

▶ Dynamic invocation is inherently unsafe because the name of the requested operation is encoded as a character string or as a token.

▶ Reflection mechanisms are needed both for discovering the type of a server object prior to making a dynamic request and for ensuring type safety of a dynamic request.

▶ Reflection mechanisms are available for both CORBA and COM. The Interface Repository of CORBA allows a client to find the interface of an object and also supports querying and traversing the universe of known types. COM's type library also enables a client to obtain an interface pointer to a representation of the object's type. The type library can then be used to traverse the universe of types known in a particular COM installation.

▶ Dynamic invocation is more expensive in terms of both execution time and development time. This is because of the additional enquiries that need to be made to ensure type safety.

Self Assessment

6.1   What is the difference between static and dynamic invocation?

6.2   What is the COM equivalent to the CORBA `InterfaceDef`?

6.3   What is the advantage of the use of COM `DISPIDs` compared to the CORBA approach of passing identifiers as strings?

6.4   What has the designer of CORBA server objects to do in order to support dynamic requests?

6.5   Dynamic invocation does not need client stubs. Which components perform the marshalling, unmarshalling and heterogeneity resolution in this case?

6.6   Why can Java's Reflection API not be applied to obtain run-time type information for Java remote method invocations?

6.7   CORBA supports three different ways to locate an `InterfaceDef`. What are these three ways?

6.8   When would you use each of them?

6.9   Why are the dynamic invocation interface and the Interface Repository always used together?

6.10 What are the trade-offs of using dynamic as opposed to static invocation?

Further Reading

Provision of primitives for genericity is included in the Smalltalk programming language [Goldberg, 1985] and its supporting environment [Goldberg, 1984]. Smalltalk is not statically-typed and therefore programmers have a need to access types at run-time. In particular, object types are stored as objects. Smalltalk programmers can use these objects in very much the same way as we used the CORBA Interface Repository and the COM type library.

Support of dynamic invocation and an implementation of run-time type information are mandatory for every object request broker that complies with the CORBA standard. A detailed specification of the dynamic invocation interface of CORBA is provided in Chapter 5 of [Object Management Group, 1998c] and a complete specification of the CORBA Interface Repository is given in Chapter 8 of the same document.

The situation with COM is slightly more diffuse. The `IDispatch` interface specification evolved from OLE. Dynamic invocation as supported by `IDispatch` is sometimes also referred to as OLE Automation. There are various specifications of `IDispatch` around, depending on whether it is for OLE on 32-bit platforms or on 16-bit platforms, or for COM. A brief introduction to dynamic invocation in COM is provided in [Box, 1998]. For a more thorough treatment of the background, the reader is referred to the OLE literature. A good coverage of the type library and dynamic invocation is included in [Platt, 1997].

Since version 1.1, the Java programming language definition includes a Reflection API [Sun, 1996] that provides run-time type information for Java. A concise introduction to this Reflection API is provided in [Flanagan, 1997]. [Jackson and McClellan, 1999] provide a number of examples that show the use of reflection and a tutorial on the use of Java Reflection is provided by [Campione and Walrath, 1998].

Object databases have a schema, which is a representation of the type of objects. The schema management facilities of object databases have similar functionality to the run-time type facilities of object middleware that we discussed in this chapter. A good description of a schema manager for the O_2 object database is included in [Bancilhon et al., 1992].

Part III

Common Design Problems

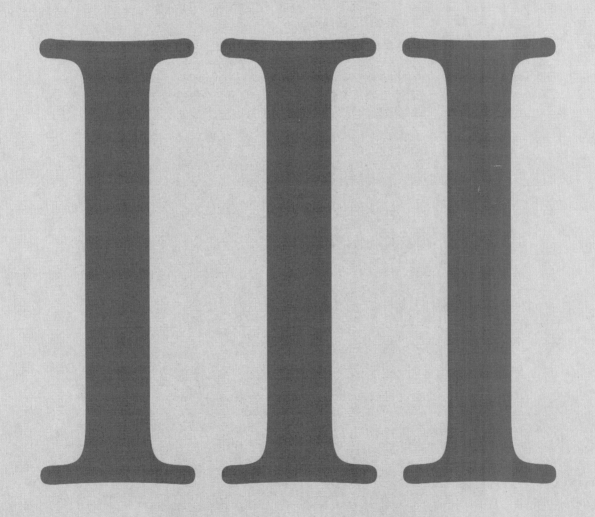

Part III: *Common Design Problems*

In Part II, we have explained how synchronous operation execution can be requested across machine boundaries. The chapters in Part III build on this ability and discuss the use of this primitive for the solution of problems that recur when building distributed systems. Because of the commonalities of these problems, object-oriented middleware provides solutions that are known as 'services'. The idea of such services originates in the Object Management Architecture (OMA) of the OMG, which is shown in Figure 6.11. The OMA includes CORBAservices, the basic services that are needed in many distributed systems in order to achieve failure transparency or location transparency, for instance.

The beauty of an object-oriented approach to distributed system construction is that services are themselves distributed objects. Service providers use the primitive of an object request to implement services and to make them available to the application developer. This, in fact, gives us the leitmotiv for Part III: we want to understand how higher-level services can be built and used by leveraging the primitive of an object request that we introduced in Part II.

As a result, the discussion in Part III will become increasingly interesting for the application programmer. Client and server stubs, marshalling and unmarshalling, resolution of heterogeneity, reflection and dynamic invocation are mostly relevant to those who build object-oriented middleware. We have included them in this book to inform application developers about what they should expect from middleware. The services that we discuss in Part III will, rather, be used directly by those who build distributed applications. The fact that only object requests are needed from middleware means that an application developer can build higher-level services in those cases where the middleware does not yet offer them.

The object requests that we introduced in Part II all involve a client and a server. In Chapter 7, we give up all these assumptions and discuss how non-synchronous requests, anonymous requests, and requests between a client and multiple server objects can be achieved. In Chapter 8, we will discuss how clients can contain the object references of servers, which then enable further communication. We will discuss naming and trading services, two principles for locating objects. In Chapter 9, we will see how the lifecycle of distributed objects can be managed. We discuss how the creation of objects on a particular machine can be requested, we see how objects can migrate across the network from one host to another and we review deletion of distributed objects. Distributed objects may be deactivated by the middleware when they have been idle for some period. If those objects maintain an internal state, that state will have to be saved onto some persistent storage. In Chapter 10, we review the principles of object persistence and discuss how persistence services assist server object programmers in storing and restoring distributed object states. We present in Chapter 11 how more than one object request can be clustered into a distributed object transaction, which is either executed completely or not at all. Moreover, the requests within a transaction are executed in isolation from any concurrent transaction and once a transaction is completed durability of the transaction results are guaranteed. Finally, object security services help application developers and administrators to prevent non-authorized use of objects and the leakage of information included in object requests. We discuss the principles underlying security services that provide authentication, access control, auditing and non-repudiation in Chapter 12.

7

Advanced Communication between Distributed Objects

Learning Objectives

We will acquaint ourselves with the primitives for distributed object communication. We have already understood synchronous communications between a client and a server object, which is the default way for object-oriented middleware to execute an object request. We will grasp the influence of non-functional requirements for distributed object systems, such as reliability or high performance, and understand why these requirements demand different forms of communication between distributed objects. We will ascertain the principles of non-standard synchronization of object requests, such as deferred synchronous, oneway or asynchronous communication between objects. We will also study request multiplicity and learn about object requests that involve more than one operation execution or more than one server object. We will then understand the different degrees of reliability with which distributed object requests can be executed and acquaint ourselves with the trade-offs between reliability and performance.

Chapter Outline

7.1 Request Synchronization
7.2 Request Multiplicity
7.3 Request Reliability

Java/RMI, COM and CORBA (see Chapter 4) all enable a client object to request an operation execution from a server object. Requests in all these object-oriented middleware systems have the same properties: they are synchronous and only involve the client and the server objects; they are defined at the time a stub or proxy invocation is compiled into the client; and they may fail, in which case, the client is informed of the failure.

An object may have to meet requirements that demand non-standard requests from its server components. Such non-standard requests may have more advanced properties than the requests we have seen so far. One example is an object that has to broadcast information to more than one object.

In general certain non-functional requirements, such as performance, genericity or reliability, may demand the use of non-standard requests. It is, therefore, important that the non-functional requirements of a system are specified during the requirements analysis stage of a project. They can then be used to decide on the properties of requests used for the interaction between objects. During the course of discussing different properties of requests, we will indicate the influencing non-functional requirements that demand their use. Such advanced requests might be more expensive, either because they are more complicated to program or because they consume more resources at run-time. It is therefore the responsibility of the engineer to carefully consider the trade-off between using the right types of request in order to meet the requirements and producing objects within budget.

This chapter reviews requests from three perspectives. These are the *synchronization* of requests, the *multiplicity* of objects involved in requests and the degree of *reliability* with which requests are transferred and processed. These dimensions are orthogonal to each other. Hence, we can discuss the extent to which object-oriented middleware supports them independently. For all of these considerations, we will discuss the underlying principles and then show how they can be implemented. These implementations can be based on the standard object requests that we discussed above and can thus be achieved in Java/RMI, COM and CORBA alike. Sometimes, however, a more efficient implementation is provided by object-oriented middleware standards or products. OMG/CORBA is the most powerful standard in this respect. Thus in addition to discussing implementations with standard object requests, we show how CORBA supports advanced communication in a more efficient way.

7.1 Request Synchronization

7.1.1 Principles

Synchronous object requests block the client until the server has finished the execution.

The standard object requests that CORBA, COM and Java/RMI support, and which we discussed in Chapter 4 are all *synchronous*. This means that the client object is blocked while the server object executes the requested operation. Control is only returned to the client after the server has completed executing the operation or the middleware has notified the client about the occurrence of an error.

Although this synchronous request execution is appropriate in many cases, high perfor-mance requirements motivate different forms of synchronization. Depending on the time it takes to execute operations, it may not be appropriate for the client to be blocked. Consider a user interface component that requests operation executions from server objects. If these operations take longer than the response-time requirements permit, synchronous requests cannot be used. Moreover if several independent operations are to be executed from different servers it might be appropriate to execute them simultaneously in order to take advantage of distribution. With synchronous requests, single-threaded clients can, however, only request one operation execution at a time. There are different ways that synchronicity can be relaxed. An overview of these approaches is given in Figure 7.1 using UML sequence diagrams.

 Non-synchronous requests are needed to avoid clients being blocked.

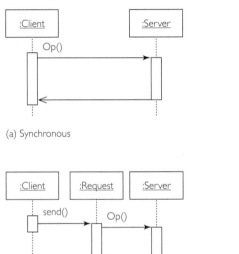

(a) Synchronous

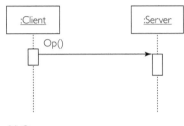

(b) Oneway

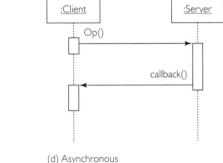

(c) Deferred Synchronous

(d) Asynchronous

Figure 7.1
Request Synchronizations

Oneway requests return control to the client as soon as the middleware has accepted the request. The requested operation and the client are then executed concurrently and they are not synchronized. Oneway operation requests can be used if there is no need for the client to await the completion of the operation. This implies that the semantics of the client must not depend on the result of the requested operation. This is the case if the operation does not produce a result that is used by the client and if the operation cannot violate the server's integrity and therefore does not need to raise exceptions.

 Oneway requests return control to the client immediately and the client and the server do not synchronize.

Similar to oneway requests, *deferred synchronous* requests return control to the client as soon as the distribution middleware has accepted the request. Unlike oneway operations, deferred synchronous requests can also be used in situations when a result needs to be transferred to the client. Deferred synchronous requests are dynamic and explicit request objects are used to represent ongoing requests. The client object is not blocked between requests and it can

 Deferred synchronous requests give control back to the client and the client polls for results later.

perform other computations. In particular, it can use other request representations to issue several requests concurrently. In that way a client can request more than one concurrent operation without using multiple threads of control. In order to obtain the result, clients invoke an operation from the request representation to get the result. A slight disadvantage of deferred synchronous requests is that clients are in charge of synchronizing with the server when they obtain the result. In particular, the result may not yet be available at the time the client invokes the operation to get the result. Then the client is either blocked or the operation needs to be invoked again at a later time. This technique is also known as *polling*.

Asynchronous requests give control back to the client immediately and the server calls the client to provide the result.

The need for polling is avoided with *asynchronous* requests. When a client uses an asynchronous request it regains control as soon as the middleware has accepted the request. The operation is executed by the server and when it has finished it explicitly calls an operation of the client to transfer the operation result. This operation is referred to as a *callback*. The callback is determined by the client when it makes the asynchronous request.

Non-synchronous requests can be achieved by synchronous requests and multi-threading.

Synchronous requests are supported by all object-oriented middleware. In the remainder of this section, we review how the other three non-synchronous forms can be implemented. We will see that they can all be implemented using synchronous requests and multi-threading. These considerations are independent of the particular middleware as CORBA, COM and Java/RMI can all be used in a multi-threaded way. Moreover, CORBA provides direct support for oneway, deferred synchronous and asynchronous requests. It is probably reasonable to assume that these implementations are more easy to use and execute more efficiently than the multi-threading implementation that is built by an application designer on top of other middleware.

7.1.2   Oneway Requests

Using Threads

Threads are used to implement concurrency, usually within one operating system process. It is much faster to start a thread than to launch an operating system process. Thus, threads are more lightweight than processes. There are a number of basic operations for threads. Spawning a new thread creates a child thread that is executed concurrently with its parent thread. Terminating a thread terminates the execution and deletes it. A thread may be suspended, thereby interrupting its execution. Suspended threads may resume execution and remain in the states in which they were suspended. If a thread is joined with a second thread, the first thread waits for the second thread to terminate and then continues execution. Threads are made available to programmers either by means of programming language constructs, such as class `Thread` in Java or co-routines in Ada, or by means of libraries, as in C++ or C.

Blocking the main thread can be avoided by making the synchronous call in a new thread

The designer of a client object may use threads in order to implement a oneway request. The general idea is that the client object spawns a child thread and executes a synchronous request using the child. Hence, the child is blocked but the client continues processing within the parent thread. Because oneway requests never synchronize the client and server objects, there is no need to synchronize the two threads; we can simply let the child thread die as soon as the request is finished.

Example 7.1 shows the implementation of oneway operations using Java/RMI. We have chosen Java because of the nice integration of multi-threading into the Java programming language. However, we note that the same strategy can be used for implementing CORBA and COM oneway requests. Depending on the programming language that is used in these systems, it may be slightly more complicated to use threads, but it is still feasible. However, the use of threads implies quite a significant performance penalty and we now discuss the implementation of oneway requests in CORBA, which provides more efficient primitives.

Threads can be used with COM, CORBA and Java/RMI to avoid blocking clients.

```
class PrintSquad {
  static void main(String[] args) {
    Team team;
    Date date;
    // initializations of team and date omitted ...
    OnewayReqPrintSquad a=new OnewayReqPrintSquad(team,date);
    a.start();
    // continue to do work while request thread is blocked...
  }
}


// thread that invokes remote method
class OnewayReqPrintSquad extends Thread {
  Team team;
  Date date;
  OnewayReqPrintSquad(Team t, Date d) {
    team=t; date=d;
  }
  public void run() {
    team.print(date); // call remote method
  }
}
```

Example 7.1
Using Java Threads for Oneway Requests

Threads are used to make a oneway request to a remote Java object team that prints a formatted representation for the squad to be used at a particular date. Class PrintSquad is the client object. OnewayReqPrintSquad extends the Java Thread class in order to implement the oneway request to print the squad data. Creation of a new OnewayReqPrintSquad object effectively spawns a new thread. The parameters passed to the constructor identify the remote server object team and the parameter for the remote method invocation date. A newly-created thread is started using the start method. This invokes the run method and the thread dies when run terminates. The remote method invocation of print is actually made as soon as the thread a has been started, i.e. the run method is executed. Then the thread a is blocked until the remote method has terminated.

Oneway Requests in CORBA

As shown in Figure 4.2 on Page 97 there are two ways in which clients can make requests: by invoking a client stub or by using the dynamic invocation interface (DII). Both of them support oneway requests.

CORBA oneway operations implement oneway requests more efficiently than threads.

As we have seen in Chapter 3, the client stubs are generated by the IDL compiler from an IDL interface definition. CORBA/IDL has a language construct for the definition of *oneway operations*. An operation exported by an object type can be defined as oneway, provided that the operation has a `void` return type, does not have any `out` or `inout` parameters and does not raise any type-specific exceptions. These preconditions for oneway requests imposed by CORBA are reasonable as they imply that the semantics of the client execution does not depend on the oneway operation. When an operation is declared as oneway, clients requesting that operation will not await completion of the operation. They will continue with the instruction after the request as soon as the request has been accepted by the object request broker.

Example 7.2
Oneway Operations in CORBA

```
interface Team {
    oneway void mail_training_timetable(in Date date);
    ...
}
```

The trainer desires an automated facility to mail training timetables to all players. This can be implemented quite easily as an operation of the object type `Team`. Instances of `Team` have references to all `Player` objects from which the player's addresses can be obtained. To format letters and have them printed, however, takes a while and it would be inappropriate to block the trainer's management application until the printing is finished. Hence, we define the operation as a oneway operation.

CORBA oneway operations are implemented by the client stub that is derived from the IDL oneway operation declaration. This means that it is not the designer of a client who chooses this form of synchronization but the designer of the server. Moreover, the synchronization is determined when the interface definition is compiled, which is when the stub is generated.

Figure 7.2
Using the DII to Implement Oneway Requests

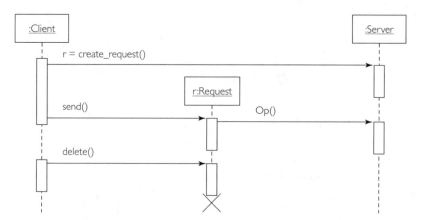

In the above example, for instance the client designer could not request synchronous execution of the operation to mail the training timetable. This restriction does not hold if oneway requests are issued using the dynamic invocation interface.

The CORBA Dynamic Invocation Interface defines `Request`, an object type that is used as an explicit representation of requests. The `send` operation exported by `Request` has a parameter that controls whether or not the client wants to wait for the result to become available. With a no-wait parameter, `send` is, in fact, a oneway request because the client regains control while the server executes the requested operation, as shown in Figure 7.2. The client can then delete the request object.

Oneway requests can also be implemented with CORBA's DII.

Comparison

In a comparison of the three approaches, oneway operations implemented with threads can be achieved in any middleware system. The implementation requires a thread to be started and deleted, which may involve a significant performance penalty. To avoid this and also to make oneway operations available in programming languages that do not have multi-threading support, CORBA provides direct support for oneway requests. The CORBA/IDL oneway operations are less flexible than oneway requests with the DII because a synchronous execution cannot be requested for them. On the other hand, an implementation with the dynamic invocation interface is less safe, because it is not validated whether the requested operation produces a result or raises exceptions to report integrity violations. Moreover oneway requests using the DII are certainly less efficient because `Request` objects need to be created at run-time. Hence, when deciding whether to use a client stub or the DII, the designer has to consider the trade-off between flexibility and lack of safety and performance.

7.1.3 Deferred Synchronous Requests

Using Threads

Oneway requests cannot be used if the client needs to obtain a result. In this case, the client and the server have to be synchronized. With deferred synchronous requests, the client initiates the synchronization. In order to achieve deferred synchronous requests with threads, we have to modify our multi-threaded oneway implementation in such a way that the client waits for the request thread to terminate before it obtains the result. We show an application in Example 7.3.

We note again, that the primitives that we use to achieve deferred synchronous invocation are multi-threading and synchronous requests and that this approach can therefore be used in COM and Java/RMI as well as CORBA. We now discuss a mechanism of CORBA that achieves more efficient deferred synchronous requests due to the lack of threading overhead.

Threads and synchronous requests can be used to implement deferred synchronous requests in CORBA, COM and Java/RMI.

Deferred Synchronous Requests in CORBA

Unlike CORBA oneway operations, deferred synchronous requests cannot be issued using client stubs. They are only available through the Dynamic Invocation Interface. The reason for this restriction is the fact that client stubs are effectively methods or procedures in the

Deferred synchronous requests are available through the DII.

Example 7.3

Using Java Threads for Deferred
Synchronous Requests

```
class PrintSquad {
  public void print(Team team, Date date) {
    DefSyncReqPrintSquad a=new DefSyncReqPrintSquad(team,date);
    // do something else here.
    a.join(this); // wait for request thread to die.
    System.out.println(a.getResult());//get result and print it
  }
}

// thread that invokes remote method
class DefSyncReqPrintSquad extends Thread {
  String s;
  Team team;
  Date date;
  DefSyncReqPrintSquad(Team t, Date d) {team=t; date=d;}
  public String getResult() {return s;}
  public void run() {
    String s;
    s=team.asString(date);// call remote method and die
  }
}
```

This example extends the oneway request implementation by re-synchronizing the two
threads. Rather than printing on a remote host, we want a formatted result of the training
schedule as a string, achieved by asString. This string is the result that requires the two
threads to be synchronized. The thread that executes the request then stores the result so
that it can be retrieved. Before the client thread retrieves the result, it uses the join
operation to wait for the request thread to die.

programming language of the client and are not suitable for representing multiple threads of
control. The approach to implementing deferred synchronous requests is the same as with
oneway requests. The Request object represents a thread of control that is ongoing on
some host of a server object. The difference between oneway requests and deferred synchronous requests is that the client invokes a get_response operation from the
Request object some time after having sent the request. This synchronizes the client
and server objects and returns control to the client as soon as the result is available.
Then the operation result is available in a data structure that was passed during the
create_request operation. Once the operation result has been obtained the request
object is deleted. Figure 7.3 shows how the dynamic invocation interface is used for deferred
synchronous requests.

The get_response operation supports two ways of synchronizing client and server. This
is necessary to give clients a chance not to be blocked if the operation result is not yet
available. A parameter of get_response controls whether or not the client will wait for
the result to become available. If set to 'no wait', get_response returns immediately
indicating whether or not the result is available. If it is not available, the client can continue
with some other processing and poll later by calling get_response again. The need for
polling is removed with asynchronous requests, which we discuss next.

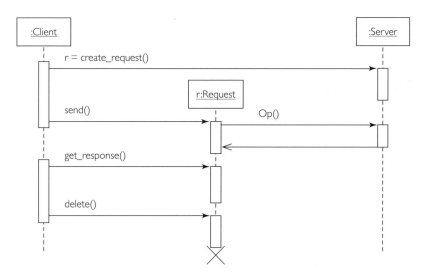

Figure 7.3
Using the DII to Implement
Deferred Synchronous Requests

7.1.4 Asynchronous Requests

Using Threads

The general idea of implementing asynchronous requests with threads and synchronous requests is very much the same as with the deferred synchronous request implementation. The difference is that it is the request thread that initiates the synchronization rather than the main thread. As soon as the request is completed, the new thread invokes a callback operation in order to pass on the result and then joins the main thread as in Example 7.4.

Note that Example 7.4 does not synchronize the two threads. The child thread dies after the callback has been completed. This is appropriate in this example as the callback prints some information on the console and does not modify the state of the client. If at some stage the client needs to access the result of the request or review whether the request has been completed, synchronization would be necessary. This can be done using the thread synchronization primitives that are available in Java. The client, for instance, could suspend its execution and then the callback could resume it, or the parent thread simply suspends its execution. Other options include the `join` operation, which makes the parent thread wait for the child thread to die, or the use of `synchronized` methods.

Although we have explained the use of threads for asynchronous requests using Java/RMI, the considerations are again directly applicable to CORBA and COM. If we used a Java programming language binding to CORBA/IDL or MIDL, we would just have to replace the remote method invocation with a call of a client stub generated by the IDL compiler.

Asynchronous requests can be implemented using synchronous requests and threads in COM, CORBA and Java/RMI.

Example 7.4

Using Java Threads for
Asynchronous Requests

```
interface Callback {
  public void result(String s);
}

class PrintSquad implements Callback {
  public void Print(Team team, Date date) {
    AsyncReqPrintSquad a;
    a=new AsyncReqPrintSquad(team,date,this);
    a.start();
    // continue to do some work here.
  }
  public void result(String s) { // callback
    System.out.println(s);
  }
}

// thread that invokes remote method
class AsyncReqPrintSquad extends Thread {
  Team team;
  Date date;
  Callback call;
  AsyncReqPrintSquad(Team t, Date d, Callback c) {
    team=t; date=d; call=c;
  }
  public void run() {
    String s;
    s=team.asString(date); // call remote method
    call.result(s); // pass result to parent thread
  }
}
```

Using Message Queues

The implementation of asynchronous requests with threads assumes that the server object is executing the requested operation while a thread in the client waits for the result. There may be situations, however, where requests need to be made that are more decoupled. Such situations often arise due to global distribution with much higher network latency or due to execution of objects in different time zones. As an example, consider a distributed application for the international stock market that is used to buy or sell shares on remote stock exchanges. The problem is that a stockbroker based in New York is working at a time when the Tokyo stock exchange is shut down and vice versa. When the New York broker uses a client object to make a request to sell shares to a server object in Tokyo, that request needs to be stored until the Tokyo stock exchange opens the next day. Also the result of the deal needs to be buffered until later in the day when business in New York reopens. Such decoupled asynchronous requests cannot be implemented using threads because the client object in New York and the server object in Tokyo are never operational at the same time and thus request information needs to be stored on some form of persistent storage.

Decoupled asynchronous requests are, rather, implemented using messages that may be temporarily stored. A request is represented as a pair of messages, a *request message* and a *reply message*. The main contents of the request message are the input parameters that are to be passed to the server object and an identifier for the requested operation. The main contents of the reply message are output parameters and the operation result, which are returned to the client.

Request and reply messages are exchanged between client and server objects by means of *message queues*. A message queue operates on the first-in first-out principle and guarantees that messages are removed in the same order in which they have been entered. Message queues often also implement persistent storage of messages in order to improve the reliability of message transport.

Message queues implement asynchronous requests that need to be stored persistently.

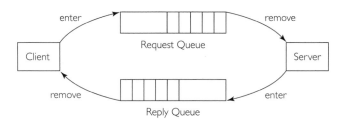

Figure 7.4
Using Message Queues for Asynchronous Requests

As shown in Figure 7.4, a pair of message queues is used to implement asynchronous requests between client and server objects. A *request queue* is used for transmission and buffering of requests and a *reply queue* transmits and buffers the replies. As queues operate on a first-in first-out basis, request messages are delivered in the order in which they arrive and the reply messages are delivered in the same order as the requests were sent to the server.

Message queues that can be used for the implementation of asynchronous requests are widely available. Implementations of message queues are generally referred to as *message-oriented middleware* (MOM). Their applicability is not restricted to object-oriented distributed systems. In fact, many MOMs that are being used today originated in mainframe operating systems. There are, however, several MOMs that integrate with object-oriented middleware. The CORBAservices include a messaging service that supports reliable queuing of messages. Implementations of that service provide an object-oriented interface to existing MOMs, such as IBM's MQSeries or DEC Message Queue. For COM, a message queuing system, currently named Falcon, is being specified while this book is being written.

7.2 Request Multiplicity

The requests that we have seen so far are *unicast* requests. This means that a client object requests an operation execution from exactly one server object. Other forms of requests can be obtained if we relax this assumption. We then have the situation of a *group request* where a client requests execution of the same operation from multiple server objects. A client may also wish to issue a *multiple request* to execute different operations from different objects.

A unicast request is made from one client object to one server object.

We discuss the principles underlying these two primitives in this section and show how they can be implemented.

7.2.1   Group Communication

A client that requests execution of the same operation from a number of servers makes a group request.

A client may wish to request execution of the same operation from a number of different objects. If these operations do not return results, there is no need for the client to know about the individual objects. The request can be made to a group of objects where the group members remain anonymous. We refer to these requests as *group requests*. They are used for notification purposes, for instance when multiple server objects need to be notified about an *event*, which occured in a client.

Group composition is managed by a channel and is unknown to the request producer.

Group composition is usually managed by a *channel*, through which group requests are posted. Objects interested in a certain type of event are referred to as *consumers*. They register with the channel and then start listening to the events and deregister if they want to stop being notified about events. The object wishing to make a group request in order to notify consumers about an event is referred to as a *producer*. It posts the request into the channel and the channel then forwards it to all registered consumers. Group requests are therefore *anonymous* forms of communication as the producer does not know its consumers.

Group requests are anonymous.

Implementing Group Requests

Group requests can be implemented using synchronous requests.

One of the CORBAservices is the *Event service*. It supports the implementation of group requests based on standard CORBA object requests. Such a service is currently not available for Java/RMI or COM. However, implementations of the CORBA Event service use synchronous, unicast object requests. These are also available in Java/RMI and COM and therefore an event service for Java/RMI or COM can easily be implemented following the design for the CORBA Event service. Thus, the discussion of the CORBA Event service should be seen as an example of how a group request can be implemented on top of synchronous unicast object requests. CORBA events are broadcast using the *event channels* mechanism to identify the subgroup of event consumer objects that are to be notified about a certain event. Event consumers therefore connect to those event channels that correspond to events in which they are interested. For an event producer, an event channel represents the community of those consumer objects that are interested in the event. The producer, however, only knows that the community exists; it does not know how large it is or which objects belong to it. The event communication between producers and consumers is entirely anonymous.

The operations that event channels provide are separated into a number of interfaces. The rationale for this split is that the designers of the CORBA Event service wanted to support the concatenation of multiple event channels. Such a concatenation might be useful if different implementations have different qualities of service. One event channel might, for example, be capable of storing event data persistently. Thus they had to devise a strategy so that event channels can also act as event consumers and producers. This is achieved by splitting the event channel interfaces into `ProxyPushConsumer` and `ProxyPushSupplier` interfaces, which represent the event consumer to a supplier and

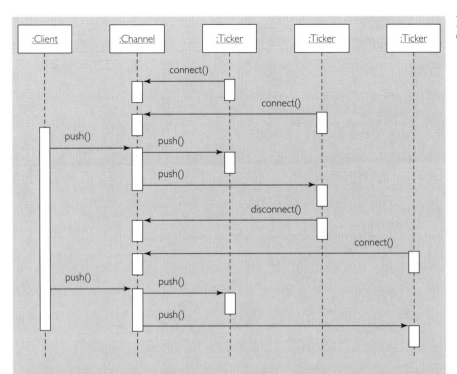

Example 7.5

Group Communication Example

Traders who deal in shares would launch a stock exchange ticker in order to see details of deals that have come through. The successful completion of a share deal would be an event about which they would want to be notified. Hence, the trading application of the stock exchange, which determines the price for a deal, broadcasts the details of the deal to every active ticker. The trading application uses group requests in order to notify all the tickers in one go and it is not and should not need to be aware of the tickers that are currently active.

the supplier to a consumer. An excerpt of the IDL interfaces to the event service is shown in Figure 7.5. The `EventChannel` interface has two operations that return administration objects, which have operations to return the proxy objects. Objects that wish to receive group requests would then implement the `PushConsumer` interface and connect with a `ProxyPushSupplier` using the `connect_push_consumer` operation.

The model of event communication discussed above is the *push* model, in which the producer takes the initiative and pushes events through the channel to the consumer. The event may contain data but the event channel does not have any knowledge about the type of this data, as it is of type `any`. It is worthwhile to note that the CORBA Event service supports several other models of event-based communication. It includes a *pull* model in which the consumer requests delivery of an event from the producer which is then pulled through the event channel. It also supports typed communication where the push and pull operations have a particular type attached to them so that it can be proven when the object is compiled that the right type of data is communicated through the channel.

Figure 7.5

Excerpt of CORBA Event
Service Interface

```
module CosEventComm {
  exception Disconnected{};
  interface PushConsumer {
    void push (in any data) raises(Disconnected);
  };
};

module CosEventChannelAdmin {
  exception AlreadyConnected {};
  exception TypeError {};
  interface ProxyPushConsumer: CosEventComm::PushConsumer {
  };
  interface ProxyPushSupplier: CosEventComm::PushSupplier {
    void connect_push_consumer(
          in CosEventComm::PushConsumer push_consumer
    ) raises(AlreadyConnected, TypeError);
  };
  interface ConsumerAdmin {
    ProxyPushSupplier obtain_push_supplier();
  };
  interface SupplierAdmin {
    ProxyPushConsumer obtain_push_consumer();
  };
  interface EventChannel {
    ConsumerAdmin for_consumers();
    SupplierAdmin for_suppliers();
  };
};
```

Example 7.6

Group Communication using
Event Channels

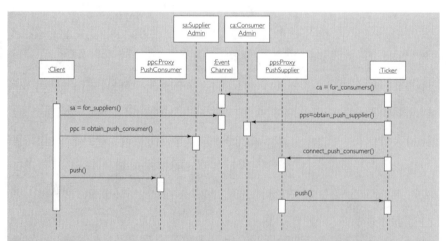

The above figure shows how the group communication scenario from Example 7.5 is
implemented using the CORBA Event service. Each Ticker object first obtains a reference
to a `ConsumerAdmin` object and a `ProxyPushSupplier` object. It then registers with
the event channel by requesting execution of `connect_push_consumer` and passing
itself as an actual parameter. The initialization for an event producer is very similar. It
obtains a reference to a `SupplierAdmin` object and a `ProxyPushConsumer` object.
The event producer can then request the `push` operation that the proxy has inherited from
`PushConsumer`. The proxy finally requests the `push` operation from each of the
currently-connected `Ticker` objects.

7.2.2 Multiple Requests

If a client wants to request a number of operation executions at the same time, it can be advantageous to cluster them together in a *multiple request*. The middleware can concurrently transfer multiple requests to the different server objects involved and the client can obtain the results when they become available. Multiple requests, however, are only viable if the requested operations are entirely independent from each other and if there are no precedence dependencies between the requested operations.

Multiple requests invoke operations from multiple server objects that are known to the client.

The main advantage of multiple requests is that the client can collect the results as they become available.

With a multiple request, the client can collect results as they become available.

We now focus on how multiple requests can be implemented. We first discuss a general solution that is applicable to all forms of distributed object middleware and relies on threads and synchronous object requests. We then discuss a more efficient solution that is available only in CORBA and uses the dynamic invocation interface.

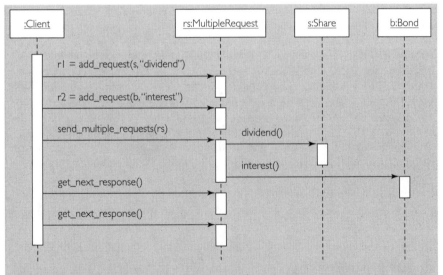

Example 7.7
A Multiple Request

Consider a portfolio of securities that includes shares and bonds. If we want to calculate the revenue for the portfolio, we need to request execution of a dividend operation from every share object and the execution of an interest operation from every bond object. If these objects reside on different machines, they can be executed concurrently and the client obtains the results in the order they become available.

Using Threads

When we discussed synchronization primitives in the first section, we saw that all forms of synchronization can be achieved by making a synchronous request in one thread. We can extend this idea for multiple requests. The difference is that we do not just create one thread to make the synchronous request, but we create a new thread for every operation that we want to request. A further difference is the synchronization of the client with the request threads. The main benefit of multiple requests, which we want to retain in any implementation, is that we obtain the results in the order in which they become available. In order to achieve this synchronization in Java, we use tuple spaces that were first proposed for so-called coordination languages [Carriero and Gelernter, 1992], in particular Linda [Gelernter, 1985]. The basic idea of tuple spaces is to have a bag that contains tagged data, which are read and updated by concurrent processes. A tuple space provides various operations for manipulating the *tuple space* content. To avoid any interference, these operations have to be executed in mutual exclusion. The out operation puts a new tuple into the space. The in operation removes a tuple from the space and returns it. The rd operation reads a tuple from the space without removing it. Both in and rd block the caller if the desired tuple is not available. Figure 7.6 shows an implementation of tuple spaces in Java that we adopted from [Magee and Kramer, 1999].

To implement multiple requests, the client spawns multiple threads and performs a synchronous object request in each thread. As soon as the request is finished, the client thread puts the result into a tuple space, using the out operation, and terminates. The client thread reads tuples from the tuple space, using the in operation, in the order in which they become available.

Multiple requests can be implemented using tuple spaces in CORBA, COM and Java/RMI.

Example 7.8 implements Example 7.7 using Java/RMI, but the idea can be applied in other object-oriented middleware systems in the same way. The Java implementation of tuple spaces is simplified due to the availability of synchronized methods that guarantee mutual exclusion. The mutual exclusion of tuple space operations can, however, also be implemented in C or C++ using operating system semaphores.

Use of threads implies performance and development overheads.

The disadvantage of this solution is that different thread classes need to be defined for each object request. Moreover, there is a performance penalty as the creation and termination of threads can be time-consuming. This may be avoided if threads are re-used and not allowed to die after the synchronous request has been performed. However, the programming overhead remains. This overhead is avoided in the CORBA-specific solution that we discuss next.

Implementing Multiple Requests with the DII

Multiple requests can be implemented with the Dynamic Invocation Interface.

We have noted above that multiple requests have to be dynamic as they cannot be defined using a static way of invoking a stub from any programming language. Indeed, multiple CORBA requests are supported by CORBA's dynamic invocation interface. Multiple CORBA requests with the DII are referred to as *multiple deferred synchronous requests*. The DII includes an operation to request multiple operation executions from several CORBA server objects. This is achieved by the operation send_multiple_requests whose interface is sketched in Figure 7.7.

The operation takes a list of Request objects, each of which was created using the create_request operation of the ORB interface. After multiple requests have been sent, the ORB can concurrently deal with them and communicate with the run-time of the server objects. Using send_multiple_requests rather than invoking the send

```
import java.util.*;
  private Hashtable tuples = new Hashtable();

  // deposits data in tuple space (ts)
  public synchronized void out (String tag, Object data) {
    Vector v = (Vector) tuples.get(tag);
    if (v==null) {
      v=new Vector();
      tuples.put(tag,v);
    }
    v.addElement(data);
    notifyAll();
  }

  private Object get(String tag, boolean remove) {
    Vector v = (Vector) tuples.get(tag);
    if (v==null) return null;
    if (v.size()==0) return null;
    Object o = v.firstElement();
    if (remove) v.removeElementAt(0);
    return o;
  }

  //extracts tagged object from ts, blocks if unavailable
  public synchronized Object in (String tag)
         throws InterruptedException {
    Object o;
    while ((o=get(tag,true))==null) wait();
    return o;
  }

  //reads tagged object from ts, blocks if unavailable
  public synchronized Object rd (String tag)
         throws InterruptedException {
    Object o;
    while ((o=get(tag,false))==null) wait();
    return o;
  }
}
```

Figure 7.6
Tuple Space Implementation in
Java

operation of the Request interface several times reduces communication costs between the client and the ORB run-time environment.

The synchronization of a multiple request is slightly different from that of a single request. Synchronisation uses get_next_response to return the next response of a server object that has terminated the requested operation. Note that the order in which responses are returned is not necessarily the order of the requests. The advantage is that no polling is necessary but responses are returned in the order in which they become available.

Example 7.8

Multiple Request
Implementation with Threads
and Tuple Spaces

```
class BondRequest extends Thread {
   TupleSpace bag; Bond bond
   BondRequest(TupleSpace ts, Bond b){ bag = ts; bond=b; }
   public void run () {
      try {
           bag.out("result",new Double(bond.interest()));
      } catch (Exception e){}
   }
}

class ShareRequest extends Thread {
// analog to BondRequest
}

public class Client {
  static void main(String[] args) {
    Bond b; Share s;
    // ... initialization of b and s omitted
    double portfolio_revenue=0.0;
    Double result;
    TupleSpace ts = new TupleSpace();
    ShareRequest sr=new ShareRequest(ts,b); sr.start();
    BondRequest br=new BondRequest(ts,b); br.start();
    System.out.println("Do something else during requests");
    try {
      for (int i=0; i<2; i++){
      result=(Double)ts.in("result");
        portfolio_revenue=portfolio_revenue+result.floatValue();
        System.out.println(result.floatValue());
      }
    } catch (InterruptedException e){}
      System.out.println(portfolio_revenue);
  }
}
```

Figure 7.7

Excerpt of ORB Interface that
Supports Multiple Requests

```
module CORBA {
  interface ORB {
    typedef sequence<Request> RequestSeq;
    Status send_multiple_requests(in RequestSeq targets);
    ...
  };
};
```

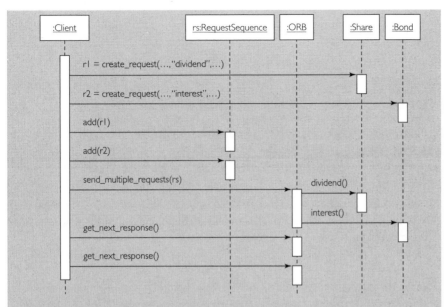

Example 7.9
Multiple Deferred Synchronous
Requests in CORBA

A client creates a number of `Request` objects and concatenates them to a `RequestSeq`. Then the client invokes `send_multiple_request` from the ORB object for requesting the respective operations all at once. After that, the client invokes `get_next_response` as many times as there are request objects in the `RequestSeq`. When the operation returns, a new operation result is available and can be processed.

As Example 7.9 suggests, the use of multiple deferred synchronous requests is less difficult than when using threads, but is still rather involved. The client has to create a request object for every object that participates in the multiple request. After successful completion of the request, request objects have to be deleted again. Moreover, the client has to manage associations between request objects and the results of the requested operation. Hence the improvement of run-time performance is paid for by higher development costs.

7.3 Request Reliability

For the implementation of several non-functional requirements, in particular, fault-tolerance, reliability and availability it is important to be aware of the reliability with which middleware handles operation execution requests. When discussing *request reliability*, we separate unicast requests, where only one client and one server interact, from multiple and group requests.

7.3.1 Unicast Requests

For unicast requests, a number of different degrees of reliability can be distinguished. These are:

1. exactly-once,

2. atomic,
3. at-least-once,
4. at-most-once and
5. maybe.

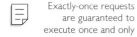

Exactly-once requests are guaranteed to execute once and only once.

Exactly-once is the highest degree of reliability for requests. If a request is handled in this way the degree of reliability is the same as with a local procedure call in an imperative programming language. It also means that failures that might occur due to distribution are entirely transparent to the client programmer. Exactly-once reliability is, however, very difficult and expensive to achieve. It cannot be achieved by the middleware alone but also requires the use of fault-tolerant and highly available hardware and operating systems platforms for the execution of server objects.

Atomic requests are either performed completely or not at all.

Atomic requests avoid side-effects when a failure occurs in the middle of the requested operation. Consider a banking application where client objects request the execution of a transfer operation to move money from one account to another. This involves a debit operation on the first account and a credit operation on the second. If the transfer request is not atomic and a failure occurs after the debit has been successfully completed, money will be lost. This is not acceptable for an application to be used by banks. Request atomicity is usually implemented using *transactions*. As transactions are such an important concept for distributed applications, we have dedicated Chapter 11 to their discussion.

At-least-once requests are guaranteed to execute once, but possibly more often.

For requests executed with *at-least-once* reliability, the middleware guarantees that the request is executed. With this degree of reliability, however, the request may be executed more than once. This happens when reply messages indicating successful completion of the request are lost. Then the middleware does not know whether the request has been executed previously and it resends the request, which might lead to an additional execution of the request. Many message-oriented middleware (MOM) systems have at-least-once delivery semantics. Thus, if such a MOM is used to implement asynchronous requests, as suggested above, these requests have at-least-once semantics.

From an application designer's point of view, at-least-once requests are not very attractive in situations where operations modify the server's state. Consider the above debit operation. If it is executed more than once, money is lost. The application designer certainly does not want this to happen. Hence, care has to been taken when requesting operations that modify server states with at-least-once semantics.

At-most-once requests notify the client if a failure occurs.

With *at-most-once* reliability, the requested operation may or may not have been executed. If the operation is not executed the client is informed of the failure. The requests we discussed in Chapter 4 have at-most-once reliability. CORBA and Java/RMI inform the client of the failure by raising an exception and COM returns HRESULT values. If, however, the exceptions are not caught or COM return values are not evaluated, the request is executed with maybe reliability.

The client does not know whether a request with maybe semantics has been executed.

Clients do not know whether requests with *maybe* reliability have been executed. Middleware does not guarantee their execution and the client is not informed when the request fails. An example of requests that have this degree of reliability are the oneway requests in CORBA. Oneway operations must not raise any operation-specific exceptions, but the object request broker also does not raise generic exceptions if they fail. Hence, the client does not know whether the requested operation has been completed.

7.3.2 Group and Multiple Requests

For group and multiple requests, a number of additional factors have to be considered when discussing reliability: there may be more than one server and, furthermore, the middleware needs time to deliver the requests. It is, therefore, rather likely that requests are not all delivered at the same time. For the reliability of group and multiple requests we distinguish:

1. k-reliability,
2. totally ordered and
3. best effort.

K-reliability adds a second dimension to the at-least-once reliability that we discussed for unicast requests. As with at-least-once reliability, the requested operations may have been executed more than once due to lost reply messages and care should be taken when using it with operations that modify server states. The CORBA Event service has been specialized into a Notification service, which has k-reliability semantics. It achieves this by persistently storing requests in those cases where the event consumer is unavailable.

K-reliability guarantees that at least k requested operations will be executed.

It is unlikely that requests will be received simultaneously by the multiple servers involved. In most cases, this does not cause further problems. It might cause problems, however, if one request overtakes a request of an earlier cycle. *Totally ordered* group and multiple requests are, therefore, always completed before the next group or multiple request can be started. The CORBA Event service achieves totally ordered requests. This is done, however, at the expense of pushing an event through an event channel in a synchronous way. Hence clients cannot continue before the last member of the group has executed the requested operation.

Totally ordered group and multiple requests disable requests from overtaking previous requests.

Best effort is the lowest degree of reliability. No explicit measures are taken to guarantee a certain quality. Best effort reliability is comparable to the maybe reliability that was introduced for unicast requests. The multiple request primitives provided by CORBA only achieve a best effort as they do not guarantee atomicity nor any order on the request delivery.

Best effort requests do not make any quality of service guarantees.

Having discussed these different degrees of reliability, we note a general trade-off between reliability and performance. Achieving a high degree of reliability is very involved. It requires persistent storage of messages or the use of transactions, which are both rather time-consuming. On the other hand, requests that may or may not have been executed can be dealt with very quickly. Oneway requests in CORBA do not require reply messages to be returned to the client and the client therefore does not need to synchronize with the server. It is the task of the application designer to trade these different characteristics against each other in order to meet the mix of performance requirements that the stakeholders have specified.

Engineers trade high reliability against performance.

Key Points

▶ Requests in Java/RMI, CORBA and COM are, by default, unicast, synchronous, and executed at-most-once. Clients need to identify servers with an object reference.

▶ Non-functional requirements may demand different request characteristics.

▶ The non-synchronous requests are oneway requests, deferred synchronous requests and asynchronous requests. Oneway requests are never synchronized. Deferred synchronous requests are synchronized by the client using polling. Asynchronous requests are synchronized by the server.

▶ All these synchronization primitives can be achieved regardless of the middleware using synchronous requests and multiple threads.

▶ CORBA provides dedicated implementations for oneway, deferred synchronous and asynchronous communication that may execute more efficiently and may be easier to use than multiple threads.

▶ Event notifications can be done in an anonymous way using group requests, in which an event producer posts events into a channel that notifies those consumers that have registered an interest in the events.

▶ Sending multiple requests at once can improve the performance of requests because the communication overhead between the client and the middleware is reduced and clients reduce the waiting time for results as they process them in the order in which they become available.

▶ Multiple requests can be implemented using tuple spaces, synchronous requests and multiple threads in all forms of object-oriented middleware.

▶ CORBA provides multiple requests as part of the dynamic invocation interface and they may be easier to use and execute more efficiently than multi-threaded implementations of multiple requests.

▶ Middleware supports different degrees of request reliability. Highly reliable requests, such as exactly-once, totally ordered or atomic requests, tend to be slow while less reliable requests that are executed at-most-once or maybe can be handled much faster.

Self Assessment

7.1   Which non-functional requirements can be addressed using CORBA's dynamic invocation interface?

7.2   Is there any dependency between dynamic and multiple requests?

7.3   What are the differences between multiple requests and group requests?

7.4   How could group requests be implemented using message queues?

7.5   Asynchronous requests seem much more efficient than synchronous requests. Why are they not used all the time?

7.6   How do the CORBA DII operations `send` and `invoke` differ?

7.7   When would you use threads and when would you use message queues to implement asynchronous requests?

7.8   Can asynchronous requests implemented with message queues perform faster than those implemented with threads?

7.9   Given that exactly-once provides the highest degree of reliability, why should designers make do with weaker reliability?

Further Reading

The multiple requests that are available in CORBA are defined as part of the Dynamic Invocation Interface that is specified in Chapter [Object Management Group, 1998c]. The CORBA group communication primitives that we sketched in this chapter are specified in Chapter 4 of [Object Management Group, 1998a].

In this chapter, we have discussed how multi-threading can be used to implement asynchronous communication. While doing so, we have assumed that the reader is familiar with the concepts and implementation of concurrency. A good introduction to the theory and practice of concurrent programming is provided by [Magee and Kramer, 1999]. In particular, they discuss models and Java implementations for message passing, which can be used for asynchronous communication between distributed objects. [Lea, 1997] gives another good introduction to concurrent programming in Java.

The group communication primitives provided by CORBA's Event service are just one example. More recently, the OMG has adopted a Notification service [Object Management Group, 1998b] that enables clients to adjust quality of service attributes for the group communication. There is currently a lot of research interest into push technology for the Internet. A good conceptual framework for Internet-scale event notification is provided by [Rosenblum and Wolf, 1997].

There is a large body of work on coordination primitives and languages. This research community has a conference series in which many approaches to communication in distributed systems based on tuple spaces have been presented. The proceedings have been edited by [Ciancarini and Hankin, 1996], [Garlan and LeMetayer, 1997] and [Ciancarini and Wolf, 1999]. With a more industrial orientation, there are various prototypes of communication systems based on tuple spaces. JavaSpaces [Freeman et al., 1999] has been developed by Sun Microsystems and TSpaces [Wyckoff et al., 1998] is a prototype developed at IBM Almaden Research Center.

There are several message-oriented middleware products in the market, which support asynchronous and group communication. One of the market leading products is IBM's MQSeries. A good overview of MQSeries is provided by [Gilman and Schreiber, 1996].

8

Locating Distributed Objects

Learning Objectives

In previous chapters, we learned that a client needs an object reference for a server object in order to be able to request an operation execution. In this chapter, we will study the principal methods by which server objects publish object references and clients find them. We will familiarize ourselves with the principles of naming and learn how naming services are provided in object-oriented middleware. We will comprehend that naming is based on the definition of external names for objects. We will compare naming with trading, which enables client objects to find objects based on the types of services that they offer. We will understand how qualities of service can be defined, both to advertise service types and to select the most suitable service offer. We will then grasp how trading is supported by the CORBA Trading service.

Chapter Outline

As we saw in Chapter 1, location transparency is a key characteristic of any distributed system. Location transparency in distributed object applications enables client objects to access the services provided by server objects without knowing the server's physical location.

Assume that we do not care about location transparency and freely use knowledge about the physical location of a server object, say the IP address of the machine executing the object, within the code of its client objects. Everything works fine when we test the system. We install it and it goes into production. After some time, the system administrator recognizes that the machine executing the server object is becoming overloaded; it becomes necessary to move the object to another machine. The administrator cannot easily migrate the object to another machine because we have to change the code of all the client objects and replace the old IP address with the new IP address. This is expensive and seriously disturbs the system operation.

The object-oriented middleware that we discussed in Chapter 4 support location transparency by maintaining object references. If client objects possess an object reference to a server object, they can request operations from that object without knowing its physical location. This principle is common to all the object-oriented middleware systems that we discussed. Hence, the concept of object references greatly contributes to achieving location transparency. The remaining problem is: how does a client object obtain a reference to a server object without using knowledge about the physical location of the object?

Obtaining references to objects in a location-transparent way is achieved by means of location services. A location service is a core component of any middleware. The service has to be known to both client and server objects. It serves two main purposes: registration of references for server objects and provision of references to client objects. There are two principle ways that a location service can reveal the identity of server objects: naming and trading. Depending on which approach is taken, we refer to the location service as a *name server* or a *trader*.

In the next section we discuss naming. Naming is based on assigning logical names to objects. The main purpose of a naming service is to manage *name spaces*, that is the sets of bindings between names and object references that are known in a distributed system. A client can submit a name to the naming service and in return obtain an object reference. This still requires clients to uniquely identify their server objects, albeit in a logical way. The second section discusses trading. Trading enables clients to locate objects based on the functionality of the server object and the quality of service required. This enables client objects to locate server objects whose identity they do not know.

8.1 Object Naming

The first part of this section analyzes the naming problem in more detail. The analysis yields requirements for a distributed object name server that state what a designer expects from a name server. We use these requirements to present the naming services of the object-oriented middleware systems that we introduced in Chapter 4. We present the naming primitives of the CORBA Naming service and discuss COM Monikers and the RMI Registry.

8.1.1 Principles of Naming

The basic idea of naming is to enable a server programmer or administrator to bind a name to a server object reference so that client objects can use the name to obtain a reference. We now discuss this idea in more detail.

Names

Abstracting from Example 8.1, we require that a name server should determine a data type for names. That data type should store names in strings of characters from a recognized character set. We denote an instance of that type as a *name*. We note that the server applications and the client applications have to have a common understanding of the semantics of names. The purpose of the name server is, then, to manage the assignments between names and server objects. We refer to these assignments as *name bindings*.

A name is a sequence of identifiers that is bound to an object reference and can be resolved into the reference.

Reaching a common understanding can be supported if servers can attach additional information to a name binding. Names in the soccer management application, for instance, would become more meaningful if team objects explicitly identified the kind of teams they represent. In that way, clients could find out more about the meaning of a name and distinguish, say soccer teams from rugby teams. In general, this means that apart from the character string representing the name bound to an object, the data type for names should support associating further information about the kind of object to which the name is bound. That additional data should, however, not influence the result of name binding operations.

When building the soccer management application, we would like to be able to obtain a reference to a `Team` server object in return for the name of the team. We can assume that teams have an official name under which they are known in the national soccer association. Hence, we can demand from local team management applications that they register a team object reference with a name server using the official team name. The national soccer management application submits these team names to the name server in order to obtain the references of the home teams.

Example 8.1
Naming

Naming is complicated by the sheer number of name bindings that name servers have to manage. In the soccer management application, there can be several thousand team objects. If there is only one name space for all these objects, name conflicts are likely to occur. Moreover, the result of a list operation will be overwhelming if it returns all name bindings that have been defined in a name server. In addition, finding an object that has a particular name is less efficient if the set of name bindings that are known in the name space is too large. Hence, the overall name space maintained by the name server should be decomposed into independent name spaces that are organized in a hierarchy.

Name spaces have to be hierarchically structured.

We refer to these separate name spaces as *naming contexts*. Naming contexts are used to store name bindings that are related to each other. Hence, the general requirement for a name server is that it should support the hierarchical decomposition of the name bindings that it manages.

This hierarchical structure is achieved through nested naming contexts.

Given that the name space is organized in a hierarchical way it becomes necessary to consult multiple naming contexts in order to locate an object. This could be achieved by resolving the names successively from the root naming context down to the naming context that contains a name binding for the desired server object. We have to bear in mind, however, that the name server is a component in a distributed application and any invocation of a resolve operation might impose a significant communication overhead. It is, therefore, highly desirable to minimize the number of times that the resolve operation has to be invoked. Name servers achieve this by means of *composite names*. A composite name is a sequence of simple names. From a given naming context, a composite name denotes a path along name bindings towards an object.

There are three fundamental naming operations that any name server must support. The *bind* operation introduces a new name binding for an object and is used by administrators for registering a server object with a name server. The bind operation has two parameters, a name and an object reference. Upon successful completion, the bind operation establishes a name binding between the name in the respective naming context and the object that was passed to the bind operation. The *resolve* operation returns an object reference for a name that is passed as a parameter. Finally, the *list* operation returns all name bindings defined in a particular naming context. A client can then review all associations between names and object references defined in a particular naming context.

Example 8.2
Hierarchical Naming Contexts

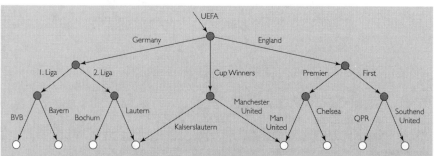

The above diagram displays naming contexts for the soccer management applications. Objects are displayed as white circles and naming contexts are displayed as black circles. An arrow leading from a naming context to an object or naming context determines a name binding. The names are displayed on top of the arrow. Note that designers have a considerable degree of freedom in organizing the name spaces of a distributed application. The strategy for structuring the overall name space is to use naming contexts for defining the different leagues. The leagues would themselves be organized by countries or international competitions and countries are organized by regional associations, such as the Union of European Football Associations (UEFA).

Example 8.3
Composite Name

In Example 8.2, the composite name for the Chelsea team object is ("UEFA","England","Premier","Chelsea"). It is used to obtain the object reference starting from the root naming context.

Behavioural Requirements for Name Servers

When setting up a naming scheme for distributed objects, it has to be decided which kinds of object are registered with the name server. We note that it is not necessary to define names for all objects. The named objects would typically be the root objects of a hierarchy of composite objects. In the soccer management application, we have decided to name objects representing teams. The player objects associated with these teams do not have external names. This assumes that there are other ways of obtaining the object references of player objects. The object-oriented model provides such facilities. Object references can be returned by an operation or clients can access an attribute that stores them. Name servers for distributed objects must avoid side-effects between name bindings and the life of an object. The existence of the object should not be affected by whether or not a name has been defined for it.

Not every server object needs to be bound to a name.

It may be necessary to register aliases for an object in order to enable different groups of client applications to locate it. In the soccer management application, teams might compete in a national league and, at the same time, play in an international competition, such as the cup winner's cup. For that reason, two names are bound to the team object for Manchester United in Example 8.2. This leads to the general requirement that the name server should avoid imposing restrictions on the number of names that can be bound to an object.

Different names can be defined for the same object.

A resolve operation can only succeed in returning an object reference if the initial sequence of the argument name refers to a naming context in which the name denoted by the last element of the sequence is bound to an object. Likewise, an object can only be bound to a name if the naming context addressed by the initial sequence of the name exists and if the name has not yet been used within that context. Clients using a naming service, however, may not always respect these pre-conditions. In a distributed setting, it is more efficient to try to bind a name to an object and be prepared for the binding to fail rather than to check the uniqueness of a name and then bind an object to the name. In the first approach, only one distributed invocation is necessary with the name server, while the second approach requires at least two remote invocations. Hence, there is a need to design name servers to be robust and behave in a deterministic way, even when used with erroneous parameters; they should raise an exception or return an error code to the client in order to indicate that the invocation failed. Clients accessing the name server, of course, should evaluate the return codes or catch exceptions raised by the server.

Name servers manage bindings of names to objects. We clearly expect that the name binding established for a server object should persist even though the server object might be deactivated. We also expect name servers to manage name bindings in such a way that the bindings persist in those occasions where the name server itself is deactivated or terminated. Any distributed object application could be seriously disrupted if clients were unable to locate server objects because the name server has lost all the name bindings after it was deliberately or accidentally shut down. Hence, it is reasonable to require from name servers that they store name bindings on persistent storage and retrieve name bindings upon re-activation or re-start. We will discuss in Chapter 10 how this can be achieved.

Name servers have to store their name spaces persistently.

Name servers should be tuned for efficient name resolution.

The performance of name server operations is critical for the performance of clients. We expect that resolving names and listing the contents of a naming context are likely to be executed much more frequently than the definition of a new name binding. Moreover, names are often bound interactively by administrators, for which performance is less important. Hence, we require from name servers that their performance is tuned for the efficient resolution of names. The application performance can also be improved by re-locating naming context objects.

We saw in Part II that the communication costs between objects that reside on different machines is usually higher than the cost of communication between objects on the same machine. This means that it is beneficial to administer the location of objects in such a way that they are located on those machines where other objects are likely to request their services. For naming context objects, this means that they should reside on those machines that run applications that are likely to request resolve operations. For the naming contexts in Example 8.2 this means that the naming context object for England should reside on a machine run by the English Football Association where the English soccer leagues are maintained. The naming context object for the cup winners' cup should reside on a machine run by UEFA, which also runs the application that manages the cup winner's cup. Hence, it should be possible to migrate naming contexts from one machine to another. The primitives needed for the migration of objects between machines will be discussed in Chapter 9.

A federation of name servers consists of intertwined naming contexts on different middleware.

We have seen reasons for having multiple object-oriented middleware, in particular, when considering wide area distribution. Each middleware system typically maintains its own name space with its own root naming context. The *federation of name servers* enables client objects to locate server objects that are connected to different name servers. In order to establish such a federation an administrator of a local name server would bind names to naming contexts of several different name servers within in the context of the naming context of the local name server. Provided that the way the different name servers identify objects is interoperable, a client locating a server object would not be able to tell whether the server object is connected to a local or a remote name server.

Documenting Name Spaces

From a software engineering point of view, naming is an interesting communication problem as different engineers are involved in naming decisions at different stages. The designer of clients locating an object needs to have an understanding of what the naming hierarchy looks like. The hierarchy, however, is only established by the administrator at the time the system is installed. The problem is further complicated as the naming hierarchy is often used by different applications. In the soccer management application, it was used by the national team's manager application as well as by applications used to organize leagues in different countries.

A naming handbook defines the layout of the name space.

It is, therefore, important that all decisions regarding the use of a name server made by designers as well as administrators are properly documented and maintained in a *naming handbook*. The handbook should determine the naming hierarchy chosen to support a set of applications, the semantics of names, the activation and de-activation of the name server, the performance profile of the name server and strategies for administering the location of naming context objects.

8.1.2 The CORBA Naming Service

Applications built with CORBA need a location service in order to enable CORBA client objects to obtain object references to CORBA server objects. The CORBA Naming service can be used as such a location service. Like any CORBA service, the Naming service is built on top of an object request broker and uses the primitives that the object request broker provides. The interface of the name server is specified in OMG/IDL. The name server is implemented by a set of CORBA server objects, which can themselves be distributed. Requests by name server clients are handled by the object request broker in exactly the same way as any other object request. In this section, we review the CORBA Naming service and assess it against the requirements for object naming that were delineated in the previous section. Apart from discussing how the service solves the naming problem, there is another motivation for looking at the service; it is a good example of a set of well-designed distributed object types.

Naming Interfaces

The CORBA Naming service supports hierarchical naming contexts and allows for composite names. The IDL type definition for names is given in Figure 8.1. As shown in the figure, a Name is a sequence of name components, each of which is a tuple of strings. Only the id field of a name component is considered in binding and resolving names. The kind attribute is used in an application-specific way to provide more information about the semantics of the object bound to a name.

We note that, unlike other name servers, the CORBA Naming service avoids using a concrete syntax for names. The rationale for this decision is to increase portability of names. The trade-off is that it requires a number of method calls to assemble a composite name.

The CORBA Naming service does not provide a concrete syntax for names to increase portability.

```
typedef string Istring;

struct NameComponent {
   Istring id;
   Istring kind;
};

typedef sequence <NameComponent> Name;
```

Figure 8.1

Names in CORBA Naming Service

The programming language bindings for CORBA/IDL map an IDL struct to classes in object-oriented programming languages. Fields of the struct become access operations of these classes. This means for the names defined above that every name component is a single object. This is a good design choice from a software engineering point of view because the internal representation of names and name components can evolve independently from name server clients. Although these objects are not distributed, there may still be too big a performance penalty; the construction of a name involves the construction of as many objects as the name has components. Each of these objects needs considerably more memory than a structure and their construction requires considerably more time than allocating memory for a structure. The CORBA Naming service, therefore, defines an IDL pseudo interface for *library names*. This interface is defined in such a way that implementations can handle name components that are not objects. It also provides conversions of library names to names as defined in Figure 8.1. These names are then used as parameters of operations exported by objects of type `NamingContext`. An excerpt of its interface is displayed in Figure 8.2 below.

The CORBA Naming service provides all required operations.

The interface includes two operations, `bind` and `resolve`, that satisfy the requirements we have discussed above. `Bind` creates a binding between the name passed as the first argument and the object passed as the second argument. Hierarchical naming contexts are traversed if a composite name is passed. `Resolve` returns an object for a given name and again hierarchical naming contexts are handled. The `unbind` operation deletes a name binding that is no longer needed and `destroy` deletes a naming context. Finally, `list` is used to enumerate the bindings that have been defined within a given naming context.

The ORB interface is used to obtain the reference of the root naming context.

In order to use the Naming service, client objects have to bootstrap and somehow obtain a CORBA object reference on the root naming context. This is a general problem, as for several CORBA services it is necessary to obtain object references on the CORBA objects that provide that service. CORBA's `ORB` interface, shown in Figure 8.3 provides

Figure 8.2

Excerpt of the
`NamingContext` Interface

```
interface NamingContext {
  enum NotFoundReason {missing_node, not_context, not_object};
  exception NotFound {
    NotFoundReason why;
    Name rest_of_name;
  };
  exception CannotProceed {
    NamingContext cxt;
    Name rest_of_name;
  };
  exception InvalidName{};
  exception AlreadyBound {};
  exception NotEmpty{};
  void bind(in Name n, in Object obj)
      raises(NotFound, CannotProceed, InvalidName, AlreadyBound);
  Object resolve (in Name n)
      raises(NotFound, CannotProceed, InvalidName);
  void unbind(in Name n)
      raises(NotFound, CannotProceed, InvalidName);
  NamingContext bind_new_context(in Name n)
      raises(NotFound, AlreadyBound, CannotProceed, InvalidName);
  void destroy( ) raises(NotEmpty);
  void list (in unsigned long how_many, out BindingList bl,
             out BindingIterator bi);
  ...
};
```

```
module CORBA {
  interface ORB {
    typedef string ObjectId;
    typedef sequence ObjectIdList;
    exception InvalidName{};
    ObjectIdList list_initial_services();
    Object resolve_initial_references(in ObjectId identifier)
           raises(InvalidName);
  }
}
```

Figure 8.3
Bootstrapping CORBA Services

the solution to that problem. It provides an operation that can return the list of all service identifiers that are supported by a CORBA implementation. The second operation can be used to obtain a CORBA object reference for a particular service. To obtain the root naming context of the name space that is associated with a particular ORB, we invoke the operation to resolve the initial services and pass the Naming service identifier as an argument.

Note the way the CORBA Naming service deals with failures. If a failure occurs, the service raises type-specific exceptions. These exceptions are defined within the `NamingContext` interface. The exceptions not only indicate that a failure occurred, but also provide a reason why the service could not be completed. As an example, consider the `NotFound` exception. It is raised by the `resolve` operation if the name addresses a naming context that does not exist or if the last name component is not bound in the context addressed by the initial sequence of the name. If it is raised, the field `why` explains the reason for the failure and the field `rest_of_name` explains those name components that could not be interpreted by the name server.

Using CORBA Naming

A distributed object application may exploit the CORBA Naming service in different ways in order to solve the location problem. We now discuss three alternatives for incorporating the Naming service: direct use by a client, specialization by proxies and specialization by inheritance.

Applications can use CORBA Naming in different ways.

The naming context objects specified by the Naming service are plain CORBA objects that can serve object requests in the same way as any other object. Clients of the naming service obtain references to root naming contexts using the initialization operations defined in the ORB interface. A system administrator registers the root naming context object in the implementation repository. Then the name server is activated by the object request broker as soon as a naming operation is requested by a client. Example 8.4 shows how a name resolution can be performed, while Example 8.5 shows how a client can modify the name space.

Applications can request operation executions directly.

This approach of directly using the Naming service interfaces is very straightforward. A disadvantage, however, is that knowledge of the name server interface is hard-coded into the client. If the standard evolves and the interfaces are changed, name server clients will have to

Example 8.4

Obtaining an Object Reference from a CORBA Naming Service

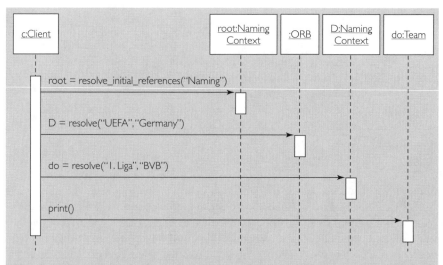

The above UML sequence diagram shows how the CORBA Naming service is used by a client object to obtain an object reference to the `Team` server object that implements *BVB Dortmund*. To do so, the client uses a reference to the root naming context that the client has obtained during its initialization procedures. It then resolves the complex name ("UEFA","Germany") to obtain a reference on the naming context that corresponds to the German Soccer Association. From there it resolves the complex name ("1. Liga","BVB") to obtain the reference to the desired server object. Note that we could have also resolved the complex name ("UEFA","Germany","1. Liga","BVB") from the root naming context to obtain the desired object reference in one step.

Example 8.5

Creating and Deleting CORBA Name Bindings

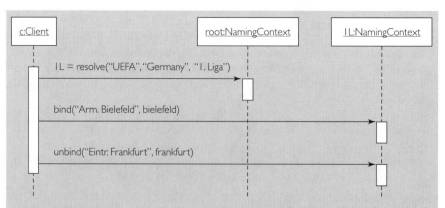

The scenario shown above assumes that one team ("Arm. Bielefeld") is being promoted to the German *1. Liga* and that another team ("Eintr. Frankfurt") is being relegated. This demands two changes to the name space of the German first division. The first change creates a name binding for ("Arm. Bielefeld") and the second step removes the name binding for ("Eintr. Frankfurt") by requesting execution of the `unbind` operation from the *1. Liga* naming context.

be adjusted. Moreover, the CORBA Naming service has been criticized for being overly complicated in cases where, for instance, hierarchical decomposition of the name space is not required.

A proxy design pattern [Gamma et al., 1995] can be used to isolate interfaces and specialize them for specific applications. The main idea of a proxy is to wrap the interface of a server object with an application-specific interface. The application-specific interface of the proxy is implemented by delegating operation requests to the wrapped interface. In the name server example, the application-specific name server interface might, for instance, define names as a character string that are easier to handle than the type `Name` defined in the CORBA Naming service. This is appropriate if applications know that there is only a flat name space or if application-specific assumptions can be made regarding special characters that delimit the component names. The application-specific name server interface then exports naming operations with the new type for names. They are implemented by translating character strings to `Name`. Then requests are delegated to a CORBA `NamingContext` object. While proxies are fairly elegant, there is a trade-off due to the overhead for the administration of additional object references and the additional run-time costs involved in delegating the request.

The Naming context interface can be wrapped in a proxy to achieve a more specific naming service.

The CORBA Naming service can also be specialized using the inheritance mechanism available in the CORBA object model. An application-specific name service declares object types as subtypes of `NamingContext`. It may then add application-specific operations to bind or resolve application-specific object types, or to implement the operations defined in the CORBA interface in a way that takes advantage of application-specific optimizations. Compared with delegation to a proxy, specialization by inheritance removes the storage and run-time overhead. It does not, however, isolate the interfaces of the Naming service. A change in the interface would not only affect the specialized name server, but also its clients.

The Naming context interface can be specialized using inheritance.

Assessment of CORBA Naming

The discussion of the ways in which the CORBA Naming service might be used has indicated that naming context objects are no different from other CORBA server objects. This allows for a relatively straightforward implementation of the Naming service and offers a lot of flexibility for its use. In particular, naming context objects can be manipulated by other CORBA services. The Life Cycle service that will be discussed in Chapter 9, for instance, can be used to move naming context objects from one machine to another one. We have seen that it is possible to have multiple name servers, a situation that will commonly arise when multiple object request brokers interoperate. By treating naming contexts as straight CORBA objects, it becomes possible to bind the root naming context object of one broker to a name in a naming context of another broker.

Naming contexts are CORBA objects and can be combined with other CORBA services.

We conclude the discussion of the CORBA Naming service by summarizing how the service supports location transparency. CORBA objects have a unique object reference. This implements location transparency to a great extent, as clients that have a server object reference can request operations from that server object without knowing its physical location. The CORBA Naming service enables clients to obtain object references in a location-transparent way by means of logical names. The service supports binding these names to objects and

The Naming service supports location transparency of CORBA objects.

obtaining objects by resolving name bindings within a naming context. The object reference of an initial naming context can be obtained in a location-transparent way by means of initialization operations exported by the object request broker interface. Hence, it is possible for a client application programmer to obtain any object reference for which a logical name is defined without any knowledge about the location of the object or the location of the name server. Location, however, is not transparent to administrators of CORBA server objects.

8.1.3   COM Monikers

 Monikers implement naming in COM.

Monikers are the naming primitives of Microsoft's COM. [Box, 1998] introduces the purpose of monikers as 'de-coupling COM clients from the algorithms and the information that is needed for finding COM server objects'. This is, in fact, another way to describe what we call location transparency in this book and is the main goal of all naming services.

Like the CORBA Naming service, COM monikers implement naming on top of the primitives that are already available. Monikers are themselves COM objects. Remote clients may use the COM primitives to invoke an operation from a moniker object that returns an interface pointer to a COM server object.

The Moniker Interfaces

Figure 8.4 shows an excerpt from the `IMoniker` interface. It gives the principle moniker operation, `BindToObject`, which returns an interface pointer to an object. Unlike CORBA naming contexts, however, monikers do not implement a binding between names and object references directly. The association is implemented when a moniker is constructed from a textual representation. This textual representation is called a *display name*. Moniker objects are constructed using `MkParseDisplayName`, an important COM API function. `MkParseDisplayName` creates a moniker object in return for a name that is passed as a parameter.

 Like CORBA, COM supports hierarchically-structured name spaces.

COM supports hierarchical naming. COM names can be complex, though they are not implemented as a composite data structure; instead, COM uses specially designated delimiters to separate the name components within one string. A delimiter that is often used with COM is '\'. `MkParseDisplayName` constructs a moniker from a name until it

Figure 8.4

Excerpt of IMoniker Interface

```
interface IMoniker : IPersistStream {
    HRESULT BindToObject([in] IBindCtx *pbc,
                         [in, unique] IMoniker *pmkToLeft,
                         [in] REFIID riid,
                         [out, iid_is(riid)] void **ppv);
    . . .
}

HRESULT MkParseDisplayName([in] IBindCtx *pbc,
                           [in,string] const OLECHAR *pwszName,
                           [out] ULONG *ppchEaten
                           [out] IMoniker **ppmk);
```

reaches the first delimiter. It informs the client through the [out] parameter ppchEaten how many characters it has used for the first name component. The client can then remove these from the name and invoke the operation again to create nested monikers. When asking a moniker to bind to an object, the parent moniker is passed as the pmkToLeft parameter to provide the context in which the binding takes place.

Using Monikers

In Chapter 4, we said that class objects provide primitives for locating instances of these classes. One of the most important uses of monikers is to locate class objects.

A class object often implements a COM Container interface and gives individual names to its instances. As it is often necessary to enable clients to locate individual instances of a class by name we need monikers for these instances, too.

A moniker that locates a class object is called a class moniker.

An *item moniker* refers to a particular instance of a class. Item monikers are usually made up of a class moniker or another item moniker. This composition also implements the parsing of composite names and, to do so, the class object that is located by a class moniker needs to implement the IParseDisplayName interface and thus the ParseDisplayName() operation. Given that class objects are often COM container objects, the implementation of this operation can, in most cases, be delegated to the GetObject operation of the container. Example 8.6 shows the use of COM monikers for locating the Dortmund team object from a display name.

Assessment

We note that the use of COM for resolving name bindings is considerably more complicated than the equivalent in CORBA. This is due to the dual representation of display names. They have both an external representation and an internal representation.

COM naming is more complicated to use than CORBA.

Moreover, naming COM objects is not orthogonal to other COM operations. It is woven into various other parts of the COM specification. Most notably, COM naming relies on the container interfaces provided by composite objects and it is also tied in with object activation. Monikers mean that clients do not have to know about containers and the way they are nested.

COM naming is not orthogonal to other COM operations.

Our most serious concern, however, is the fact that naming in COM is not entirely transparent to designers and programmers of COM server objects. In order for the above example to work, various COM objects have to implement the IParseDisplayName interface. Hence, COM class object implementations and objects that are identified by composite names have to take explicit measures to participate in the resolution of name bindings. Therefore naming is not entirely transparent to the server programmer.

Naming is not transparent for designers of COM server objects.

8.1.4 The Java/RMI Registry

Java's Remote Method Invocation specification addresses naming through the Java/RMI *Registry*. Though slightly less sophisticated than the CORBA and COM naming services, the Java/RMI Registry meets most of our requirements for a distributed object naming

Example 8.6
Resolving a COM display name

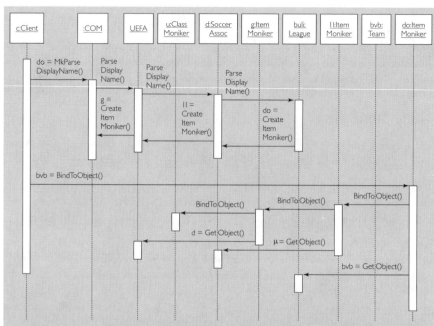

"clsid:571F1680-CC83-11d0-8C48-000CBA:!Germany!1.Liga!BVB" is the display name that is resolved in this example. First, the display name is parsed by calling MkParseDisplayName from the COM library. The COM library then uses the GUID that is part of the first name component to locate the identified class object. It creates the ClassMoniker u and then removes the first name component from the display name and invokes ParseDisplayName from UEFA class object. This removes the second name component and forwards the ParseDisplayName call to the COM object d that implements the German soccer association. This, in turn, forwards the ParseDisplayName call to the League object buli that contains all teams playing in the 1. Liga. After parsing the display names, each of these implementations of IParseDisplayName also creates item moniker objects for the objects designated by the names they parsed. They compose these item monikers and associate them with their left-most moniker. Once these moniker objects have been constructed, the BindToObject operation of do forwards the call to each moniker to its left until it can be resolved in the ClassMoniker u. That moniker returns an interface pointer to the COM container object that is capable of resolving the name and it does so using the GetObject operation. This is repeated for all the monikers in the hierarchy until the leaf moniker do can resolve the name 'BVB' using GetObject from buli.

service. Like the CORBA Naming service and COM Monikers, the Registry provides naming services by using the ability to invoke remote methods.

The Registry Interfaces

The Java/RMI Registry offers all required operations for naming.

Figure 8.5 shows the principle operations of the Java/RMI Registry. These are, in fact, the operations that we would expect by now. The registry supports resolving a name binding using lookup, creating a name binding using bind and deleting a name binding using

```
package java.rmi.registry;
  public interface Registry extends java.rmi.Remote {
    public static final int REGISTRY_PORT = 1099;
    public java.rmi.Remote lookup(String name)
                throws java.rmi.RemoteException,
                java.rmi.NotBoundException,
                java.rmi.AccessException;
    public void bind(String name, java.rmi.Remote obj)
                throws java.rmi.RemoteException,
                        java.rmi.AlreadyBoundException,
                        java.rmi.AccessException;
    public void rebind(String name, java.rmi.Remote obj)
                throws java.rmi.RemoteException,
                        java.rmi.AccessException;
    public void unbind(String name)
                throws java.rmi.RemoteException,
                        java.rmi.NotBoundException,
                        java.rmi.AccessException;
    public String[] list() throws java.rmi.RemoteException,
                        java.rmi.AccessException;
  }
```

Figure 8.5
The Java/RMI Registry Interface

unbind. In addition, it also supports an operation rebind that allows clients to change the object reference to which the name is bound.

The RMI specification includes a class LocateRegistry for bootstrapping the name server. That class performs the same task as the CORBA operation to resolve the initial services. LocateRegistry enables client objects to locate a registry. That class is not a remote interface, but its static operations are called using local method calls. The operations return a reference to a registry object. This registry object can either be on the local host or on a remote host. Note that clients need to pass a host name to obtain a registry object reference on a remote host.

```
package java.rmi.registry;
  public final class LocateRegistry {
    public static Registry getRegistry()
                throws java.rmi.RemoteException;
    public static Registry getRegistry(int port)
                throws java.rmi.RemoteException;
    public static Registry getRegistry(String host)
                throws java.rmi.RemoteException,
                java.rmi.UnknownHostException;
    public static Registry getRegistry(String host, int port)
                throws java.rmi.RemoteException,
                java.rmi.UnknownHostException;
    public static Registry createRegistry(int port)
                throws java.rmi.RemoteException;
  }
```

Figure 8.6
Interface to Locate Java/RMI Registries

The Java/RMI Registry differs from the CORBA Naming service and from COM Monikers in one important aspect. It does not allow clients that reside on a different host from the registry implementation object to modify the name space. This means that administrators cannot create, delete or modify name bindings on remote machines.

There are two ways in which administrators can cope with the above restriction. They either use another naming service that is built on top of the Java/RMI Registry primitives or they establish a `Registry` object on every host of an Java/RMI server object. They then need to create name bindings for every registry object in all other registries, creating a federated name service that connects them.

Using the Registry

It is possible, in principle, to define hierarchical name spaces because registry objects can be inserted into a name binding, too. However, the Registry does not support hierarchical lookups in the same way as CORBA and COM, because it does not support the concept of composite names; they have to be implemented by the client, as in Example 8.7.

Example 8.7
Obtaining an Object Reference
from an Java/RMI Registry

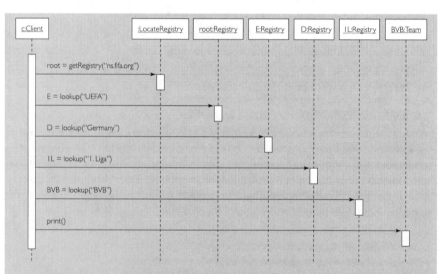

The root registry is operated by the federation of international football associations (FIFA). In order to obtain the root registry, we perform a local method call to class `LocateRegistry`, passing the name of the machine that hosts the FIFA registry. From there, we perform repeated `lookup` operations and obtain the registry objects of UEFA, of the German football association and so forth until we obtain the reference to the desired team object. We can then communicate with that team object independently.

Assessment

As suggested by the complexity of the sequence diagram in Example 8.7, the lack of complex names makes it more difficult to write clients that access a hierarchical name space. Clients

have to manipulate composite names themselves and must use multiple `lookup` operations in order to find a server object at a leaf of a hierarchical name space. This lack of complex names also has performance consequences. The lookup operation is a remote method invocation. When using the CORBA Naming service we can traverse from the root of the name space to any leaf with one `resolve` operation request. In the case of the Java/RMI Registry, as many `lookup` invocations are needed as there are naming contexts.

Like its CORBA and COM counterparts, the Registry supports achieving location transparency. The support however does not reach as far. The bootstrapping of naming services, however, is not necessarily location transparent as clients may have to supply hostnames in order to obtain a reference to the registry on that particular host. In Example 8.7, we have actually broken the location transparency principle to obtain the root registry object. We have hard-coded the host name of the registry that hosts the root naming context for FIFA.

Bootstrapping naming in RMI is not necessarily location transparent.

Moreover, the restriction that non-local clients must not create name bindings violates the transparency principle. It effectively means that the structure of the name space has to reflect physical hosts and that bind operations can only be performed locally. In our example, it is not possible for a soccer team that has changed its name to reflect this in the name space of its associated soccer association. This is because the two are likely to run on different hosts and the soccer team is not allowed to execute the `rebind` operation. This operation can only be performed by an administration application that resides on the soccer association's host.

Disabling remote modifications breaks location transparency.

8.2 Object Trading

Object naming assumes that clients identify server objects by name. While this is fully appropriate to achieve location transparency without a significant overhead, it assumes that the client knows the server's name. However, in a distributed system it is not desirable that clients have to have this knowledge. In particular, it reduces the flexibility of the system administrator if the identity of the server is determined at the time the client is constructed. Let us consider an example where naming is not the most appropriate way to locate objects.

Clients may not always be able to identify their servers by name.

An electronic commerce system to buy and sell shares has a front-end component that is used by customers to determine the transaction details. The front-end interacts with a back-end component at a particular stock exchange to execute the transaction. The front-end has to solve a location problem to find a back-end component to deal with. Ideally, a customer wants the electronic commerce system to find the stock exchange that offers the best deal at the time the transaction is executed. Hence, the selection of the back-end stock exchange component cannot be done statically at the time the front-end is constructed. The stock exchange has to be selected dynamically on the basis of the current state of the market for the particular shares that are to be bought or sold rather than by identifying the name of the stock exchange.

Example 8.8
Inappropriateness of Naming

Trading solves these problems. The principle idea is to have a trader that makes the selection on behalf of the client. The trader selects a service provider on the basis of a specification of the characteristics of a desired service. These include the functionality of the server object as defined by the interface and the quality of the service provision. In the above example, a trader would select the stock exchange that is most appropriate for a deal with a particular share.

In this section we first introduce the concepts involved in trading as determined in the ISO/ ITU ODP Trading function standard. These concepts are concerned with the way services are specified and how the trader matches requested services against available services. We then review the CORBA Trading service and show how it implements the concepts in an object-oriented way.

8.2.1   Principles of Object Trading

Trading participants can export, import or trade services.

The components involved in trading can have three different roles: it can be an *exporter*, an *importer* or a *trader* of services. The relationship between these roles is displayed in Figure 8.7. The exporter and the importer are both clients of the trader. In the electronic commerce example above, the front-end for defining share transactions is an importer. The back-ends at various stock exchanges are exporters and a trader locates back-ends for the front-end. The exporter uses the trader to advertise its services. In the example, the back-ends tell the trader that they offer two services, namely to sell and to buy shares. The importer uses the trader to locate an exporter. In the example, the front-end would use the trader to locate the most suitable stock exchange for a transaction. Once the importer has located a suitable exporter, the trader is no longer involved in the interaction between the exporter and the importer. In the example, the front-end would request the service to buy or sell shares directly from the back-end, without involving the trader. Note, that the roles are abstract and that the same object can be an exporter and an importer at the same time.

Figure 8.7
Roles of Components involved in Trading

Figure 8.7 also shows the two principal interactions between clients and a trader: *service export* and *service query*. When exporting a service, the exporter passes a *service offer* to the trader. The offer contains the exporter's identity and a specification of its service characteristics. As part of the query operation, the importer passes a *service request* to the trader. The service request contains the specification of the service functionality and the characteristics desired by the importer. Exporter, importer and trader need to have a common understanding of service characteristics. These characteristics are specified in service types.

Service Type Specification

Service types define functionality and quality of services.

The specification of a service has to determine two major concerns: the functionality of the service and the quality that the exporter guarantees for the service or that the importer desires. The functionality of an object providing a service is determined by the operations that the object exports. As most object models used in distributed object computing are typed, object type names are sufficient to specify the functionality. In the example of the electronic commerce system, the back-ends that are operated by the stock exchanges have an interface that includes two operations: to sell and buy shares.

Unfortunately, the specification of quality of service is not as simple as determining the functionality. Quality of service is specified by means of properties. A *property* is a name–value pair that determines a particular aspect of the service characteristics.

Properties support quality of service definition.

The value of a property named `fee` might be used in the example to express the handling fee charged for a successful share transaction. An exporter uses the property value to assure a certain characteristic of the service. A back-end of the electronic commerce system might for instance use the property `fee` to express that the stock exchange charges 0.5% of the shares value for a transaction. An importer uses the property in conditions to enable the trader to make a suitable selection. The electronic commerce front-end might, for instance, express that it wants to restrict the search to those stock exchanges that charge a fee of less than 1%. Note that it is essential that both importer and exporter have a precise common understanding of the semantics of properties. It would lead to fatal errors if the front-end considered the value of `fee` as a fixed amount while the back-end used it to determine a percentage of the transaction volume.

Example 8.9
Properties for Quality of Service Definition

To improve the common understanding, service properties are considered as instances of *service property types*. This type definition has three constituents: a *property name*, a *property type* and a *property mode*. The type is used to restrict the domain of the property value. Trading systems usually determine a pre-defined set of types that can be used as property types. The property mode determines whether a property is *mandatory* or *optional* and *readonly* or *modifiable*. Exporters must provide a value for a mandatory property, but it is not required for an optional property. The value of a readonly property is determined upon service export and never changed. The exporter can change the value of a modifiable property during its operation in order to reflect a change in the quality of service it can deliver. The service property type `fee` in the electronic commerce system would be mandatory and readonly. A modifiable property in the electronic commerce example would be the list of shares that are currently offered or sought-after at a particular stock exchange. Although types and modes contribute to expressing property semantics more clearly, we think the definition of properties should be accompanied by a textual description of their semantics.

Properties are defined in service property types.

Service property types are used for the specification of *service types*. The definition of a service type comprises the service type name, an object type definition and the list of service property types. Note that the same object type can occur in different service types. This implies that the object type must provide all the properties demanded by all those service types.

Service types define a name, an object type and a set of property types.

As an object type may be used in different services, there is a possibility that a trader can replace one exporter with another. In our example, there might be a service `CheapAndFastTransaction` that has an additional property `duration` ensuring that the transaction is executed within a given time limit. A trader could also return a

`CheapAndFastTransaction` service provider when just a cheap transaction service is demanded. To enable the trader to decide on such replacements efficiently, it is necessary to reflect the relationship between services that can be substituted for each other in a *service type hierarchy*. In this type hierarchy, a service S is a subtype of S' if the object type determining the functionality of S is identical to or a subtype of the object type of S' (i.e. the functionality of S is a superset of the functionality of S') and if S has all properties defined for S' (i.e. the qualities of service of S are at least as good as those for S').

The consistency of exported and imported services can be validated against the definition of service types. Trading systems, therefore, often include a service type definition language by means of which the known service types can be expressed. A compiler for this language inserts a representation of services into a *service type repository*, which provides information about services at run-time. The repository is used by the trader to check for the consistency between the service definition and a service import. It may also be used by importers to review the service types known by the trader.

The Trading Process

The principal trading operations are register, withdraw, query and change.

The trader exports a number of principal trading operations. The exporter uses the *register* operation in order to export services and the *withdraw* operation in order to revoke previously registered services. The exporter might change the value of modifiable properties of previously registered services using the *change* operation. The importer uses the *query* operation to query for services.

When registering a service, service providers *offer* to perform the service in the future. An offer can be regarded as an instance of a service type. The offer identifies the object that can execute the service. The object has to be an instance of the object type identified in the service type. Moreover, the offer determines values for all mandatory properties of the service type. An offer might determine additional property values for optional properties. A trader maintains an internal offer database, storing all registered offers. When an exporter registers an offer, traders return a unique offer identifier that is used by the exporter to identify offers that are to be withdrawn or changed.

Constraints use properties to express required or guaranteed quality of service.

When querying a service, the importer uses a service type name to identify the service in which it is interested. The service type, however, is not sufficient to restrict the search for a suitable exporter. The importer also has to provide values for property types in order to enable the trader to make a reasonable selection. The trader should, therefore, offer a *constraint definition language* so that the importer can specify constraints that the trader can use to make a selection suitable for the importer. It is again a matter of trader design how expressive the constraint definition language is. It should, however, include suitable operations for all the property types and all operations of the boolean algebra.

Example 8.10
Constraint Definition

A constraint of `fee<1 AND duration<30` could be specified by a front-end in our electronic commerce example for a `CheapAndFastTransaction`.

The query operation returns a sequence of offers to an importer. It might be necessary to restrict the size of the sequence further. Trading systems support different *policies* that importers use to determine how the trader should restrict the number of offers. A trading system might support a large variety of policies. For example, an importer may specify an upper limit on the cardinality of the sequence of offers returned by a trader; it may specify whether or not it would consider service replacements; or it may specify whether the offers should include modifiable properties. In the electronic commerce example, we might not want to deal with stock exchanges that suddenly increase the fees. We would then specify in a policy that offers with a dynamic `fee` property should be excluded.

Trading policies determine how results of queries are handled.

It is desirable that the sequence of offers returned by the trader is ordered so that it is easier for the importer to select the most appropriate service provider. The import operation might therefore enable the importer to specify its *preferences* for sorting the sequence of offers. In our example of buying and selling shares, we might determine that the fee is more important than the transaction duration. The preferences would then determine that offers are ordered using the values of the `fee` property.

Federated Traders

In a large distributed system, such as the Internet, it is unlikely that just one trader can cope with all service queries and service exports. It might be difficult to manage the large number of service offers in one trader and to cope with an even higher load of queries. Moreover, the consideration of fault-tolerance also applies to trading; if the system has more than one trader it is possible for an importer to query services, even though some traders may be unavailable. We refer to the integration of different traders as *federated traders*. A trader participating in such a federation would maintain *links* to related traders. If the trader receives a query, it may forward the query to the related traders and would then merge the offers returned by those traders with the ones it found itself. Hence in federated trading, traders that have a link to another trader also have the role of an importer.

Federated traders export services to, and query, each other.

By linking a trader to other traders, the offer databases of those traders become implicitly available to the clients of the trader. It is not necessary to link a trader to every other trader as the availability relationship is transitive. The federated traders form a directed graph in which traders form the nodes and the links between traders form the edges. We refer to this graph as the *trading graph*.

Queries in federated traders may cause two problems: non-termination of an import and duplication of matched offers. If the trading graph contains cycles there is a chance that a loop is created by forwarding queries to other traders. If that loop remains undetected, the import operation does not terminate. The second problem occurs if a trader is visited more than once during a federated query. Then the trader might return duplicate offers. Note that this problem may occur even if the graph is acyclic. Both problems are very difficult to resolve statically due to the complexity of the graph algorithms involved. They are efficiently treated at run-time by traders using heuristics.

8.2.2 The CORBA Trading Service

Of the middleware that we discussed in Part II, only CORBA supports trading and we now discuss this service in order to study how the above trading principles are applied. The

CORBA supports trading.

traders complying with the trading service are implemented by CORBA objects themselves. Their interfaces are fully specified in CORBA/IDL. The specification also includes a service type definition language and proposes a structure for a service type repository. The CORBA Trading service standardizes a constraint definition language for use in queries. The trader also determines policies and preferences to control the way offer sequences are computed by the query. The CORBA Trading service supports federated traders. The purpose of this section is to give a concise overview of how CORBA implements the concepts and requirements that were outlined in the previous section.

Figure 8.8

Interfaces of the
CORBA Trading Service

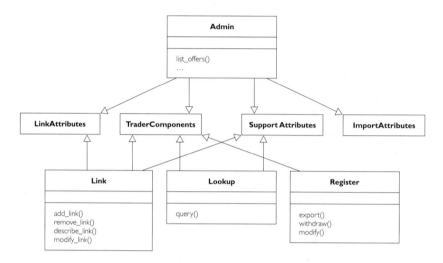

Figure 8.8 depicts an overview of the various interfaces defined in the CORBA Trading service specification as a UML class diagram. The trader specification contains the abstract interfaces `LinkAttributes`, `TraderComponents`, `SupportAttributes` and `ImportAttributes`. They define read-only attributes that are inherited by the functional interfaces. Interface `Lookup` is the principal interface used by importers. It exports operation `query`, which returns a sequence of offers for a service type name, a constraint, a policy and a preference specification. Interface `Register` is the principal interface used by exporters. It offers an `export` operation, which implements the register operation of the ISO ODP Trading function. Likewise, `modify` implements the change operation and `withdraw` implements the operation to revoke a registered service. The `Admin` interface is the principal interface used by a trader administration facility. It exports attributes and operations to review the internal trader state. An example is the `list_offers` operation, which returns a sequence of all offers contained in the service offer database. The `Link` interface exports operations to federated traders. Interface `ServiceTypeRepository` exports operations that support queries and updates of service types at run-time.

Example 8.11 shows the use of the service specification language suggested in the CORBA Trading service. It shows two service types that we derived for the electronic commerce example. The service type hierarchy is defined using the same syntactic constructs used for the IDL interface hierarchy. The identifier that follows the `interface` keyword identifies the CORBA object type name that determines the functionality of the service. The property

```
    service CheapTransaction {
        interface BackEnd;
        readonly mandatory property float fee;
        mandatory property sequence<Shares> on_offer;
        mandatory property sequence<Shares> sought;
    };

    service CheapAndFastTransaction : CheapTransaction {
        mandatory property float duration;
    };
```

CheapTransaction and CheapAndFastTransaction are two service types. An object of type BackEnd can register itself with a trader as a provider for CheapTransaction services using the export operation of the Register interface. The back-end object passes its own object reference, the service type name CheapTransaction and a property sequence list as parameters to export. The elements of the property sequence list are name–value pairs of the property types identified in the service type definition. A client object that is looking for a CheapTransaction service invokes the query operation and passes CheapTransaction as a service name, a constraint, a policy definition, a preference specification. The query returns a sequence of offers that the client can traverse using an OfferIterator.

Example 8.11
Service Type Examples in the CORBA Trading Service

definition enumerates a list of property types that are used to specify the quality of service. Note that the use of trading enables clients to locate server objects, without having to know them. Thus, it complements naming as a location service.

Key Points

▶ The two principal techniques for locating distributed objects are naming and trading.

▶ A name server manages hierarchical naming contexts. Server objects are bound to a logical name. The name identifies a path from a naming context along name bindings to the object. Client objects can resolve a name binding to locate an object.

▶ The CORBA Naming service implements a name server for CORBA objects. It can be used directly in distributed applications. It can also be specialized using proxies or inheritance.

▶ In trading, a service type determines an interface type and a set of property types. An offer is an instance of a service type. A trader manages an offer database containing service offers and a repository of service types. Traders have two types of clients: exporters and importers.

▶ Exporters register offers with the trader. The trader inserts that offer into its offer database. During export, values are provided for all mandatory property types of the service; in that way, exporters assure a certain quality of service.

▶   Importers use service types, constraints, policies and preferences to query the trader. Traders respond to queries by returning a sequence of those offers from their database that conform to the service type and meet the constraints and policies. The sequence is sorted according to the preferences.

▶   Traders may be federated in a trading graph. A trader in such a graph may forward queries to other traders. They make their offer database available to the connected traders.

▶   The CORBA Trading service specifies federated traders for CORBA objects. It is an object-oriented adaptation of the ISO/ITU Trading function standard.

Self Assessment

8.1   Why do naming and trading not contribute to achieving access transparency?

8.2   CORBA object identifiers contribute to achieving location transparency as clients can use them to request a service from the objects. Why is this not sufficient?

8.3   Give reasons for organizing name servers hierarchically.

8.4   What are the advantages of composite names?

8.5   How many different CORBA naming context objects can successfully reveal the same object?

8.6   What are the two most important operations of any name server?

8.7   Why does the list operation of the CORBA Naming service return multiple name bindings rather than one binding at a time?

8.8   What is the difference between the scope of names in CORBA/IDL and the scope of names in the CORBA Naming service?

8.9   Why does the CORBA Naming service not have a lookup operation that only checks whether a name has been defined?

8.10   How can two different ORBs make their respective name servers known to each other?

8.11   Explain the differences between naming and trading.

8.12   When would you use naming and when would you use trading for locating objects?

8.13   Who decides which technique is to be used, the engineer of the client object or the engineer of the server object?

8.14   Apart from those engineers, who else is concerned with location of objects?

8.15   What roles do components play in trading?

8.16   Who plays the trader role when considering locating services in the yellow pages of the telephone directory?

8.17   What are the principal trading operations?

8.18   What is the difference between a service type and an object type?

8.19   How are service type hierarchies and object type hierarchies related?

8.20   Give examples where it is not sufficient to use a readonly property in service types.

8.21   What is the disadvantage of a modifiable property type definition?

8.22   What are policies used for in trading?

8.23   What is the impact of preferences passed to a trader query on the sequence of offers returned?

Further Reading

The detailed definition of the CORBA Naming service is given in Chapter 3 of [Object Management Group, 1996]. A more readable description of these two services is provided by [Orfali et al., 1997]. An example of the use of the Naming service implementation in Orbix is given by [Baker, 1997].

The Java/RMI Registry is specified in Chapter 7 of [RMI, 1998] and an introduction to monikers is given in Chapter 3 of [Box, 1998]. A detailed discussion of the non-object-oriented name services is provided in Chapter 9 of [Colouris et al., 1994].

Chapter 16 of [Object Management Group, 1996] defines the CORBA Trading service. The ISO Standard 13235-1 defines the ISO/ITU Trading function. The document is also available as recommendation X.950 from the International Telecommunications Union (ITU). A readable and more accessible introduction to these two standards is provided by [Bearman, 1993].

[Meyer and Popien, 1994] define a formal language for the definition of service exports and imports. The syntax of the language is defined in a BNF and the semantics of the language is defined in first-order logic.

[Bearman and Raymond, 1991] suggested the federation of traders. The paper delineates requirements for the federation of traders and has influenced the definition of federation in both the ISO/ITU Trading function standard and in the CORBA Trading service.

9

Life Cycle of Distributed Objects

Learning Objectives

In this chapter, we will study the life cycle of distributed objects. We will understand how the creation and deletion of distributed objects is different from the creation and deletion of local objects. We will recognize the importance and the principles of migration, that is copying or moving objects from one host to another. We will acquaint ourselves with how different relationships can be defined between distributed objects. We will see how relationships can be implemented without related objects being aware of the relationships in which they participate. We will comprehend the difference between reference and composition relationships and grasp the concept of composite objects. This allows us to learn about the life cycle operations for composite objects.

Chapter Outline

9.1 Distributed Object Life Cycle
9.2 Distributed Object Composition
9.3 Composite Object Life Cycle

When discussing the life cycle we are concerned with operations that affect an object's existence. An object comes into existence through execution of an object creation operation. Objects might be copied or moved to different locations and their life cycle terminates when they are deleted.

The life cycle of distributed objects is generally more complicated than that of centralized objects. Creation is more complicated because the new object might have to be created on a remote host. Object constructors of programming languages (for example C++ or Java) cannot specify these locations. Secondly, the application of the location transparency principle to the creation problem means that the physical identification of the host where the object is to be created must be transparent for both the client that wants to create the object and also the object itself.

An additional problem arises for copying and moving objects due to the potentially hetero-geneous source and target platforms. Copying and moving is not only complicated by heterogeneity of the object's data representation but also by heterogeneity of the machine code that executes operations when the source and target platforms have different processors and operating systems. If an object is to be copied, for instance from a UNIX Workstation to a personal computer, not only must the data representation in the object attributes be changed, but also the operations are executed by a different processor architecture and operating system. Moreover, it may happen that an object that needs to be moved is currently executing an object request. Should the move operation be delayed until after the operation is completed or will the execution state of the object be moved with the object?

The destruction of objects is also more difficult in a distributed setting. Garbage collection techniques, which are available in Smalltalk and Java, assume that all objects are available in one address space. Deletion of distributed objects is more complicated. In particular, it is never the case that all objects are activated all the time. The techniques can therefore not be applied directly and even if they are, as in the case of Java/RMI, there is a need for the application programmer to be aware that objects might have been deleted.

Related to the discussion of the object life cycle is the concept of object composition. A composite object is built by aggregating component objects. When the components are on different hosts, the composite object will itself be distributed. Object composition and the object life cycle are related, because moving or deleting a composite object should move or delete its components, too.

In this chapter, we will follow the leitmotiv that we established in the introduction to Part III and see how we can use the ability to request operation executions from remote objects to support the life cycle of possibly composite objects. We will use the Life Cycle service of CORBA to illustrate our discussion because it is the most mature one. We note, however, that the principles of using and implementing life cycle support that we discuss in this chapter apply in similar ways to COM and Java/RMI.

In the next section, we introduce concepts that support the location-transparent creation, migration and deletion of objects on remote locations. We then present the use of aggrega-tion and reference relationships between distributed objects in order to achieve object composition. Finally, we combine the two ideas and illustrate the life cycle of composite objects.

9.1 Object Life Cycle

Figure 9.1 shows an overview of the states of an object's life cycle and the operations that trigger transitions between these states. We discuss each of those operations in this section.

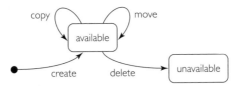

Figure 9.1
States and Transitions of the Object Life Cycle

9.1.1 Creating Distributed Objects

In object-oriented programming languages, objects are created using object construction operators. C++ and Java, for example, provide a new operator that is applied to a class in order to instantiate that class and create a new object. After having allocated memory for the new object, the operator executes a constructor in order to initialize the object's attributes. The constructor can be a default constructor which executes default initializations. It may also be a constructor determined by the programmer of the class in order to execute type-specific initializations that may be parameterised by the formal parameters of the constructor. These features are also needed for the construction of distributed objects.

Constructors, however, always allocate memory within the process that executed the new operator. Hence, constructors alone cannot create an object on a remote host. Two problems arise with the creation of distributed objects.

 Constructors of object-oriented programming languages cannot specify the location of the new objects.

First, the component that implements the object creation on the remote host needs to be identified. Secondly, there is a problem with policies for deciding the location of the new object. These policies may determine fixed or varying locations and may also differ in the time when the location is decided. It may be determined when the client or the server is compiled or be installed, when the client is executed. We discuss object creation from the points of view of a client designer, a server designer and an administrator.

Client Designer's Perspective on Creation

The client object that initiates the creation of a new distributed object cannot rely solely on object-oriented programming language constructs because then the new object would be created in the client's memory and be executed on the client's host. This problem is solved by using the primitive of an object request to request the creation of a new object from an object on another host.

Objects that are capable of creating other objects are referred to as *factories*. The term was coined by [Gamma et al., 1995], who introduced the *abstract factory* design pattern. Abstract factories are used whenever details of object creation should be hidden from clients. These hidden concerns may include the concrete type of object (as in Example 9.1) or the location of an object. Thus, the use of factories is not restricted to distributed objects.

A factory is an object that creates other objects. An abstract factory hides creation details and is refined in concrete factories.

Example 9.1
Abstract Factory Pattern

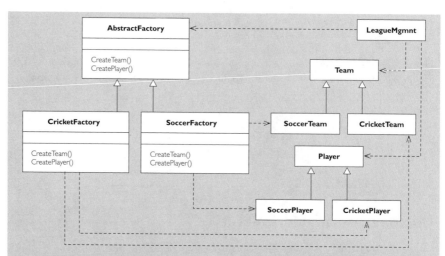

This UML class diagram shows an application of the abstract factory design pattern in order to hide the type of objects that are created. A client for league management should not have to be aware whether it is managing a soccer league, a cricket league or any other league. The client, however, needs to be able to decide whether to create instances for soccer leagues or for cricket leagues. This dilemma is resolved by using the abstract factory design pattern. The league management application uses an abstract factory that exports operations to create teams and players. The two operations in the factory are abstract; that is they are not implemented. Concrete factories, such as the cricket factory and the soccer factory, inherit from the abstract factory and redefine the operations that create objects in such a way that they create soccer teams and soccer players or cricket teams and cricket players. The league management class has a polymorphic reference of a soccer to a cricket factory, depending on which type of league it is managing. The static type of that factory reference is, however, an abstract factory. The league management class does not have to be aware of the existence of the more specific factory objects.

In fact, [Gamma et al., 1995] do not consider object distribution. Abstract factory objects, however, are also useful for the creation of distributed objects. An abstract factory object represents a particular location and it creates a new object in the location in which it operates. As the location of the factory is transparent to the client, the location of the newly-created object is also transparent (see Example 9.2).

The location of new objects, however, should not be transparent to everybody. Administrators will want to influence the location of new objects. They will want to devise

Example 9.2
Using Factories to Create
Distributed Objects

In distributed league management, different instances of a soccer team factory might exist in different locations. Whenever the league management requests a factory instance to create a new team or player object, it is created on the machine that hosts the factory. The location of the newly-created object is therefore transparent to the user of the application, to the designer of the league management application and even to the designer of the factory.

policies that achieve certain goals for the location of new objects. Such a policy in the league management application might be that a player object is created on the machine that hosts the player's team object. Assuming that multiple instances of factory objects have been distributed, devising policies for the location of new objects can be implemented through strategies for finding factory objects.

Policies for locating objects are often implemented using *factory finder* objects. We will discuss the implementation of factory finders when we discuss the administrator's perspective below. However, clients that wish to create, copy or move objects will need to use factory finders to refer to a location. Factory finders export an operation `find_ factories` that returns a reference to one or more factories. That operation, therefore, implements the location policy by returning a factory in an appropriate location. Factory finders are themselves located by clients using the naming or trading services that we discussed in Chapter 8.

A factory finder is an object that locates a factory.

A client wishing to create a new team object first obtains a reference to a factory finder from a location service. The client then uses the factory finder to locate a factory. The `find_factories` operation returns a factory according to the finder's policy. After that, the client requests creation of the team object from the factory revealed by the factory finder. Thus by returning a factory on a particular host, the factory finder implements the decision about the host on which the new object is created. We note that this avoids clients having to specify the physical location of a new object.

Factory finders implement policies about where to create new objects.

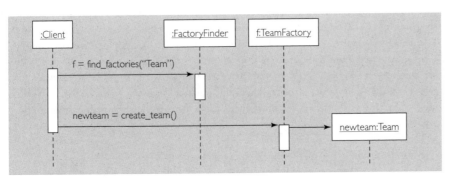

Example 9.3
Object Creation Scenario from Client's Perspective

From a client's point of view, the use of factories for creating objects is entirely independent of the particular distribution middleware that is being used. Clients only need to be able to request execution of an object creation operation from a factory. This is supported by the middleware that we discussed in Chapter 4. The way factories are implemented, however, is middleware-dependent. We now discuss principles for the implementation of factories and factory finders, using examples drawn from CORBA.

Use of factories is independent of the middleware.

Server Designer's Perspective on Creation

When a server designer defines application-specific types, the designer also has to think about how instances of these types are created. This means the designer also needs to design the factories for the application-specific types.

Server designers need to design factories that create objects.

In order to create a new distributed object of a particular type, a factory needs to complete a number of tasks. It first needs to create a new object in main memory. Secondly, it should initialize the object's instance variables, probably using application-specific values that were passed as parameters to the object creation operation. The first two steps do not need any further explanation in the context of this book as they are done using standard object-oriented programming language concepts, such as constructors.

Factories register objects with the middleware and obtain object references for them.

As a third step, the factory registers the object as a server object with the middleware. In this way, the middleware knows where the new server object is located. During the fourth step, it obtains an object reference from the middleware, which it returns to the client that requested the object creation.

Registration is achieved using the middleware interface.

Registration of new objects with an object request broker is achieved through CORBA's Portable Object Adapter (POA), COM's Service Control Module (SCM) or the Java Activation interfaces. The POA exports the operation `activate_object`. Activation in this context means the ability of the server object to execute requested operations. The `activate_object` operation returns an internal identifier to the object. Using that object reference, the factory can request creation of an object reference from the object adapter. The factory will return this object reference to client and the client will then be able to request operation executions.

The factory needs to determine the activation strategy for the object.

The above explicit activation strategy means that newly-created objects are active all the time. This may not be appropriate if the factory creates a high number of objects. Instead, an implicit activation strategy might be more appropriate. The idea of implicit activation is to activate the object only when necessary, that is when it needs to execute a requested operation. With implicit object activation the factory registers the object with an instance manager that knows about all the objects on a server, whether they are currently active or not. When the object request broker forwards a request for an object, the POA's instance manager starts the object if necessary, initializes the object's internal state from persistent storage and then invokes the operation through the implementation skeleton.

Example 9.4
Use of a Generic Factory in a Type-Specific Factory

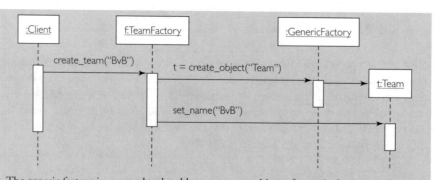

The generic factory is assumed to be able to create an object of a particular type and return an object reference for it. The type-specific factory then performs initializations and returns the object reference to the client. The client does not interact with the generic factory. Its existence is entirely transparent to the client.

Several tasks that need to be done by a factory are independent of the particular type of object that needs to be created. Registration of the object with the middleware and creation of an object reference are examples of those. It is therefore appropriate to implement object registration and reference creation in a generic and reusable manner. These implementations are often provided by the distribution middleware in the form of *generic factories*. The CORBA Life Cycle service includes such a factory, which is used by application-specific factories.

Application-specific factories may wrap generic factories that are provided by the middleware.

Administrator's Perspective on Creation

As with any distributed object, administrators need to register implementations of factories and factory finders with the distribution middleware. This involves registering the executable code of both factory finders and factories with the distribution middleware on particular hosts and registering object references of factory finders with a location service. The latter is then used as a mechanism to implement policy decisions about where new objects should be created.

As with any other server object, the administrator has to register the executable code of both factories and factory finders with the middleware implementation repository. In CORBA, this means that the executable is entered into the implementation repository. In COM, it is entered into the Windows registry and with Java/RMI, the Activator needs to know the URL of the server object. Then the middleware is in a position to activate the factory finder or the factory whenever a `find_factories` or object creation request arrives at the object adapter of the host where the factory finder or factory is located. The administrator might want to register factory implementations on more hosts than strictly necessary in order to be able to change location policies for new objects.

The executables of the factory and the factory finder are registered with the middleware.

In order to enable client applications that need to create new objects to locate a factory finder, object references of factory finders need to be registered with a location service. A naming or trading service might be used for that purpose.

The factory finder needs to be inserted into the naming or trading service.

To change location policies, administrators may replace factory finder objects in name servers or traders. They do so by replacing an old factory finder implementation with a new implementation. Clients that locate the factory finder by name or by service characteristics will then obtain a different factory finder object that implements the changed location policy.

9.1.2 Migrating Objects to Remote Locations

We refer to *object migration* as moving or copying an object from its current host to some other host. Moving an object preserves its reference but changes the host on which the object's operations will be executed. Copying creates a new object with a new object reference on the target host. Administrators might want to migrate objects from one host to another, for instance in order to relieve the source host from the processing load that is caused by requests served by the object. Copying an object is often used with stateless objects to share an increasing load across additional hosts.

Object migration denotes the copying or moving of a server object from one machine to another.

The migration of an object from one host to another may be performed by the middleware entirely transparently to the client designer, for example, when the middleware implements *load balancing.* Balancing the load between the different hosts on which a distributed system executes may make it necessary to move objects from overloaded hosts to those hosts that currently operate with a lower load. Migration may also be explicitly triggered by client programmers, for example, when it is part of an application semantics that an object needs to visit different hosts, for example to collect information local to that host.

 Middleware cannot always implement migration in an entirely transparent way.

There are several reasons why migrating objects to remote hosts cannot be implemented by the distribution middleware alone. First, the middleware may not be able to identify the target location if this location is application-specific. Secondly, the middleware may not always have full knowledge of the private data structures that the object implementation may have defined. For the object to be operational on a remote host, however, these data structures have to be transferred to the object or its copy on the remote host. This problem is related to persistence and we will revisit it in Chapter 10. Thirdly, in CORBA and COM systems, the source and the target host may be heterogeneous. They may differ in the processor architecture, the operating system and the available programming languages. Hence, in those systems it is not possible to load the machine code of an object implementation from a different host and then execute it locally. Thus the class loading mechanism that is known from Java cannot be applied for CORBA and COM systems.

An important design principle that we discussed in Chapter 1 is migration transparency. Migration transparency means that client programmers and users do not see when components migrate from one host to another. We want to keep this important principle in mind when discussing migration.

We are going to consider object migration from the same perspectives that we used for discussing distributed object creation. A client designer is interested in the interface by means of which migration requests can be made, an implementor should be aware of what has to be done in order to make migration happen and an administrator should know the obligations that are created when objects have to be migrated from one host to another.

Client Programmer's Perspective on Migration

Client programmers need just one interface to migrate any type of object.

From a client programmer's point of view, object migration is independent of the particular type of object. Hence, it is feasible to define a common interface that clients use to request the migration of an object. Such an interface exports two operations: a copy operation that returns an object reference to the newly-created object and a move operation that does not return anything.

Migration uses factories to create objects on remote hosts and factory finders as location proxies

Copying objects in an object-oriented programming language is done by *copy constructors*. These are constructors that take the object to be copied as an argument. Copy constructors cannot be used in a distributed setting because the new location has to be defined, too. As with object creation, the location of the new copy can be determined by factory finders. The implementation of a copy operation will use that factory finder to obtain a reference on a factory that is capable of creating a new object in the appropriate location.

As an example of a life cycle interface, consider Figure 9.2. The interface `LifeCycleObject` exports two operations `copy` and `move`. Copy returns a reference to an object of type `LifeCycleObject` or a subtype thereof. Move does not return any object. Both operations have a parameter of type `FactoryFinder`. It serves as a proxy for the location of the migrated object. The operations raise exceptions if the factory finder is incapable of finding a suitable factory for the type or if the object cannot be migrated.

```
module CosLifeCycle{
  exception NoFactory { Key search_key; };
  exception NotCopyable { string reason; };
  exception NotMovable { string reason; };
  exception InvalidCriteria{ Criteria invalid_criteria; };
  exception CannotMeetCriteria { Criteria unmet_criteria; };
  interface LifeCycleObject {
    LifeCycleObject copy(in FactoryFinder there,
                         in Criteria the_criteria)
                 raises(NoFactory, NotCopyable, InvalidCriteria,
                        CannotMeetCriteria);
    void move(in FactoryFinder there, in Criteria the_criteria)
                 raises(NoFactory, NotMovable, InvalidCriteria,
                        CannotMeetCriteria);
    ...
};
```

Figure 9.2
Excerpt of the CORBA Life Cycle Service Specication

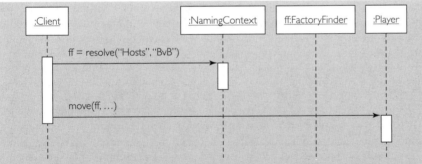

Example 9.5
Moving a `SoccerPlayer` to Another Host

If a player is 'bought' from one team by another, the player object should be moved from the host of its former team to the host of the new team in order to achieve processing locality. The league management has to approve of the move and consequently it would also implement the move. It would rely on objects of type `Player` (and team objects) being able to be migrated; this means that they would have to implement the `copy` and `move` operations. Player interfaces in CORBA-based systems would be subtypes of `LifeCycleObject`. The league management application is a client of the player object and requests execution of the `move` operation. As shown above, it would obtain a reference on a factory finder object that identifies the host of the new team and pass it as a parameter to the move operation. The player object would then move itself to the host determined by the factory finder.

Server Designer's Perspective on Migration

 Every migratable object must implement life cycle operations.

In order to enable an object to migrate from one host to another, the designer of a server object implements the two operations copy and move. The signatures of these operations do not contain any type-specific information and the operations therefore appear to be the same for all objects. The implementations of these two operations, however, are type-specific. This is because not only exported attributes but also all instance variables that are hidden in object implementations need to be transferred from one host to the other. In our soccer management example, the code needed for moving a player object is different from the code needed for moving a team object. In general, it is necessary that the migration operations are specifically implemented for each type of migratable object. In CORBA-based systems, this is done by redefining the `copy` and `move` operations in any subtype of `LifeCycleObject`.

 New copies need to be created for both creating and moving objects.

The first step of implementing the copy operation is to create a new copy of the same object type. The implementation of the copy operation asks the factory finder for a reference of a suitable factory in the desired location and requests the factory to create a new copy. Even for moving an object, a new copy has to be created. This is necessary as, at least in CORBA and COM-based systems, we cannot make any assumptions about the particular data representation that is being used for the attributes and instance variables of objects. These will be different, for instance, if the object is copied or moved from a mainframe to a UNIX machine.

 Data heterogeneity resolution during attribute transfer uses the mechanisms discussed in Chapter 5.

Heterogeneity of data representations is resolved while values of public attributes and private instance variables of objects are transferred from the object to the newly-created copy of the object. These transfers are implemented by object requests that pass attribute and instance variable values as arguments. Hence, the standard mechanism of marshalling to a common external data representation is used to resolve data heterogeneity of object migration.

 Move operations need to transfer the object reference to achieve migration transparency to clients.

The only difference between copying and moving an object is the treatment of the external CORBA object reference or the COM UID. When copying an object, other clients are not affected as the original object remains operational. When moving an object, other clients should not be affected either. The object reference they possess on the object should remain operational and requests they make using the reference should now be executed on the new host. Hence, for the move operation, the implementation of the factory has to assign the same CORBA object reference or COM UID to the new object. Migration is then transparent to clients.

 Heterogeneity of machine code is resolved by registration of factories and object implementations on different hosts.

Creating new copies of objects, even if they only need to be moved, also resolves potential heterogeneity of the machine code that is needed to execute requested operations. The new copy is created by a factory on the target host and uses the same machine code, operating system calls and address space as the factory. Note, however, that this assumes that there is an implementation of both the factory and the object type available on any potential target host. We discuss the administration obligations that result from this assumption next.

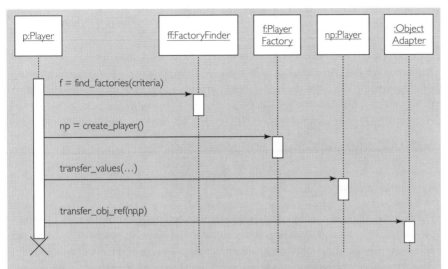

Example 9.6

Implementation of the Move
Operation

This UML sequence diagram shows the interactions that are necessary for moving an object
from one machine to another. The move operation first obtains a factory finder. To enable
the factory finder to find a suitable factory, the criteria passed to the move operation are
passed through to the factory finder. The factory finder returns a reference to a factory. The
move operation then requests creation of a new object of type Player from that factory.
Finally, it transfers values of attributes and instance variables to the new copy and then
assigns its object reference to the newly-created object using the object adapter, before
destroying itself.

Administrator's Perspective on Migration

Object migrations are often initiated by administrators. In general, their motivation for
doing so is to improve performance and reliability. Improving performance can be broken
down to two goals of preserving locality and load balancing. *Locality* means to locate those
objects that often request operations from one another on the same host or on hosts that are
efficiently connected. When request patterns change, there might be a need to relocate
objects. Load balancing might imply moving objects from an overloaded host to a new or
less-loaded host. In both cases, administrators would not perform these tasks manually but
rather employ administration applications. These applications would be clients of the life
cycle operations that we have discussed above.

Administrators, however, also have a number of obligations in order to implement object
migration. They are analogous with object creation:

Administration tasks
for migration are the
same as for creation.

1. installation of factory finders that are capable of locating suitable factories;
2. installation of factories capable of creating objects; and
3. registration of factory finders with naming or trading services.

There is again a need for communication between the designers of server objects and
administrators. Factories are designed and implemented with the types of server objects

that they create. Factory finders are implemented and installed by administrators. When life cycle operations are implemented within server objects, the implementation relies on factory finders to locate factories that implement the object creation operation that is used by the copy and move operations. Designers of server objects must make explicit assumptions about the interfaces of factory objects that they use. It is, therefore, advisable to start writing an administration handbook during the design of server objects and include information on factory usage in that handbook.

Location and Migration Transparency

To conclude, let us review the extent to which the migration operations support the transparency principles of distributed systems.

Migration is transparent to client, but not to server, designers.

We note that migration of objects is transparent to users of distributed applications and to client designers. Client programmers can continue to use object references even though the object has migrated from one host to another. Migration, however, is not transparent to designers of server objects and to administrators. Engineers building server objects need to implement migration operations. Administrators need to decide and implement policies about when migration operations are used.

Factory finders achieve location transparency.

The two migration operations can be used without having to determine the new physical location. The new location is even transparent to designers of server objects when they implement the object migration operations. They rely on a factory finder to reveal an object reference of a suitable object factory in a particular location. The way this location is determined is hidden within the factory finder objects that administration clients pass as arguments to the migration operations.

Migration does not achieve replication transparency.

Note that the copy operation that we have discussed does not achieve replication transparency for clients. This is because the result of copying is an entirely new object with its own object reference. Clients are aware of this fact as they obtain the object reference of the new copy. Moreover, if the copied object maintains an internal state, the state evolves differently from the time the object has been copied. With replicated objects, the existence of multiple replicas is concealed from clients. Clients are aware of only one object reference. Requests are dispatched to particular replicas according to a dispatch scheme that takes load balancing into account. Moreover, if a replicated object has an internal state the replication mechanism will propagate any updates to all replicas. Replication is generally transparent from developers of both client and server objects.

9.1.3 Deleting Objects

It is desirable to delete objects whose services are no longer needed in a distributed system. This frees resources in both the distribution middleware and the server host. It thus contributes to improving the overall efficiency of the distributed system. When considering object deletion, two concerns have to be separated:

1. How are objects deleted?
2. When are objects deleted?

In object-oriented programming languages *destructors* determine how objects are deleted. Destructors are used by programmers in order to determine type-specific actions that need to be taken when objects are destroyed. This is exactly the same with distributed objects. Specific operations that are similar to destructors need to be implemented in order to determine the actions to be taken upon object deletion.

The question of when objects can be deleted is more difficult. It is tightly related to the concept of *referential integrity*. This integrity constraint demands that references to objects must remain valid. In this context, it means that objects must not be deleted if other objects still refer to them. A violation of referential integrity in our soccer management example would be the deletion of a soccer player object that is still in a team. During printing of the squad plan, when all player objects are being visited, the team management application will then fail because it requests an operation from a non-existent object.

Referential integrity means that the validity of server object references held by a client is guaranteed.

In the remainder of this section, we will again use three different perspectives to discuss object deletion. We discuss the client's perspective of deletion, the way that deletion is implemented and finally we sketch object deletion from an administrator's point of view.

Client Designer's Perspective on Deletion

The time when objects are to be deleted can either be determined explicitly by clients of the object or implicitly by some run-time component that detects that objects will not be used any more. In both cases referential integrity needs to be ensured.

Many modern object-oriented programming languages (Java, Eiffel or Smalltalk) perform *implicit object deletion* by means of a *garbage collection* algorithm. These algorithms occasionally visit all objects and delete those to which no other objects refer. This approach is rather elegant as it deletes unused objects in a way that is transparent for clients and guarantees referential integrity. Hence, client programmers do not need to worry about tidying up and therefore cannot make any mistakes during that process. The problem with garbage collection algorithms in a distributed setting is that middleware does not necessarily know how many references to an object there are. In CORBA-based systems, for instance, object references can be held by other request brokers or even be stored in an externalized form outside the broker. In addition, garbage collection in a distributed setting is more expensive than in a centralized system; the approach taken for distributed Java objects keeps track of how many references exist to the object. This implies remote communication to the object whenever object references are duplicated, for instance when they are passed as arguments to a Java method.

Garbage collection means the implicit deletion of objects that are no longer needed.

Some object-oriented programming languages, such as C++, do not have garbage collection mechanisms. This choice was deliberately made in order to avoid the performance overhead of garbage collection, which had disabled the use of these languages in several classes of applications where performance is paramount (e.g. operating system implementations). In these languages, object deletion has to be explicitly requested by clients. C++ uses a delete operator; during execution of that operator, the code of the destructor and all inherited destructors is executed. The problem that arises with explicit deletion is that the burden of ensuring referential integrity is put on the client. In particular, the client must

Destructors are operations that define what needs to be done when an object is deleted.

make assumptions about whether other objects have a reference to the object to be deleted. While this might be possible in a centralized system that was designed in a coherent way, a client of a distributed server object does not know whether other distributed objects possess references to the server object. If an object has been registered with a location service any client of that service could have obtained an object reference. With federated location services, any client of some component in the federation might have a reference.

In practice, implicit object deletion where clients do not delete objects seems most desirable for distributed objects. A middleware implementation might be able to maintain a precise count of how many references exist for a server object within its domain. The middleware would then implicitly delete objects whose reference count has become zero. This would ensure referential integrity as long as the middleware is aware of every object reference that a client holds.

 Referential integrity cannot be assured across middleware boundaries.

Unfortunately, referential integrity cannot always be ensured and thus object deletion is not entirely transparent to client designers. It is generally not feasible to extend distributed garbage collection algorithms across middleware boundaries. Thus, clients that obtained an object reference from another middleware using the interoperability or interworking primitives that we discussed in Chapter 5 have to be aware of the fact that a server object they use might not be available anymore. When a client requests an operation execution from a non-existent object, the distribution middleware will inform the clients that the object does not exist. This is done by raising a Java or CORBA exception or by returning a COM error code. Designers of clients need to be aware of this fact and build clients that react appropriately to such error conditions.

Server Designer's Perspective on Deletion

Objects need to revoke their availability as service providers from the middleware.

Designers of server objects are concerned with actions that need to be taken when objects are deleted. Some actions are independent of the object type, for example deregistration of the object reference from the POA, SCM or Activation interfaces, others are type-specific. Type-specific operations usually involve actions that are needed to retain the semantic integrity of the remaining objects. In our soccer management example, deleting a team object requires release of all player object references (assuming the players continue to exist). These actions can, therefore, not be implemented by the middleware. In CORBA objects, they are implemented within the `remove` operation of the `LifeCycle` interface shown in Figure 9.3.

Figure 9.3
Interface of CORBA Deletion Operation

```
module CosLifeCycle{
  exception NotRemovable { string reason; };
  interface LifeCycleObject {
    ...
    void remove() raises {NotRemovable};
  }
  ...
};
```

An implementation of a destructor in a C++ class or the remove operation in the CORBA Life Cycle service should free all resources that are used by the server object implementation. This involves releasing all references that the object might have to its own server objects, releasing the memory used by its private data structures and finally deleting the object itself and telling the middleware that it is no longer available. In CORBA-based systems, the server object needs to deactivate itself through the object adapter. Example 9.7 shows such a CORBA-based implementation for the removal of a team object.

Objects need to free resources.

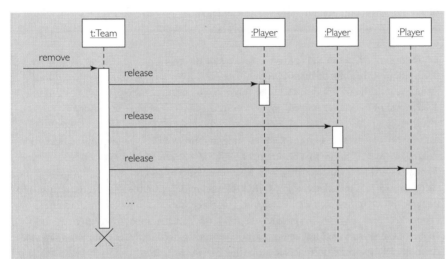

Example 9.7
Implementing the Deletion Operation

When executing the remove operation, the Team object releases all object references of the objects implementing the players of the team. For each player, this decrements the number of references that the broker maintains for the player. If a player object does not have any object references assigned to it any more the broker might also remove the player object.

Once an object has been deleted, the middleware will discontinue the object's identity. Any reference to the object that may exist will cease to be valid. This means in particular that the middleware will raise an exception or return an error code if clients continue to use the references in order to request operations from the object.

Administrator's Perspective on Deletion

Very often it is the administrator who decides on final object deletion. That decision is derived from management decisions that applications are not needed any more. The server objects constituting those applications are then deletion candidates. Object deletion from an administrator's point of view has two facets: the deletion of instances and the deletion of object types.

Administrators need to consider deletion of instances and deletion of types.

To implement the deletion of instances, administrators remove the object from a location service. This may involve deleting a name binding in a naming service or revoking a service from a trader. If the object is not used by any other objects, the object references held by the location service will be the last references to the object and the garbage collection

Instance deletion involves the removal of object references from the location service.

mechanism of the middleware will be able to delete the object. If the object is used by other objects, they will possess object references to the object. The middleware will then not delete them. New usages, however, will not be possible as the server objects cannot be located.

Deletion of a type involves removal of the object type from the Interface Repository, removal of code from the implementation repository, and removal of factories and factory types.

When the last instance of an object type has been deleted, the object type may itself be obsolete. It is obsolete when the administrator is convinced that no new instances of that type will need to be created. Then the administrator may decide to remove the object type from the middleware, too. Deletion of an object type involves a number of activities:

1. deletion of all factories that create instances of the type,
2. deletion of the type of these factories,
3. removal of the object type from the Interface Repository, and
4. removal of the object implementation from the implementation repository.

The factory objects that are capable of creating instances of the type in question need to be deleted in order to ensure that no attempts are made to create objects of a non-existent type. The factory types themselves may then have to be deleted too, in order to ensure that no such factories are created again. For CORBA-based middleware the type definition needs to be removed from the Interface Repository. This will ensure that middleware does not know about the object type any more and usages of the dynamic invocation interface and the Interface Repository will not rely on a non-existent type. Finally, the implementation of the object needs to be deregistered from the implementation repository. This will disable the object adapter from starting processes or threads that execute the object code that implements the type. For COM-based systems similar deregistration actions are needed in the COM registry.

9.2 Composite Objects

Often a group of objects have the same life cycle and composing them enables us to apply life cycle operations to the group.

In the previous section we have considered the life cycle of individual objects. It is quite common for more than one object to have the same life cycle because applications are often composed of several server objects. In our soccer management application, for instance, a team object is composed of a number of player objects. If the application is to be created, moved or deleted then all of its component objects have to be created, moved or deleted. If the team is to be moved to a different server then all the player objects that are part of the team should be moved, too. If we designate individual objects into a composite object, a life cycle service can implement these operations for a composite object. Object composition is usually determined by relationships. We have already discussed different forms of relationship in Chapter 2; refer back to that chapter for the notations; and we will now review how we can implement them.

In the next section we will discuss ways that object composition can be modelled statically, that is at a type level of abstraction. Then we will show how object composition can be implemented on the basis of a relationship service, an example of which is the CORBA Object Relationship service.

9.2.1 Modelling Distributed Object Composition

The motivation for modelling object composition is to determine a composite object in terms of its root object and all the components that belong to it. This information is used by programmers and administrators. Programmers use the model as a specification for decomposing applications into component objects. The model tells administrators the types of root objects of a composite object. Moreover, if they want to migrate or delete an object, they can query the composition model about the implications for other objects. We have already seen that we can use UML class diagrams to model relationships.

 UML class diagrams provide administrators and programmers with a model for the composition of objects.

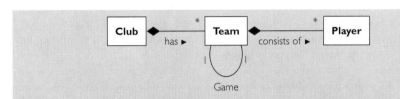

Game is an association between two teams. This association has reference semantics because it does not have diamonds at either end. A Club has a certain number of teams and a Team consists of a number of players. The use of composition relationships in this context means that a team can only be a component of one club and a player can only play in one team. Hence, an instance of type Club is a composite object and the related teams are its components. As composition is transitive, the Player objects that are components of a Team are also components of the Club that the team belongs to. Because of the reference semantics of relationship Game, however, a team that plays against another team is not a component of the other team's club.

Example 9.8
Modelling Composite Soccer Application Objects

A number of questions can be used as guidelines to validate an object composition model:

 Composition relationships need to meet a number of criteria.

1. If this composite object is moved, can all its component objects go with it?
2. If this composite object is copied, should all its component objects be copied to the new composite object?
3. If this composite object is deleted, can all its component objects be deleted, too?
4. Can this component object migrate without deleting the composition relationship?

If any of the above questions is negated then the object composition model is flawed and should be rectified by introducing additional object types or by changing composition relationships to reference relationships.

9.2.2 Implementing Distributed Object Composition

The implementation of object composition is based on object relationships. It would be desirable to have a service that uses the primitives available in object-oriented middleware to implement relationships between objects. We now discuss requirements that such a service must meet.

 Composition should be implemented using a relationship service.

One might ask why object references would not be sufficient for this problem as they can also be used in an attribute of one object to refer to another object. In fact we have used attributes in this way in the examples of Chapter 4. Relationships are implemented by objects rather than references for the following reasons:

Relationships should be objects in their own right.

1. Object types need to be changed in order to relate two objects, as new attributes have to be introduced that store references to related objects. This might not be possible if objects have to be related whose type definitions cannot or should not be changed (for instance if their source code is unavailable). If objects are used they can refer to the related objects without actually having to change their type definition.
2. References are only navigable in one direction. In order to implement bi-directional navigation, circular references are needed and the two object types are mutually dependent on each other. If relationships are implemented as objects they can store all the references to the related objects and implement navigation.
3. It is sometimes useful to attach attributes to relationships or to associate a certain behaviour with a relationship in order to give it a particular semantics. If objects are used to implement relationships their attributes and operations can implement such semantics, but this is not possible with object references.

This section discusses the implementation of object composition using relationships as they are supported by the CORBA Relationship service. We discuss the CORBA Relationship service as no equivalent service is available for Java or COM. It should, however, be a straightforward exercise to engineer a relationship service for those two middleware systems having understood the considerations given in this section.

The CORBA Relationship service supports three levels of abstraction. The lowest level of abstraction standardizes interfaces for the creation of relationships and for connecting objects using these relationships. The second level of abstraction uses these relationships to provide different forms of traversals through the graphs of objects that are related. The highest level of abstraction provides two specific services that are of particular importance for the implementation of composite objects. These are reference and containment relationships, with the containment relationship service having the same semantics as the composition relationships that we have found in UML. We now discuss these three levels of support.

Base Relationships

A role object is a proxy for an object that participates in a relationship.

The CORBA Relationship service addresses the above requirements by implementing relationships as objects. These relationship objects do not connect the related objects directly but rather refer to so-called *role* objects. Relationships use roles as proxies for the related objects. Roles have a reference to the related objects as well as to the relationship. The related objects, however, have no knowledge of the roles they play in a relationship nor of the relationship itself. This means that their types do not need to be changed for them to be able to participate in relationships.

To implement these relationships, in general one needs role objects, relationship objects and factory objects to create the role and relationship objects. These can be defined in a generic way as part of a service for implementing relationships. Figure 9.4 displays a UML class

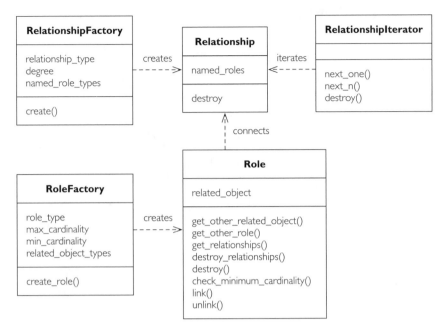

Figure 9.4
Relationship Interfaces in the CORBA Relationship Service

diagram that identifies object types contained in the base level of the CORBA relationship service.

Relationships come into existence through the `create` operation exported by the `RelationshipFactory` interface. `Create` takes a list of pairs of names and role objects as an argument and creates a new relationship object that connects all these role objects. While doing so, the factory also checks the cardinality of the relationship, the degree and the typing of the relationship.

Relationships are created by factories that check cardinality, degree and typing constraints.

The *cardinality* of a relationship is concerned with how many different relationships can be connected to the same role object. In Example 9.8, the cardinality of relationship `consists of` between `Player` and `Team` is one-to-many meaning that one team has many players. The `Contains` role that refers to the team object in Example 9.9 therefore may have many different instances of the relationship type `has` connected to it. On the other hand the `ContainedIn` role object must only be connected to one `has` relationship object. The `create` operation of interface `RelationshipFactory` raises an exception if the cardinality is exceeded in any roles involved in the relationship to be created. Hence cardinality constraints are checked at run-time by the factory.

Cardinality constrains the number of relationships that can be connected to the same role.

Most relationships are *binary*, that is they connect two server objects through two roles. The CORBA Relationship service, however, also supports relationships higher *degree*. The relationship factory raises an exception if the degree constraints for a relationship type are violated. This is the case if the list of named role objects does not contain exactly as many role objects as the degree of the relationship demands. Hence, compliance with the relationship degree is dynamically checked at run-time.

Degree defines how many roles a relationship has.

Example 9.9
Relating Objects using Roles and
Relationships

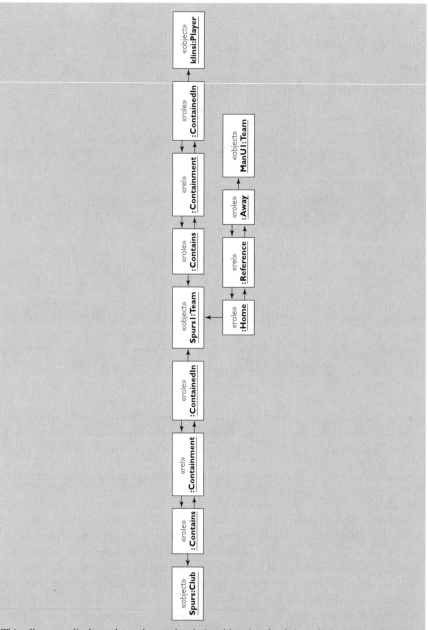

This diagram displays the roles and relationships involved in relating `Club`, `Team`, `Player` and `Game` objects as modelled in Example 9.8 in a UML object diagram. Stereotypes are used to indicate whether objects implement server objects, roles or relationships. The implementation-oriented relationships in that figure are directed and can be implemented directly with object references. Note that there are no outgoing relationships from any server objects which means that the server objects are unaware that they are related and their types do not have to be adjusted.

The factory may also check whether the relationship is correctly typed. While the relationship Game is reasonable to relate two team objects playing the roles Home and Away, it would be meaningless to use it to relate two League objects. The factory may raise an exception indicating a typing error if the wrong types of role objects are passed to its create operation. Hence, typing constraints are also checked dynamically at run-time.

Typing constraints restrict the types of object to which roles can refer.

This consistency checking at run-time is not feasible within general-purpose relationship factories. Hence any use of the Relationship service would implement relationship factories in an application type-specific way. They would then create application-specific relationships that are subtypes of object type Relationship by connecting objects of application-specific role types that are subtypes of Role.

Application-specific role and relationship types specialize the role and relationship types provided by the service.

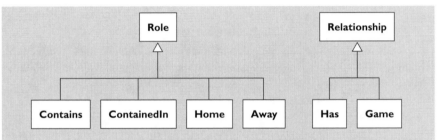

Example 9.10
Relationships and Role Types

The above diagram shows the relationship and role types that were used in Example 9.9. It shows the four application-specific role types Contains ContainedIn, Home and Away as subtypes of Role. Moreover, the two relationships has and Game are subtypes of object type Relationship as defined in the base level of the relationship service.

Graphs of Related Objects

The second layer of the CORBA Relationship service supports determining graphs of related objects which clients can traverse using different graph traversal algorithms. This graph layer is exploited by the Life Cycle service to visit all components of a composite object during a 'deep' migration or deletion operation.

Graphs are built from nodes and edges. Nodes are objects that implement the Node interface defined in the Relationship service. In particular they have knowledge of all role objects that refer to them. They also have a reference to the related server object. Therefore nodes are used as proxies of server objects by the relationship service and its clients. Edges are implemented as relationships that connect roles. Example 9.9 is extended to a graph of related objects in Example 9.11.

Traversal through graphs of related objects are supported by the Relationship service through interfaces TraversalFactory, TraversalCriteria and Traversal. The TraversalFactory exports an operation that takes a node, a traversal mode and a TraversalCriteria object as a parameter and creates a Traversal object. The traversal object will start from the node given to the factory and return all nodes of the graph according to the specified mode. The Traversal object is the principal server object to

Relationship services can implement graph traversal algorithms.

Example 9.11
Graph of Related Objects

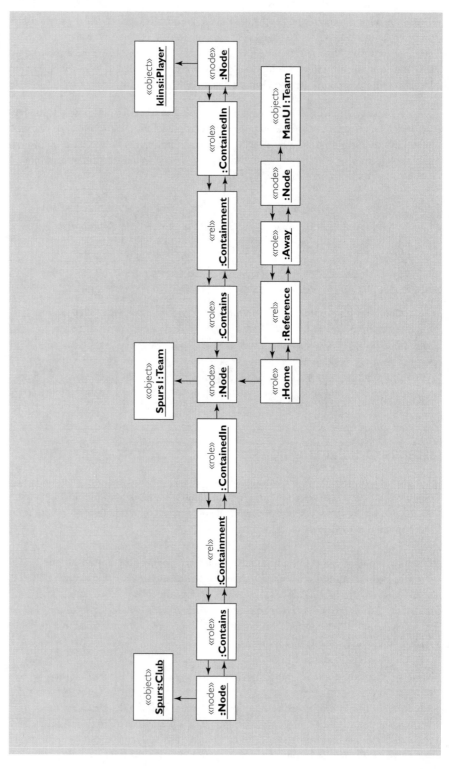

clients and exports operations to get the next or the *n* next node objects. The supported traversal modes are depth-first, breadth-first and best-first. The traversal criteria object implements the different traversal modes. It is invoked during a traversal by the traversal object transparently to clients. The traversal object will tell the `TraversalCriteria` object which node is currently being visited and then the object emits edges according to the chosen traversal strategy.

Reference and Containment Relationships

The final layer of the CORBA Relationship service defines two specific types of relationship with a reference and a containment semantics. They are defined with the roles needed to connect relationships of these types to objects. Figure 9.5 shows a UML class diagram that indicates the interfaces of these relationships and roles. The reference and containment relationships are each defined in separate IDL module that is shown as a UML package. They are subtypes of the relationship type that is defined in the package `CosRelationships` that constitutes the base layer.

Relationship service can provide a direct implementation for the semantics of UML compositions.

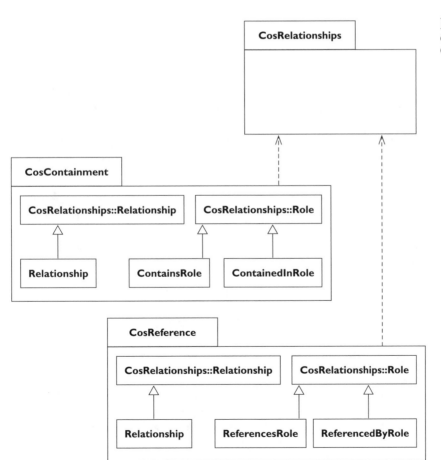

Figure 9.5
CORBA Reference and Containment Relationships

Both relationships are binary relationships. The reference relationship has many-to-many cardinality, which means that one object can refer to many further objects and also be referenced by many other objects. The containment relationship has one-to-many cardinality which means that a container can refer to many contained objects but an object is contained in at most one container. The objects to which the four role objects refer to have to be of type `CosGraph::Node`. This means that the relationships form traversable graphs of objects. Instances of reference relationships relate a role object of type `ReferencesRole` with a role object of type `ReferencedByRole`. Likewise, instances of containment relationships relate a role object of type `ContainsRole` with a role object of type `ContainedInRole`. If any of these constraints are not met, the Relationship service raises exceptions.

The containment relationship of the CORBA Relationship service meets the requirements that we have for composition relationships: it has an aggregation semantics and it demands that each containee is at most contained in one container. Moreover, the objects interconnected by the Relationship service are of type `Node` or any subtype thereof. Hence the container and all its containees can be traversed by a life cycle service for implementing migration and deletion of composite objects.

9.3 Composite Object Life Cycle

 Composite object life cycle is concerned with migration and deletion of composite objects.

The life cycle operations of composite objects are a subset of the life cycle of component objects. We do not consider creation of composite objects. They are created by relating their component objects and we have already discussed how to create individual objects and how to relate them. The services that we have discussed in the previous two sections are sufficient for that. We do, however, consider the migration operations to copy and move composite objects to a different host and the deletion operation that removes a composite object with all its components from a host.

A composite object is a root node and the transitive closure of the containment relationship.

We are in a position now to refine our definition of a composite object. A composite object is determined by a root node. All role objects that are in the transitive closure of the containment relationships belong to the composite object. All containment relationship objects that are connected to these node objects belong to the composite object. All node objects that are connected to the role objects in the composite object belong to the composite object and all server objects to which node objects refer also belong to the composite object.

The semantics of these three operations for the life cycle of composite objects are slightly more complicated than those of the life cycle operations for individual objects. We not only have to deal with individual server objects, but also with the node, roles and relationship objects that belong to the composite object.

 A deep life cycle operation is an operation applied to a composite object and all the relationship and role objects that it contains.

Hence when a composite object is copied to a different host, all node, role, relationship and server objects that belong to the composite object are also copied to the new host. This is referred to as a *deep copy*. In addition, we connect the newly-created objects with newly-created reference relationship objects if their respective source nodes had reference relations. A *deep move* operation is similar, except that we move all constituents of the composite object and redirect existing reference relationships to them. A *deep delete* operation removes all constituents of the composite object and deletes reference relationships too.

We now discuss the client and server designer perspectives on the composite object life cycle. We note that there is no need to cover the administrator's perspective as the composite objects consist of simple distributed objects and the primitives for administering the life cycle of these have been discussed already.

9.3.1 Client Designer's View of the Composite Object Life Cycle

We assume that a client wishing to request a life cycle operation for a composite object has a reference to the root node of a graph of objects that is related by containment relationships. In the composite life cycle specification, nodes are also life cycle objects. Hence they export `move`, `copy` and `remove` operations. In order to request a life cycle operation of a composite object, the client programmer only requests execution of the `copy`, `move` or `remove` operation of the root node. The implementation of the composite life cycle operations would then handle the rest in a way transparent to the client programmer.

Life cycle operations for composite objects are applied via its root object.

We note that from a client's perspective, life cycle operations for composite objects are no different from life cycle operations for individual objects. Hence as far as the life cycle is concerned, object composition is transparent to clients.

9.3.2 Server Designer's View of Composite Object Life Cycle

Each node object in a graph of objects related by a composition relationship refers to a server object. When performing a composite object life cycle operation, a node object needs to request the respective life cycle operation from its server object. Hence the server objects that participate in a composite object each need to support the `LifeCycle` interface. This is achieved by the fact that the `Node` type used for the life cycle of composite objects refers to server objects of type `LifeCycleObject`, which was shown in Figure 9.2. Other than that, the designer implementing a composite life cycle does not have to do anything. It is again done by the implementation of a relationship service in a transparent way.

Every component object needs to implement the life cycle interface.

The life cycle approach for composite objects that was discussed above is rather elegant. It combines composition relationships with the life cycle of individual objects in such a way that server objects are not aware that they participate in a composition. This is an important property that simplifies the administration of composite objects.

There is, however, a price to be paid for this elegance. If you consider how many objects are needed for the implementation of four objects and three relationships in Example 9.11 and how that number increases with every copy of the object as shown in Example 9.12 then the price becomes obvious. There are considerable storage and run-time overhead costs involved with implementing relationships in this way. This implies that these relationships should only be used with rather coarse-grained objects. Using them with a large quantity of fine-grained objects is likely to exhibit poor performance characteristics.

Object composition with a relationship service can incur performance problems.

Example 9.12
Copying a Composite Object

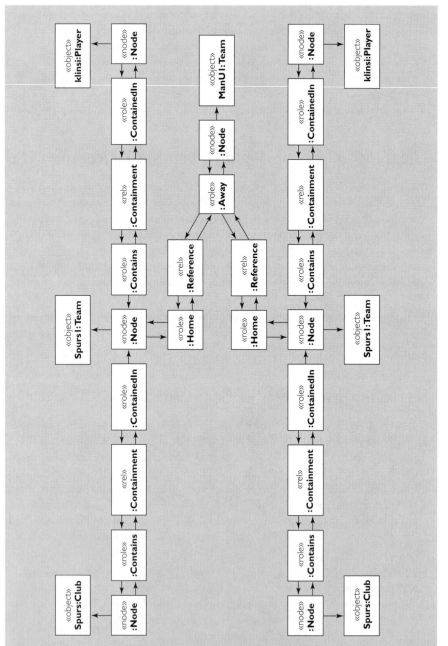

When we request copy from the composite object shown in Example 9.11, the result is shown above. The copy operation has performed a deep copy and copied the Team and Player objects as well as the node, role and relationship objects that are in the transitive closure of the containment relationship. It has copied the reference relationship object implementing the Game relation but it has stopped copying at the Away Role and only related the newly-created object to this role.

Key Points

▶ The four life cycle operations are creation, copying, moving and removing objects. The life cycle of distributed objects is considerably more complicated than the life cycle of central objects due to location and heterogeneity considerations.

▶ Object creation is supported by factories. A factory is a distributed object that exports operations that create new objects. The newly-created objects operate initially in the same location as the factory.

▶ Copying and moving an object from one host to another is referred to as object migration. Factory finders are used by migration operations to determine the location of the host in a way that is transparent to both the client and the server.

▶ Object deletion can be done either explicitly or implicitly. Objects are deleted explicitly when authorized clients request a remove operation. In that case, clients have to ensure referential integrity. Objects are deleted implicitly by the middleware if no client object possesses a reference to the object.

▶ Composite objects are determined by composition relationships. A composition relationship is an aggregation relationship where each component is at most part of one aggregate. All objects that are in the transitive closure of a root object belong to the composite object induced by that root object.

▶ Object composition can be supported by a relationship service. A relationship service for distributed objects should be able to relate objects without the objects being aware that they are related.

▶ An integration between a relationship service and a life cycle service can be used to implement the life cycle of composite objects. The fact that an object does not only support its individual life cycle but may also be part of the life cycle of a composite object can be kept transparent to both clients of the composite object and the implementation of the individual objects.

▶ Due to the overhead in space and time complexity, the relationship service should only be used for relating and composing rather coarse-grained server objects.

Self Assessment

9.1 What is the object life cycle?

9.2 Why is the concept of constructors not sufficient for creating objects in a distributed setting?

9.3 What is the difference between a factory and a factory finder?

9.4 Should a newly-created object always be registered with a name server or a trader?

9.5 How is the host to which objects should be migrated specified?

9.6 Why does this support location transparency and to whom is it transparent?

9.7 What are the differences between explicit and implicit object deletion?

9.8 In which situations do CORBA clients have to be aware of the fact that an object might have been deleted?

9.9 What are the differences between aggregation and reference relationships?

9.10 What distinguishes composition relationships from other aggregation relationships?

9.11 How are the objects that are components of a composite object determined?

9.12   What are the three support layers of the CORBA Relationship service?

9.13   How does the Relationship service contribute to implementing composite objects?

9.14   What ensures that objects that are related by CORBA relationships do not need to be changed?

9.15   What has to be traded off against the fact that CORBA server objects are unaware that they might be involved in a CORBA relationship?

Further Reading

We suggest that the reader compares the distributed object life cycle discussed in this chapter with the much simpler life cycle of objects in object-oriented programming languages. The model of explicit object construction and destruction that has been chosen for C++ is discussed by [Ellis and Stroustrup, 1990]. [Meyer, 1988b] gives a good introduction to the concepts of object creation in Eiffel. Meyer also argues convincingly in favour of garbage collection as opposed to explicit object removal. A good summary of how object construction and deletion is treated in Java is presented in [Flanagan, 1997].

Data structures and algorithms for garbage collection techniques are presented by [Aho et al., 1983] and their application in compiler construction are discussed in [Aho et al., 1986]. They suggest two techniques for garbage collection: reference counting and mark and sweep. While the former technique is applicable to collecting distributed object garbage, the latter assumes that there is only one process at a time working on the objects and that it can be stopped to find out which objects are unused. Reference-counting algorithms in their pure form also do not work if there are circular reference structures, which occur regularly in composite distributed objects.

Factories are introduced by [Gamma et al., 1995]. The applications of factories they refer to, however, is not to hide location information as in our case but to avoid distributing knowledge about which particular type of object needs to be created into client objects.

Entity–relationship modelling was introduced by [Chen, 1976] as a mechanism to model the relationships between tuples of relational databases. The first object-oriented approach to modelling these relationships, still for relational databases, was presented in [Blaha et al., 1988]. A more elaborate introduction on how to use relationships in class diagrams is given by [Rumbaugh et al., 1991]. The reader should also refer to the Unified Modeling Language, which we use throughout this book. It is introduced quite comprehensively in [Muller, 1997].

Two chapters of the CORBAservices specification are relevant to what has been discussed in this chapter. The CORBA Life Cycle specification is in Chapter 7 and the CORBA Relationship service in Chapter 9 of [Object Management Group, 1996]. The appendix of Chapter 7 determines interfaces for the life cycle of composite objects. The appendix can thus be seen as a specification for the integration between the Life Cycle service and the Relationship Service.

There is a growing interest in code mobility, which is related to the discussion in this chapter. A very good conceptual framework is provided by [Fuggetta et al., 1998]. Theories that provide a formal treatment of code mobility have been developed by [Milner,

1999] and [Cardelli and Gordon, 1998]. A good coverage in the programming of object mobility in Java is provided by [Nelson, 1999].

Mobile Agents are primitives that are usually layered on top of the primitives that we discussed in this chapter. They transfer both code and data. One of the most successful frameworks for mobile agents is Aglets, which were developed at IBM Japan by [Lange and Oshima, 1998].

10

Object Persistence

Learning Objectives

A persistent object is capable of storing its state in such a way that it survives termination of the process in which it is being executed. We will grasp the importance of persistence for distributed objects and comprehend the relationship between persistence and deactivation policies in object-oriented middleware. We will learn how persistence can be achieved by storing and reading the state of distributed objects to and from secondary storage. We will study the techniques that are supported by object-oriented middleware for achieving persistence. We will see that none of them uses raw disk formats, but rather that they rely on higher levels of abstractions, such as file systems and relational and object databases. We will ascertain the circumstances in which each of these mechanisms is most appropriate and comprehend their influence on the design of distributed objects.

Chapter Outline

The meta-object model for distributed objects that we introduced in Chapter 2 includes the concept of attributes. According to our definition, attributes make a server's state information available to client objects. Server objects that do not make their state available to their clients may maintain an internal, hidden state, which may influence the behaviour of the object operations. For the integrity of a server object, it is therefore important that its state is retained even though the process that executes the server object is terminated.

In Chapter 9, we discussed composite objects. The need to secure state information also applies to composite objects. If the process executing a composite object is terminated then often the processes that execute its component objects are terminated, too. If these component objects maintain state information, this state has to be retained alongside the data about the composition of the composite object itself.

Processes that execute server objects terminate for various reasons. They may be terminated due to a deactivation policy that determines, for example that objects that have been idle for some time should release the resources that they occupy. Processes may be terminated by administrators when hosts need to go out of operation. Processes also terminate accidentally when, for example the host's operating system cannot meet the memory demands.

In Chapter 11, we will discuss how the concept of transactions can be used to secure the integrity of server objects against accidental termination of processes. We will see that transactions demand that once they are finished the state of the objects that they modified is retained or *durable*. This means that the state must survive failures and host shutdown. Durability is usually achieved by using the same primitives that are used to implement deliberate termination of processes.

A persistent state service helps server object programmers to implement persistence.

To meet the demand that objects do not lose their state, it becomes necessary to store the state on secondary storage before the process terminates and to load the state from secondary storage when the object is activated again. The implementation of this storage and recovery is supported by a *persistent state service*.

In the next section, we discuss the principles of when and how persistence can be achieved. We then discuss the CORBA Persistent State Service, to exemplify these principles. After that we review how a persistent state service can be implemented and outline a general architecture for it. In the last section, we will review how object states can be mapped into files and relational or object-oriented database management systems.

10.1 Principles of Persistence

Persistence is the ability of an object state to survive termination of the process in which the object executes.

While an object is active, its state is retained in memory that is allocated to the process that executes the object. *Persistent* objects survive the lifetime of the process. Objects that are not persistent are referred to as *transient*. In order to achieve persistence, objects have to transfer their state to non-volatile, that is secondary, storage such as battery-powered RAM, Flash RAM, tapes or CDs. The most common media for implementing persistence, however, are hard disk drives.

It may not be necessary for every distributed object to implement persistence. Whether persistence needs to be supported depends on whether the object maintains a state. We now distinguish stateful from stateless objects. Designers of server objects need to be aware of this distinction and they need to implement persistence for stateful server objects only.

10.1.1 Stateful versus Stateless Objects

We have seen that distributed object models support the concept of attributes. Server designers use attributes to make state information available to client programmers. One might, therefore, consider implementing persistence for those objects that have declared attributes in their interfaces. This choice, however, would not include those objects that have an internal state that they do not disclose in their interface. It is therefore not appropriate to regard the fact that an interface declares attributes as the only indicator for having to support persistence in the interface implementation.

A much better indication of the need to implement persistence is the fact that server object implementations have instance variables. These instance variables retain state information, which will be lost when the object is deactivated or the object's process terminates otherwise. We therefore define distributed objects to be *stateful* if and only if their object implementation declares any instance variables; otherwise, they are *stateless*.

Stateful objects have instance variables in their implementation.

In the soccer management application, the team objects are stateful, as they store object references to the team's players. Likewise, player objects are stateful, as they store the player's name. An iterator object that visits every player of the team, however, is a stateless server object, as it does not maintain an internal state.

Example 10.1
Persistence in Soccer Management Application

The situation is slightly more complicated with composite objects. The individual component objects can be either stateful or stateless. In the previous chapter, we noted as a general principle that objects are unaware of whether they are related to other objects or not. A stateless server object that is related to stateful component objects, therefore cannot take responsibility for implementing persistence of its component objects; the designer of the composite object would not know anything about the composition relationship. Hence, the role objects, which implement the relationships have to be considered as stateful and they need to implement persistence.

10.1.2 Transparency of Persistence

The previous section has helped us to understand which objects need to support persistence. We now review which engineers need to be aware of the different aspects of persistence.

We have already discussed that different media types, of which hard disks are the most common, can be used for implementing persistence. Persistence may be achieved by writing onto a file or by utilizing a database system. We will discuss these mechanisms in detail in later sections of this chapter. It is worthwhile to note that the particular mechanism that is

Server object designers have to implement persistence.

chosen for achieving persistence may be transparent to some engineers, while it may not be transparent to others. The use of a persistent state service is usually transparent to designers of client objects. The client programmer only considers the published interface of the object and is not aware how persistence is achieved in the implementation of that interface. The designer of a stateful server object, however, generally has to be aware of the mechanism that he or she uses to implement persistence. Hence the target audience for the discussions in this chapter are designers who want to implement persistence of stateful server objects.

Persistent state services hide the details of data stores from server objects.

Stateful server objects are quite common. Implementing persistence for stateful server objects can be quite involved. It usually requires mapping server objects to some data store, such as a file system, or a relational or object-oriented database and it is highly desirable to support engineers in implementing those mappings. As shown in Figure 10.1, such support is generally provided by a *persistent state service*. The service implements the mapping of object states to file systems or databases in such a way that the particular details of a data store are transparent to a server object designer.

Figure 10.1

Interfaces of Stateful Server Objects

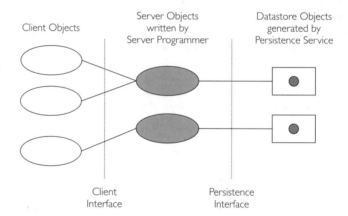

Achieving persistence involves the transfer of data from main memory to secondary storage or vice versa. We refer to this data transfer as a *swap*. We expect that this transfer is managed by the persistent state service. There may be many different strategies for when a swap is best achieved and accordingly who triggers the transfer. If persistence needs to be achieved due to the activation or deactivation of a server object, it is the object-oriented middleware implementation that chooses the point in time when the swap is triggered. If stateful server objects participate in transactions in order to secure updates to those objects, the transaction coordinator will trigger the swap. Hence, the time of swaps is not only transparent to client designers, but also to server designers.

10.1.3 Persistent State Services

We now introduce concepts that are commonly used in the discussion of persistent state services. We refer to Figure 10.2 for an overview of these concepts. The figure refers to the objects that are shown as Datastore Objects on the right-hand side of Figure 10.1.

Persistent state services often define a *persistent state service definition language* (PSSDL) and their implementations include a compiler for this language. The purpose of the PSSDL is to specify what has to be stored persistently and to enable a PSSDL compiler to derive programming language representations that a server object designer can use. Many concepts shown in Figure 10.2 have a representation in such PSSDLs. The PSSDL compiler then derives the implementations of these concepts.

Persistent state service definition languages define object persistence independently of a data store.

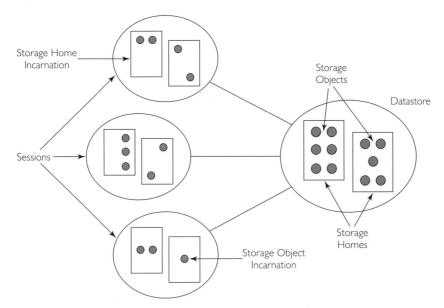

Figure 10.2
Concepts in Persistent State Services

Datastores

A datastore is an abstract concept that subsumes technologies such as files, relational databases, object–relational databases, object-oriented databases, hierarchical databases and network databases. These technologies can be used to store the state of objects in a persistent manner. Datastores manage storage objects and storage homes. A storage home is a container that manages the persistent representations for storage objects. For a relational datastore, a storage home is a table. A storage object is the representation of the state of a stateful server object within the storage home. In the case of the relational datastore, this would be a row of the table that contains a set of attributes for the server object's state.

Datastores are storage technologies that are used to achieve persistence of data.

Storage Types

A persistent state service may take the attributes of server objects and store them in a persistent datastore. However, the representation of attributes in server objects might not be best suited for a direct and automatic mapping onto a datastore. Moreover, there may be attributes in a server object that do not need to be stored persistently. We therefore introduce an additional layer of objects that are in charge of persistence. This layer contains storage objects. They will be defined in such a way that their attributes can be directly and

Storage types define the representation of storage objects.

automatically mapped to persistent storage. They will provide operations for server objects to obtain and modify the attribute values that are stored persistently.

Storage type specifications are interfaces to storage objects.

Storage objects have an interface and an implementation. The interface is referred to as a *storage type specification*. It defines the storage object from the server object designer's point of view. The implementation of this specification is called a *storage type*. The storage type defines sufficient information for the persistent state service to automatically generate all the code that is necessary for the implementation of a swap.

Storage objects may be nested within other storage objects. In our soccer management example, a storage object for a player may be nested within the storage object of the player's team. In the realm of COM, this nesting is referred to as *structured storage*. The nesting is usually done only for composite objects, because the lifetime of the nested storage object is the same as the lifetime of the container in which it resides. In the soccer management example, the player would be implicitly deleted when the team storage object is deleted.

A storage object incarnation is a programming language representation of a storage object.

Storage objects are instances of storage types. Storage objects have a representation in the datastore that achieves persistence. They have further representations in the processes that execute distributed server objects. To distinguish the two, the latter are referred to as *storage object incarnations*. A storage object incarnation is always a programming language object, while the storage object may be a tuple in a relational database or a node in a network database. The programming language representation of the storage object incarnation's type is usually derived from the storage type by the persistent state service.

Storage Homes

A storage home manages the life cycle of types of storage objects. Its interface is defined in a storage home specification.

Storage homes are the containers for storage objects. They provide operations to create new storage objects and to look up existing storage objects. The concepts for storage homes are similar to those of the storage objects they contain. A *storage home specification* defines the interface that server object programmers see for the storage home. The implementation of the specification is specified in a *storage home*. Again, the concrete implementation of the storage home is often derived fully automatically by a persistent state service.

Storage home incarnations are programming language representations of storage homes.

Storage home incarnations are programming language representations of instances of storage homes. Like storage object incarnations, they execute in the same process as the server objects that use them. The type of a storage home incarnation is often generated fully automatically from the storage home type by the persistent state service.

Keys

As suggested in Figure 10.2, storage homes act as containers for collections of storage objects. There may be a large number of these objects. In order to be able to efficiently identify storage objects, persistent state services may support the concept of keys. A *key* is an attribute of a storage object that uniquely identifies the storage object within its storage home. The designer of a server object will have to use the PSSDL to specify which attributes uniquely identify a storage object.

Keys are a very important concept in databases, too. They are often used to speed up access. Databases maintain an index, usually in the form of a B-tree, that efficiently maps key values to objects or tuples. Identification of objects in a collection can then be done in logarithmic rather than linear time. A persistent state service may use the keys that are specified in the PSSDL definition of storage objects to derive such indexes.

Sessions

A session denotes the time during which a connection is established between a datastore and a process that executes a server object. During sessions, the persistent state service transfers storage object incarnations and storage object home incarnations to the server object process. The persistent state service also swaps storage object or storage home incarnation data that a server object has modified back onto the persistent storage object or storage home.

> A session is a logical connection between a datastore and a process that executes a server object.

The persistent state service will offer an interface to the server object for session management purposes. This interface will support creating sessions, closing sessions, flushing storage object incarnation onto persistent storage and refreshing storage object incarnations from persistent storage. During the creation of a session, security checks will be performed. We will discuss security in more detail in Chapter 12.

10.2 Using the CORBA Persistent State Service

In this section we use the CORBA Persistent State Service (PSS) to review an example of a persistent state service and to show what server object designers need to do to achieve persistence in practice. PSS, which was adopted in August 1999, replaces the Persistent Object Service, which was one of the first CORBAservices. The Persistent Object Service was never fully implemented because it was both too ambitious and too loosely specified. Moreover, it was not properly integrated with the CORBA Transaction Service and the Portable Object Adapter, both of which were defined at a later point.

The PSS is used by designers of stateful CORBA server objects to implement persistence. Implementations of the PSS achieve persistence in various datastores, including files, relational databases and object databases. Example 10.2 shows a persistent implementation of the CORBA Naming service, which we discussed in Chapter 8. The Naming service defines `NamingContext` objects, each of which manages different name bindings. Clients that use the Naming service obviously expect the name bindings that they register to remain available even though the name server may be temporarily deactivated. Hence, the need arises for `NamingContext` server objects to store the name bindings persistently. The objects that implement the second interface of the Naming service and iterate over name bindings do not have to be considered here as they are transient.

Example 10.2 suggests that persistence can be kept transparent for designers of client objects. The IDL interface `NamingContext` has no relationships with the storage home and storage type specifications.

Example 10.2
Interfaces and Classes for a
Persistent Name Server

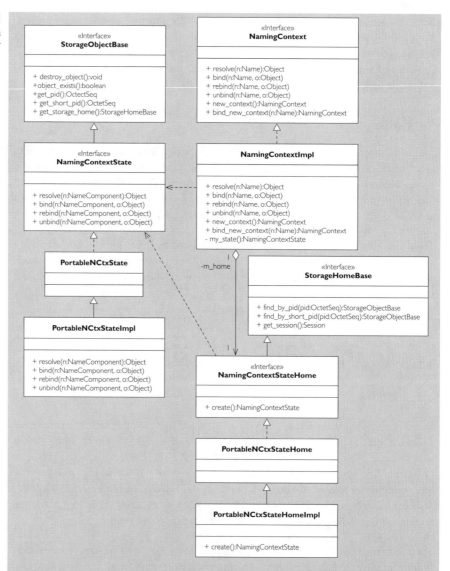

This UML class diagram shows IDL interfaces, the specification of storage types and storage homes, and the classes that implement storage types and storage homes for a persistent naming service. Clients access the service through `NamingContext`. Its implementation, `NamingContextImpl`, uses `NamingContextStateHome` and `NamingContextState` to achieve persistence. `NamingContextStateHome` is a storage home specification. `NamingContextState` is a storage object specification that is capable of storing and manipulating the binding of simple names to CORBA object references. The binding and resolution of composite names is achieved in `NamingContextImpl`. Each `NamingContextImpl` object maintains a reference to a `NamingContextStateHome` object that it uses to create `NamingContextState` storage objects for new naming contexts.

10.2.1   Persistent State Service Definition Language

The service specification includes the *Persistent State Service Definition Language* (PSSDL), an example of a persistence definition language. PSSDL is a strict superset of CORBA/IDL. PSSDL extends IDL with mechanisms to specify storage objects, storage homes and keys.

PSSDL storage type and storage home specifications then need to be implemented. This implementation is specified at a high level of abstraction and the implementation is then generated from this specification by the PSSDL compiler. Example 10.3 continues our persistent naming service discussion and shows how PSSDL is used to specify the implementation of `NamingContextState` and `NamingContextHome`.

Persistence is transparent to client designers.

Server object implementations cannot directly use the storage home and storage type implementations shown in Example 10.4. To render PSSDL usable, PSS defines a number of programming language bindings that are similar to the bindings between CORBA/IDL and programming languages. A PSSDL compiler will translate the definitions and produce classes in Java or C++. These classes are used for two purposes. Server object implementations use them to instantiate and invoke storage object incarnations and storage home incarnations. Moreover, the classes are used to implement the operations that are declared in the storage home and storage type specifications.

```
// file NamingContextState.pssdl
#include <CosNaming.idl>
storagetypespec NamingContextState{
   Object resolve(in CosNaming::NameComponent n)
         raises(CosNaming::NotFound, CosNaming::CannotProceed,
         CosNaming::InvalidName);
   void bind(in CosNaming::NameComponent n, in Object obj)
      raises(CosNaming::NotFound, CosNaming::CannotProceed,
            CosNaming::InvalidName, CosNaming::AlreadyBound);
   void unbind(in CosNaming::NameComponent n, in Object obj)
       raises(CosNaming::NotFound, CosNaming::CannotProceed,
            CosNaming::InvalidName);
   void rebind(in CosNaming::NameComponent n, in Object obj)
       raises(CosNaming::NotFound, CosNaming::CannotProceed,
            CosNaming::InvalidName);
};

storagehomespec NamingContextStateHome of NamingContextState{
   ref<NamingContextState> create();
};
```

Example 10.3
Storage Type and Storage Home Specifications in PSSDL

PSSDL specifies the storage types and storage homes that are used to persistently store name bindings on behalf of `NamingContext` server objects. The specifications refine the interfaces `NamingContextState` and `NamingContextStateHome` that were shown in Example 10.2.

Example 10.4

Implementation of Storage
Home and Storage Types in PSS

```
#include "NamingContextState.pssdl"
struct ListElement {
   CosNaming::NameComponent name;
   Object obj;
};

typedef sequence List;

storagetype PortableNCtxState implements NamingContextState{
   attribute List m_list;
};

storagehome PortableNCtxStateHome of PortableNCtxState
   implements NamingContextStateHome {};
```

The implementation of the storage object for persistent naming contexts is defined in
`PortableNCtxState` and the implementation of the storage home is provided in
`PortableNCtxStateHome`. In particular, we define that the persistent representation
of a naming context state has an attribute that stores a list of bindings between simple name
components and CORBA object references.

10.2.2 Programming Language Bindings

The bindings for Java and C++ extend the IDL language bindings. They define how
the PSSDL-specific constructs are mapped to constructs available in the Java and C++
programming languages. In particular, they map the base interfaces that are defined in PSS
to interfaces and classes in the programming language. We now focus on the Java programming language binding.

The PSSDL/Java language binding defines that storage home and storage object specifications are mapped to Java interfaces. Storage objects and storage homes are mapped to Java
classes that implement these interfaces. The PSSDL compiler generates both interfaces and
classes. The server object programmer who wants to achieve persistence can then subclass
the generated classes to add specific behaviour (see Example 10.5).

Whenever a new object is created, the storage home has to be involved. It needs to create
and return a reference onto a new storage object and use the portable object adapter to
create a new object reference for a naming context object and associates it with the persistent
identifier of the newly-created storage object. Example 10.6 continues our example to
demonstrate this aspect.

10.2.3 Integration with Object Adapter

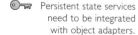 Persistent state services
need to be integrated
with object adapters.

In the introduction to this chapter we indicated that one of the motivating factors for
persistence is object activation and deactivation. Activation and deactivation are implemented by object adapters. One of the CORBA object adapters is the Portable Object Adapter

```
public class NamingContextImpl extends POA_NamingContext {
  private NamingContextStateHome m_home;
  private POA m_poa;

  private NamingContextState my_state() {
    return((NamingContextState)
          m_home.find_by_short_pid(_object_id()));
  }

  NamingContextImpl(NamingContextStateHome home, POA poa) {
    m_home = home; m_poa = poa;
  }

  public CORBA.Object resolve(NameComponent[] n) {
    if (n.length == 1)
      return my_state().resolve(n[0]);
    else {
      NamingContext new_target = NamingContext.narrow(
                          my_state().resolve(n[n.length-1]));
      NameComponent[] rest_of_name=new NameComponent[n.length-1];
      System.arraycopy(n,0,rest_of_name,0,n.length-1);
      return new_target.resolve(rest_of_name);
    }
  }
  // similar implementations for bind, unbind, rebind, etc

  public NamingContext new_context() {
    NamingContextStateRef ref = m_home.create();
    return NamingContext.narrow(m_poa().create_reference_with_id(
    ref.short_pid(),"IDL:omg.org/CosNaming/NamingContext:1.0"));
  }
}
```

Example 10.5
POA-Based Java Server Class

This code uses the PSSDL/Java binding to implement naming context server objects. The implementation maintains a reference m_home to the storage home object that contains the naming context storage objects. Note that this is a standard Java and not a CORBA object reference. All storage homes can look up storage objects based on Persistent IDs (PIDs) using find_by_short_pid. We will see below how this PID is related to the CORBA object identifier. Method my_state uses this lookup mechanism to establish the one-to-one relationship between the CORBA naming context server object and the storage object that stores name bindings persistently. The code then shows as an example how the resolve operation of NamingContext is implemented.

(POA), which supports persistence. The POA defines a number of persistence-related policies with which server object implementors can control the way the server object is activated and deactivated. We discuss these policies alongside our Naming service implementation example. In particular, we now review how the naming service is initialized in Example 10.7.

Example 10.6

Implementation of Storage
Homes and Storage Objects

```java
public class PortableNCtxStateImpl extends PortableNCtxState {
  public CORBA.Object resolve(NameComponent n)
        throws NotFound, CannotProceed, InvalidName {
  for (int i = 0; i < m_list.length; i++)
    if (m_list[i].name.id==n.id)
      return m_list[i].obj;
  throw new NotFound;
  }
  ...
}


public class PortableNCtxStateHomeImpl
                      extends PortableNCtxStateHome{
  public NamingContextStateRef create() {
    return _create(CosPersistentState.YIELD_REF);
  }
}
```

The above Java code shows the implementation of storage homes and storage objects, including an example for the creation of new persistent CORBA objects. This creation is delegated to the storage home. The implementation of `new_context` creates a new naming context. The example also shows how the resolve operation is implemented using the PSSDL Java binding.

 Storage home keys can be used in CORBA object identifiers.

Every CORBA object has a unique object identifier, which is encoded in its object reference. Object references are generated by the object adapters. The POA supports different policies so that object identifiers can be either user- or system-defined. With persistent objects, it is often appropriate to use user-defined object identifiers. Following this policy it becomes possible to utilize the keys of persistent storage objects to identify the associated CORBA objects. We have, in fact, employed this strategy in the above Naming service implementation. The object identifiers that we assigned to `NamingContext` objects are, in fact, the persistent identifiers that were provided by the storage homes. This enables the persistence service implementation to transparently map between its persistent object identifiers and the CORBA object references.

 Multiple storage objects can be executed in one server process.

Persistent storage objects are often rather fine-grained. In our example, every naming context has a storage object associated with it. If there is a one-to-one mapping between persistent objects and CORBA server processes this may potentially lead to too large a number of server processes. Hence, it may be necessary to map many logical CORBA server objects in one physical server process. The POA Multiple_ID policy that we used in our example supports such a mapping. It achieves that just one instance of a `NamingContextImpl` object implements all conceptual `NamingContext` objects. The POA achieves this by routing every request that uses any of the object references of the different naming contexts to the one instance of the `NamingContextImpl` object.

```
public class NamingServer {
  public static void main(String[] args) {
    CORBA.ORB myOrb = CORBA.ORB.init(args);
    ... // initialize mySession and rootPOA
    NamingContextStateHome home = (NamingContextStateHome)
      mySession.find_storage_home("PortableNCtxStateHomeImpl");
    CORBA.Policy policies[5];
    policies[0]=rootPOA.create_lifespan_policy(
      PortableServer.LifespanPolicyValue.PERSISTENT);
    policies[1]=rootPOA.create_request_processing_policy(
      PortableServer.RequestProcessingPolicyValue.
        USE_DEFAULT_SERVANT);
    policies[2]=rootPOA.create_id_uniqueness_policy(
      PortableServer.IdUniquenessPolicyValue.MULTIPLE_ID);
    policies[3]=rootPOA.create_id_assignment_policy(
      PortableServer.IdAssignmentPolicyValue.USER_ID);
    policies[4]=rootPOA.create_servant_retention_policy(
      PortableServer.ServantRetentionPolicyValue.NON_RETAIN);

    PortableServer.POAManager poaMgr=rootPOA.the_POAManager();
    PortableServer.POA poa=rootPOA.create_POA("Naming",
                                        null,policies);

    if (firstTime) {
      byte[] root_id = home.create().short_pid();
      CORBA.Object root_nc=poa.create_reference_with_id(
          root_id,"IDL:omg.org/CosNaming/NamingContext:1.0");
      System.out.println(myOrb.object_to_string(root_nc));
    }
    // create and set servant
    NamingContextImpl servant(home, poa);
    poa.set_servant(servant);
    // start server
    poaMgr.activate();
    myOrb.run();
    mySession.close();
  }
}
```

Example 10.7
Use of Object Adapter in
Persistent Server
Implementation

CORBA object references are only valid when the persistent object adapter that created the reference is actually operational. When a persistent object adapter has been instructed to create CORBA object references from persistent object identifiers, it can happen that an object reference is used in an object request for which an object adapter is not operational. To cope with this situation, object references of persistent objects always have to maintain an association with the object adapter that created them. If such an object reference is used in a request, the object adapter will be started by the ORB, if necessary, before control is passed to the adapter to handle the request. As some overhead derives from employing this strategy,

Persistent objects have
to maintain a
relationship with the
object adapter on the
host.

the object adapter can be parameterized using the Persistent or Transient Policies to define its life-span.

10.2.4 Summary

In this section we have reviewed the CORBA PSS, a particular example of a persistent state service. The service specification defines a persistence definition language, which is expected to be implemented in service implementations. Designers of CORBA server objects use this PSSDL to specify storage objects and storage homes. We have seen that there is a need for programming language bindings to this PSSDL and how this programming language binding is used for implementation of both server objects and storage objects and storage homes. We also discussed how the persistent state service is integrated with the CORBA Portable Object Adapter.

 Persistent state services simplify the implementation of stateful server objects.

We note that the persistent state service simplifies the implementation of stateful server objects quite considerably. The service makes achieving persistence entirely transparent for the user and the client programmer. The client programmer sees a CORBA server object but does not know when and how persistence of information that the client establishes is achieved. The server object programmer obtains an object-oriented perspective on achieving persistence, even though persistent state service implementations might use file systems or relational database technology. This is entirely transparent for the server object designer. The persistent state service entirely performs the mapping of IDL data types to data types that are available in the persistent datastore. This is achieved because PSSDL is a strict superset of CORBA IDL. Finally, the integration of the object adapter, and as we shall see of the transaction service, with the persistence service achieves transparency of when swaps are executed, that is when data values of storage objects are actually transferred onto persistent storage.

10.3 A Persistent State Service Architecture

We will now switch perspective and take the point of view of a persistent state service implementor. We will discuss a general architecture of a persistent state service and identify the components that it must have. We then review how this architecture can be instantiated using different data storage technologies. This discussion will enable an appreciation of the non-functional characteristics that can be expected from a persistent state service. We will focus in the next section on how file systems can be used in a persistent state service implementation. We will then review the use of relational databases and finally we will see how object databases can be used to implement a persistent state service.

10.3.1 Architecture Components and their Interactions

Figure 10.3 shows a high-level overview of the components that are involved in achieving persistence of server objects. Rectangles identify components and arrows represent usage relationships. Each of these components consists of a number of objects.

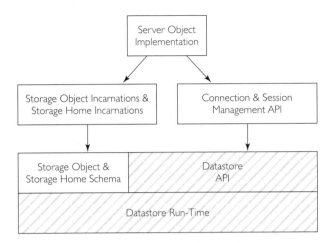

Figure 10.3
Components of a Persistent
State Service and their
Interactions

The datastore generally has a run-time environment that performs the mapping of data onto secondary storage. File systems provide the ability to manage sequences of bytes or homogeneous data records. Relational databases manage sets of tables, each of which consists of a set of tuples that have similar attributes. Object-oriented databases are capable of storing objects persistently and encapsulate the persistent data through operations. Datastores offer an Application Programming Interface (API), which applications use to interface with the datastore. These APIs typically include primitives for data definition and data manipulation purposes, session management (for example to open and close a file) and concurrency control (for example to lock resources). The same datastore run-time environment and the datastore API can be used for different server object implementations; they are independent of object types. To indicate this, these components are shown with a shaded background.

Datastore APIs are
independent of storage
types.

We have already discussed that the persistent state service must manage sessions. These sessions have to be reconciled with sessions that are managed by the datastore. For example, the file has to be opened before the first write operation and, to be sure that the state is properly retained, the file has to be closed after the last write operation. Unfortunately the session management of different datastores is rather heterogeneous. Session management in files is different from session management in databases. In order to facilitate portability of server object implementations across different forms of datastore, the datastore must provide a standardized API for session and connection management that the server object implementation can use.

Session management
of the persistent state
service has to be
integrated with the
session management
of the datastore.

Some datastores expect that a *schema* is established prior to being able to create and manipulate data. The schema defines the type of data that the datastore manages on behalf of the application. In a relational database, the schema determines the number of tables in the database, the name of columns and the data types that can be stored in these columns. In object-oriented databases, the schema defines classes including attributes and operations for the persistent objects. If we want to use a database as a datastore to manage storage homes and storage objects we have to build a schema.

A schema is a type
definition of
information that is
defined in a language
specific to the
datastore.

From Figure 10.3 we can also observe that the server object implementation does not rely on the schema. This independence is important, because the schema and the way the

Server object
implementations are

independent of schemas and thus not dependent on particular datastore technology.

schema information is utilized in programs is dependent on the type of datastore. It would be difficult to port the server object implementation from one type of datastore to another if schema information would be used in the implementation. Instead, the storage object and storage home incarnations hide the schema from the server object implementation.

Storage object and storage home implementations are dependent on datastore technology.

The server object implementation will therefore need to use an implementation of the incarnations of storage objects and storage homes. We noted above that the programming language bindings of the persistence definition languages determine how server objects can use them. The objects, however, also have to be implemented. This implementation is usually dependent upon the specification that designers provided.

10.3.2 Generating Architecture Components

Storage object and storage home incarnations can be generated automatically.

We note that incarnations of storage objects and homes, as well as the schema definition are specific for every different persistent server object type. The way that the schema is defined is unfortunately dependent on the type of database that is being used; a relational schema consists of a set of tables, while an object-oriented schema consists of classes. Hence schema definitions that server object designers build manually would not be portable. Because storage object incarnations are programming language representations of the objects as defined in the schema, the same consideration applies to storage object home implementations. Fortunately, all the information that is needed to determine the schema and the persistence storage object and storage home implementations is already specified in a PSSDL. Hence, it is possible for a generator to derive schemas as well as storage object and storage home implementations in a fully automatic way.

Figure 10.4
Generation of Components for Persistence Architecture

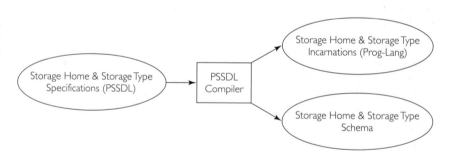

As shown in Figure 10.4 this generation task is done by a PSSDL compiler. The compiler first checks syntactic and static semantic consistency of the PSSDL specification. It then translates that information into a datastore schema and the implementations of storage homes and storage objects that utilize the schema.

The PSSDL compiler achieves datastore independence of server objects.

Note that it is this generation mechanism that achieves datastore independence in the server objects. All those parts of the architecture that are dependent on server types and the datastore are generated automatically by the PSSDL compiler. The PSSDL compiler, however, is dependent on the type of datastore. Thus persistent state service providers will need to implement a different PSSDL compiler for every type of datastore that the persistent state service supports.

10.4 Datastore Technology for Persistence

In this section, we review strategies for how the mapping between objects and various types of datastores can be achieved. Hence, we investigate the target that a PSSDL compiler needs to generate in order to implement storage homes, storage object incarnations and, if necessary, a schema.

We note that the considerations that we made in the earlier sections were of a general nature and did not focus on a particular object-oriented middleware approach. In this section, however, we will make middleware-specific assumptions and review the different approaches towards persistence that CORBA, COM and Java support. Thus, we discuss in this section the most popular datastores that are used to make distributed objects persistent. We look at file systems, where object states are stored in sequential or structured files. We then review how relational databases can be used to store object state and we investigate object–relational mappings. Finally, object-oriented databases, as we shall see, provide the most seamless integration with a PSS. The fact that different datastores can be used to achieve persistence leaves designers of persistent state services with a selection problem. In the last part of this section, we discuss the different properties of these datastores and review the circumstances in which each of them is best applied.

10.4.1 Persistence in File Systems

In this section, we will see how persistence in files is supported by the different forms of object-oriented middleware. We first review the CORBA Externalization service, which supports writing CORBA objects, possibly composite, onto a file. We then review the serialization interfaces of Java, which can be used to achieve persistence of stateful Java remote objects. Finally, we discuss structured storage in COM. As files do not have a schema, the discussion of this subsection is concerned with how implementations of storage homes and storage object incarnations can be achieved using files.

We note that there are two different principles that can be used to store objects onto a file. The first approach is to flatten objects into a sequential form and then store that sequential representation onto a file. This approach is employed when using the CORBA Externalization service and the Java serialization architecture. The second approach is to retain the structure of objects in the file so as to be able to update portions of the file incrementally. This approach is taken in COM's structured storage.

Files can store data sequentially or in a structured form.

The CORBA Externalization Service

The CORBA Externalization service was adopted in 1994 as part of the CORBAservices RFP2. The purpose of the service is to standardize interfaces that enable CORBA objects to write their state into a sequential byte stream and to read the state from that byte stream. In order to enable interoperability between different implementations, the Externalization service specification standardizes the format in which atomic data types are stored and also the way constructed types are represented.

In order to use the Externalization service for the implementation of persistence, implementors of a PSS would associate the byte stream with files in which the byte stream is stored and from which it is loaded.

Figure 10.5 shows the CORBA Externalization interfaces and their relationships as a UML class diagram. The central abstraction is `Streamable`, which is an interface for externalizing state into, and internalizing it from, a stream. `StreamIO` provides the primitive operations to do so, such as writing a string or an object reference. `Stream` is an interface that can take a streamable object and externalize it. `StreamFactory` is capable of creating objects that implement `Stream` and `StreamableFactory` will create instances of subtypes of `Streamable` during internalization.

Figure 10.5
Using the CORBA
Externalization Service

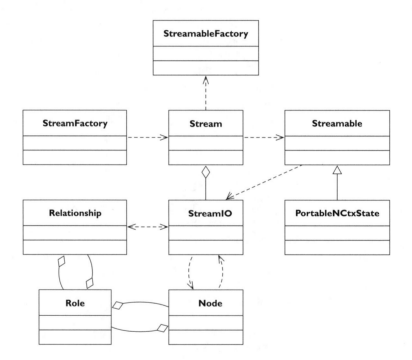

To implement storage object or storage home incarnations, the PSSDL compiler has to generate the code in such a way that it conforms to the expectations of the Externalization service. Example 10.8 shows how a persistent Naming service could be implemented using externalization.

Object Serialization in Java

 Java serialization is very
similar to CORBA
externalization.

Implementations of storage objects and storage homes that are written in Java can utilize the Java serialization architecture to achieve persistence. The serialization architecture is very similar to the Externalization service of CORBA and specifies how Java objects and all

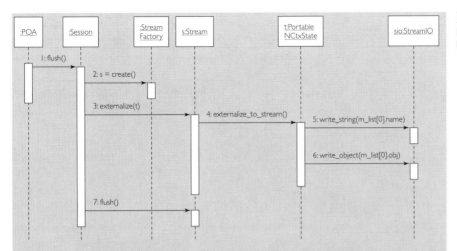

Example 10.8
Interactions with the CORBA
Externalization Service

Interface `PortableNCtxState` is a subtype of `Streamable`. This determines that implementations of `PortableNCtxState` implement operations `externalize_to_stream` and `internalize_from_stream`. If an object adapter detects the need to deactivate an object, it will request the session object to flush all modified objects onto persistent storage. The session object might then detect that a particular naming context has been modified. It creates a `Stream` object and a `StreamIO` object using the `StreamFactory` and then requests the `Stream` to `externalize` the modified storage object incarnation t that it passes as an argument. The storage object incarnation will then serve the request to externalize itself by iterating over its `m_list` attribute and writing all name–value pairs onto the stream. During activation, the reverse operation would be performed. The stream would then use an implementation of the `StreamableFactory` to create objects of type `PortableNCtxState` and request execution of `internalize_from_stream` in order to restore their state.

objects that they reference are serialized into a byte stream and how they can be restored from that byte stream. We have already seen a usage of Java serialization in Chapter 4 when we discussed how it is used to pass objects by value in remote method invocations. Now we review how serialization is used to achieve object persistence.

The serialization architecture defines the interface `Serializable` and instances of any Java class that implements `Serializable` can be written into a byte stream or be read from a byte stream. `Serializable`, in fact, does not define any operations, hence there are no obligations to implement operations. Classes that implement `Serializable` have to identify the attributes that are serializable. By default, these are all attributes, but Java programmers can exclude attributes from serialization by declaring them as transient. Figure 10.6 shows the relationships between storage object incarnations that achieve persistence using Java's serialization architecture and Example 10.9 shows how a storage object home can be implemented using Java serialization.

Figure 10.6
Using Java Serialization for
Object Persistence

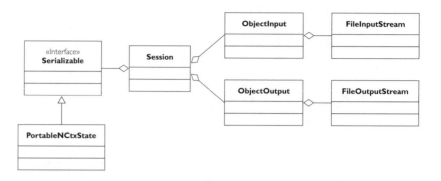

Example 10.9
Interactions for Object
Persistence with Java
Serialization

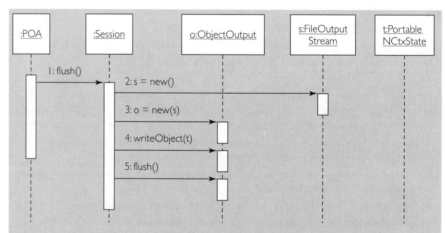

This diagram shows the interactions that occur between the session implementation, the storage object home class and the serialization classes. These are, in fact, very similar to the interactions that the storage object implementation had with the CORBA Externalization service. In order to serialize a class, we create a `FileOutputStream` object and pass that as a target upon construction to the `ObjectOutput` stream. That stream implements the operation `writeObject` that can be used to serialize objects and write them into the target stream.

Structured Storage in COM

The techniques for externalization/serialization and successive storage of possibly composite objects that we have discussed in the previous sections are also supported by COM. Figure 10.7 shows an overview of the various persistence interfaces provided by COM. They include the `IPersist` interface. `IPersist` is specialized into `IPersistStream`, which supports serialization of objects into a byte stream, that can then be stored in a file using `IPersistFile`. In addition to serialization, COM also supports a mechanism that is referred to as *structured storage*, which we will discuss in this section.

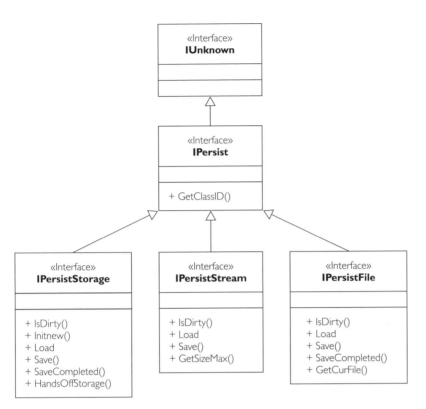

Figure 10.7
Persistence Interfaces Available in COM

COM supports the composition of objects. COM objects can be held in *container* objects, which control the life cycle of all objects they contain. A good example of a COM container is a Word document, which may include figures that were produced by Powerpoint and spreadsheets produced by Excel. We have also seen in Chapter 8 that monikers can be nested and this nesting is achieved using containers, too. Structured storage facilitates persistence of containers while retaining the container/contained relationship even on the persistent storage. This has the advantage that incremental load and storage operations can be achieved more efficiently compared to a fully-serialized representation of the contained object.

The structured storage model of COM can be considered as a lightweight file system that is used by a container to manage all its contained objects within one file. The file is referred to as *root storage*. For each container that is contained in another container, the file includes a nested *storage*, which can be considered equivalent to a file system sub-directory. For objects that are contained in a container, the storage refers to a *stream*. The object represents its state in that stream in a serialized form in a similar way to that we have seen in previous sections.

10.4.2 Persistence in Relational Databases

We have discussed how files can be used for the implementation of storage homes and storage object incarnations. The usage of files for achieving persistence, however, is overly simplistic. File systems usually do not support concurrency control and transactional access.

File systems do not support concurrency control and transactional access.

This inhibits the provision of transactional sessions in a persistent state service, which means that files are rarely used when fault-tolerance of server objects is important. Moreover, the mapping of objects to files is computationally complex due to the transformation of possibly composite objects into byte streams. In circumstances where fault-tolerance and scalability are important, persistence is often achieved using database management systems (DBMS). There are different types of DBMS that can be used to achieve persistence of objects.

Relational database management systems provide development and run-time support for data organized in relational tables.

A large number of relational database management systems (RDBMSs) exist in practice. The most prominent systems include IBM's DB2, Oracle, Sybase, Ingres, Microsoft's SQLServer and Access products. An important part of these systems is a processor for the *Standardized Query Language* (SQL), which is used to define, query and update relational databases.

Relational databases overcome the problems of file systems in that they support concurrency control and transactions. In this section, we discuss how relational databases can be used in an implementation of a persistent state service. We note that the discussion in this section applies to all three object-oriented middleware systems. Hence, it is possible to use the same mechanisms for the persistence of CORBA, COM and Java objects.

Mapping Objects into Tables

Relational databases contain a set of tables and their structure is defined in a relational schema.

RDBMSs are used to develop and manage relational databases. A *relational database* consists of a set of tables, with associated index and query information. A very important component of every relational database is its *schema*. A schema defines the tables that comprise the database. It defines for each of these tables a set of columns. For each column, the schema defines the data type that can be stored in the column.

PSS implementation demands mapping objects to tables.

An implementor of a PSS wishing to utilize a relational database for the persistent implementation of storage objects and storage homes needs to derive an appropriate schema. In order to do so, an *object–relational mapping* has to be provided between types defined in the persistence definition language and the primitives that are available in the relational data model.

The object–relational mapping has to create a table for every type of storage object. The attributes of the table derive from the attributes of the storage object. Additional tables may be needed for constructed attributes. Object references that the storage object may have to other objects will have to be externalized. In CORBA, this can be done by converting an object reference into a string using the operations provided in interface `Object`. In COM, CLSIDs can be used as external references.

Embedded Queries

Example 10.10 uses the data definition capabilities of SQL to define a database schema for storage objects and storage homes. In order to retrieve data from, and update data in, a relational database, PSS designers use the querying and modification capabilities of SQL. Example 10.11 demonstrates how the resolve operation can be implemented as an SQL query by a PSSDL compiler.

Example 10.10
Relational Database for Naming
Contexts of Example 8.2

```
CREATE TABLE NamingCtxts (id TEXT, objref TEXT,
  CONSTRAINT c1 PRIMARY KEY (id))
CREATE TABLE Bindings (
  id TEXT, name TEXT, kind TEXT, objref TEXT,
  CONSTRAINT c2 PRIMARY KEY(id))
CREATE TABLE NameBindings (
  nctx TEXT, bind TEXT,
  CONSTRAINT c3 FOREIGN KEY(nctx) REFERENCES NamingCtxts(id),
  CONSTRAINT c4 FOREIGN KEY(bind) REFERENCES Bindings(id))
```

The above definitions show the schema of a relational database that is suitable for managing the data for storage objects of our name server example. The first table `NamingCtxts` stores the relevant information for `NamingContext` objects by maintaining tuples of internal identifiers and representations of object references. The `Bindings` table stores details of name bindings. It associates an internal name binding identifier with the two parts of a name component and an externalized object references. The last table stores the association between naming contexts and name bindings and captures, which name binding is associated in which naming context. We note that, in practice, the schema would be derived from the storage object specification by a PSSDL compiler. The tables below show how the schema is instantiated for the naming contexts of Example 8.2 on Page 206.

NamingCtxts	
id	objref
1	lasd098asjasfd08lasdsfhasdf0
2	kljsadpoweurasldkfjasofduqels
3	aslkjdksahdfksgdf9qeijksadhfs
4	ashkw09we4ty0slajdfhisafsgfs
5	saldkjfdasldkjfalsdkfh0828lsdj
6	sosdihfw9y4t02-1jwohfkasjdnf
7	lsadkfh924357109ejaojkasbja
8	asldkjfh29y35r-q[ofdhdasldgj2

Bindings			
id	name	kind	objref
1	UEFA	NCtx	lasd098asjasfd08lasdsfhasdf0
2	Germany	NCtx	kljsadpoweurasldkfjasofduqels
3	England	NCtx	aslkjdksahdfksgdf9qeijksadhfs
4	Cup Winners	NCtx	ashkw09we4ty0slajdfhisafsgfs
5	Premier	NCtx	saldkjfdasldkjfalsdkfh0828lsdj
6	First	NCtx	sosdihfw9y4t02-1jwohfkasjdnf
7	1. Liga	NCtx	lsadkfh924357109ejaojkasbja
8	2. Liga	NCtx	asldkjfh29y35r-q[ofdhdasldgj2
9	BVB	Team	ksaldfhqweoiry[pa-sonasglsas

NameBindings	
nctx	bind
1	2
1	3
1	4
2	7
2	8
3	5
3	6
7	9

Example 10.11
SQL Query for Resolving a
Name Binding

```
SELECT Bindings.objref
FROM Bindings,NameBindings,NamingCtxts
WHERE NamingCtxts.objref="lsadkfh924357109ejaojkasbja" AND
            Bindings.name="BVB" AND
            Bindings.id=NameBindings.bind AND
            NamingCtxts.id=NameBindings.nctx
```

This is an example of an SQL query that resolves a name binding. We assume that we want to resolve the binding of "BVB" in the Naming Context with the object reference "lsadkfh924357109ejaojkasbja". In order to do so, the query first performs a join of our three tables. A *join* is the cartesian product of the three tables. The tables that are to be joined are specified in the FROM clause. The query then selects a subset of the join as specified in the WHERE clause. We declare that we are interested in a particular naming context and a particular name binding and we want only those bindings with that name that are actually defined within the naming context (remember that the same name could be used in different contexts) and our Bindings table includes them all.

All database management systems provide ad hoc query facilities that can be used to type in and execute SQL queries. In practice, however, these SQL queries need to be parameterized and have to be embedded into programs. In our case, these programs are the programming language incarnations of storage objects and storage homes. Hence, we wish to write a C++ or Java class that requests the database to execute the above query. There are several ways to achieve this embedding.

One approach is to embed queries into the source code of the storage object incarnation using *embedded SQL*. These embedded queries are macros, which are expanded by the preprocessors that are part of most RDBMSs. Programmers formulate queries using these macros and use *query variables* in order to parameterize queries with variables of the programming language. The RDBMSs offer application programming interfaces to traverse through query results.

Embedding of SQL queries is not standardized.

A major problem with using embedded SQL is that the macros, the way that query variables are passed and the APIs that are used to retrieve query results are not standardized. As a result, the way SQL is embedded into programming languages is different for every RDBMS and programming language. For the implementation of a persistent state service, this means that the PSS will not be portable among different RDBMSs. This is unfortunate because the SQL query language that is used to define the schema and to formulate queries is standardized and common to all RDBMSs.

ODBC and JDBC provide a standardized interface for making queries from within storage object and storage home incarnations.

Standardized database access interfaces rectify this portability problem. Microsoft's Open Database Connectivity (ODBC) is a standardized application programming interface for accessing all major SQL databases. ODBC supports the definition and execution of SQL queries. ODBC also standardizes database connection and transaction control. Java Database Connectivity (JDBC) was defined by Sun as part of the Java language definition effort. It standardizes access to SQL databases from programs that are written in Java. Like ODBC, it supports the creation of new connections from a Java program to a SQL database.

It also defines a `Statement` class that can be used to define an SQL query, execute it, and obtain the results.

10.4.3 Persistence in Object Databases

We have seen in the section above how relational databases can be employed to store the state of objects persistently. A complicating factor is the mapping that is needed between objects and relational tables. This mapping is not always straightforward. The gap is often referred to as *impedance mismatch* between the relational and the object-oriented paradigms. The impedance mismatch leads to situations in which information that conceptually belongs together is split across several tables. In practice, this means that tables need to be joined in order to retrieve the information. To resolve a name binding in the above example, we had to join three tables. These joins are computationally expensive if the tables that are to be joined are of substantial size.

Object–relational mappings are complicated due to the impedance mismatch between relational and object-oriented paradigms.

In order to avoid the impedance mismatch, research has been devoted from the mid 1980s to the development of object databases. The idea of these databases is to combine object-oriented programming languages and database technology in order to store objects onto persistent secondary storage directly. From the beginning of the 1990s, products such as GemStone, O_2, ObjectStore, Objectivity, Poet and others became available. Vendors of these products aspired to achieve a similar standardization as for relational databases. They associated themselves with the OMG in a group called Object Database Management Group (ODMG) and published the ODMG object database standard in 1993.

Object databases overcome this impedance mismatch.

The ODMG-93 standard defines an object definition language (ODL) and an object query language (OQL). Moreover, it defines a number of programming language bindings that are used to implement objects defined in the database schema and that are used to query objects from application programs. In this section, we review the ODMG-93 standard and see how it can be employed in the implementation of a persistent state service.

Object databases have been standardized in the ODMG-93 standard.

Object Definition Language (ODL)

The ODMG-93 ODL is a strict superset of CORBA/IDL. It extends IDL with mechanisms to specify the extent of interfaces, that is to provide access to the set of all instances that implement an interface. ODL also supports the concept of relationships, which are treated as an add-on service in CORBA. Given that ODL is a superset of IDL, the mapping of storage home and storage object specifications is very straightforward. Storage object specifications can be implemented as ODL interfaces, with attributes being transformed into attributes of ODL interfaces in a one-to-one manner. Storage homes, that is the containers of storage objects, can be implemented as ODL extents.

Because object databases also support methods, it is actually possible to define and implement the operations that we declared for storage objects and storage homes as parts of the schema. The implementation of the operation bodies is usually done in a programming language, for which ODMG-93 defines a number of language bindings.

Programming Language Bindings

Programming language
bindings support
operation
implementation in
ODMG schemas.

The ODMG-93 standard defines three programming language bindings. Initially bindings were defined for Smalltalk and C++. The second edition of the standard added a programming language binding for Java.

In our setting of implementing a persistent state service, we will use the programming language bindings to access the storage homes and storage objects from their programming language incarnations. In particular, the persistence definition language compiler generates operations that will implement the operations that were specified in the storage home and storage object type specifications.

Example 10.12
Implementation of Naming
Service Storage Objects in ODL

```
typedef NameComponent struct {
    string id;
    string kind;
};
typedef struct ListElement {
    NameComponent name;
    Object obj;
};
interface ODLPortableNctxState {
    list<ListElement> m_list;
    extent ODLPortableNctxStateHome;
    Object resolve(in NameComponent n);
    void bind(in NameComponent n, in Object obj);
    void unbind(in NameComponent n, in Object obj);
    void rebind(in NameComponent n, in Object obj);
};
```

The above code shows the ODL declarations that are needed for a persistent storage home and storage object implementation using the ODMG-93 standard. Interface ODLPortableNctxState uses the ODMG-93 list type constructor to define a list of name bindings, where value kind pairs are associated to object references. Note that the object references defined here are ODMG-93 object references and that we assume that a POA allows for a mapping between CORBA and ODMG-93 object references. We then define the storage home for storage objects ODLPortableNctxState using the extent mechanism of ODL.

Object Query Language

The ODMG-93 standard defines an object-oriented query language (OQL). OQL extends SQL with mechanisms to invoke methods during the execution of queries. OQL has standardized programming language bindings and it is therefore possible to embed OQL queries in operations in the schema as well as in programs that access the schema.

The availability of both imperative and associative means of accessing the data stored in an object database provides an interesting choice to designers of a PSS. The imperative access using a programming language binding is best utilized with navigational access, that is when it is clear in which way to navigate. The associative access using OQL is best utilized when searches have to be performed over large amounts of data. These can usually be executed in a more efficient way by a query processor than in a programmatic way.

10.4.4 Comparison

Using the file system to implement a persistent state service is the most lightweight approach. It does not involve any licensing costs for databases. The PDL compiler does not have to generate a database schema but only utilizes serialization or structured storage techniques. The use of files, however, does not scale to large-scale, multi-user applications due to the lack of concurrency control and fault-tolerance.

The use of relational databases overcomes this problem as they support concurrency control and transaction processing. To employ relational databases, a PDL compiler generates a set of tables for the persistent representation of storage homes and storage objects. Storage object and storage home incarnations have embedded SQL or database connectivity in order to query and update the database. The large installation base of relational databases may make them the persistence mechanism of choice because no additional licensing costs are incurred.

This section should have demonstrated that object databases are the most elegant way to implement a persistent state service. They do not suffer from the scalability problems of file systems and overcome the impedance mismatch that occurs when using relational database technology. It is, therefore, not surprising that most object database vendors have a strong interest in providing mechanisms for persistence of distributed objects. Most of the main vendors were party to the specification of the CORBA persistent state service. Object databases, however, do not have the market penetration that relational databases have and for managing large amounts of similarly-structured data, RDBMSs may still be the best choice.

> Despite the impedance mismatch, relational databases are most commonly used because of their market penetration.

Key Points

▶ We distinguish between stateless and stateful server objects and note that persistence only needs to be implemented for stateful server objects.

▶ The way persistence is achieved should be, and can be, kept transparent to users and designers of the clients of stateful server objects. Only server programmers are concerned with implementation of persistence.

▶ Achieving persistence should be supported by a persistent state service, which ensures that the implementation of persistence is independent of the particular type of datastore.

▶ A persistent state service provides a persistence definition language that is used to specify storage objects and storage homes to which server objects transfer data that they need to store persistently.

▶ A compiler for a persistence definition language automatically derives the implementation of persistence. This usually involves the generation of a schema for a relational or object-oriented database and the generation of code that accesses these schemas so that storage object and storage home incarnations are provided in the server object implementation.

▶ The most common forms of achieving persistence is to use file systems, relational database management systems or object database systems as datastores that map data onto disk-based secondary storage.

▶ The use of a file system involves serializing object representations into streams that are then stored in a file. If composite objects need to be made persistent, structured storage can be used to achieve incremental persistence

▶ Relational databases achieve persistence by storing object attributes in tables. This involves an object–relational mapping, which may result in an impedance mismatch.

▶ Object databases avoid this impedance mismatch by mapping structured objects directly onto secondary storage. Object databases, therefore provide the most seamless approach to persistence.

Self Assessment

10.1 What is persistence?
10.2 Which server objects need to take care of persistence?
10.3 To whom is persistence transparent?
10.4 What is the relationship between persistence and activation?
10.5 Why is persistence so important in distributed systems?
10.6 What are the components of a persistent state service?
10.7 When would you prefer files over relational databases for achieving persistence?
10.8 Who makes the choice of which datastore to use for achieving persistence?
10.9 When would you prefer relational databases over files for achieving persistence?
10.10 What is the impedance mismatch?
10.11 When are relational databases more appropriate for achieving persistence than object databases?

Further Reading

Many of the concepts that we used for discussing persistence in this chapter have been borrowed from the CORBA Persistent State Service specification [Object Management Group, 1999]. This service specification reflects broad consensus between the vendors of ORBs, object databases, relational databases and persistence middleware on how stateful server object implementations should achieve persistence.

The Externalization architecture of CORBA, which we suggested for implementing persistence based on files, is discussed in detail in Chapter 8 of the CORBAservices
specification [Object Management Group, 1996].

Object serialization in Java is specified in [Sun, 1998]. While the specification is
complete and unambiguous, there are more easily readable introductions to serialization in
Java, for example in Chapter 10 of [Eckel, 1998] and in [Winder and Roberts, 1997].

The theory and application of relational databases is probably one of the best
understood fields of computer science. Consequently there is a large body of research
publications and textbooks available on the subject. The initial ideas of using tables for
structuring data were published by [Codd, 1970]. Ingres [Stonebraker et al., 1976] was one
of the very first database systems that fully implemented the relational data model and the
SQL query language. Good introductory texts on relational database theory and practice are
provided in [Ullmn, 1988a] and [Ullman, 1988b]. In this chapter, we have discussed how
databases are used in a distributed setting, where distribution is resolved on top of the
database. A different approach is taken by distributed databases, which aim to resolve
distribution transparently including the distribution of data and the processing of queries
across distributed databases. A good introductory text on distributed databases is [Ceri and
Pelagatti, 1984]. The JDBC interface to relational databases is described in detail in
[Hamilton et al., 1997].

There is also quite a broad literature on object databases. The first ideas on
combining Smalltalk with database management techniques were published by [Copeland
and Maier, 1984]. A broad consensus on what constitutes an object-oriented database is
outlined in the *object-oriented database manifesto* [Atkinson et al., 1990]. A very comprehensive discussion of what it takes to build an object database system is provided by
[Bancilhon et al., 1992]. The Communications of the ACM include a special issue on object
databases that provides a good overview of available systems, which among others discusses
ObjectStore [Lamb et al., 1991] and O_2 [Deux, 1991].

There have been about two decades of research into persistent programming
languages [Atkinson et al., 1983]. The idea underlying this strand of research is to introduce
persistence into programming languages with a minimal level of changes to the programming language. This has been achieved in the PS-Algol and Napier-88 systems. [Atkinson
et al., 1996] report about the PJama project which aims to introduce persistence into Java
without having to serialize Java objects and store them in files.

11

Distributed Object Transactions

Learning Objectives

In this chapter, we study the concepts of concurrency control and transactions. We will comprehend why we need to perform concurrency control in a distributed object system. We will acquaint ourselves with two-phase locking, which is the basic concurrency control protocol. We will study the concurrency control primitives that are available in object-oriented middleware. We will then familiarize ourselves with the properties of a transaction and investigate how distributed object transactions can be implemented. We will then investigate the relationship between concurrency control and distributed object transactions and realize that concurrency control is needed in order to implement the isolation property of transactions. We will then study the two-phase commit protocol and understand how it implements the atomicity property of transactions. We investigate the distributed transaction services provided by object-oriented middleware and comprehend how designers use these services.

Chapter Outline

We have discussed in the introductory chapters that distributed systems may have multiple points of failures. While centralized systems either do or do not work, distributed object systems may work only partially, which may lead to integrity violations.

Example 11.1
Consequences of Failures

A good example is a funds transfer from an account in one bank to an account in another bank. The banks use different hosts for their account management objects. In an Internet banking application, the object from which the funds transfer is initiated resides on yet another host, for example the client's home PC. The funds transfer involves executing a debit operation on the account object from which the funds are transferred and a credit operation on the account object of the target bank. If one account-holding object is unavailable to serve requests, only one of the operations will succeed and the other one will fail. This will result in either funds being lost or funds being generated. Neither situation is acceptable.

Integrity violations can also occur due to concurrent accesses to objects. If two clients invoke operations concurrently and the object adapter used on the server-side supports concurrent execution of requests, we may find situations where changes performed by one object are overwritten by another object. To prevent such integrity violations we have to control the concurrent execution and only permit those schedules that respect the integrity of objects' data.

Transactions are the main concept that we introduce in this chapter. Transactions cluster several object requests into a coarse-grained unit for which a number of properties hold: the transaction is either performed completely or not at all; the transaction leaves objects in a consistent state; the transaction is performed in isolation from any concurrent transaction; and once completed, the result of the transaction is prevented from being lost.

In the last chapter, we saw how objects can make their states persistent. The ability to retain state on persistent storage is a powerful measure in the struggle against failures. We will see that transactions utilize the ability to persistently store state information. We will first introduce the main principles and concepts of transactions. In the second section we discuss the techniques for concurrency control that a transaction uses in order to guarantee an execution of its requests in isolation from any concurrent transactions. We then discuss that at least two phases are needed to implement the commit of a transaction in a distributed setting. We conclude by reviewing the technologies that object-oriented middleware provides for implementing distributed object transactions.

11.1 Transaction Principles

11.1.1 Concepts

Before we can see how transactions can be implemented, we need to understand what exactly transactions are. We also need to develop a feeling for when they are used. We therefore first define a transaction and its defining properties. We then discuss flat versus nested transactions and we classify the roles that objects can play in transactions.

A *transaction* clusters a sequence of object requests together in such a way that they are performed with ACID properties. This means that the transaction is either performed completely or not at all; it leads from one consistent state to another one; it is executed in isolation from other transactions; and, once completed, it is durable.

A transaction is an atomic, consistent, isolated and durable sequence of operations.

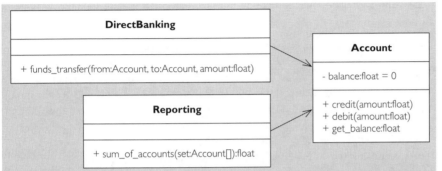

Example 11.2
Types of Objects in Banking Example

This class diagram shows the types of objects that participate in example transactions that we use for illustration purposes throughout this chapter. The examples will use objects of type Account, which have an internal state. The state captures the balance of the account as a float number. Objects of type Account can debit or credit a sum to the account and use get_balance to find out what the account currently holds.

A funds transfer, which involves requesting a debit operation from one account and a credit operation from another account, would be regarded as a transaction. Both of these operations have to be executed together or not at all; they leave the system in a consistent state; they should be isolated from other transactions; and they should be durable, once the transaction is completed.

Example 11.3
Funds Transfer as Transaction

As Example 11.3 suggests, more than one object may be involved in a transaction and the object requests modify the states of these objects. However, a sequence of read operations could also be executed as a transaction. These operations do not perform any modifications, but it may be necessary to execute them as a transaction to ensure that they are not modified while the reading goes on. Hence, transactions allow us to attach particular execution semantics to a sequence of object requests. This semantics is characterized by the ACID properties that we discuss now.

The execution semantics of transactions cannot be defined for single operations.

Atomicity

Atomicity denotes the property of a transaction to be executed either completely or not at all. When a failure occurs in the middle of a sequence of object requests, some object request may have been completed while others will never be completed due to the failure. If the sequence of requests is executed as a transaction, the transaction manager will ensure that the effect of those requests that have been completed are undone and that the state of the

A transaction is either executed completely or not at all.

distributed object system is restored to the situation in which it was before the transaction was started.

Atomicity is an important concept because it enables application programmers to use transactions to define points to which the system recovers in a transparent way if failures occur. This is an important contribution to failure transparency.

Example 11.4
Atomicity of Funds Transfer Transaction

To implement a funds transfer, we need to perform a `debit` operation on one account object and a `credit` operation on another account object. Usually these operations are executed in sequential order. Let us assume without loss of generality that we start with the `debit` operation and then perform the `credit` operation. If a failure occurs during the execution of the `credit` operation, we must also undo the effect of the `debit` operation, which was completed successfully. If we do not do this the system will lose money due to the failure. If we execute the two operations as a transaction, the transaction manager will ensure that the effect of the `debit` operation is undone.

Consistency

A transaction preserves consistency.

In every system there are application-specific consistency constraints that must not be violated. Transactions preserve *consistency* in that they lead from one consistent state to another one. This does not mean that inconsistencies do not occur, but they are confined within the boundaries of one transaction. If a transaction does not reach a consistent state it cannot be allowed to commit; it has to be aborted and all previous changes have to be undone.

Example 11.5
Consistency in Funds Transfer Transaction

In our funds transfer transaction, a consistency constraint would be that banks do not lose or generate monies during their operation. Hence, every account management transaction has to ensure that it credits monies to accounts in exactly the same amount as it debits monies. Note also that inconsistencies are bound to occur during the transaction. There is a point in time when an amount has been debited but the credit operation is still outstanding. Hence, the transaction temporarily violates the consistency constraint.

We have seen in the preceding chapters that consistency can also be defined at an object level. An account object can, for example, reject execution of a debit operation if it would leave a negative balance (or a balance that exceeds some previously-agreed overdraft limit). One object, however, can usually not decide on the consistency of more global information that spans multiple objects. In our example, this would be that the sum of balances on all account objects is equal to the assets of the bank. It is for these more global consistency constraints that transactions are needed.

Consistency is such an important concept of a transaction because it gives designers the assurance that, once a transaction is completed, it has left the system in a consistent state. Transactions provide this mechanism to define consistency constraints among all the objects that are accessed during a transaction.

Isolation

Transactions are performed in isolation from any other concurrent transactions. The *isolation* property of a transaction means that there cannot be any interference between two concurrent transactions. This means that no changes that a transaction does to a system are shown to concurrent transactions until the transaction is complete.

Transactions are isolated from each other.

> The transaction manager ensures that two transactions that attempt to access the same accounts concurrently are forced to a sequential execution schedule so as to exclude integrity violations.

Example 11.6
Isolation of Funds Transfer Transactions

To achieve isolation property, transaction managers have to perform concurrency control and this motivates the next section, where we will discuss the concurrency control problem and its solutions in more detail. Note, however, that isolation does not mean that transactions are not executed concurrently at all. This would be highly undesirable because distributed objects are potentially used by a high number of concurrent users. In the bank system example that we presented in Chapter 1, there are about 2,000 employees that manipulate account information concurrently. It would be unsatisfactory if their accesses had to be performed in a strictly sequential order. The focus of the isolation property is on avoiding interference.

The isolation property of transactions provides concurrency transparency (see Page 52). In particular, it means that application programmers that use transactions are guaranteed exclusive access to all participating objects without taking any further measures.

Durability

Once a transaction has successfully been completed, its changes persist and cannot be undone. This *durability* is usually achieved by integrating distributed objects with the persistent state services that we discussed in Chapter 10. The difference is that now it is the transaction manager rather than the object adapter or service control manager that calls upon the service to make persistent the states of all objects that participated in a transaction.

The changes of every completed transaction persist.

> Upon completion of the funds transfer transaction, the account objects would need to store their changed balance attributes onto persistent storage. To do so, they would utilize a storage object that could either be stored in a file or in a relational or an object database.

Example 11.7
Durability in Funds Transfer Transaction

Durability is an important property of a transaction because it means that the processes that execute objects may deliberately or accidentally terminate after the transaction and the changes that the transaction made are still preserved.

Summary

We note that the power of transactions lies in the combination of these ACID properties. The combination of atomicity and durability means that only the effect of completed transactions are stored on persistent storage. Together with atomicity, consistency means that transactions can always recover to a consistent point. The combination of consistency and durability means that only consistent information is stored on persistent storage. The combination of isolation and consistency properties implies that no concurrent processes can see the inconsistent information that may arise during the course of a transaction. Transactions can only see the consistent information that was established at previously committed transactions.

11.1.2   Transaction Operations

It is generally client objects that implement a particular application in order to determine the start and end of a transaction. To do so, the client application needs to use a number of operations for transaction manipulation purposes. These operations form the client's perspective on transaction management. Figure 11.1 shows an overview of these operations and their effects.

Figure 11.1
Client Perspective on
Transaction Management
Operations

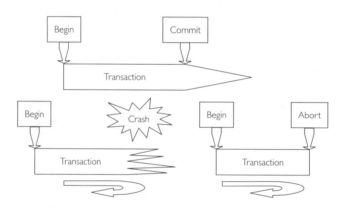

Begin starts a transaction.

All operation executions that are requested after a transaction has *begun* are executed under transaction control. Hence, their effect is not visible to concurrent transactions until after the transaction has been finished successfully.

Commit completes a transaction.

During a transaction *commit*, all the changes are stored onto persistent storage and they are made available to other transactions. Moreover, the transaction leaves the resources that it modified in a consistent state.

Abort cancels the effect of a transaction.

A transaction may also terminate unsuccessfully. *Aborts* can either be implicit, due to a failure that terminates one of the participating objects, or explicit by invoking an abort operation. Clients may invoke an abort operation explicitly if they have reached an inconsistent state from which they cannot recover. The effect of implicit and explicit aborts is the same: all changes that the transaction has performed to participating objects are undone so that the state that these objects had before the transaction started is re-established.

Client and server programmers use transaction commands to design transaction boundaries.

We note that the determination of transaction begin, commit and abort is application-specific. Whether client or server objects determine transaction boundaries cannot be defined in general; both are viable options. It is usually the client or server object designer that determines the transaction boundaries and thus client or server object programmers use the transaction commands. We note, however, that the designer of server objects has to inform the client designer whether the operation of the server object defines a transaction or not so as to avoid double use or omission of transaction protection.

11.1.3   Flat versus Nested Transactions

The most basic, and also the most common, form of transaction is a *flat transaction*. This means that a new transaction is only begun if the previous transaction has been either committed or aborted. Flat transactions are easy to implement but they are limited in that an abort leads to the potential loss of all the results that have been achieved during the course of the transaction.

Alternating begin and commit commands lead to flat transactions.

Nested transactions overcome this limitation. A *nested transaction* is embedded in another transaction. This other transaction is referred to as *parent transaction* while the nested transaction is sometimes also called a *child transaction*. Nested transactions are used to set continuation points during the course of the parent transaction so that parts of a more complex transaction can be undone without losing all changes. This is achieved by the following execution semantics of the transaction.

A nested transaction is embedded in another transaction.

Child transactions can commit or abort independently of their parent transactions. Figure 11.2 visualizes this behaviour. If a child transaction aborts, only those changes that were done within the child transaction are undone. If a child transaction is completed, the changes are made visible to the parent transaction and successive sibling transactions. However, if a parent transaction aborts, all the changes made by its child transactions will be undone.

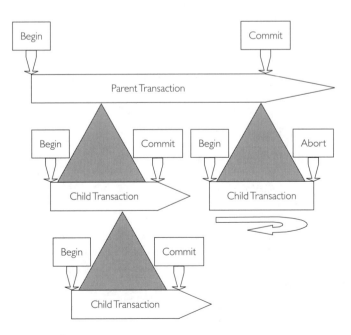

Figure 11.2
Client Perspective on Nested Transactions

Hence, nested transaction give additional degrees of freedom to the designer of an application. It should, however, be noted that the additional flexibility gained by nested transactions does not come for free. It is considerably more complicated to implement the concurrency control and commit protocol of nested transaction than those needed for flat transactions.

11.2 Concurrency Control

After having introduced the transaction concepts, we will now switch perspective and review how transactions can be implemented. We will start with concurrency control techniques, which are used to achieve the isolation property of transactions.

The application of concurrency control techniques is transparent to designers of transactional clients. Whether or not it is also transparent to the designers of transactional servers depends on the way persistence is achieved. If relational or object databases are used to achieve persistence, then the concurrency control mechanisms of these database systems are generally sufficient to guarantee isolation. If persistence is achieved in a different way, for example by storing state information in files then the server object designer has to implement concurrency control manually and the techniques discussed here should be applied.

Before we study the concurrency control techniques in detail, we will first investigate why concurrency control is necessary. We will review two typical issues that make concurrency control necessary, lost updates and inconsistent analysis. We will then study two-phase locking, which is the most commonly-used concurrency control technique in databases as well as for distributed objects. We will then see that deadlocks can occur in two-phase locking and we will investigate how to detect and resolve deadlocks. We will finally discuss hierarchical locking techniques and see how concurrency control is supported by the CORBA concurrency control service.

11.2.1 Motivation

Servers usually have more than one client object. It can, therefore, happen that these client objects make object requests in parallel. The object requests will then arrive at the CORBA object adapter or the COM service control manager (SCM) or the Java activation interfaces on the host where the server object executes. Depending on the configuration of these adapters or SCMs, concurrent threads may be spawned. These threads are then used to execute the requested operations of the server object concurrently. In order to make these points more clear, we use an example.

If the requested server objects include operations that modify the server's state, two problems may occur: lost updates and inconsistent analysis. We now investigate these problems in detail to provide a reason for why concurrency control is so important. In order to study the concurrency control problems with our example, it is necessary to make assumptions on the way that the methods of `Account` are actually implemented. Figure 11.8 shows an example implementation.

```
        class Account {
          private:
            float balance;
          public:
            float get_balance() {return balance;};
            void debit(float amount){
              float new=balance-amount;
              balance=new;
            };
            void credit(float amount) {
              float new=balance+amount;
              balance=new;
            };
        };
```

This class declaration refines the Account class designed in the class diagram of Example 11.2.

Example 11.8
Implementation of Account Operations

Lost Updates

A *schedule* is a particular interleaving of operations of concurrent threads. Generally concurrent execution allows many schedules to occur and the aim of concurrency control is to reject those schedules that lead to unwanted interference between the concurrent processor threads. Lost updates are an interference that we wish to avoid.

A schedule results in a *lost update* if one concurrent thread overwrites changes that were performed by a different thread. Lost updates are not confined to distributed objects or databases, but they can occur in concurrent programs in general. Example 11.9 shows an occurrence of such a lost update.

Lost updates are modifications done in one thread that are overwritten by another.

Inconsistent Analysis

Lost updates occur when two threads modify a shared object in an improper way. A different form of concurrency anomaly occurs between a reading and a writing thread. The anomaly is referred to as *inconsistent analysis* and denotes a result that is invalid because the object on which the analysis was performed was modified during the course of the analysis. Example 11.10 shows a schedule leading to an inconsistent analysis.

Inconsistent analysis occurs when an object is modified concurrently while the analysis is performed.

Serializability

A system where updates are lost or incorrect results are produced is clearly undesirable. In order to solve this problem, we have to control concurrency in such a way that those schedules that cause lost updates or inconsistent analysis are avoided. In order to characterize such schedules we define the concept of serializability.

Example 11.9
Concurrent Schedule Leading to
Lost Updates

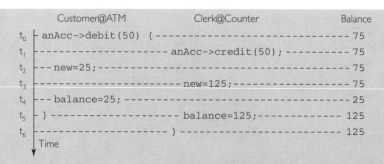

	Customer@ATM	Clerk@Counter	Balance
t_0	anAcc->debit(50) { ----------------------------------		75
t_1	-------------------- anAcc->credit(50); ----------		75
t_2	--- new=25; ---		75
t_3	------------------------ new=125; ------------------		75
t_4	--- balance=25; ---------------------------------------		25
t_5	} -------------------- balance=125; ------------		125
t_6	-------------------- } -----------------------		125

Time

The above figure shows `credit` and `debit` operations that are performed concurrently on the same `Account` object. The column on the right-hand side traces the evolution of the `balance` attribute of the account. Our implementation stores the result of the subtraction and addition operations in the temporary variable `new`. Programmers might not write code like this, however most processors perform the addition and subtraction in this way and we have made that explicit for illustration purposes. The time passes from the top to the bottom. The schedule interleaves operations in such a way that the modification performed by the `debit` operation is overwritten by the `credit` operation; the update performed by `debit` is lost.

Example 11.10
Concurrent Schedule Leading to
Inconsistent Analysis

	Funds Transfer	Inland Revenue Report	Acc1	Acc2	Sum
t_0	Acc1->debit(7500) { - sum=0; --------------------		7500	0	0
t_1	--- new=0; --		7500	0	0
t_2	--- balance=0; ------- sum+=Acc2->get_balance(); ----		0	0	0
t_3	} ---		0	0	0
t_4	Acc2->credit(7500) { ---------------------------		0	0	0
t_5	--- new=7500; -----------------------------------		0	0	0
t_6	--- balance=7500; ----- sum+=Acc1->get_balance(); ----		0	7500	0
t_7	} ---		0	7500	0

Time

Assume that a customer has two accounts. The first thread performs a funds transfer between the two accounts by debiting an amount of 7,500 from the first account and crediting it to the second account. The second thread adds the account balances for a report about the customer's assets to the Inland Revenue. The analysis reveals a result of a balance of 0, though the customer commands assets in the amount of 7,500. The reason for this inconsistent analysis is that the accounts were modified by the fund transfer thread while the sums were computed.

Transactions are
serializable if the same
result can be achieved
by executing them in
sequential order.

Two transactions are *serializable* if the same result can be achieved by executing them one after the other, that is in serial order. Serializability is the objective of every concurrency control technique. Concurrency control techniques that achieve serializability inhibit every non-serializable schedule by delaying operations that would cause non-serializability. It is rather complex for a concurrency control technique to reject every non-serializable and admit every serializable schedule. For the sake of efficiency, concurrency control techniques often employ simplifications, which might also reject some serializable schedules. However, they never permit non-serializable schedules.

11.2.2 Two-Phase Locking

Two-phase locking (2PL), which guarantees serializability, is the most popular concurrency control technique. It is used in most database systems and by many distributed object systems. *Two-phase locking* is based on the idea that transactions ask the concurrency control manager for a lock for a shared resource; they *acquire* locks prior to using resources. In the realm of this book, resources are objects, but the mechanisms apply as well to tuples of relational databases or pages, the storage granularity of object databases. The concurrency control manager only *grants* the lock if the use of the object does not conflict with locks granted previously to concurrent transactions. If the transaction does not access an object any more, it will *release* the lock so that it can be acquired by other transactions.

2PL consists of a lock acquisition and a lock release phase.

Two-phase locking guarantees serializability.

Locking Profile

Two-phase locking demands that once a transaction has released a lock, it cannot acquire other locks. The two phases of 2PL are consequently referred to the *lock acquisition* and the *lock release* phases. If these phases are strictly distinguished, serializability is guaranteed by 2PL. For a proof of this theorem we refer to [Bernstein et al., 1987].

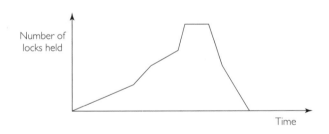

Figure 11.3
Typical Two-Phase Locking Profile

Figure 11.3 shows a typical locking profile of a transaction. The number of locks held by the transaction grows up to a certain maximum. The transaction can release the lock for an object only when it knows that it will no longer need the object and has acquired all the locks that it needs.

2PL never acquires a lock after it has started releasing locks.

It is desirable to release locks as early as possible so that concurrent transactions that need access to the object can acquire their lock. However, due to the complexity involved in deciding whether the it is safe to release a lock, transactions often retain locks to objects and only release them together at the end.

Locks

There are two perspectives on locking that have to be distinguished. The above locking profile showed the perspective of a transaction, which knows which locks it holds for the objects that it wants to access. The concurrency control manager, on the other hand, has to decide which locks to grant. It has to base this decision on the locks that have already been granted to concurrent transactions for that object.

Binary locks on a resource can either be held or not held.

A very simplistic locking approach would be to consider locks as binary information where objects are either locked or not. We refer to these locks as *binary locks*. The implementation of synchronized methods and blocks in Java use such binary locks. If a Java thread tries to acquire a lock on an object that is already locked the concurrency control manager will force that thread to wait until the existing lock has been released.

Binary locks are overly restrictive.

This approach, however, restricts concurrency unnecessarily. Many transactions only read the state of an object, which does not interfere with other transactions that are reading the object as well. The concurrency control manager can permit multiple transactions to read the object's state, but it has to prevent a transaction that wishes to write to an object's state to proceed if other transactions are reading or writing to the object. To avoid unnecessary concurrency restrictions between transactions, concurrency control managers distinguish locks with different *modes*.

Lock modes determine operations that transactions can request from objects.

A *read lock* is acquired by a transaction that wishes to access the state of an object. A transaction that wishes to perform a modification to the state of an object will require a *write lock*. Following the principle of information hiding, the state of objects is often hidden and only exposed by operations. These operations therefore often also perform the lock acquisition and then locking can be kept transparent to clients.

Lock Compatibility

Lock compatibility matrices determine compatibility and conflicts between locking modes.

Given that there are different locking modes, the definition of a concurrency control scheme always includes the definition of compatibility between locks. Figure 11.4 shows the lock compatibility matrix for a concurrency control scheme that includes only read and write locks. This is the minimal lock compatibility matrix. More complicated ones are used in practice. The scheme defines that a read lock is compatible with another read lock, but incompatible with a write lock. Furthermore, write locks are incompatible with each other.

Figure 11.4
Minimal Lock Compatibility Matrix

	Read	Write
Read	+	−
Write	−	−

Given that concurrency control managers may grant multiple locks to different transactions, they have to keep track of which locks they have granted. This is necessary for them to have a basis for future decisions on lock acquisition requests. Hence concurrency control managers associate *locksets* with every shared object. The lockset will then include a lock for every transaction that has been granted access to an object in a particular mode.

The situation when access cannot be granted due to an incompatibility between the requested lock and a previously-granted lock is referred to as a *locking conflict*. The previously-granted locks that cause the conflict are referred to as *conflicting locks*. There are

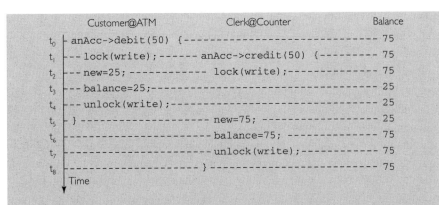

Example 11.11
Preventing Lost Updates
through Locking

The above figure continues Example 11.9 on Page 298. The difference between the two figures is that we now acquire a lock for every object that we access and release it when we do not need to access the object any more. Following this 2PL strategy, lost updates are prevented. At time t_2 the concurrency control manager detects a concurrency control conflict between the write lock that was granted to the first transaction at t_1 and the lock that is requested by the second transaction. This locking conflict is handled by delaying the second transaction and only granting the write lock at t_5, that is after the first transaction has released the conflicting lock. Hence, the use of locking delays the second transaction and avoids the lost update.

different options as to how a concurrency control manager handles locking conflicts. The first approach is to make the requesting transaction wait until the conflicting lock is released by the other transaction. The second approach is to return control to the requesting transaction indicating that the requested lock cannot be granted. The third approach, which is most commonly used in practice, is a combination of the two. The concurrency control manager returns control to the requesting transaction only when a certain amount of time has passed (time-out) and the conflicting lock has not been released.

11.2.3 Deadlocks

Forcing a transaction that requests a conflicting lock to wait solves the problem of lost updates and inconsistent analysis; it does however, introduce a new class of *liveness* problem.

It could happen, that while the transaction is waiting for the conflicting lock to be released, another transaction comes along that obtains the lock. *Starvation* problems can be solved by the concurrency control manager. It has to ensure fairness, which means that every transaction will eventually obtain the resources that it wants.

A different class of liveness problem is deadlocks. Transactions may request locks for more than one object. It may then happen that a transaction T_1 has a lock on one object O_1 and waits for a conflicting lock on a second object O_2 to be released. If this conflicting lock is held by another transaction T_2 and that transaction requests a lock on O_1 then the two transactions are mutually waiting for each other's locks to be released.

Liveness refers to the property of a concurrent system that something desirable will eventually happen.

A transaction starves if it waits indefinitely to obtain a shared resource.

Transactions that are waiting for each other to release locks are in a deadlock.

2PL is not deadlock-free!

We refer to such a blockage situation as a *deadlock*. The above example has sketched a situation where we employed two-phase commit and have reached a deadlock.

Deadlock Detection

 Transaction waiting graphs record the 'waits-for' relationship between transactions.

 We can find deadlocks by detecting cycles in waiting graphs.

Deadlocks not only occur between two transactions but they can also occur when three or more transactions are mutually waiting for each other. In order to characterize deadlocks more precisely, we need to define the *transaction waiting graph*. The nodes in this graph are the transactions that are currently active. For every conflict between a lock that is requested by transaction T_1 and another lock that has been granted to transaction T_2, the graph includes an edge from T_1 to T_2 to denote the waiting relationship. We note that deadlocks can involve more than one transaction (see Example 11.12).

Example 11.12
Deadlock Involving More Than Two Transactions

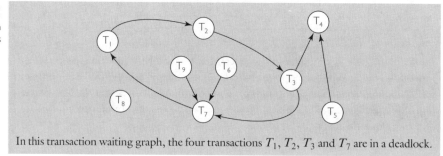

In this transaction waiting graph, the four transactions T_1, T_2, T_3 and T_7 are in a deadlock.

In order to detect the occurrence of deadlocks efficiently, the concurrency control manager has to maintain an up-to-date representation of this transaction waiting graph. It has to create a new node for every transaction that is started. It has to delete the node for every transaction that is committed or aborted. The concurrency control manager then needs to record every locking conflict that it detects by inserting an edge into the graph. Furthermore whenever a transaction resolves a locking conflict by releasing a conflicting lock the respective edge has to be deleted.

 Deadlock detection is linear in relation to the number of concurrent transactions.

The concurrency control manager can use the transaction waiting graph to detect deadlocks. This is done by checking for cycles in the graph. The complexity of this operation is linear in relation to the number of nodes, that is the number of transactions. This complexity is so low that the concurrency control manager can perform this operation on a regular basis, for example, whenever a new locking conflict has been recognized.

Deadlock Resolution

 Deadlocks are resolved by aborting involved transactions.

When a deadlock occurs, the transactions involved in the deadlock cannot proceed any more and therefore they cannot resolve the deadlock themselves. The isolation property of transactions, in fact, means that they do not know about the other transactions that are involved in the deadlock. Deadlocks therefore have to be resolved by the concurrency control manager. The transactions that participate in a conflict are represented in the transaction waiting graph as those nodes that are connected by the cycle. In order to resolve the deadlock, the concurrency control manager has to break this cycle by selecting a transaction from the cycle and aborting it. A good heuristic for doing this is to select the transaction that has the maximum incoming or outgoing edges so as to reduce the chance of further deadlocks. In Example 11.12 this would be transaction T_7. Selecting it would not only resolve the deadlock, but also facilitate progress of T_6 and T_9.

We have seen in the first section that transactions can be aborted implicitly due to hardware or operating system failures, or explicitly if they cannot reach a consistent state. We now add the occurrence of deadlocks as another reason why transactions may be aborted. We note that depending on the application, deadlocks may actually be a regular occurrence and therefore transactions have to be implemented in such a way that they abort properly, even in a distributed setting.

11.2.4 Hierarchical Locking

While two-phase locking is fully appropriate to transactions that only access a few objects, it is inefficient for those transactions that have to access a high number of objects. At the close of business of a bank branch, for example, the branch has to perform a transaction summing up all balances of all account objects managed at this branch in order to check whether the bank's overall accounts balance. This transaction might have to access many thousands of account objects. Inefficiencies with accessing large numbers of objects arise for two reasons: transactions have to acquire and release a lock for every object; if there are many concurrent transactions that have a similar profile, the chances of deadlock occurrence are high.

 2PL is inefficient if transactions need large number of objects.

Locking Granularity

We can observe that objects that are accessed by transactions concurrently are often contained in more coarse-grained composite objects. For example,

1. files are contained in directories, which are contained in other directories;
2. relational databases contain a set of tables, which contain a set of tuples, which contain a set of attributes; or
3. distributed composite objects may act as containers for component objects, which may again contain other objects.

A common access pattern for transactions is to visit all or a large subset of the objects that are contained in a container. The concurrency control manager can save a lot of effort if it manages to exploit these containment hierarchies for concurrency control purposes.

Hierarchical Locking Protocol

The basic idea of the *hierarchical locking protocol* is to lock all objects that are contained in a composite object simply by locking the composite object. Then a large number of objects can be locked or unlocked in a single locking operation. Nevertheless, some transactions will still need to be able to lock single objects. It is necessary for these transaction to also record at the more coarse-grained objects that they are locking some objects contained in the

 Hierarchical locking protocols lock all component objects with one locking operation applied to the composite object.

Example 11.13
Different Locking Granularities
in Financial Transactions

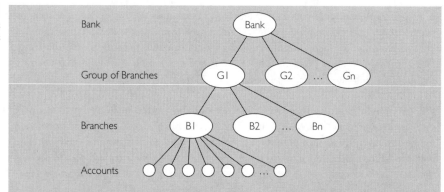

Consider the containment hierarchy of account objects of a bank as shown above. The bank can be seen as a set of groups of branches, each group has a set of branches, and each branch manages its own account objects.

composite objects. To be able to record this, concurrency control protocols use intention locks.

 An intention lock on a composite object highlights that a transaction has acquired a real lock on a component.

An *intention lock* is a lock acquired for a composite object before a transaction requests a real lock for an object that is contained in the composite object. Intention locks are used to signal to those transactions that wish to lock the entire composite object that some other transaction currently has locks for objects that are contained in the composite object. Hence, the complexity of the decision about whether or not a concurrency control manager can grant a lock on a composite object is independent of the number of objects contained in the composite object. In practice, concurrency control schemes will use different modes of intention locks, for the same reason as there are different modes for real locks.

 The hierarchical locking protocol locks every composite object of a component object.

In order to be able to read or write an object, it is necessary in the hierarchical locking protocol to acquire intention locks on all composite objects in which the object is contained. This is done from the root of the containment hierarchy to the object that is to be locked. In Example 11.13, in order to obtain a write lock on a particular account object, a transaction obtains intention write locks on the bank, the group of branches and the branch object that the object is contained in.

Figure 11.5
Lock Compatibility for
Hierarchical Locking

	Intention Read	Read	Intention Write	Write
Intention Read	+	+	+	−
Read	+	+	−	−
Intention Write	+	−	+	−
Write	−	−	−	−

Figure 11.5 shows the lock compatibility matrix between the locking modes that are used for hierarchical locking. This matrix extends the minimal lock matrix that we presented in Figure 11.4 with two new locking modes: intention read and intention write. The *intention read* locks indicate that some transaction has acquired or is about to acquire read locks on the

objects in the composite object. The *intention write* locks indicate that some other transaction has or is about to acquire write locks on the objects in the composite object. Intention read and intention write locks are compatible among themselves because they do not actually correspond to any locks. An intention read lock is also compatible with a read lock because a read access to all elements of the composite object can be done while some other transactions are accessing components of that object. However, an intention read lock is incompatible with a write lock because it is not possible to modify every element of the composite object while some other transaction is reading the state of an object of the composite. Likewise, it is not possible to write all objects while some other transaction is writing some objects.

Example 11.14
Hierarchical Locking of Bank Accounts

Let us assume that there are three transactions. T_1 produces a sum of the balances of a particular customer, whose accounts are managed at branch B1. T_2 performs a funds transfer between two accounts held at branch B1. T_3 produces a sum of the balances of all accounts held at a group of branches to which B1 belongs. T_3 locks the root note in intention read and the group of branches in read mode. T_1 locks the root node, the group of branches and the branch objects in intention read and the account objects of the customer in read mode. T_2 locks the root, the group of branches and the branch object in intention write mode and the two account objects in write mode. The hierarchical lock compatibility matrix determines that T_1 can be performed at the same time as T_3. T_1 and T_2 can be performed concurrently if the set of account objects is disjoint. T_2 and T_3, however, cannot be performed at the same time.

Hierarchical locking has enabled us to lock all account objects of a group of branches with two locking operations. The overhead is that for every individual object, we also have to use intention locks on every composite object in which the object is contained. This overhead is justifiable if there are some transactions that access a large number of objects and the composition hierarchy is not very deep.

11.2.5 The CORBA Concurrency Control Service

Now that we have seen the principles of two-phase and hierarchical locking, let us now review how they are applied to distributed objects in practice. To do so, we review the CORBA Concurrency Control service. It was adopted in 1994 as part of the CORBAservices RFP2 and specifies standard interfaces for controlling the concurrency between distributed CORBA objects.

Lock Compatibility

The Concurrency Control service supports hierarchical two-phase locking of CORBA objects. Figure 11.6 shows the lock compatibility matrix.

In addition to the locking modes that we have discussed already, the service defines upgrade locks. *Upgrade locks* are used when a transaction initially needs read access to an object, but already knows that it will at a later point also need to acquire a write lock for the object.

Upgrade locks are not compatible with themselves.

Upgrade locks reduce
the likelihood of
deadlocks.

Upgrade locks have the same compatibility as read locks, but two upgrade locks are not mutually compatible. Two update locks are not granted for an object as that would very likely result in a deadlock. Hence, the use of upgrade locks avoids deadlocks.

Figure 11.6

Lock Compatibility of CORBA
Concurrency Control Service

	Intention Read	Read	Upgrade	Intention Write	Write
Intention Read	+	+	+	−	−
Read	+	+	+	−	−
Upgrade	+	−	−	−	−
Intention Write	+	−	−	−	−
Write	−	−	−	−	−

Locksets

The CORBA Concurrency Control service defines the interface `Lockset` in order to standardize operations for the acquisition and release of locks. Instances of this type are associated with any CORBA object to which concurrent access needs to be controlled. The interface is contained in the `CosConcurrencyControl` module, an excerpt of which is shown in Figure 11.7. In addition to the obvious operations to `lock` and `unlock`, `LockSet` also defines an operation `try_lock` that allows a transaction to check whether it can acquire a lock in a particular mode and `change_mode` in order to upgrade or downgrade the mode of a lock.

Figure 11.7

Excerpt of CORBA
Concurrency Control Interfaces

```
module CosConcurrencyControl {
  enum lock_mode{
          read,write,upgrade,intention_read,intention_write
  };
  exception LockNotHeld{};
  interface LockCoordinator {
    void drop_locks();
  };
  interface LockSet {
    void lock(in lock_mode mode);
    boolean try_lock(in lock_mode mode);
    void unlock(in lock_mode mode) raises(LockNotHeld);
    void change_mode(in lock_mode held_mode, in lock_mode new_mode)
                    raises(LockNotHeld); ...
  }; ...
  interface LockSetFactory {
    LockSet create();
    LockSet create_related(in LockSet which); ...
  };
};
```

In addition to the locking operations of `LockSet`, the Concurrency Control service also standardizes the operations of a factory to create locksets. The `create` operation creates a lockset and the `create_related` operation creates a lockset that is associated to a related lockset. Related locksets release their locks together and therefore unlocking of a set of related objects can be achieved with just one object request.

11.2.6 Summary

We have seen how concurrency control can be applied to distributed objects. We have identified the need for concurrency control when shared objects are accessed by concurrent transactions outside the control of a database. In these circumstances the designer of a server object has to apply two-phase locking in order to achieve serializability of the transactions. We have discussed hierarchical locking, a mechanism to efficiently implement the locking of large numbers of objects and we have seen how both two-phase locking and hierarchical locking are supported by the CORBA Concurrency Control service.

11.3 The Two-Phase Commit Protocol

In the previous section, we saw how the isolation property can be implemented. We have also already identified that the durability property of transactions will be achieved using a persistent state service, as discussed in Chapter 10. We have also seen that the implementation of consistency preservation is the responsibility of the client programmer. Hence we are only missing atomicity. In order to discuss how atomicity of distributed object transactions is achieved, we first present the roles that objects can adopt in distributed transactions. We then discuss that committing a distributed transaction involves distributed decision-making and that two phases are needed for implementing a commit. The communication between the objects involved with the transaction is therefore called the *two-phase commit protocol* (2PC).

11.3.1 Roles of Objects in Distributed Transactions

There are different distributed objects involved in transactions. It is beneficial to identify the roles that these distributed objects play for transaction management in order to understand their obligations for a successful implementation of the transaction properties. The roles that we identify now are the most basic ones that are commonly found in all distributed transactional systems. It should be noted that some middleware adds more specific roles.

We already identified that it is usually the application that starts and ends transactions. The objects executing these applications are generally referred to as *transactional clients*. In the examples that we have used above, objects of types `DirectBanking` and `Reporting` acted as transactional clients. They invoke the begin, commit and abort operations from a transaction coordinator.

A transactional client issues transaction commands.

Each transaction has a *transaction coordinator*. The coordinator knows the identity of all server objects that participate in a transaction. In distributed systems, there are usually many transaction coordinator objects, as otherwise an artificial bottleneck would be created. The

A transaction coordinator controls the execution of the transaction.

transaction coordinator is often provided by transaction services because, unlike transactional clients and transactional servers, it is application-independent.

 Transactional servers are server objects that participate in transactions.

Transactional server objects are the application-specific server objects. They are often stateful. Prior to participating in the transaction they register their involvement with the transaction coordinator. The transactional server objects implement the protocols that are necessary to ascertain the ACID properties of the transaction. In our bank example, the different instances of `Account` objects are transactional server objects. In the examples used in this chapter, all instance are accounts but it is quite possible that instances of different types can participate in the same transaction.

11.3.2 Two-Phase Commit for Flat Transactions

There may be many concurrent transactions in a distributed object system. Every transaction coordinator manages a subset of those concurrent transactions. It is therefore necessary for a transactional client to identify the transaction that they wish to manipulate and for the transactional servers to indicate in which transactions they participate. This is achieved by system-wide *unique transaction identifiers*. The transaction identifier is acquired by the co-ordinator during the start of a new transaction and then passed to clients. Clients may either explicitly or implicitly pass the transaction identifier to transactional servers.

 Distributed transaction commits can only be done in two phases.

A transaction involves the operation of multiple transactional servers. Each of these transactional servers may perform modifications to its state during the transaction. For the transaction to commit successfully every single participating transactional server has to be able to commit. It is therefore not possible for the transaction coordinator to decide for itself whether or not to commit the transaction. For the transaction to be atomic, every single transactional server that participated in the transaction has to be able to commit. The coordinator has to obtain agreement from every single participating transactional server to be able to commit. Only after that agreement has been given can the coordinator trigger the completion of the commit. It is therefore necessary to split the implementation of the commit into two phases: the voting phase and the completion phase.

Voting Phase

 In the voting phase, servers decide whether they can commit.

The purpose of the *voting phase* of the two-phase commit protocol is to see whether or not the transaction can be committed. This is done by voting. Obtaining the votes is initiated by the transaction coordinator. We have to assume that the coordinator knows all the transactional servers that are participating in a transaction. Servers therefore have to register with the coordinator as soon as they participate in the transaction. To implement the voting phase, the transaction coordinator then asks every participating server for a vote. The transaction commits if every single transactional server has voted for the commit. If a single server has not voted in favour of committing, the transaction will be aborted.

There are many reasons why a transaction may have to be aborted. It could be because a transactional server detects a state of inconsistency from which it cannot recover. The server would then vote against the commit. Another reason could be that the transactional server has crashed at some point after registering its participation but before returning its vote. The coordinator will then receive an exception, time-out or other failure indication saying that the transactional server is unavailable, which it will interpret as a vote against the commit. Finally, the transactional coordinator itself may decide that it is not a good idea to commit and vote against the commit itself.

Completion Phase

The purpose of the *completion phase* of the two-phase commit protocol is to implement the commit. After receiving votes from all participating transactional servers, the coordinator collates the votes and, if all servers voted for the commit, it requests every server to do the commit. This involves storing modified states on persistent storage. The transactional servers confirm completion of the commit with the transactional server.

In the completion phase, servers perform the commit.

From Example 11.15, we note that the implementation of transactions is transparent to the client. It only starts and commits the transaction. However, the implementation of transactions is not transparent to the designers of transactional servers. They have to implement the operations that are necessary for the two-phase commit protocol. These are, in particular, the `vote` and the `doCommit` operations.

Transaction implementation is transparent to the client, but not to the server.

Message Complexity

Let us now investigate the overhead of processing distributed transactions. The overhead is dominated by the number of messages that are needed for the object requests that implement the transaction. We can also observe that the only variable in the number of participating objects is the number of transactional servers. Let us therefore assume that N transactional servers participate in a transaction.

Every transactional server needs to register with the coordinator which leads to N registration requests. The transactional coordinator needs to request a vote from every participating server. This results in a total of N voting requests. Moreover, the coordinator needs to request N `doCommit` requests from the servers. This adds up to about $3 \times N$ requests in the case where there is no failure. Additional requests may be needed if a failure occurs, but we can note that the complexity of transaction processing is linear in relation to the number of participating transactional servers.

The complexity of two-phase commit is linear in relation to the number of participating servers.

Server Uncertainty

The sequence diagram in Example 11.15 slightly oversimplifies the picture. Transactions are not so easy to implement as it may seem from this example. The reason for this is the so-called *server uncertainty*. It denotes the period after a transactional server has voted in favour of a commit and before it receives the request to do the commit. During this period the server is ready to commit but does not know whether the commit is actually going to happen.

Example 11.15

Object Requests for Two-Phase
Commit

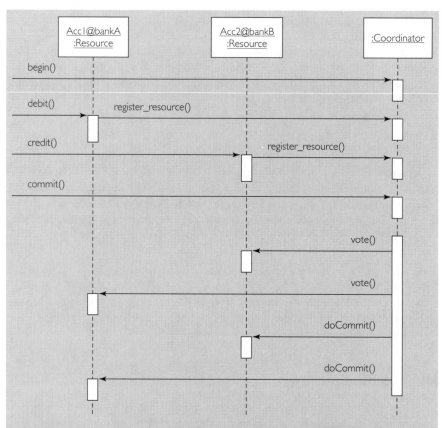

This sequence diagram shows the two-phase commit for a distributed funds transfer transaction between two accounts residing on the hosts of different banks. First the transactional client requests the begin of a new transaction from the transaction coordinator. Then the transactional client invokes the `debit` and `credit` operations from the two account objects that are transactional servers. The implementation of these two operations know that they are part of a transaction and they therefore register their transaction involvement with the coordinator. The client then requests execution of the commit. To implement the commit, the coordinator first asks the two account objects for their vote to commit. In this example, both transactional servers vote in favour of the commit and the coordinator requests the `doCommit` operation from them. The coordinator then returns control to the client, indicating that the transaction was completed successfully.

The server uncertainty has to be bridged by the transactional server. After having voted in favour of a commit, the server must be able to complete the transaction. This means, in fact, that the server has to cope with a situation when it crashes after returning the vote. This is usually done by storing the changes of the transaction on some temporary persistent storage, for example a log file, that is used to recover the transaction result during a restart of the server.

The transactional coordinator also has to store some information on persistent temporary storage after the decision has been reached to do the commit. In particular, it has to store the transaction identifier, the references of participating transactional servers and the decision whether to commit the transaction. The server will use this information after a recovery from a failure that happened after the collation of the votes to re-transmit the `doCommit` requests to participating transactional servers.

Recovery

Let us now discuss what can go wrong during a transaction in order to reveal how the two-phase commit protocol recovers from failures. The aim of this discussion is to show how 2PC achieves atomicity.

Failure prior to commit: If any object involved with a transaction (including the transactional client) fails prior to requesting the commit message, the transaction coordinator will eventually abort the transaction by requesting an explicit abort from participating servers.

Failure of server before voting: If any server fails prior to voting, the coordinator will interpret the absence of a vote from the server as a vote against a commit and abort the transaction.

Failure of coordinator during voting: If the coordinator fails before or during the vote, the transactions will never receive a `doCommit` request and eventually abort.

Failure of server after voting: If a server fails after it has voted in favour of committing, after restarting it will ask the coordinator about the commit decision for the transaction. If the decision was to commit, it will commit using the data it recovered from the temporary persistent storage; otherwise it will abort.

Failure of coordinator after first `doCommit`: If the coordinator fails after it has started the completion phase, the coordinator has to use the data it stored on temporary persistent storage to re-transmit the `doCommit` requests to participating transactional servers.

Summary

All the changes that were performed by transactional servers are performed either completely or not performed at all. In order to achieve this atomicity, both transactional servers and the transaction coordinator utilize temporary persistent storage. The request of the first `doCommit` operation from a transactional server marks a decision point. Before that point, the coordinator might undo all changes by sending abort messages. From that point forward, recovery is used to complete the transaction.

Two-phase commit achieves atomicity of transactions.

11.3.3 Open Distributed Transaction Processing

In the previous chapter, we suggested that database management systems (DBMS) may be used to implement persistence. DBMSs also support the concept of transactions, though these transactions were traditionally confined to data that is stored in databases that are under full control of the DBMS. If some transactional servers use a relational database, another server uses an object database and a third server uses files to achieve persistence, how

Example 11.16

Two-Phase Commit
Implementation using ODTP/
XA Protocol

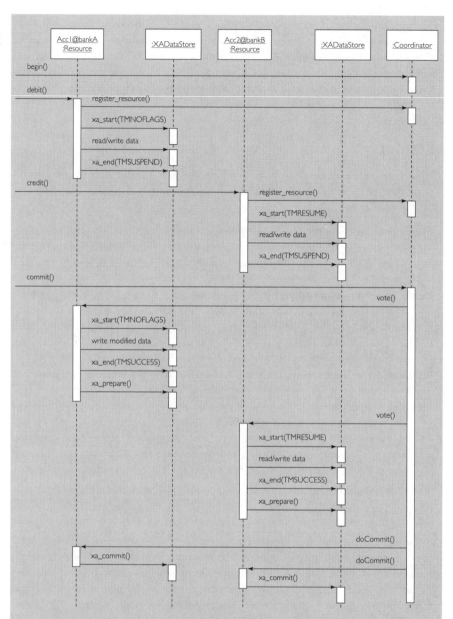

The above diagram shows the interactions between transactional servers and different databases that are used to store persistently the state of the account objects of Example 11.15. Access or update operations of the state of account objects are encapsulated by `xa_start` and `xa_end` operations so that the database uses its own locking mechanisms to achieve the isolation property. Note how the implementation of the voting phase uses the database to store the modified data temporarily. The database then uses its own mechanisms to make those changes permanent and then release all locks on the accessed and modified data during the `xa_commit` operation.

can we use the two-phase commit protocol to implement distributed object transactions between these databases?

Fortunately all database vendors have understood the importance of distributed transaction processing. In addition to their internal transaction processing capabilities, they offer interfaces so that their transaction execution can be externally controlled. This enables databases to participate in transaction implementations that follow the two-phase commit protocol. In order to facilitate the portability and interoperability, a standard interface has been defined for Open Distributed Transaction Processing (ODTP) by the Open Group.

The XA protocol is part of the ODTP standard and defines the application programming interface that database management systems have to implement for transaction processing. In particular, it includes operations to start a transaction (`xa_start`), to end or suspend a transaction (`xa_end`), to vote on committing a transaction (`xa_prepare`) and to do the commit (`xa_commit`). The XA protocol standardizes the parameterization and the semantics of these operations. Example 11.16 shows how this XA protocol is used in a transactional server implementation.

Thus, transactional servers that delegate persistence to a DBMS will use the XA protocol for also delegating the implementation of the two-phase commit operations. This delegation will considerably simplify the implementation of transactions in transactional servers and should be chosen by server object designers whenever possible.

 Servers can delegate transaction implementations to a DBMS.

11.4 Services for Distributed Object Transactions

We have explained the principles of distributed object transactions. We have identified how the isolation property can be implemented in those cases when it is not addressed already by a database management system. We have shown how the atomicity property of transactions is implemented using the two-phase commit protocol. We will now review standard technologies that are available for the implementation of distributed object transactions.

In this section, we discuss the CORBA Transaction Service that is used for implementing CORBA-based distributed object transactions. We then see how COM objects can implement transactions using the Microsoft Transaction Service and finally we review Sun's Java Transaction Service that is used by distributed Java objects.

11.4.1 CORBA Transaction Service

The CORBA Transaction Service was adopted as part of the CORBAservices RFP2 in 1994. It standardizes CORBA interfaces to implement the principles that we have discussed in this chapter. We now discuss excerpts of these interfaces in order to show how a sequence of CORBA object requests can be executed with transaction semantics.

CORBA Transaction Architecture

Figure 11.8 shows an overview of the interfaces of the CORBA Transaction service. For reasons of brevity, the figure includes only those operations that show that the Transaction Service implements the principles that we discussed above. We note also that we have omitted a number of less important interfaces.

Figure 11.8
Interfaces of the CORBA Transaction Service

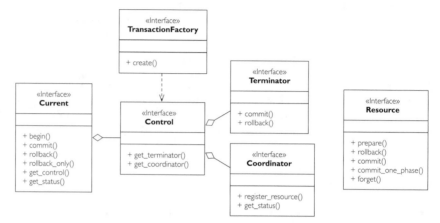

The CORBA transaction service uses the two-phase commit protocol for transaction management. The operations for transaction coordination purposes are distributed among several CORBA interfaces in order to provide dedicated interfaces for transactional clients and transactional servers. Every CORBA thread has an implicit current transaction associated with it. If implicit transaction contexts are used, the transaction operations are provided by the `Current` object. In addition to the implicit transaction control, CORBA supports the creation of explicit transaction contexts. They are created using the Transaction service's `TransactionFactory`, a reference to which can be obtained using the `FactoryFinder` interface of the cycle service. Transactional clients can start a new transaction using the `create` operation and are given a reference onto a transaction control object, which can pass a reference on a transaction terminator object. The terminator object is then used to commit or rollback (that is, abort) a transaction.

The `Coordinator` and the `Resource` interfaces are relevant for transactional servers. CORBA objects that are transactional servers register their involvement in a transaction using the `register_resource` operation to which they pass a reference to themselves as a parameter. CORBA transactional server objects have to implement the `Resource` interface. It includes the operations needed for the two-phase commit. Their vote is requested using the `prepare` operation and requesting `commit` demands the server to commit the transaction. The `rollback` operation is requested from a server in order to abort a transaction and `forget` is invoked when the server can forget all knowledge about the transaction.

Using CORBA Transactions

There are two ways that transactional clients can start a transaction. Transactional clients can obtain a reference on an object representing the current transaction using the CORBA initialization operation `resolve_initial_references`, which returns an object of type `Current`. They then use the operations provided by `Current` to start, commit or abort a transaction. The second way to start a transaction is to create a new `Control` object using the `TransactionFactory`. The transaction is then completed using a `Terminator` object to which the client can obtain an object reference from the `Control` object.

To implement transactional servers in CORBA, designers need to implement the `Resource` interface. In particular, they need to implement the `prepare`, `commit` and `rollback` operations. If a relational or object database is used for persistence, they can delegate these calls using the XA protocol to the DBMS.

11.4.2   Microsoft Transaction Server

A sequence of COM operation executions can be executed as a transaction using the Microsoft Transaction Server (MTS). Like the CORBA Transaction service, MTS uses the two-phase commit protocol for the execution of distributed transactions. MTS originates in the SQL Server relational database product of Microsoft, but it will become part of the next generation of the Windows operating system.

MTS Architecture

Figure 11.9 provides an overview of the main components of MTS. The transaction coordination is performed in MTS by the *Distributed Transaction Coordinator (DTC)*. There is one DTC object on every MTS. The DTC manages the transaction context objects on behalf of MTS.

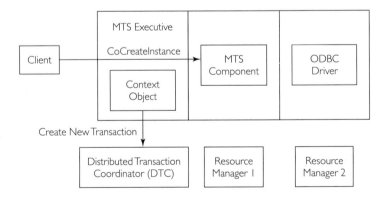

Figure 11.9
Distributed Object Transactions using MTS

There is one *context object* for every transaction. The context object implements the interface that is used by MTS Components in order to identify whether they are able to commit or whether a transaction should be aborted. The context object also provides a redefined `CreateInstance` operation that facilitates the creation of COM components that execute under MTS control.

MTS Components are the equivalent to resources in the CORBA Transaction service. Unlike CORBA resources, however, they do not have to implement a particular interface. They use the context object to indicate whether they can commit transactions or want to abort the transaction in which they participate.

Resource Managers

Resource managers store the state of MTS components persistently and therefore they participate in the two-phase commit protocol. When an MTS Component calls a resource manager for the first time, the resource manager registers itself with the MTS. This registration is referred to as *enlistment*, in Microsoft's terminology. From then on, the MTS will ensure that the resource manager is involved in the two-phase commit protocol. At the time of writing this book, the only type of resource manager that was supported by MTS was Microsoft's SQL Server product. It can, however, be expected that MTS will soon support other resource managers, in particular database management systems implementing the XA protocol and the NT file system.

Using MTS Transactions

The use of MTS is more transparent to client and server programmers than the use of the CORBA Transaction service. COM clients that use MTS components are generally unaware of transactions. The transactions are started by the MTS based on transaction attributes that are established using MTS Explorer, the administration tool that is provided for MTS.

In order to write transactional servers, COM designers need to build an MTS component. MTS components have to be in-process servers (also known as DLLs). The component needs to have a class factory that MTS can use for creating instances of the component. Moreover, the component must interface with the context object in order to indicate whether it is ready to commit a transaction or whether the transaction should be aborted.

11.4.3 Transactions in Java

Sun recently released the Enterprise Java Beans (EJB) specification. Enterprise Java Beans are Java Beans that use RMI to communicate with clients and other beans across distributed Java VMs. Because client applications may wish to execute a series of different EJB operations in an atomic, consistency-preserving, isolated and durable fashion, the EJB specification demands provision of transactions. In order to support the implementation of such transactions, Sun defined the Java Transaction API and the Java Transaction Service. The Java Transaction API defines the interfaces that are used by transactional clients and transactional servers. EJB providers use this Java interface to implement transactions. The Java Transaction Service defines how transaction coordinators can be implemented based on the CORBA Transaction service.

Java Transaction Architecture

Figure 11.10 shows an overview of the different layers of the Transaction Management architecture for Java.

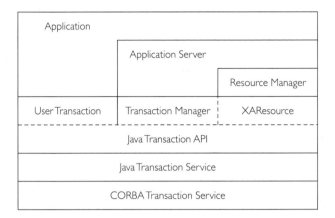

Figure 11.10
Distributed Transaction
Management in Java

The Java transaction management uses the two-phase commit protocol for transaction management purposes and defines three main interfaces in the Java Transaction API (JTA). The `UserTransaction` interface is used by applications in order to control transactions. The `TransactionManager` interface is implemented by application servers, such as transaction monitors or Enterprise Java Beans implementations in order to provide a transaction coordinator. Finally, the `XAResource` interface is implemented by transactional servers. Figure 11.11 shows an excerpt of the operations provided by the most important interfaces of the JTA.

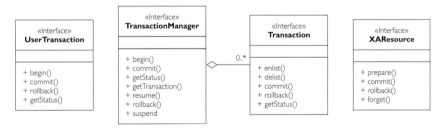

Figure 11.11
Interfaces of the Java
Transaction API

`UserTransaction` provides the operation for a transactional client to start new transactions (`begin`), to commit a transaction (`commit`) and to abort a transaction (`rollback`). In fact, the purpose of `UserTransaction` in the Java Transaction API is identical to interface `Current` in the CORBA Transaction service. `TransactionManager` is the coordinator interface. It provides operations to implement the transaction begin and end. Implementations of `UserTransaction` will delegate transaction management operations to `TransactionManager`. The `TransactionManager` interface also provides a mechanism to return a reference to one of the `Transaction` objects that it manages. The `Transaction` interface has the same purpose as the `Coordinator` interface of the CORBA Transaction service. The `enlist` operation of a `Transaction` object is used by a transactional server to register its participation in a transaction. Finally, the `XAResource` interface corresponds to the `Resource` interface of the CORBA Transaction service and has to be implemented by all transactional servers that wish to participate in two-phase commit transactions.

Using Java Transactions

The use of the Java Transaction API is very similar to the use of the CORBA Transaction service. They both support the XA protocol and the Java Transaction API can be seen as an extension of the CORBA Transaction service.

The transactional client obtains a reference onto the `UserTransaction` object using an interface provided by the JTA. It can then use `UserTransaction` operations to control start, commit and abort transactions.

A transactional server has to implement the `XAResource` interface and it will most often do so by delegating calls to an XA-capable database. Moreover, it has to register its involvement with the transaction coordinator using the `enlist` operation that is available through the `Transaction` interface. The resource can obtain a reference to its `Transaction` object using the `TransactionManager`.

Summary

We have seen that all object-oriented middleware systems support transaction management through dedicated services. All of these services offer an integration with database systems. In the case of CORBA and Java this integration is the XA industry standard, which is not yet supported by MTS. MTS uses a proprietary protocol for an integration with SQL Server.

The isolation property is generally achieved using the locking mechanisms supported by the database. In cases where no database is used, the designer of a transactional server has to use concurrency control mechanisms, such as the CORBA Concurrency service to avoid lost updates and inconsistent analysis.

We have also seen that all transaction services use the two-phase commit protocol that we have explained in this chapter. They all standardize interfaces for transactional servers to register their involvement in a transaction and then the servers are called upon by the transaction coordinator to vote and to do the commit.

Distributed object transactions are well supported by object-oriented middleware.

Transaction services are integrated with DBMSs using the XA protocol.

Middleware uses two-phase commit to implement transactions.

Key Points

- ▶   In this chapter we have introduced the basic principles of distributed transaction management. A transaction is an atomic, consistency-preserving, isolated and durable sequence of object requests.
- ▶   The objects involved in distributed transaction management play different roles. A transactional client determines the beginning and end of the transaction. A transactional server maintains a state and performs modifications to that state under transaction control. A transaction coordinator determines whether or not a transaction can be committed using the two-phase commit protocol.

▶ The implementation of transactions involves concurrency control, which can be done explicitly by a transactional server designer or it can be delegated to a database system.

▶ Explicit concurrency control is implemented using the two-phase locking protocol. It achieves serializability, but is not deadlock free.

▶ Deadlocks are detected by a concurrency control manager and they are resolved by aborting a transaction involved in the deadlock.

▶ The two-phase commit protocol consists of a voting phase and an implementation phase. During voting, the transaction coordinator checks whether every participating transactional server is able to commit the transaction. During commit, the servers save their changes to persistent storage and thus implement durability.

▶ The phase after a transactional server has voted for a commit and before it receives the commit request is called server uncertainty. It has to be covered by storing the modifications of the transaction on temporary persistent storage.

▶ Object-oriented middleware provides services for the implementation of transactions. We have discussed the CORBA Transaction service, MTS and the Java Transaction API. All of these services use the two-phase commit protocol and an integration with database systems for the implementation of transactions.

Self Assessment

11.1 What are the ACID properties of transactions?

11.2 What is the difference between two-phase locking and two-phase commit?

11.3 What is lock compatibility?

11.4 When is the hierarchical locking protocol applied?

11.5 What is the purpose of upgrade locks?

11.6 Why are upgrade locks mutually incompatible?

11.7 For which designers is concurrency control transparent?

11.8 When do designers of transactional servers not have to implement concurrency control?

11.9 How does 2PL prevent inconsistent analysis?

11.10 What are the three roles that objects can play in distributed object transactions?

11.11 Why do distributed transactions need two phases to commit?

11.12 How are the ACID properties implemented in distributed object transactions?

11.13 What is server uncertainty?

11.14 How is server uncertainty dealt with?

11.15 Of which tasks do the CORBA Transaction Service, MTS and JTS relieve the designer?

Further Reading

The idea of transactions and the four ACID properties were first introduced by [Gray, 1978] in a course on operating systems. [Gray, 1981] reports on the application of transactions in databases, an area where they have been most successful.

A number of extensions were suggested to the transactions as suggested by Gray. [Moss, 1985] suggested the concept of nested transactions as we have discussed them in this section. Mechanisms for the implementation of nested transactions are still not widely available in either databases or object-oriented middleware, which is why we have refrained from discussing them further.

The transactions that we have discussed here are very suitable when the overall amount of processing can be completed in a short period of time. Transactions have also been suggested for long-lived tasks, such as designing a circuit or a software architecture. These long transactions give up one ACID property or another in order to be suitable for collaborative and interactive long-lived activities. A good overview of these non-standard transactions and their application to software engineering is provided by [Barghouti and Kaiser, 1991]. The survey includes CAD transactions [Bancilhon et al., 1985], design transactions [Katz, 1984] and split—join transactions [Kaiser, 1990].

[Bernstein et al., 1987] wrote the definitive textbook on database concurrency control. The book includes a very thorough discussion of the different locking techniques that we could only briefly discuss in this chapter. The Concurrency Control service of CORBA is discussed in Chapter 7 of [Object Management Group, 1996]. Java provides built-in primitives for concurrency control. Java operations can be declared as synchronized, which means that only one of these synchronized operations can be executed at any point in time. The locking mechanism that is used to implement synchronization, however, does not distinguish different locking modes and thus may be overly restrictive. A good discussion of the concurrency primitives of Java is provided by [Magee and Kramer, 1999] and [Lea, 1997].

The discussion of the services that are available to implement distributed object transaction had to be rather brief in this chapter, as we felt it more important to focus on the underlying principles. The CORBA Object Transaction service is defined in detail in Chapter 10 of [Object Management Group, 1996]. A professional text book that covers Microsoft's Transaction Service rather well is [Hillier, 1998]. The Java architecture for transaction management is defined in the Java Transaction API [Cheung and Matena, 1999]. It relies on the Java Transaction Service, a Java binding to the CORBA Transaction Service. The Java Transaction Service is defined in [Cheung, 1999]. [Sun, 1999] specifies transactions for Jini, the Java-based middleware for physically mobile devices. Again, those transactions are implemented using a two-phase commit protocol.

Distributed transactions do not necessarily have to be implemented in an object-oriented way. *Transaction monitors* support the implementation of distributed transactions between non-object-oriented programs. Examples of these transaction monitors include CICS from IBM and Tuxedo from BEA. CICS is extensively described by [Hudders, 1994]. A comprehensive introduction to Tuxedo is given by [Andrade, 1996]. These transaction monitors are also often used to implement distributed object transaction services. The integration of both transaction monitors and distributed object transaction services with database systems relies on the Open Distributed Transaction Processing Standard of the Open Group. The XA Protocol for database transaction control is defined in [X/Open Group, 1994].

12

Security

Learning Objectives

In this chapter, we study the principles of engineering secure distributed objects. We will understand the potential security threats to which distributed objects are exposed. We will then learn about the principles of encryption and recognize that they provide the basic primitives upon which higher levels of security are built. We will comprehend these higher levels, which are concerned with the authenticity of objects, restriction of requests to authorized clients, auditing of security-relevant events, and provision of non-repudiable evidence. We investigate how higher-levels of security are supported by the CORBA Security service.

Chapter Outline

In the previous chapters we have started to address how reliable distributed objects can be built. We have investigated how to store the state of objects onto persistent storage so that it is retained after deliberate or accidental termination of server objects. We have also seen how transactions are used to limit the impact of failures. Reliability, however has a different facet that we have neglected so far. Using object-oriented middleware, we can build server objects and make them available to clients anywhere on a local area network, or even the Internet. This means that every client that can obtain an object reference to a server object can request operation execution from the server. Very often it is necessary to restrict access to a more limited community of client objects, to allow client objects only to execute particular operations, to secure the parameters of object requests against unauthorized access while in transit on a public network, to provide non-repudiable evidence that a client has indeed requested execution of a particular operation, and to record any incidents that may compromise the overall system security. We continue our banking example from the previous chapter in Example 12.1 to illustrate this point.

Example 12.1
Why We Need Security in Distributed Object Systems

Consider the availability of server objects on the Internet that is necessitated by a direct banking application. A bank will have to keep tight control over the client objects that it permits to execute credit or debit operations on account objects. The bank will also have to be convinced that the principal who executes the client object is actually who he or she claims to be. Moreover, the bank will have to provide non-repudiable evidence that the principal requested a particular operation. In the Internet direct banking application, the bank will have to generate evidence that the principal executing the client has, for example, requested a funds transfer. Finally, the auditors of the bank will demand from the application that it provides details about any attack or other security-relevant event that occurred within the system. All these requirements demand the provision of high-level primitives for security.

In order to understand the importance of security and the measures against which distributed systems have to be secured, we discuss the different security threats and the methods that are used for attacking security. The higher levels of security we ultimately want to achieve are implemented using encryption techniques. We then review public and secure key-based encryption methods and the key distribution techniques that are associated with them. We review high-level security services, such as authentication, access control, non-repudiation and auditing, that are built on top of the encryption primitives. Finally, we review the security services provided by object-oriented middleware to provide examples of how these principles are applied.

12.1 Security Attacks

12.1.1 Insecurity of Distributed Systems

The components of distributed systems, whether object-oriented or not, have to communicate via a network. If hosts are directly connected to public networks, such as the Internet, any network traffic to or from the host is publicly accessible. Individuals wishing to launch security attacks can obtain connections to a public network, because there are no restrictions on connecting machines to a public network. This means that an attacker can use a public network to send messages to distributed system components in an attempt to compromise the system security.

An obvious approach to avoiding security problems is to physically separate the network from the public network. These separated networks are called private networks and are still often employed by banks and telecommunications operators to secure their mission-critical systems. As a consequence of such a separation, however, we cannot have distributed system communication across the two networks. With the advent of electronic commerce, distributed system components often cannot have such a physical separation and even critical systems have to be connected to public networks. Even when networks are private, or the connection between hosts on a private network and hosts on a public network is tightly controlled, security can be compromised. Individuals who have authorized access to machines connected to the private network may use these machines to launch security attacks.

This leads us to the observation that distributed systems are inherently insecure. If an attacker succeeds in breaking the security of a system, the legitimate users will lose confidence in the system. They may sue the engineers or operators of the system for the damages that were caused as a result of the security attack. For the engineering of distributed objects this means that one should not trust any other distributed object, because it may be written by an attacker, who wants to compromise security. We thus have to engineer both client and server objects in such a secure way that confidence and trust can be re-established. In order to do this, we first have to develop a better understanding of the security threats to which distributed objects are exposed.

Distributed systems are inherently insecure.

12.1.2 Threats

There are different forms of security threat. [Colouris et al., 1994] classify them into four different categories and we follow this classification. The first class is concerned with leakage of information to non-authorized parties. The second class includes threats of non-authorized parties modifying information that is stored or manipulated in a distributed system. The third class is concerned with the unauthorized use of resources, such as network bandwidth, disk space or CPU time. The last, and probably most serious, threat involves the destruction of information or the distributed system itself by unauthorized parties. We now discuss each of these threats and provide examples that show why they can be very serious.

Leakage

A *leakage* is the disclosure of information to unauthorized parties. The damage that can be caused through leakage greatly varies depending on the nature of the information and the relationship between the attacker and the owner of the information. Leakage may lead to loss of business: if videos are leaked from a video-on-demand server then attackers can watch the videos without paying. Leakage may also lead to a loss of privacy, for example, if the financial standing of an account owner is disclosed to third parties. Leakage may also have effects that are more damaging than the loss of privacy.

Leakage is the unauthorized disclosure of information.

Example 12.2
Leakage of Account Information

The balance of a personal or company account is considered to be private to that person. Yet, sometimes it would be advantageous for competitor companies or companies planning to buy a company to have detailed insights into account balances. If a company manages to hack into the bank database and obtain this information, this is an example of leakage of information.

Tampering

Tampering is unauthorized modification of information.

Tampering denotes the unauthorized modification of information that is stored or manipulated in a distributed system. Tampering with information implies leakage but goes beyond it, in that the information is not only accessed but also modified. Tampering is potentially a more dangerous threat than leakage, because the attacker modifies an organization's perception of the world as it is captured in the organization's data.

Example 12.3
Tampering with Bank Accounts

Attackers that can tamper with the information that is held about accounts in a distributed system of a bank can effectively modify account balances. They can, for example, increase the balances of their own accounts to increase the funds that they can command.

Resource Stealing

Resource stealing denotes the unauthorized use of computing resources.

The class of threats that are subsumed under *resource stealing* use the resources provided by the distributed system in an unauthorized way. Such unauthorized usage often coincides with usage for which the attackers are not paying, which is why we refer to the use as stealing. Stolen resources can be CPU time, main memory, network bandwidth, air-time of mobile phones, secondary storage memory or even human resources who operate a computer system.

Example 12.4
Resource Stealing

Telephone network management applications are often distributed systems. By violating the security of these distributed systems, attackers may be able to use the resources of a telephone network provider without paying. They may, for example, attempt to modify the distributed billing system of the provider in such a way that they can use their telephone without being charged.

Vandalism

Vandalism is the destruction of information.

Vandalism is potentially the most serious threat and in the context of distributed system security it denotes the destruction of information stored by distributed objects or the distributed object system itself.

Example 12.5
Vandalism

There have been examples where attackers obtained administrator rights and then formatted hard disks and thus destroyed data and code alike.

Combined Threats

Attackers very often combine the different threats discussed above. They steal resources such as telephone network access in order to connect themselves to a public network. They then attempt to obtain sensitive information, such as passwords or login details. Once they obtain those, they login to a machine and launch security attacks using another user's identity and may tamper with data in a way that is beneficial to them.

12.1.3 Methods of Attack

Now that we have understood the different forms of security threats that distributed object systems are exposed to, we can investigate the methods that attackers use to exercise these threats. Understanding these methods is important in order to engineer distributed objects in such a way that these methods cannot be applied.

The methods can be classified into four categories. Methods in the first category involve concealing the attacker's identity so that they can pretend to be an authorized user of a distributed object. The second category involves listening to network traffic in order to obtain the contents of object requests. The third category includes methods that modify object requests. And the last category includes methods that are based on repeating requests that have previously been exchanged between distributed objects. We now discuss each of these methods in more detail.

Masquerading

Masquerading is a method of attack where the attacker obtains the identity of a different, usually an authorized, user. Masquerading is also sometimes referred to as *spoofing*. The attacker can then use the access rights and privileges of that user to perform malicious actions. Identity in centralized systems is usually validated at session startup time. In distributed object systems, however, the identity has to be passed and validated with each object request.

Masquerading attacks obtain the identity of legitimate users.

The operations to credit and debit accounts in our banking example should obviously only be executed by authorized personnel of the bank in such a way that there is never a credit without a debit operation. A secure implementation of the banking example would have to distinguish different groups of users and grant the right to execute the `credit` and `debit` operations only to a particular group. An attacker wishing to credit monies on his account would then have to use masquerading to obtain the identity of one of the authorized users.

Example 12.6
Masquerading Attack on a Bank Account

In order to prevent attackers from using masquerading, we will have to make it difficult for them to obtain the identity of authorized users. *Authentication* is used for that purpose. Authentication supports proving that a user is who the user claims to be. The implementation of authentication is based on encryption techniques, which we will study in the next section.

Eavesdropping

The request parameters and request results that are sent from a client object to a server object or vice versa may include sensitive information. We have seen that the client and server stubs marshal these parameters into a transmittable form. Very often the format that is used for this transmission is well known to an attacker, because it is based on a standard data representation, such as NDR, XDR, or CDR. By listening to or sniffing the network packets that are transmitted when implementing an object request, attackers can therefore obtain and decode the request parameters. We refer to this method of attack as *eavesdropping*.

Eavesdropping is possible because the attacker knows how object requests are encoded. Object requests, however, have to be encoded in a standardized form in order to facilitate interoperability. In order to prevent eavesdropping, we must, therefore, avoid transmitting object request data in an encoding that is known to other people. This is generally achieved by encrypting the messages before they are sent through the network and decrypting the messages immediately after they have been received.

Example 12.7
Eavesdropping Attack on a Bank
Account

In the banking application discussed in Example 11.2 on Page ●●●, an object request `get_balance` returns the balance of an account object. If we assume that the object request is executed using CORBA, the floating point number that represents the balance will be encoded using CORBA's CDR representation. Moreover, the IIOP protocol demands that the name of the operation is included in the marshalled representation of the object request, too. The message will also identify whether it is a request or a reply. An attacker who wants to obtain balances of account objects can then eavesdrop and wait for packets that include the string `get_balance`. The requester will then know from the encoding of the type of message whether it is a reply message and can then obtain the balance that is encoded as float in CDR.

Request Tampering

Request tampering builds on, and goes beyond, eavesdropping. The idea of request tampering is that request messages are intercepted before they reach the server object. The attacker modifies request parameters and then passes the message on. Using request tampering, an attacker can modify information without having to masquerade some other user's identity. The ease with which request tampering can be used depends on the type of network protocol that is being used. We should however assume that network protocols do not exclude the modification of information between senders and receivers.

Example 12.8

Let us assume that an attacker wants to tamper with a credit request in order to unlawfully increase his or her account balance. Assuming again a CORBA-based distributed object system, the credit request will be implemented using an IIOP request message. The attacker could force the generation of such a message, for example by banking a cheque with a small amount of money. The attacker would then intercept the message and modify the parameters of the `credit` request to a high amount of money before passing the message on to the intended receiver. Instead of generating the request message, the attacker uses a request message generated by an authorized user of the system and just modifies the message to credit a higher amount.

Request tampering can be prevented in the same way as eavesdropping. If a requester cannot decode the request message then he or she can also not modify it. Hence encrypting request and reply messages that implement object requests is the basic mechanism that is used to prevent request tampering.

Replaying

Attackers may compromise the security of a distributed system, even if they are not able to tamper with any request or reply messages. They can intercept and store a request message and then have a server repeatedly execute an operation by *replaying* the message. Note that the attacker does not have to be able to interpret the message and therefore the encryption mechanisms that can be applied to defeat eavesdropping and request tampering cannot prevent replaying.

Replaying denotes the repetition of request messages.

Consider that an authorized client requests a `credit` operation to an account. In order to prevent eavesdropping and tampering, the designer of the banking application has ensured that the message is encrypted. An attacker who captures a message is not able to interpret the message. However, the attacker can repeatedly send the captured message and thus compromise the integrity of the banking application because the server object will not execute the credit operation once but multiple times. This leads to the balance of the account being unduly increased. An attacker who has other ways than reading the message context to associate the encrypted credit message with a particular account will then be able to increase the balance on that particular account.

Example 12.9
Replaying Attack on a Bank Account

Replaying is difficult to prevent. The obvious solution is to tightly control the flow of network packets. This reinforces the concern we raised earlier about separating private from public networks, which is achieved by firewalls that we will discuss below.

12.1.4 Infiltration

For all of the above methods it is necessary that the attacker obtains access to the network to which server objects are connected. There are three ways that an attacker can obtain the necessary network access.

Attacks by Legitimate Users: Many security attacks are, in fact, launched by legitimate users of the system, who attempt to use the system beyond what they are authorized to do. Thus they abuse their existing authorization for attacks. Auditing is an important measure to tackle such infiltration by detecting and recording any illegitimate usage. We will discuss auditing in the sections below.

Obtaining a Legitimate User's Identity: Most operating systems force users to identify themselves with a password during login. The security of the system critically depends on how these passwords are chosen. It is not difficult to obtain the list of legitimate users of a system and then an attacker can write a *password-cracking program*, which tries words from a dictionary for each of the legitimate users. The system administrators of my Computer Science department once found that 40% of the passwords were girls' first names. As those

A password cracker tries to break the login of a legitimate user with a large dictionary of words.

are commonly included in a dictionary, attackers have a significant number of user identities at their disposal. Again these attacks can be identified by auditing. They can be prevented by choosing proper passwords, which is the responsibility of every user. Because this cannot be enforced and validated, organizations often connect the hosts on which their users work to a private network and strictly control the network flow between the private network and public network with a firewall.

Smuggling Client or Server Objects: The most subtle form of infiltration is the smuggling of executable objects that act as servers or clients into a private network. This can be achieved by means of viruses or worms.

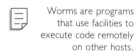
A virus is code that travels with an object to overcome a security barrier.

Viruses exploit object mobility. A virus attaches itself to an object and when the object migrates from one host to another, for example as a result of a load-balancing operation, the virus replicates itself by attaching a copy to other objects that it finds. The execution of a virus is often triggered by a particular date.

Worms are programs that use facilities to execute code remotely on other hosts.

The basic mechanisms to write and execute *worms* are provided by the mobility mechanisms of the middleware. The code of an object may be written on some host and then migrated to another host. An attacker can request execution of some operations after it has been migrated to that host. Whether it is actually possible to execute a worm depends on the installation and administration of the factories that are necessary for object migration purposes.

A distributed object virus or worm would typically start by investigating the interface repository or the type library that is available within the domain of an object-oriented middleware in order to discover information about the types of server objects that are known in that domain. It may traverse name servers in order to discover the object references of server objects that are available in a particular domain. It would transmit that information back to the attacker who then has the object references and the type information that is necessary to write more meaningful attacks, which could again be infiltrated using a virus or worm.

12.2 Encryption

We have seen above that eavesdropping and message tampering are based on the assumption that the network packets that implement an object request between a client and a server object can be interpreted by an attacker. In order to prevent those methods, we will have to avoid sending object requests in plain messages across the network. Masquerading assumes that an attacker can use another user's identity. To prevent masquerading distributed objects must not trust any object that has not been authenticated, that is the objects must prove that they are who they claim to be. The basic primitives both for avoiding plain messages and authentication are provided by encryption techniques.

Encryption uses an algorithm and a key to convert plain text into cypher text and vice versa.

Encryption is a very old technique. It was used by the Romans to avoid messages carried by a messenger being meaningful if the messenger was captured by an enemy. *Encryption techniques* use an algorithm that encapsulates a large set of encryption functions and the key selects one such function. The encryption functions have to be chosen in such a way that it is difficult to perform the inverse function. That means it has to be computationally difficult to create the plain text from the cypher text without having the key.

Two methods of encryption can be distinguished. The first method uses *secret keys*, which are disclosed to only the two parties wishing to communicate securely. The second method uses *public keys* which each party makes generally available for secure communication with that party. A problem that arises then is how keys are distributed in a trustworthy way between two parties and we discuss protocols for the secure distribution of keys.

12.2.1 Secret Key Encryption

Secret key encryption is based on the idea that every pair of components that wish to exchange messages securely have a key that is not known to any other component; the key is kept secret by these two components. Secret key methods typically use the same key for both encrypting and decrypting messages. This means that the encryption algorithms are chosen in such a way that the same key selects a function and its inverse function. Since the secret keys used for the encryption are not publicly available, the encryption and decryption functions may be public.

Secret keys are known to two parties and not disclosed to any others.

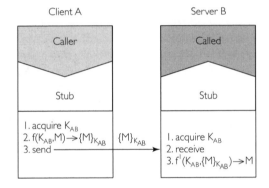

Figure 12.1
Secure Distributed Object Communication with Secret Keys

Figure 12.1 shows how secret key methods work. Sender A acquires key K_{AB}, which has been set up for communication with the receiver B. It then applies the encryption function to the message M that is to be transmitted and parameterizes the encryption with K_{AB}. This results in an encrypted message $M_{K_{AB}}$, which is transmitted to the receiver. The receiver B also has to acquire the same key K_{AB} to decrypt any message received from A and it does so by applying the inverse encryption function f^{-1} to the encrypted message $M_{K_{AB}}$ and the key K_{AB}.

Figure 12.1 also suggests how to employ secret key methods to secure the communication between distributed objects. To implement a request, the client object is the message sender and the server object is the message receiver. The encryption and decryption is performed after the stubs have completed request marshalling and unmarshalling and it has been recognized that the server object is not local. Then the marshalled object request is transmitted in an encrypted form via the network and secured against eavesdropping and message tampering. When receiving the message on the server-side, the message is decrypted and then passed on to the server stub. The same key can then be used for the reply message. We also note that encryption can be kept entirely transparent for client and server programmers as it is done either by the middleware or by the stubs that are created by the middleware.

 Distribution of secret keys to large numbers of objects is too complex. The disadvantage of secret key encryption for distributed objects is that the number of keys that need to be created and distributed increases quadratically by the number of objects. Public key encryption overcomes this problem.

12.2.2 Public Key Encryption

 Public key encryption generate pairs of keys of which only one is made publicly available and the other is kept private. Methods based on secret keys use the same key for both encryption and decryption. It is therefore necessary to keep that key secret. If different keys are used for encryption and decryption, there is no need to keep secret the key that is used for encryption. This is the basic idea of public key encryption methods. They provide mechanisms to generate pairs of matching keys. The first key is made public and the second key is kept private. Public key methods can be used to ensure that a message has been sent from a particular sender or that only a particular receiver can receive the message.

Figure 12.2

Secure Distributed Object Communication with Public Keys

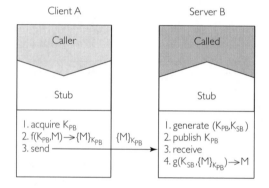

Figure 12.2 shows the steps involved in transmitting messages securely using public keys. First the receiver B generates a pair of keys (K_{PB}, K_{SB}) where K_{PB} denotes the public and K_{SB} denotes the secret key. B publishes K_{PB} in a key database and retains the key K_{SB}. A sender A wishing to transmit a message M securely to B can then acquire the public key K_{PB}, apply the encryption function f with the key to the message and obtain an encrypted message $M_{K_{PB}}$. Transmission of the message across the network is secure because only B has the matching secret key and therefore only B can decrypt the message upon receipt. It does so by applying a decryption function g to the private key K_{SB} and the encrypted message.

Figure 12.2 also shows how public key encryption can be used for secure distributed object communication. The difference between public and secret key methods is that just one pair of keys is generated for every object and thus the number of keys needed is linear in relation to the number of objects. Because different functions f and g are used on the client side and on the server side, the use of public keys is more complicated for the reply message than with secret keys. For the reply message, A needs to generate a pair of keys and publish its public key K_{PA}, which B acquires to encrypt the reply message.

Public key methods have the advantage that the number of keys is only linear in relation to the number of objects. Public key encryption is used in Pretty Good Privacy (PGP) [Zimmermann, 1995]. However, they have a slight disadvantage in that execution of the encryption and decryption function is more complex. With the steady increase in computing power this is often not a problem any more. If the complexity is an issue, *hybrid encryption* approaches that combine secret and public keys are used. A typical hybrid approach that uses a public key to encrypt a secret key is the Secure Socket Layer (SSL) protocol of Netscape.

Public key encryption can be used to protect distributed object requests from eavesdropping and tampering.

SSL uses *Rivest Shamir Adelmann* (RSA) [Rivest et al., 1978] encryption, which is a public key approach and therefore RSA was incorporated into Netscape to support secure downloads of information from the Web. The SSL client generates a secret key for one session, that secret key is encrypted using the server's public key, and the session key is then forwarded to the server and used for any further communication between client and server. Most object-oriented middleware uses SSL rather than straight TCP as a transport protocol in order to prevent eavesdropping and message tampering of object request traffic.

12.2.3   Key Distribution

For both public and secret key encryption, the problem arises as to how keys are distributed in a secure manner. For secret key methods this is an obvious problem. Both a client and a server object need to be equipped with the same key. They need to obtain the key in such a way that no other object gets access to the key. In military encryption applications, keys are distributed by non-networked means, such as a messenger, but this is not feasible in a distributed object system. Hence, for distributed object applications, keys need to be distributed via the network too. While in transit, however, the key must be secured against eavesdropping and tampering, otherwise third parties could use the key for successive eavesdropping or message tampering.

Key distribution is also a problem, though less obvious, for public key methods. The request parameters that a client transmits should only become known to the desired server object. It is therefore important that the public key that the client uses for encrypting the message is the public key of the desired server object rather than a public key that was generated by an attacker. This can be achieved if a trusted key distribution service is used.

A *key distribution service* for both public and secret key encryption methods takes care of distributing keys between objects. A key distribution service has to be a trusted service and the registration of objects with that service has to be trustworthy, too. We now discuss the *Needham/Schroeder protocol*, upon which most key distribution services are based. There are different versions of the Needham/Schroeder protocol for secret and for public keys. We first consider the secret key distribution protocol because it is simpler.

Secure key distribution mechanisms are needed for both secret and public key encryption.

Distributing Secret Keys

Figure 12.3 shows an overview of the parties that are in involved in and the steps that are necessary to securely distribute secret keys. In general, the objects are a client C, a server S and a key distribution server AS. The protocol assumes that every participating object's

Figure 12.3

Needham/Schroeder Protocol
for Secret Key Distribution

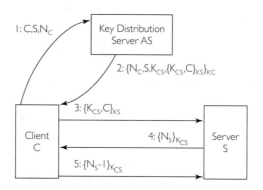

identity is registered with AS and that AS and the object share a secret key for mutual communication, which has been transmitted by different means.

 A nonce is a piece of information that is used temporarily in order to detect replaying of messages.

As a first step, the client C requests generation of a secret key for communication with server S. As part of the request, the client also submits a nonce N_C that is used to avoid replaying. In response to that request, the key distribution service generates a key K_{CS} that C and S use for their communication. It then encrypts K_{CS} and the identity of the client C using the secret key KS that S uses to communicate with the key distribution service. It then encrypts this together with the nonce, the identity of S and the key K_{CS} using the key K_C that C uses for the communication with the key distribution service. In this way it is ensured that only C can decrypt the key K_{CS}. The client then provides S with the key and its identity that was encrypted by the key distribution server, knowing that only S can decrypt it. After decrypting this message, the server tests the key. To do so, the server generates a nonce N_S and returns it encrypted using K_{CS}. The client performs an agreed computation to the nonce and returns the result to the server in a message encrypted by K_{CS}.

Distributing Public Keys

The components that participate in the protocol for securely distributing public keys are the same as for secret key distribution. The protocol, however, is slightly more complicated as it is has to distribute two keys for every pair of objects that wish to communicate. Client C needs to obtain the public key of S in order to send messages to S that only S can decrypt and S has to obtain the public key of C.

Figure 12.4

Need/Schroeder Protocol for
Public Key Distribution

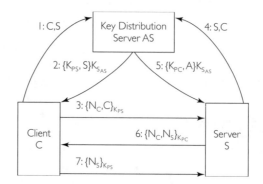

The protocol starts when client C requests transmission of a public key for server S from the key distribution service AS. The server then returns the public key of S encrypted with its own secret key $K_{S_{AS}}$. By decrypting it with AS's public key, the client can be certain that it can only be the key distribution service that has provided the public key of S. The client then sends its identity together with a nonce to the server encrypted with the server's public key K_{PS}. The server interprets this as a signal to obtain the public key for the client from the key distribution service in step 4. The service then provides that key encrypted using its own secret key, which the server decrypts using the public key of AS. The server then sends back the nonce created by the client with a freshly-generated nonce and encrypts this using the public key of the client K_{PC}. The client acknowledges receipt by transmitting the nonce back to the server encrypted using the server's public key.

12.2.4 Summary

We have seen how encryption can be used to prevent eavesdropping on and tampering with messages that are exchanged during the implementation of requests and replies between distributed objects. We have seen the two facets of encryption, secret and public key. They both assumed the availability of keys for the encryption of messages. We have discussed two variants of the Needham/Schroeder protocol with which the necessary key distribution can be achieved.

12.3 Higher-Level Security Services

We will now study higher-level security mechanisms and we will see that the encryption primitives that we have discussed above will also be used for preventing masquerading and for providing evidence that can be used in legal proceedings.

12.3.1 Firewalls

Figure 12.5 shows the principal idea of a *firewall*. The aim of all firewalls is to create a barrier that makes it as difficult as possible for an intruder from a public network to obtain network access to objects that execute within in the private network. To achieve this, access to the host of the firewall is usually extremely restricted and the security is administered with exceptionally great care to make it difficult to break into the host and somehow circumvent the firewall. The host of the firewall is therefore also sometimes referred to as a *bastion host*.

The levels of control that are exercised by a firewall can vary greatly. A firewall may provide only the facilities to monitor and audit the network traffic that passes the public–private network boundary. A firewall may also be set up in such a way that it only routes packets

Firewalls are gateways that tightly control message traffic between private and public networks.

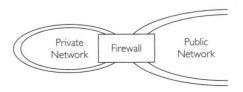

Figure 12.5
Separating Private and Public Networks with a Firewall

from certain authorized users through or that it does not allow particular types of network packet, such as telnet or rlogin requests, from the public network into the private network.

A firewall between a private and a public network does not impact a distributed object system if object request and reply messages do not have to pass the firewall, that is if client and servers are either all connected to the private network or all on the public network. However, sometimes clients that reside on a host connected to a public network want to request operations from a server that is behind a firewall. Our direct banking application is a good example again. The client uses the Internet to connect to the direct banking server, which should for obvious reasons be shielded against attacks by a firewall. The problem is that the client needs to establish a network connection to a host that is hidden behind a firewall and that the firewall might not allow the client to establish a transport connection to the server.

Firewalls between distributed objects have to understand the encoding of object requests.

It is therefore necessary that the firewalls that are used with distributed object systems understand the message traffic that is exchanged between clients and servers. We refer to such firewalls as *distributed object firewalls* and they are designed for monitoring and controlling object requests that pass the public–private network boundary in either direction. Distributed object firewalls support filtering of object requests. These filters can be based on the identity of the server object, the requested operation, or the client that originated a particular request.

Distributed object firewalls base their decision about whether or not a transport connection can be established and whether or not to pass on request and reply messages on the content of the message. They therefore have to understand the representation for requests and replies that is used at the transport level. This means that the distributed object firewall has to understand the standard data representation that is used for marshalling object requests. A firewall for CORBA-based systems would, for example, utilize knowledge about the GIOP protocol and the OMG's Common Data Representation, which is used for marshalling requests and replies.

Firewalls have to be integrated with encryption techniques.

The fact that firewalls need to be able to interpret messages also has implications for the use of encryption. It is highly desirable to encrypt request and reply messages that are transported in a public network. A firewall, however, cannot interpret an encrypted message. Request and reply messages therefore have to be decrypted before they can enter the firewall. Whether or not the message is encrypted on the way from the firewall to the host on the private network is application-specific. The firewall therefore has to be integrated with the encryption mechanism that is used by the distributed object middleware. If, for example, the Secure Socket Layer protocol is used, the middleware has to know the secret session key so that it can decrypt the message before deciding whether to pass it on. Messages that the firewall passes on are then encrypted again using the session key.

12.3.2 Authentication

Authentication techniques establish trust in a principal and its credentials

The purpose of *authentication* is to establish a trusted association between the *principal*, who is using a client or on whose behalf a server is acting, and the credentials that the system maintains about this principal. Authentication is necessary to ensure, for example that the user who is using an Internet banking application is authorized by the account holder whose bank account is manipulated. It is not only client objects that have to be authenticated, but authentication is frequently necessary for server objects, too. For example, a principal who is requested to provide bank account details or a credit card number wants to be assured that the server belongs the bank or the e-commerce site with which the principal wants to conduct business.

In order to achieve such a trusted association, clients and servers authenticate themselves with the security service of the object-oriented middleware. The security service provides authentication operations with which the client can obtain a certified set of their credentials. In order to do so, the clients and servers provide a *security identifier*, such as the login name, and the *authentication data* of the principal. The authentication data is used by the service as evidence that the principal is an authorized user of the system.

The middleware stores the credentials that the authentication service provides in an attribute that the middleware keeps to store information about the session of the current principal. The CORBA `Current` object is such a session object. It uses the credentials for implementing the security of further object requests. As the credentials include, for example, the access rights that were granted to the principal, the middleware can then decide whether the principal is allowed to execute a certain operation or not.

The security service implements authentication using encryption techniques and both public and secret keys can be used for this purpose. The use of encryption avoids storing the authentication data of principals as plain text when their disclosure could be used by an attacker for masquerading purposes.

> Authentication is implemented using encryption.

Authentication might also be performed using a *challenge–response protocol*, where the security service challenges the principal during login with a phrase and the principal responds by encrypting the phrase using its private key (see Figure 12.6) The security service can then use the principal's public key to decrypt the phrase and authenticate the principal based on the assumption that only the principal could have encrypted the phrase. Using challenge–response protocols, the authentication server avoids storing authentication information at all.

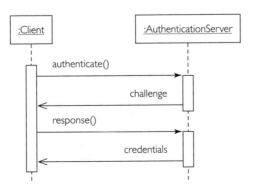

Figure 12.6
Use of the Challenge–Response Protocol for Authentication

12.3.3 Access Control

Access control mechanisms decide whether or not an object request can be granted to a client object.

We have so far assumed that a client object that has the object reference of a server object can actually request operation executions from the server. From a security point of view, this assumption is largely unreasonable. In our banking example, this would mean that a client object that can obtain an object reference of an account object can request execution of a credit operation. However, not all client objects that can obtain a reference to a server object should be able to request all operations. The *Access control mechanisms* that we discuss now provide the primitives that are needed for deciding whether an object request is granted to a particular client object or not. We discuss access control concepts using the terminology established in the CORBA Security service.

Access Control Concepts

A principal is a human user or a system entity that is registered in and authenticated to a system.

Credentials contain the security attributes of a principal.

Whether or not an object request can be granted does not so much depend on the identity of the client object, but rather on the principal on whose behalf the client object requests an operation. A principal has at least one *identity*, such as a user name, which is used as the computerized representation of the principal. Principals have security attributes that determine what they are allowed to do. These attributes are referred to as *credentials*. Figure 12.7 shows a conceptual overview of the constituents of credentials. We separate security attributes that are generally defined for all users of the system and attributes that are specific to a particular user. These specific attributes have to be validated upon login using authentication mechanisms that we discuss below.

Figure 12.7
Security Attributes in Credential

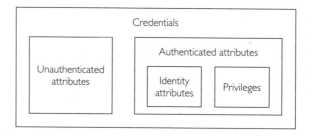

A particular subset of the security attributes of a principal is relevant to access control. Those are referred to as *privileges*. Privileges can, for example, record that a principal has a particular role and may execute all operations that are granted to that role. Privileges are used in access policies. Two forms of access policies can be distinguished: object invocation access policies and application object access policies.

Object invocation access policies determine whether a particular principal is allowed to perform an object request.

Object invocation access policies are implemented by the object-oriented middleware. Object invocation access policies are enforced by the middleware and are implemented in *access decision functions*. The parameters to these access decision functions are the object reference that is to be accessed, the name of the operation that is requested and credential objects that characterize the access control privileges of the principal on whose behalf the operation is requested. Access decision functions base their decision on these parameters, on system-wide configurations and on the control attributes of individual server objects. *Control attributes* are very often *access control lists*, which identify the principals or groups of principals that will be granted which operation executions.

Application object access policies are enforced at an application level and are, therefore, implemented by the application developer. They may use application-specific data in the implementation of the access decision function.

Application object access policies use request-specific data for access decisions.

> Using object invocation policies, we can determine that only principals who have the role 'bank clerk' may execute the credit operation. Using application object access policies, we can determine that principals with the role 'bank clerk' may execute credit operations up to $5,000, while operations that credit more than $5,000 can only be executed by a principal that has the role 'bank manager'.

Example 12.10
Invocation and Application Object Access Policies

Client's Perspective on Access Control

The client programmer's perspective on access control is rather simple: a request is either granted or not. Object-oriented middleware might provide an explicit interface that a client object programmer can use to check whether the right to execute a particular object request will be granted or not. If a client requests an operation execution that the principal associated with the client is not allowed to execute, an exception will be raised. In the case of object invocation access policies, the middleware will raise the exception. In the case of application object access policies, the application programmer of the server will raise the exception.

Server's Perspective on Access Control

The server object programmer's point of view on access control distinguishes two cases, depending on whether an object invocation or an application object access policy is used. In case of the object invocation policy, access control is transparent on the server programmer as it is performed by the object-oriented middleware. If, however, an application object access policy is required access control is not transparent to the server programmer. The server object programmer has to implement the access decision function. Object-oriented middleware may provide standardized interfaces for these functions in *access decision objects* in order to support the use of a common infrastructure for application object access policy implementation. Access decision object implementations provide a boolean access decision function that determines whether or not to grant access. The parameters to these access decisions normally include:

Access decision objects provide common functionality for application access policies to server programmers.

1. the credentials of the principal that requested an operation execution,
2. the reference of the server object from which an execution is requested,
3. the requested operation, and
4. the parameters of the requested operation.

Administrator's Perspective on Access Control

We have seen above that implementations of the object invocation access policy are transparent to both client and server object designers. The implementation is not transparent to administrators. Administrators have to establish the credentials of principals and control the attributes of objects in such a way that only those principals that should be allowed to request operation executions can actually do so. The security mechanisms of object-oriented middleware have to provide the primitives that support administrators in implementing these access control policies.

Access rights define the modes of access that principals have to server objects.

Access control policies determine the principals that are allowed to execute a particular operation based on *access rights*. Access rights are usually formulated in terms of access modes. An access mode might be the ability to get an attribute value or to set an attribute value or to use a particular operation. There are three parts to an access control policy. First, access rights have to be granted to a principal and stored in the principal's credentials. Secondly, a set of access rights for being able to execute an operation has to be defined. Finally, the policy has to define how the rights in the set of required access rights have to be combined in order to determine whether or not access is granted. A principal who wishes to execute a particular operation must previously have been granted those rights that are required for this operation, as determined by the policy.

Access rights are often defined for types rather than objects.

Administrators may wish to set access rights for individual objects, but this may be too impractical if there are many instances of a type. The definition of access rights is therefore often determined based on the types of object. This means that all instances of the object type then share the same set of required access rights. It is also desirable to be able to determine access rights for object types that have not been designed to have access rights. This means that definition of access rights should be isolated from the interfaces and be done by a separate required rights object.

The *required rights object* can be seen as an interface to a database of access rights. The database contains, for the operations in each type of object or even in individual objects, the access rights that are required. Object-oriented middleware products will provide user interfaces so that administrators can set up and maintain this database. At run-time, the middleware will utilize the database in order to perform access control checks.

12.3.4   Non-Repudiation

Non-repudiation makes principals accountable for their actions.

Secure object-oriented middleware often include non-repudiation services, which make users and other principals accountable for their actions. They achieve this accountability by the collection of evidence

1. that a principal has requested a particular operation, which prevents a requester falsely denying a request for an operation, and
2. that a server has received a request for a particular operation, which prevents a servers falsely denying receipt of a request.

It is important that the non-repudiation service collects the evidence in such a way that the principals using the client or server cannot repudiate the evidence later, and that the evidence can be used by an *adjudicator* to settle disputes.

Figure 12.8 shows an overview of the different components of a non-repudiation service according to the ISO 7498-2 standard [ISO 7498-2, 1989]. The most important of those components generates verifiable evidence about creation and receipt of object requests. A

Example 12.11
Non-Repudiation in the Banking
Example

Consider a funds transfer between two accounts. In a conventional setting, a customer walks into a bank branch and asks for a funds transfer of $1,000 from one account to another. The bank will make him write a cheque and sign it. The bank will archive the cheque and the signature and date on the cheque will be used as evidence that the customer actually demanded the funds transfer. The bank needs to collect similar evidence in a direct banking setting, where the funds transfer is requested via the Internet.

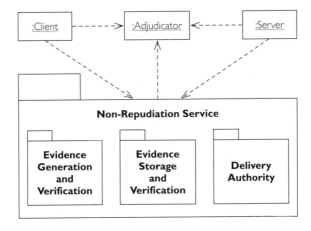

Figure 12.8
Overview of Non-Repudiation
Service Components

non-repudiation service may store this evidence on behalf of clients and servers so that evidence can be retrieved when a dispute arises. A delivery authority generates proof of origin so that clients and servers cannot repudiate that it was actually them who created or received an object request. Note that these components of a non-repudiation service have to be trusted by both clients and servers so that they both accept the evidence that is provided by the service.

It is worthwhile to note that non-repudiation may involve significant overheads. Therefore, such evidence is only collected for those object requests that have legally binding implications in the domain in which the distributed object system executes. In our direct banking application, for example, evidence will be needed for funds transfer requests, but no evidence will be needed for the request of an operation to return the account balance if we can assume that these requests are performed free of charge. Non-repudiation services are therefore only provided when client or server objects explicitly demand the creation of evidence. Hence the usage of non-repudiation is not transparent to designers of client and server objects.

Evidence is provided in the form of *non-repudiation tokens* that are handed out to clients when servers have received an object request and to servers when clients have created an object request. There are two types of token. The first form of token includes all data that is needed for the evidence. The second form of token is a key that can then be used in a request to the non-repudiation service to produce the data that is needed for the evidence.

Non-repudiation is
implemented using
digital signatures, which
rely on encryption.

The implementation of non-repudiation relies on encryption techniques, just as the implementation of authentication does. In particular, non-repudiation uses the concept of *digital signatures*. To create a digital signature, the client encrypts the principal's identity with the secret key of that principal. Non-repudiation services demand that clients include such a digital signature in the data that is submitted for the generation of a non-repudiation token. The non-repudiation service then stores that data together with the signature as evidence that the principal whose signature was included has requested the service. The same mechanism applies for servers that generate evidence that a certain request has been achieved. If a dispute arises an adjudicator uses a certified public key of the principal to validate that indeed that particular principal has requested generation of the non-repudiation token.

12.3.5 Security Auditing

The services that we have discussed above have in common that they provide proactive measures to prevent attacks. Administrators also need to react to attacks that were attempted or that actually succeeded. Hence, it is necessary that a distributed object system maintains records about security incidents. *Security auditing mechanisms* are concerned with logging security-relevant events on persistent storage so that they can be analyzed by administrators.

Auditing policies
determine the analysis
of logs of security
events.

Potentially, many different events can be logged and administrators want to be able to restrict the amount of information to events that are relevant to their particular distributed object system. Security auditing mechanisms provide the basic primitives for administrators to establish *auditing policies*. These auditing policies determine which events should be logged, how long the logs should be kept and which analyses should be performed on these logs. Two kinds of auditing policy can be distinguished. *System audit policies* determine the system events that the middleware logs in a way that is transparent to both client and server programmers. Examples of system events that may be considered relevant to security are authentication of principals, updates to a principal's credentials or the success or failure of object requests. *Application audit policies* determine the application events that client and server objects log to assist with security auditing; they are obviously not transparent to programmers. Examples of application events in our Internet direct banking application might be the request of a funds transfer including the request parameters.

Example 12.12
Security Auditing Requirements

An audit policy for our direct banking application should, for example, log the credentials of a principal of the bank and whether or not they are successfully authenticated. The policy should also record any failures in access to the credit or debit operation of a bank account.

Events can be logged on files in order to provide *audit trails* for later security analyses. Administrators may, however, also wish to use automated analysis facilities for more serious security incidents. These facilities analyse those events that correspond to serious security breaches and take active measures to alert the administrator if such an event occurs so that the administrator can take measures to locate the attacker and record evidence about the attack.

12.4 Security Services in Object-Oriented Middleware

The previous section presented the principles of higher-level security services and showed how encryption is used in their implementations. We have identified how security services support controlling the access of authorized principals. We have seen how they validate that principals are who they claim to be; we have seen how irrefutable evidence can be generated in order to make principals accountable for what they do; and we have identified how security audits can be achieved.

Java has had a security model from when it was first released. The Java security specification focuses on how to shield the host from (potentially malicious) applet code that may be downloaded from remote servers to execute in a Java Virtual Machine. While this is an important security concern for Java as an Internet programming language, this does not address the security problems that we raised above.

The security models available in CORBA, COM and Java/RMI are quite similar. COM does not support non-repudiation but it does cover the other higher-level services that we discussed in the previous section. RMI does not support non-repudiation or object invocation access policies but enables server designers to specify application access security policies. We now discuss the higher-level security services that are provided by OMG/CORBA in order to show an example of how the security principles that we discussed above are supported in current object-oriented middleware.

CORBA, COM and Java/RMI security models are similar.

The OMG determines security mechanisms for CORBA as part of the CORBAservices. It includes the CORBA Security service specification and defines how to secure distributed CORBA objects against attacks. The CORBA security service defines the CORBA interfaces that are provided to client developers, server developers and administrators for access control, authentication, non-repudiation and auditing purposes. We briefly discuss these interfaces in this section now and indicate by whom they would be used.

12.4.1 Authentication

The CORBA Security service assumes that a client object establishes the credentials of its principal using authentication prior to requesting any operations from a secure distributed object system. The `Credentials` interface shown in Figure 12.9 defines the interfaces that are available for a CORBA credentials object. A `Credentials` object is provided by operation `authenticate` that is part of interface `PrincipalAuthenticator`. To authenticate a principal, a client identifies an authentication method, such as password-based authentication, the security identifier of the principal and the authentication data, which is a password in the case of password-based authentication. Moreover, the client submits a list of attributes that identify the access rights that the principal will need in order to access distributed server objects during a session.

After a successful authentication, the CORBA Security service stores the credentials of a principal in the `Current` object that is associated with the session. We have already seen a

Figure 12.9

Authentication Interface of
CORBA Security Service

```
interface Credentials {
  Credentials copy();
  void destroy();
  ...
  boolean set_privileges(in boolean force_commit,
                         in AttributeList requested_privileges,
                         out AttributeList actual_privileges);
  AttributeList get_attributes (in AttributeTypeList attributes);
  boolean is_valid (out UtcT expiry_time);
  boolean refresh();
};

interface PrincipalAuthenticator {
  AuthenticationStatus authenticate(
                         in AuthenticationMethod method,
                         in SecurityName security_name,
                         in Opaque auth_data,
                         in AttributeList privileges,
                         out Credentials creds,
                         out Opaque continuation_data,
                         out Opaque auth_specific_data);
  ...
}
```

use of the `Current` object when we discussed distributed transactions. In addition to transaction contexts, the `Current` object also stores the credentials of the principal on whose behalf the session is executed and they are then used for access control purposes.

12.4.2 Access Control

Figure 12.10 shows the interfaces that are available for the management of access rights in credentials. These interfaces are used to construct administration tools so that administrators can set and revoke access rights for individual principals. The definition of access rights is based on *privileges*. Privileges are assigned to a principal's credentials object using `set_privileges` shown in Figure 12.9. Access to this operation is usually restricted to an administrator. The `DomainAccessPolicy` interface allows an administrative tool to grant, revoke, replace and get the set of access rights that are defined for a privilege.

In order for an administrator to effectively control the access to objects, the CORBA Security service defines the `RequiredRights`. CORBA performs access control at a type-level of abstraction, which means that it is not possible to define different access rights for different instances of a type. `RequiredRights` enables an administrator to associate a set of rights with an operation that is part of an interface and demand that any principal wishing to execute that operation must possess those rights. A `RightsCombinator` defines how sequences of more than one required right are determined.

```
interface DomainAccessPolicy : AccessPolicy {
  void grant_rights(in SecAttribute priv_attr,
                    in DelegationState del_state,
                    in ExtensibleFamily rights_family,
                    in RightsList rights);
  void revoke_rights(in SecAttribute priv_attr,
                     in DelegationState del_state,
                     in ExtensibleFamily rights_family,
                     in RightsList rights);
  void replace_rights (in SecAttribute priv_attr,
                       in DelegationState del_state,
                       in ExtensibleFamily rights_family,
                       in RightsList rights);
  RightsList get_rights (in SecAttribute priv_attr,
                         in DelegationState del_state,
                         in ExtensibleFamily rights_family);
  };
```

Figure 12.10
CORBA Interfaces for
Administering Credentials

```
// Declarations related to Rights
struct ExtensibleFamily {
  unsigned short family_definer;
  unsigned short family;
};
struct Right {
  ExtensibleFamily rights_family;
  string right;
};
typedef sequence <Right> RightsList;

interface RequiredRights{
  ...
  void set_required_rights(
                      in string operation_name,
                      in CORBA::RepositoryId interface_name,
                      in RightsList rights,
                      in RightsCombinator rights_combinator);
};
```

Figure 12.11
CORBA Access Control
Interface for Administrators

To summarize the administration of access rights we note that access rights are defined in a three-stage process. First, credential objects capture the assignment of privileges to principals. Secondly, access policies capture the access rights that are granted to privileges. Finally, for each operation of each interface, required rights define the rights that principals must hold (through their privileges) in order to be able to use the operation.

CORBA access rights
have three parts:
credentials, access
policies, and access
rights.

Figure 12.12 shows the rather simple client interface to access control. A client can test whether the credentials of the principal currently using the client are sufficient to execute a particular operation in a particular interface.

Figure 12.12
Figure 12.12
CORBA Access Control
Interface for Clients

```
typedef sequence <Credentials> CredentialsList;

interface AccessDecision {
   boolean access_allowed(
                     in CredentialsList cred_list,
                     in Object target,
                     in CORBA::Identifier operation_name,
                     in CORBA::Identifier target_interface_name);
};
```

12.4.3   Non-Repudiation

The essential operations for the client interface to the non-repudiation interfaces of the
CORBA Security service are shown in Figure 12.13. The NRCredential supports the
creation of a non-repudiation token that represents a particular type of evidence. The client
provides the data that is needed for the generation of the evidence in input_buffer and
determines the type of evidence that is to be generated. The client then receives a token that

Figure 12.13
CORBA Non-Repudiation
Interface

```
enum EvidenceType {
   SecProofofCreation,
   SecProofofReceipt,
   SecProofofApproval,
   SecProofofRetrieval, ...
};

interface NRCredentials : Credentials {
   ...
   void generate_token(in Opaque input_buffer,
                     in EvidenceType generate_evidence_type,
                     in boolean include_data_in_token,
                     in boolean generate_request,
                     in RequestFeatures request_features,
                     in boolean input_buffer_complete,
                     out Opaque nr_token,
                     out Opaque evidence_check);

   NRVerificationResult verify_evidence(
                     in Opaque input_token_buffer,
                     in Opaque evidence_check,
                     in boolean form_complete_evidence,
                     in boolean token_buffer_complete,
                     out Opaque output_token,
                     out Opaque data_included_in_token,
                     out boolean evidence_is_complete,
                     out boolean trusted_time_used,
                     out TimeT complete_evidence_before,
                     out TimeT complete_evidence_after);
   ...
};
```

it can record or pass on whenever evidence is necessary. Servers or adjudicators can use the evidence token in an evidence check to retrieve the original evidence data and a verification that the token was generated.

The CORBA Security service further includes a number of interfaces that support the construction of tools for the administration of non-repudiation policies. These rules determine the involvement of trusted third parties in the evidence generation, the roles in which they may be involved and the duration for which the generated evidence is valid. Moreover, policies may determine rules for adjudication, which for example determine the authorities that may be used for the adjudication of disputes.

12.4.4 Auditing

Auditing of system events relevant to security is transparent for programmers of client and server objects. The AuditPolicy interface in Figure 12.14 shows CORBA interfaces that are used by administrative tools for the definition of system auditing policies.

Security auditing can be kept transparent for CORBA server and client programmers.

Figure 12.14
CORBA Interfaces for Administering Auditing Policies

```
typedef unsigned long SelectorType;
const SelectorType InterfaceRef = 1;
const SelectorType ObjectRef = 2;
const SelectorType Operation = 3;
const SelectorType Initiator = 4;
const SelectorType SuccessFailure = 5 ;
const SelectorType Time = 6;
struct SelectorValue {SelectorType selector; any value;};
typedef sequence <SelectorValue> SelectorValueList;

typedef unsigned long AuditChannelId;
typedef unsigned short EventType;
const EventType AuditAll = 0;
const EventType AuditPrincipalAuth = 1;
const EventType AuditSessionAuth = 2;
const EventType AuditAuthorization = 3;
const EventType AuditInvocation = 4;
const EventType AuditSecEnvChange = 5;
...
struct AuditEventType {
   ExtensibleFamily event_family;
   EventType event_type;
};

typedef sequence <AuditEventType> AuditEventTypeList;

interface AuditPolicy : CORBA::Policy {
  void set_audit_selectors (
        in CORBA::InterfaceDef object_type,
        in AuditEventTypeList events,
        in SelectorValueList selectors);
  ...
  void set_audit_channel (
        in AuditChannelId audit_channel_id);
};
```

In particular, `AuditPolicy` allows administrators to determine the channel that is used for logging security event occurrences. `AuditPolicy` further defines operation `set_ audit_selectors`, which can be used to determine the types of events for which an entry should be written into the audit channel. For example, by passing a list including event types `AuditPrincipalAuth` and `AuditSessionAuth` only authentication events will be logged. Finally, the `selectors` parameter allows administrators to determine which auditing information is to be written for each event.

Summary

In this section, we have seen an example of how object-oriented middleware supports the higher-level security concepts that we have introduced in previous sections. We have discussed how the CORBA Security service supports authentication, access control, non-repudiation and auditing. As with other CORBA services, the security service standardizes the interface of objects that are needed for security management purposes. We have seen that client programmers, server programmers and administrators need different interfaces for controlling the security of a distributed object-based system.

Key Points

▶   Distributed objects have to rely on networks to be able to communicate with each other. The message traffic on these networks can be eavesdropped on and tampered with by non-authorized third parties. The construction of trustworthy distributed object systems therefore demands that message traffic is secured against such attacks and that infiltration of distributed object systems by attackers is prevented.

▶   Encryption techniques are used to prevent eavesdropping and message tampering. Public or secret key methods are used to encrypt a marshalled object request before it is transmitted using an insecure network.

▶   The distribution of public or secret keys is achieved by a trusted key distribution service which implements a key distribution protocol. The Needham/Schroeder protocol is such a protocol.

▶   Encryption is also used for authentication. Authentication establishes the evidence that principals are who they claim to be. It can be achieved by demonstrating that the principal possesses a key, which can then be seen as evidence that the principal is authorized to perform certain operations.

▶   Access control is based on authentication. Middleware associate credentials with principals during authentication. These credentials determine the rights or privileges that have been granted to the principal to use the distributed object system. Administrators then assign the required rights to operations of objects or object types and the access control of the middleware ensures that only those principals who possess sufficient access rights can execute these operations.

▶   Non-repudiation is concerned with the generation of irrefutable evidence that principals have requested certain operations or that servers have received these requests. Non-repudiation thus makes principals accountable for their activities within the distributed object system.

▶ Auditing is a passive security mechanism that enables administrators to identify security incidents. Auditing policies determine the events and the details that have to be recorded for these events so that they can be viewed or analyzed by security administrators.

Self Assessment

12.1 Why are distributed systems inherently insecure?

12.2 What are the security threats to which distributed systems are exposed?

12.3 What are the principle methods of attacking a distributed system?

12.4 How can distributed systems be infiltrated?

12.5 What role does encryption play in securing distributed systems?

12.6 What is the difference between secret key and public key encryption?

12.7 What is a key?

12.8 How are keys distributed?

12.9 Why is the Needham/Schroeder protocol for public keys more complicated than the one for secret keys?

12.10 Why are nonces used in the Needham/Schroeder protocol?

12.11 What is authentication?

12.12 How are credentials managed in object-oriented systems?

12.13 What is the relationship between authentication and access control?

12.14 Why is non-repudiation important for electronic commerce?

12.15 Why does non-repudiation hand out tokens for evidence rather than handing out the signed evidence?

12.16 What is the difference between auditing and the other distributed system security mechanisms?

12.17 How is eavesdropping and message tampering prevented in CORBA-based systems?

Further Reading

[Colouris et al., 1994] includes a chapter on the security of general distributed systems. This chapter covers encryption and key distribution in greater depth than we did, but it does not address all of the higher levels of security that are currently supported by object-oriented middleware.

[Garfinkel and Spafford, 1996] is a good professional book on UNIX and Internet security. It provides a good introduction to operating system and network security for the beginner and reviews security from the user and administrator points of view. Its discussions on RPC and Kerberos are also somewhat relevant to security of distributed object systems.

Various encryption techniques have been proposed. The Distributed Encryption Standard (DES) was among the first and originated at IBM in 1977. It was then promoted to a US ANSI standard. DES is based on secret key encryption technology. Phil Zimmermann has gained quite some attention with his public-key-based Pretty Good

Privacy (PGP) [Zimmermann, 1995] due to a legal battle he had to fight with the US government. PGP uses strong 128-bit public key encryption and enables the creation of cypher text that even the most powerful computers of the National Security Agency (NSA) cannot break. When Zimmermann made PGP publicly available under the Gnu License Agreement this was considered by the US Government an illegal export of weapon technology. The US government, however, recently dropped the charges against Zimmermann. SSL was initially used to secure the transport between data entered into a HTML form and a web server where the data is processed by a server script or program. SSL is now also used with object-oriented middleware to secure the data transfer.

The CORBA Security specification of the OMG is defined in Chapter 15 of the CORBAservices specification [Object Management Group, 1996]. It is the result of merging three specifications: the CORBA Security service, revision 1; the Common Secure Interoperability specification; and the CORBAsecurity/SSL interoperability specification. These three specifications are all available from the OMG ftp server ftp.omg.org.

[Needham and Schroeder, 1978] first published the Needham/Schroeder protocol. It is used in MIT's Kerberos system [Neumann and Tso, 1994]. Kerberos, in turn, is the basis for key distribution and access control in systems based on remote procedure calls that follow the OSF/DCE standard, upon which Microsoft's COM is based. Microsoft's COM supports authentication, access control and auditing in very much the same way as CORBA. A reasonable introduction to COM Security is provided in Chapter 7 of [Grimes, 1997].

A

Full CORBA C++ Implementation of Soccer Example

For didactic reasons, the example given in Chapter 4 is incomplete and oversimplified. The code included in this appendix provides the complete IDL and C++ source code of that example.

The example has been developed on Solaris 2.5 using Orbix 1.3.5 and the GNU C++ compiler. Since the compiler version used did not yet support C++ exception, an explicit approach for exception information passing was chosen using additional parameters of type Environment. The example deploys the basic object adapter with a shared server activation strategy.

It consists of the following source files:

Makefile   Dependencies and rules to derive the executables using Make.

Example.idl   IDL Interface definitions of distributed objects

Client.cc   C++ Client program using static invocations

PlayerServer.hh   C++ class definition for the implementation of Player and PlayerFactory Objects.

PlayerServer.cc   C++ method implementations of Player and PlayerFactory operations.

TeamServer.hh   C++ class definitions for the implementation of Team and TeamFactory Objects.

TeamServer.cc   C++ method implementations of Team and TeamFactory Objects.

After compilation of the program, it has to be ensured that an orbix daemon is running and then the PlayerServer and TeamServer executables can be registered with Orbix's implementation repository. Then the Client application can be started and it will start issuing requests and the object adapter will startup the PlayerServer and TeamServer processes. Orbix's implementation of the basic object adapter is configured in a way that it deactivates the server processes after they have been idle for 30 seconds.

```
#////////////////////////////////////////////////////////
#// Makefile
#// 20 March 1999
#////////////////////////////////////////////////////////

include /vol/Orbix-1.3.5/demos/orbixsol2gnu.mk
C++             = g++ -g
IDLFLAGS        = -B
SVR_OBJS        = exampleS.o
CLIENT_OBJS     = Client.o exampleC.o

all: TeamServer PlayerServer Client

example.hh: example.idl

TeamServer.o: TeamServer.cc TeamServer.hh example.hh

PlayerServer.o: PlayerServer.cc PlayerServer.hh example.hh

TeamServer: $(SVR_OBJS) TeamServer.o
            $( C++) -o TeamServer TeamServer.o $(SVR_OBJS) \
            $(LDFLAGS) $(ITSRV) $(SYSLIBS)

PlayerServer: $(SVR_OBJS) PlayerServer.o
            $( C++) -o PlayerServer PlayerServer.o \
        $(SVR_OBJS) $(LDFLAGS) $(ITSRV) $(SYSLIBS)

Client: $(CLIENT_OBJS)
        $( C++) -o Client $(CLIENT_OBJS) $(LDFLAGS) \
        $(ITCLT) $(SYSLIBS)

clean: /bin/rm -f *.o PlayerServer TeamServer Client \
        example.hh exampleS.cc exampleC.cc

////////////////////////////////////////////////////////
// example.idl
// 20 March 1999
////////////////////////////////////////////////////////

typedef string<80> NameStr;

interface Player {
    readonly attribute NameStr name;
};
```

```
interface PlayerFactory {
    Player createPlayer(in NameStr name);
};

interface Team {
    readonly attribute NameStr name;
    exception InvalidNumber{};
    exception NumberOccupied{};
    exception NoPlayerAtNumber{};
    void add(in Player aPlayer, in short number)
        raises (InvalidNumber,NumberOccupied);
    void remove(in short number)
        raises (InvalidNumber,NoPlayerAtNumber);
    string print();
};

interface TeamFactory {
    Team createTeam(in NameStr teamname);
};

//////////////////////////////////////////////////////////
// Client.cc
// 20 March 1999
//////////////////////////////////////////////////////////

#include "example.hh"
#include <iostream.h>
int main(int argc, char* argv[]) {
   PlayerFactory * pf;
   TeamFactory * tf;
   Team * t;
   Player *goalkeeper, *centreforward,
          *left_winger, *right_winger;
   char * output;

TRY {
   pf=PlayerFactory::_bind(":PlayerFactory","", IT_X);
   tf=TeamFactory::_bind(":TeamFactory","", IT_X);
 } CATCHANY {
    // an error occurred while trying to bind to factories.
    cerr << "Bind to object failed" << endl;
    cerr << "Unexpected exception " << IT_X << endl;
    exit(1);
 } ENDTRY

  TRY {
     t=tf->createTeam("Germany",IT_X);
  } CATCHANY {
     cerr << "could not create Team" << endl;
     cerr << "Unexpected exception " << IT_X << endl;
     exit(1);
  } ENDTRY
```

```cpp
      cout << "successfully created team " << t->name() << "\n";

      TRY {
         goalkeeper=pf->createPlayer("Stefan Klos",IT_X);
         centreforward=pf->createPlayer("Andy Moeller", IT_X);
         left_winger=pf->createPlayer("Christian Ziege",IT_X);
         right_winger=pf->createPlayer("Stefan Reuter",IT_X);
      } CATCHANY {
         cerr << "could not create players" << endl;
         cerr << "Unexpected exception " << IT_X << endl;
         exit(1);
      } ENDTRY

      output=goalkeeper->name();
      cout<<"successfully created player "<<output<< "\n";
      delete output;
      output=centreforward->name();
      cout<<"successfully created player "<<output<< "\n";
      delete output; output=left_winger->name();
      cout<<"successfully created player "<<output<< "\n";
      delete output;
      output=right_winger->name();
      cout<<"successfully created player "<<output<< "\n";
      delete output;

      TRY {
        t->add(goalkeeper,1);
        t->add(centreforward,10);
        t->add(left_winger,2);
        t->add(right_winger,4);
      } CATCHANY {
        cerr << "could not add players to team" << endl;
        cerr << "Unexpected exception " << IT_X << endl;
        exit(1);
      } ENDTRY

      TRY {
        output=t->print();
        cout << output;
        delete output;
      } CATCHANY {
        cerr << "could not print team" << endl;
        cerr << "Unexpected exception " << IT_X << endl;
        exit(1);
      } ENDTRY
}

////////////////////////////////////////////////////////////
// PlayerServer.hh
// 20 March 1999
////////////////////////////////////////////////////////////
```

```cpp
#ifndef PLAYERSERVER_hh
#define PLAYERSERVER_hh_
#include "example.hh"

class PlayerServer : public virtual PlayerBOAImpl {
 private:
   char * the_player_name;
 public:
   PlayerServer();
   virtual NameStr name(CORBA::Environment &
                  env = CORBA::default_environment);
   virtual void set_name(char *);
};

class PlayerFactoryServer:public virtual PlayerFactoryBOAImpl {
  virtual Player * createPlayer(NameStr name,
                  CORBA::Environment &
                  env = CORBA::default_environment);
};
#endif

//////////////////////////////////////////////////////////
// PlayerServer.cc
// 20 March 1999
//////////////////////////////////////////////////////////
#include "PlayerServer.hh"
#include <iostream.h>

PlayerServer::PlayerServer(){
  the_player_name=NULL;
};

void PlayerServer::set_name(char * name){
  if (the_player_name != NULL)
    delete the_player_name;
  the_player_name = new char [strlen(name)+1];
  strcpy(the_player_name,name);
  cout << "Created Player object for " << name << "\n";
};

NameStr PlayerServer::name(CORBA::Environment &
                        env = CORBA::default_environment){
  char * ret = new char[strlen(the_player_name)+1];
  strcpy(ret,the_player_name);
  return(ret);
};

Player * PlayerFactoryServer::createPlayer(NameStr name,
                        CORBA::Environment &
                        env = CORBA::default_environment){
  PlayerServer * aPlayer = new PlayerServer;
  aPlayer->set_name(name);
```

```
 aPlayer->_duplicate();
 return aPlayer;
};

int main(int argc, char* argv[]) {
 PlayerFactoryServer myplayergenerator;
 TRY {
   CORBA::Orbix.impl_is_ready("PlayerFactory",IT_X);
 }
 CATCHANY {
   // output error that occured calling impl_is_ready()
   cout << IT_X;
 }
 ENDTRY
}


//////////////////////////////////////////////////////////////
// TeamServer.hh
// 20 March 1999
//////////////////////////////////////////////////////////////
#ifndef TEAMSERVER_hh
#define TEAMSERVER_hh
#include "example.hh"
#define MAXPLAYERS 22
class TeamServer : public virtual TeamBOAImpl {
 private:
   Player * the_team[MAXPLAYERS+1];
   char * the_team_name;
 public:
   virtual void set_name(char *);
   virtual NameStr name(CORBA::Environment &
                 env = CORBA::default_environment);
   virtual void add(Player * aPlayer, short number,
              CORBA::Environment &
              env = CORBA::default_environment);
   virtual void remove(short number,
              CORBA::Environment &
              env = CORBA::default_environment);
   virtual char * print (CORBA::Environment &
                env = CORBA::default_environment);
};

class TeamFactoryServer : public virtual TeamFactoryBOAImpl {
 virtual Team * createTeam(NameStr name,
              CORBA::Environment &
              env = CORBA::default_environment);
};

#endif
```

```
//////////////////////////////////////////////////////////
// TeamServer.cc
// 20 March 1999
//////////////////////////////////////////////////////////
#include "TeamServer.hh"
#include <iostream.h>
#include <stdio.h>

TeamServer::TeamServer(){
  int i;
  the_team_name = NULL;
  for (i=0; i<=MAXPLAYERS; i++)
    the_team[i]=NULL;
}

void TeamServer::set_name(char * name) {
  if (the_team_name !=NULL) delete the_team_name;
  the_team_name = new char [strlen(name)+1];
  strcpy(the_team_name,name);
  cout << "Establishing Team Name to " << name << "\n";
};

NameStr TeamServer::name(CORBA::Environment &
                       env=CORBA::default_environment){
  char * ret = new char[strlen(the_team_name)+1];
  strcpy(ret,the_team_name);
  return(ret);
};

void TeamServer::add(Player * aPlayer, short number,
                 CORBA::Environment &
                 env = CORBA::default_environment){
  cout << "Adding Player " << aPlayer->name() <<
          " as number " << number << "\n";
  if (number<1 || number > MAXPLAYERS) {
    // raise InvalidNumber
  }
  else
    if ((the_team[number]!=NULL)) {
      // raise NumberOccupied
    } else {
      aPlayer->_duplicate();
      the_team[number]=aPlayer;
    }
};

void TeamServer::remove(short number,
                   CORBA::Environment &
                   env = CORBA::default_environment){
  if(number<1 || number > MAXPLAYERS) {
    // raise InvalidNumber
```

```cpp
    } else
     if (the_team[number]==NULL) {
        // raise NoPlayerAtNumber
     } else {
       the_team[number]->_release();
       the_team[number]=NULL;
     }
};

char * TeamServer::print(CORBA::Environment &
                            env = CORBA::default_environment) {
  char output[2000], tmp[10];
  char * Player;
  int i;
  sprintf(output,"No | Player\n");
  for (i=1;i<=MAXPLAYERS; i++) {
    sprintf(tmp,"%2d | ",i);
    strcat(output,tmp);
      if (the_team[i]!=NULL) {
        player = the_team[i]->name();
        strcat(output,player);
        delete player;
      }
      strcat(output,"\n");
  }
  return(output);
};

Team * TeamFactoryServer::createTeam(NameStr name,
                          CORBA::Environment &
                          env = CORBA::default_environment){
  TeamServer * aTeam = new TeamServer;
  aTeam->set_name(name);
  aTeam->_duplicate();
  return(aTeam);
};

int main(int argc, char* argv[]) {
  TeamFactoryServer myteamgenerator;
  TRY {
    CORBA::Orbix.impl_is_ready("TeamFactory",IT_X);
  }
  CATCHANY {
    // output error that occured calling impl_is_ready()
    cout << IT_X;
  }
  ENDTRY
}
```

Bibliography

Aho, A.V., Hopcroft, J.E., and Ullman, J.D. (1983). *Data Structures and Algorithms.* Addison Wesley.

Aho, A.V., Sethi, R., and Ullmann, J.D. (1986). *Compilers – Principles, Techniques and Tools.* Addison Wesley.

Andrade, J.M., editor (1996). *The Tuxedo System: Software for Constructing and Managing Distributed Business Applications.* Addison-Wesley.

ANSA (1989). The Advanced Network Systems Architecture (ANSA). Reference manual, Architecture Project Management, Castle Hill, Cambridge, UK.

Apparao, V., Byrne, S., Champion, M., Isaacs, S., Jacobs, I., Hors, A.L., Nicol, G., Robie, J., Sutor, R., Wilson, C., and Wood, L. (1998). Document Object Model (DOM) Level 1 Specification. W3C Recommendation http://www.w3.org/TR/1998/REC-DOM-Level-1-19981001, World Wide Web Consortium.

Arnold, K., O'Sullivan, B., Schneider, R.W., Waldo, J., and Wollrath, A. (1999). *The Jini Specification.* Addison-Wesley.

Atkinson, M.P., Bailey, P.J., Chisholm, K.J., Cockshott, W.P., and Morrison, R. (1983). An Approach to Persistent Programming. *Computer Journal*, 26(4):360–365.

Atkinson, M.P., Bancilhon, F., DeWitt, D., Dittrich, K., Maier, D., and Zdonik, S. (1990). The Object-Oriented Database System Manifesto. In Kim, W., Nicholas, J.-M., and Nishio, S., editors, *Proc. of the 1st International Conference on Deductive and Object-Oriented Databases, Kyoto, Japan*, pages 223–240. North-Holland.

Atkinson, M.P., Daynes, L., Jordan, M.J., Printezis, T., and Spence, S. (1996). An Orthogonally Persistent Java. *ACM SIGMOD Record*, 25(4).

Baker, S. (1997). *CORBA Distributed Objects using Orbix.* Addison Wesley.

Bancilhon, F., Delobel, C., and Kanellakis, P. (1992). *Building an Object-Oriented Database System: the Story of O_2.* Morgan Kaufmann.

Bancilhon, F., Kim, W., and Korth, H.F. (1985). A model of CAD transactions. In Pirotte, A. and Vassilou, Y., editors, *Proc. of the 11th International Conference on Very Large Databases, Stockholm, Sweden*, pages 25–33, Morgan Kaufmann.

Barghouti, N.S. and Kaiser, G.E. (1991). Concurrency Control in Advanced Database Applications, *ACM Computing Surveys*, 23(3):269–317.

Barret, D.J., Kaplan, A., and Wileden, J.C. (1996). Automated Support for Seamless Interoperability in Polylingual Software Systems. In *Proceedings of the 4th*

International Symposium on the Foundations of Software Engineering (SIGSOFT '96), San Francisco, Cal. ACM Press.

Bearman, M. (1993). ODP-Trader. In *Proc. of the IFIP TC6/WG6.1 International Conference on Open Distributed Processing, Berlin, Germany*, pages 341–352. North-Holland.

Bearman, M. and Raymond, K. (1991). Federating Traders: An ODP Adventure. In *Proceedings of the IFIP TC6/WG6.4 International Workshop on Open Distributed Processing, Berlin, Germany*, pages 125–141. North-Holland.

Bernstein, P.A., Hadzilacos, V., and Goodman, N. (1987). *Concurrency Control and Recovery in Database Systems.* Addison Wesley.

Birman, K.P. (1997). *Building Secure and Reliable Network Applications.* Manning Publishing.

Blaha, M.R., Premerlani, W.J., and Rumbaugh, J.E. (1988). Relational Database Design using an object-oriented Methodology. *Communications of the ACM.* 31(4):414–427.

Booch, G. (1991). *Object-Oriented Design with Applications.* Benjamin Cummings.

Booch, G. (1996). *Object Solutions: Managing the Object-Oriented Project.* Addison Wesley.

Booch, G., Rumbaugh, J., and Jacobson, I. (1999). *The Unified Modeling Language User Guide.* Addison Wesley.

Box, D. (1998). *Essential COM.* Addison Wesley Longman.

Bradley, N. (1998). *The XML Companion.* Addison Wesley.

Bray, T., Paoli, J., and Sperberg-McQueen, C.M. (1998). Extensible Markup Language. Recommendation http://www.w3.org/TR/1998/REC-xml-19980210, World Wide Web Consortium.

Campione, M. and Walrath, K. (1998). *The Java Tutorial.* Addison Wesley, 2nd edition.

Cardelli, L. and Gordon, A. (1998). Mobile Ambients. In *Proceedings of Foundations of Software Science and Computation Structures (FoSSaCS), European Joint Conferences on Theory and Practice of Software (ETAPS'98)*, volume 1378 of *Lecture Notes in Computer Science*, Lisbon, Portugal. Springer.

Carriero, N. and Gelernter, D. (1992). Coordination Languages and Their Significance. *Communications of the ACM*, 35(2):97–107.

Cattell, R., editor (1993). *The Object Database Standard: ODMG-93.* Morgan Kaufman.

Ceri, S. and Pelagatti, G. (1984). *Distributed Databases: Principles and Systems.* McGraw Hill.

Chang, D. and Harkey, D. (1998). *Client/Server Data Access With Java and XML.* Wiley.

Chen, P.P. (1976). The Entity-Relationship Model: Toward a unified view of data. *ACM Transactions on Database Systems*, 1(1):9–36.

Cheung, S. (1999). *Java Transaction Service (JTS).* Sun Microsystems, 901 San Antonio Road, Palo Alto, CA 94303.

Cheung, S. and Matena, V. (1999). *Java Transaction API (JTA).* Sun Microsystems, 901 San Antonio Road, Palo Alto, CA 94303.

Chung, P., Huang, Y., Yajnik, S., Liang, D., Shin, J., Wang, C.-Y., and Wang, Y.-M. (1998). DCOM and CORBA: Side by Side, Step by Step, and Layer by Layer, *C++ Report*, pages 18–29.

Ciancarini, P. and Hankin, C., editors (1996). *Proceedings of the 1st International Conference on Coordination Models and Languages, Cesena, Italy*, volume 1061 of *Lecture Notes in Computer Science.* Springer.

Ciancarini, P. and Wolf, A., editors (1999). *Proceedings of the 3rd International Conference on Coordination Models and Languages, Amsterdam, The Netherlands*, volume 1594 of *Lecture Notes in Computer Science*. Springer.

Codd, E.F. (1970). A Relational Model of Data for Large Shared Data Banks. *Communications of the ACM*. 13(6): 377–387.

Colouris, G., Dollimore, J., and Kindberg, T. (1994). *Distributed Systems: Concepts and Design*. Addison Wesley, 2nd edition.

Copeland, G. and Maier, D. (1984). Making Smalltalk a Database System. *Proceedings of the ACM SIGMOD 1984 International Conference on the Management of Data, Boston, MA, ACM SIGMOD Record*, 14(2): 316–325.

Couch, J. (1999). *Java2 Networking*. McGraw-Hill.

Dahl, O.-J. and Nygaard, K. (1966). Simula: An Algol Based Simulation Language. *Communications of the ACM*, 9(9): 671–678.

Deux, O. (1991). The O_2 System. *Communications of the ACM*, 34(10).

Eckel, B. (1998). *Thinking in Java*. Prentice Hall.

Ellis, M.A. and Stroustrup, B. (1990). *The Annotated C++ Reference Manual*. Addison Wesley.

Feldman, S.I. (1979). Make: A Program for Maintaining Computer Programs. *Software – Practice and Experience*, 4(3): 255–256.

Flanagan, D. (1997). *Java in a Nutshell*. O'Reilly & Associates, Inc., 2nd edition.

Fowler, M. and Scott, K. (1997). *UML Distilled: Applying the Standard Object Modeling Language*. Addison Wesley Longman.

Freeman, E., Hupfer, S., and Arnold, K. (1999). *JavaSpaces: Principles, Patterns, and Practice*. Addison Wesley.

Fuggetta, A., Picco, G., and Vigna, G. (1998). Understanding Code Mobility. *IEEE Transactions on Software Engineering*, 24(5): 342–361.

Gamma, E., Helm, R., Johnson, R., and Vlissides, J. (1995). *Design Patterns: Elements of Reusable Software*. Addison Wesley.

Garfinkel, S. and Spafford, G. (1996). *Practical Unix and Internet Security*. O'Reilly & Associates.

Garlan, D. and LeMetayer, D., editors (1997). *Proceedings of the 2nd International Conference on Coordination Models and Languages, Berlin, Germany*, volume 1282 of *Lecture Notes in Computer Science*. Springer.

Gelernter, D. (1985). Generative Communication in Linda. *ACM Transactions on Programming Languages and Systems*, 7(1): 80–112.

Ghezzi, C., Jazayeri, M., and Mandrioli, D. (1991). *Fundamentals of Software Engineering*. Prentice Hall.

Gilman, L. and Schreiber, R. (1996). *Distributed Computing with IBM MQSeries*. Wiley.

Goldberg, A. (1984). *Smalltalk-80: The Interactive Programming Environment*. Addison Wesley.

Goldberg, A. (1985). *Smalltalk-80: The Language and its Implementation*. Addison Wesley.

Gray, J.N. (1978). Notes on Database Operating Systems. In Bayer, R., Graham, R., and Seegmüller, G., editors, *Operating systems: An advanced course*, volume 60 of *Lecture Notes in Computer Science*, chapter 3.F., pages 393–481. Springer.

Gray, J.N. (1981). The Transaction Concept: Virtues and Limitations. In *Proceedings of the 7th International Conference on Very Large Data Bases, Cannes, France*, pages 144–154.

Grimes, R. (1997). *DCOM Programming*. Wrox.

Hall, C.L. (1996). *Building Client/Server Applications Using TUXEDO*. Wiley.

Hamilton, G., Cattell, R., and Fisher, M. (1997). *JDBC Database Access with Java*. Addison Wesley.

Harel, D. (1987). Statecharts: A Visual Formalism for Complex Systems, *Science of Computer Programming*, 8(3):231–274.

Henderson-Sellers, B., Simons, T., and Younessi, H. (1998). *The OPEN Toolbox of Techniques*. Addison Wesley.

Hillier, S. (1998). *Microsoft Transaction Server Programming*. Microsoft Press.

Hoare, C.A.R. (1978). Communicating Sequential Processes. *CACM*, 21(8):666–677.

Hudders, E.S. (1994). *CICS: A Guide to Internal Structure*. Wiley.

Hughes, M., Hughes, C., Shoffner, M., and Winslow, M. (1997). *Java Network Programming*. Manning.

Ion, P. and Miner, R. (1998). Mathematical Markup Language. Recommendation http://www.w3.org/TR/REC-MathML, World Wide Web Consortium.

ISO 10303-1 (1994). Industrial automation systems and integration – Product data representation and exchange. Technical report, International Standards Organisation.

ISO 20746-2 (1996). Information Technology – Open Distributed Processing – Reference Model: Foundations. Technical Report ISO/IEC 20746-2:1996, International Standardization Organization.

ISO 7498-2 (1989). Information processing systems – Open Systems Interconnection – Basic Reference Model – Part 2: Security Architecture. Technical report, International Standards Organisation.

ISO 8824-1 (1998). Abstract Syntax Notation One (ASN.1): Specification of Basic Notation. Technical report, International Standards Organisation.

ISO 8879 (1986). Information processing – Text and Office Systems – Standardised General Markup Language SGML. Technical report, International Standards Organisation.

Jackson, J.R. and McClellan, A.L. (1999). *Java 1.2 by example*. Sun Microsystems Press & Prentice Hall.

Jacobson, I., Booch, G., and Rumbaugh, J. (1999). *The Unified Software Development Process*. Addison Wesley.

Jacobson, I., Christerson, M., Jonsson, P., and Övergaard, G. (1992). *Object-Oriented Software Engineering: A Use Case Driven Approach*. Addison Wesley.

Jalote, P. (1991). *An Integrated Approach to Software Engineering*. Springer.

Kaiser, G.E. (1990). A Flexible Transaction Model for Software Engineering. In *Proceedings of the 6th International Conference on Data Engineering, Los Angeles*. IEEE Computer Society Press.

Katz, R.H. (1984). Transaction Management in the Design Environment. In Gardarin, E. and Gelenbe, E., editors, *New Applications of Data Bases*, pages 259–273. Academic Press.

Lamb, C., Landis, G., Orenstein, J., and Weinreb, D. (1991). The ObjectStore Database System. *Communications of the ACM*. 34(10):51–63.

Lange, D.B. and Oshima, M. (1998). *Programming and Deploying Java Mobile Agents with Aglets*. Addison Wesley.

Lea, D. (1997). *Concurrent Programming in Java*. Addison Wesley.

Lewandowski, S.M. (1998). Component-Based Client/Server Computing. *ACM Computing Surveys*, 30(1):3–27.

Lindholm, T. and Yellin, F. (1998). *The Java Virtual Machine Specification*. Addison Wesley, 2nd revised edition.

Liskov, B. and Zilles, S. (1974). Programming with Abstract Data Types. *ACM SIGPLAN Notices*, 9(4):50–55.

Magee, J. and Kramer, J. (1999). *Concurrency: Models and Programs – From Finite State Models to Java Programs*. Wiley.

Mazza, C., Fairclough, J., Melton, B., De Pablo, D., Scheffer, A., and Stevens, R. (1994). *Software Engineering Standards*. Prentice Hall.

Meyer, B. (1988a). Eiffel: A Language and Environment for Software Engineering. *Journal of Systems and Software*.

Meyer, B. (1988b). *Object-oriented Software Construction*. Prentice Hall.

Meyer, B. and Popien, C. (1994). A Service Request Description Language. In *Proc. of FORTE '94, Bern, Switzerland*, pages 17–32. Chapman and Hall.

Milner, R. (1989). *Communication and Concurrency*. Prentice Hall.

Milner, R. (1999). *Communicating and Mobile Systems: the π-Calculus*. Cambridge University Press.

Monson-Haefel, R. (1999). *Enterprise Javabeans*. O'Reilly UK.

Moss, J.B. (1985). *Nested Transactions: An Approach to Reliable Distributed Computing*. MIT Press.

Mowbray, T. and Zahavi, R. (1995). *The Essential CORBA: Systems Integration Using Distributed Objects*. Wiley.

Mullender, S., editor (1993). *Distributed systems*. Addison Wesley.

Muller, P.-A. (1997). *Instant UML*. Wrox Press.

Needham, R. and Schroeder, M. (1978). Using Encryption for Authentication in Large Networks of Computers. *Communications of the ACM*, 21(12):993–999.

Nelson, J. (1999). *Programming Mobile Objects*. Wiley.

Neumann, B.C. and Tso, T. (1994). Kerberos: An Authentication Service for Computer Networks. *IEEE Communications*, 32(9):33–38.

Object Management Group (1995). *The Common Object Request Broker: Architecture and Specification Revision 2.0*. 492 Old Connecticut Path, Framingham, MA 01701, USA.

Object Management Group (1996). *CORBAservices: Common Object Services Specification, Revised Edition*. 492 Old Connecticut Path, Framingham, MA 01701, USA.

Object Management Group (1997a). *OMG Semantics Guide*. 492 Old Connecticut Path, Framingham, Mass., ad/97-08-04 edition.

Object Management Group (1997b). *The Meta Object Facility*. 492 Old Connecticut Path, Framingham, MA 01701, USA.

Object Management Group (1997c). *UML Notation Guide*. 492 Old Connecticut Path, Framingham, Mass., ad/97-08-05 edition.

Object Management Group (1998a). *CORBAservices: Common Object Services Specification, Revised Edition*. 492 Old Connecticut Path, Framingham, MA 01701, USA.

Object Management Group (1998b). *Notification Service*. 492 Old Connecticut Path, Framingham, MA 01701, USA.

Object Management Group (1998c). *The Common Object Request Broker: Architecture and Specification Revision 2.2*. 492 Old Connecticut Path, Framingham, MA 01701, USA.

Object Management Group (1998d). *XML Meta Data Interchange (XMI) – Proposal to the OMG OA&DTF RFP 3: Stream-based Model Interchange Format (SMIF)*. 492 Old Connecticut Path, Framingham, MA 01701, USA.

Object Management Group (1999). *Persistent State Service 2.0*. 492 Old Connecticut Path, Framingham, MA 01701, USA.

OMF (1998). Chemical markup language reference. Technical Report http://www.xml-cml.org/cmlref.html, Open Molecule Foundation.

Open Group, editor (1997). *DCE 1.1: Remote Procedure Calls*. The Open Group.

Orfali, R., Harkey, D., and Edwards, J. (1996). *Client/Server Programming with CORBA Objects*. Wiley.

Orfali, R., Harkey, D., and Edwards, J. (1997). *Instant CORBA*. Wiley.

Overgaard, M. and Strinfellow, S. (1985). *Personal Computing With the Ucsd P-System*. Prentice Hall.

Parnas, D.C. (1972). A Technique for the Software Module Specification with Examples. *Communications of the ACM*. 15(5):330–336.

Platt, D.S. (1997). *The Essence of OLE with ActiveX: A Programmer's Workbook*. Prentice Hall.

Pressman, R.S. (1997). *Software Engineering: A Practitioner's Approach (4th Edition)*. McGraw Hill.

Quatrani, T. (1998). *Visual Modeling with Rational Rose and UML*. Addison Wesley.

Rivest, R.L., Shamir, A., and Adelmann, L. (1978). A Method of Obtaining Digital Signatures and Public Key Cryptosystems. *Communications of the ACM*, 21(2):120–126.

RMI (1998). *Java Remote Method Invocation Specification*. JavaSoft, revision 1.50, JDK 1.2 edition.

Roodyn, N. and Emmerich, W. (1999). An Architectural Style for Multiple Real-Time Data Feeds. In *Proceedings of the 21st International Conference on Software Engineering, Los Angeles*, pages 564–572. ACM Press.

Rosen, M., Curtis, D., and Foody, D. (1998). *Integrating CORBA and COM Applications*. Wiley.

Rosenblum, D.S. and Wolf, A.L. (1997). A Design Framework for Internet-Scale Event Observation and Notivication. In Jazayeri, M. and Schauer, H., editors, *Software Engineering — ESEC/FSE '97, Zurich, Switzerland*, volume 1301 of *Lecture Notes in Computer Science*, pages 344–360. Springer.

Rumbaugh, J., Blaha, M., Premerlani, W., Eddy, F., and Lorensen, W. (1991). *Object-Oriented Modeling and Design*. Prentice Hall.

Rumbaugh, J., Jacobson, I., and Booch, G. (1999). *The Unified Modeling Language Reference Manual*. Addison Wesley.

Schill, A. (1993). *DCE: Das OSF Distributed Computing Environment*. Springer.

Siegel, J. (1996). *CORBA Programming*. Wiley.

Sloman, M. and Kramer, J. (1987). *Distributed Systems and Computer Networks*. Prentice Hall.

Soley, R.M., editor (1992). *Object Management Architecture Guide*. Wiley, 492 Old Connecticut Path, Framingham, MA 01701, USA.

Sommerville, I. and Sawyer, P. (1997). *Requirements Engineering: A Good Practice Guide*. Wiley.

Spitzner, J.H. (1998). Bioinformatic sequence markup language. Technical Report http://visualgenomics.com/sbir/rfc.htm, Visual Genomics Inc., 1275 Kinnear Rd, Columbus, OH 43212, USA.

Stevens, W.R. (1990). *UNIX Network Programming*. Prentice Hall.

Stonebraker, M., Wong, E., Kreps, P., and Held, G. (1976). The Design and Implementation of INGRES. *ACM Transactions on Database Systems*, 1(3):189–222.

Stroustrup, B. (1986). *The C++ Programming Language*. Addison Wesley.

Summerville, J.E. (1987). *Advanced CICS Design Techniques Concepts And Guidelines*. Chapman and Hall.

Sun (1996). *Java Core Reflection*. Sun Microsystems, 901 San Antonio Road, Palo Alto, CA 94303, USA.

Sun (1998). *Java Object Serialization Specification*. Sun Microsystems, 2550 Garcia Avenue, Mountain View, CA 94043, USA.

Sun (1999). *Jini Transaction Specification*. Sun Microsystems, 901 San Antonio Road, Palo Alto, CA 94303, USA.

Tanenbaum, A.S. (1989). *Computer Networks, 2nd Edition*. Prentice Hall.

Ullman, J.D. (1988a). *Principles of Databases and Knowledge-Base Systems Vol. 1*. Computer Science Press.

Ullman, J.D. (1988b). *Principles of Databases and Knowledge-Base Systems Vol. 2*. Computer Science Press.

Vogel, A. and Duddy, K. (1997). *Java Programming with CORBA*. Wiley.

Watterson, K. (1998). Turbocharging Object Projects. *SunExpert Magazine*, pages 45–52.

Winder, R. and Roberts, G. (1997). *Developing Java Software*. Wiley.

Wyckoff, P., McLaughry, S.W., Lehman, T.J., and Ford, D.A. (1998). Tspaces. *IBM Systems Journal*, 37(3):454–474.

X/Open Group (1994). Distributed Transaction Processing: The XA+ Specification, Version 2. X/Open Company, ISBN 1-85912-046-6, Reading, UK.

Zimmermann, P. (1995). *The Official PGP User's Guide*. MIT Press.

Index